# Fear and Anxiety
# On the Florida Frontier

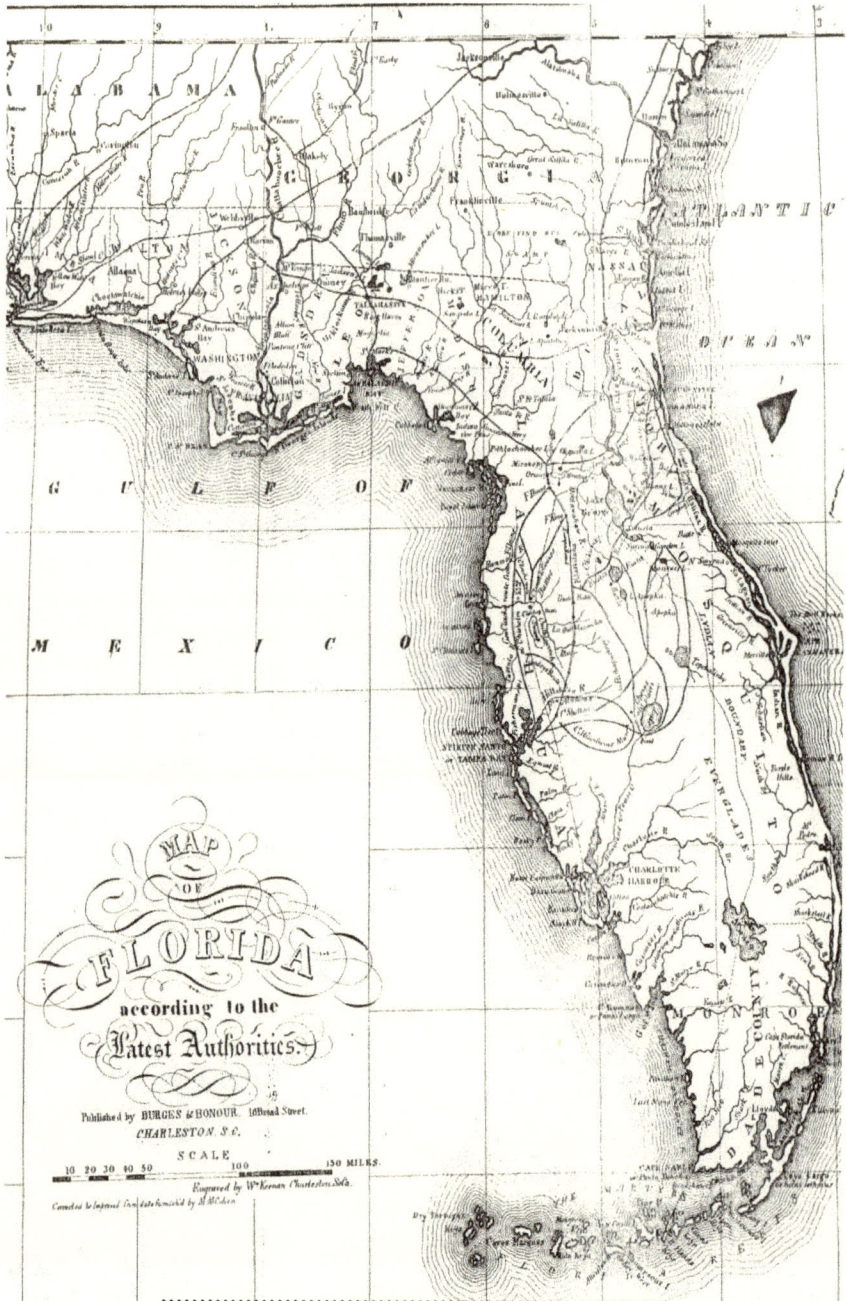

MAP
OF
FLORIDA
according to the
Latest Authorities.

Published by BURGES & HONOUR, 108 Broad Street.
CHARLESTON S.C.

SCALE
10  20  30  40 50        100        150 MILES.

Engraved by W.<sup>m</sup> Keenan Charleston S.C.

Corrected to Improved Survey data furnished by H. M.Cohen

**Florida in 1836**

# Fear and Anxiety
# On the Florida Frontier
## Articles on
## The Second Seminole War

## Joe Knetsch

**Contribution Number Five**

**Seminole Wars Foundation, Inc.**

Dade City, FL

Copyright 2008 by Joe Knetsch

Published by the Seminole Wars Foundation Press
(dba: The Seminole Wars Historic Foundation, Inc.)
35247 Reynolds Street, Dade City, FL 33523
www.swhfoundation.org

Cover painting "The Captive Osceola" by Jackson Walker,
copyright the Museum of Florida Art, Deland
Jacket design by Jackson Walker Studio
www.jacksonwalkerstudio.com

Layout and design by John Missall

ISBN 978-0-9821105-4-6
Library of Congress Catalog # 2008930474

# CONTENTS

# ILLUSTRATIONS

# The Seminole Wars Foundation

The Seminole Wars Foundation, (dba: Seminole Wars Historic Foundation, Inc.) was founded in 1992 with the goal of preserving sites significant to the Seminole Wars, establishing educational programs to disseminate information about the wars, and to publish books and other matter pertaining to these important but little understood conflicts.

The Foundation has been instrumental in the preservation of the Camp Izard battle site, has purchased portions of the Fort Dade site and funded excavations upon it, and has assisted in the purchase and preservation of the Fort King site in Ocala. Foundation members have given numerous talks to civic organizations, student groups, and the general public.

This is the fifth book-length publication by the Foundation, and the first under our own imprint. Our earlier titles were published in partnership with the University of Tampa Press and are listed on the back cover of this volume. The Foundation has also published a series of small educational booklets on various aspects of the wars.

For further information, contact the Seminole Wars Foundation at 352-583-2711, by mail at 35247 Reynolds St., Dade City, FL 33523, or visit our website, www.seminolewars.us.

# Foreword

This foreword is intended for those few readers who *do not* already know "Dr. Joe." As will become apparent when you read the introduction and acknowledgments, Joe Knetsch's address book is like the "who's who" of Florida historians. As will also become apparent when you read the excellent articles contained in this volume, his knowledge of Florida history is encyclopedic. If you have a question concerning the Seminole Wars, Joe probably knows the answer, and if he doesn't, he will certainly know who to refer you to.

When holding a conversation with Joe, he will often mention "his good friend . . ." There is a reason so many people consider Joe their good friend: He is ever-willing to share knowledge and resources with his fellow scholars and give a hand to aspiring students. I speak from personal experience. My wife Mary Lou knew Joe professionally from her work in the engineering/surveying field. When she mentioned our interest in the Seminole Wars, Joe became an instant mentor. He told us what to look for and where to find it. He sent us articles and microfilms. He introduced us to people who have become treasured friends. Most of all, his enthusiasm inspired us. Without a doubt, our book "The Seminole Wars" would not exist if it had not been for Joe's encouragement and support. I'm sure there are plenty of other people who could tell similar stories.

Although this is the fifth book offered by the Seminole Wars Foundation, it marks the beginning of a new endeavor for our organization. This is the first book to be published by the Foundation on its own and not in partnership with the University of Tampa Press. As an organization, the Foundation has grown confident in the abilities of its members to create and produce quality publications dealing with the Seminole Wars and related subjects. Two other original works are already in progress, and several other projects are under consideration, including reprints of books that have gone out of print.

As the layout designer and one of the editors of this book, I was presented with a number of interesting challenges. One of the most difficult had to do with the nature of this work as an anthology of articles previously printed in other publications. Because each article originally had to stand on its own, a certain amount of background information had to be included with it. If you read the book from front to back, some of that material may seem repetitious. There was some discussion as to eliminating the redundant portions, but in the end we decided to leave them in. Although we hope you'll read the book from cover to cover, we also realize that it is an excellent reference work. The extensive endnotes and thorough bibliography are invaluable resources on their own. It is the sort of book you go back to again and again, and if you choose to read just one article at a time, those redundant portions need to be there.

We hope you enjoy "Fear and Anxiety on the Florida Frontier" and find it both useful and enlightening. The Seminole Wars Foundation is proud to bring it to you.

*John Missall*

# INTRODUCTION

The following essays represent nearly twenty years of research and writing on the Seminole wars. I had discussed these important wars when I did a short monograph on the history of Broward County for my students at Ramblewood Middle School in the early 1980s and became fascinated with their impact on the southeastern portion of the state. My first article on the Seminole Wars appeared in 1988 with the publication of my essay, "A Second Ending: Broward and the Indian Scare of 1849," and was edited by one of my many mentors in Florida history, the late Dr. Cooper Kirk, then the historian for Broward County and editor of the *Broward Legacy* magazine. Spending many days at the Broward County Historical Commission offices with Cooper and a young scholar and friend, Rodney Dillon, taught me how diligent one must be to research these wars and how so much depended upon the primary sources of that era. These essays are, in their own way, a small tribute to Cooper Kirk and the late John Mahon, Florida's finest military historian and outstanding scholar.

I clearly remember the very first meeting with Dr. John Mahon. I was sent by the Department of Natural Resources to research the history of the Wekiva River in Orange and Seminole Counties. I had already read Dr. Mahon's *History of the Second Seminole War* and was not expecting to meet him in the old P. K. Yonge Library of Florida History on that day. Being naïve and still working on a doctorate in another area of history, I asked the librarian on duty, the legendary Elizabeth Alexander, about sources for this project. She pointed out John Mahon and introduced me to him. I had never attended any classes of his, and had never even seen him in person until this day. He was obviously a well disciplined man, stern of look but gentle of soul. John took me under wing and taught me more about the wars, the sources and the context than almost anyone could have the right to expect. With his guidance and help I was able to acquire enough material to help the Attorney General's Office win the case. More importantly for my own development, I gained a confidant and friend that I never expected. John's willingness to share research, assist young scholars, and stringent work ethic helped me realize what true scholarship was all about. I have tried to follow his example in my career.

But there is more to these essays and articles than imitation and following in someone's footsteps. In the approach I have taken in interpreting the Seminole wars, I have attempted to be as thorough and wide-ranging as possible. It has taken many years of research to accumulate the sources I use and I continue to find new ones every year. Working with colleagues like Patsy West, Frank Laumer, Rodney Dillon, Pam Gibson and others has made me sharpen my tools to keep up with their knowledge and abilities. Primary sources for these wars abound in the documents at the National Archives, Library of Congress, Congressional documents, the Florida Room at the State Library of Florida, the Florida Historical Society collections, many of the universities in Florida and a large number of local historical societies and archives. During the time I have been researching Florida history in general, I have found useful collections concerning the Seminole Wars at the Huntington Library, the Detroit Public Library, Bowdoin College in Brunswick, Maine, the Georgia State Archives. Almost everywhere I go, something turns up. My dear wife Linda can attest to the excitement I felt when we delved into the Poinsett Papers and the George Gordon Meade Papers at the Historical Society of Pennsylvania. Because so many of the men in uniform who fought in these wars came from outside Florida, there is no telling where one will find pertinent information regarding these wars. As many of the sources were untapped or underutilized at the time of my inspection, I have had the good fortune to bring many of these finds to light and offer new interpretations of facets of the wars.

Sharing information has been important, both as a means to an academic end and as a way to get to know other scholars who share similar interests. One of the best at this technique is Dr. Canter Brown, Jr. whose large body of work needs no introduction. Canter has been a friend, cohort and sharer of information since I first met him nearly twenty years ago. He introduced me to a number of sources in Maryland, Detroit and Yale University that I would have been years in finding had it not been for his willingness to share and teach. As will be seen in some of the following essays and articles, I totally agree that slavery was a major cause of these wars. I also point out that this was not the only cause of these wars. As the first chapter indicates, cattle and land played important roles too.

In the second series of these essays it will be seen that the Second Seminole War was experienced differently in the scattered locations throughout Florida. St. Augustine, for example, felt the panic of being surrounded by an enemy force after the disaster at Dunlawton exposed it to almost direct assault. The Florida Keys also felt a sense of urgency but went about defending themselves quite differently than the citizens of Tampa or St. Augustine. Tampa was almost abandoned by the army in 1836 and truly felt the sense of isolation after the news of Dade's battle came home. Few communities suffered more than the residents of Micanopy. This well educated, prosperous community was more vulnerable than most because of its location in the middle of the Territory and the lack of an infrastructure to transport goods and military materials to and from it. Almost every plantation in the area was burned to the ground and what the Indians did not burn was destroyed on orders of the military as it abandoned the settlement in 1836. Tallahassee was isolated from the rest of the Territory and away from the bulk of the action and did not suffer much in the way of damage. However, it too felt the sense of panic when outlying plantations and families were destroyed and killed. Even Jacksonville, with the handy St. Johns River and fairly good transportation facilities, had its moments of anxiety, but this town reacted very differently than others and became a refuge for many of the "suffering inhabitants" from the frontier. In these essays I try to document these reactions and how the inhabitants relied upon each other for strength and courage in the face of danger.

As a military historian I have become fascinated with the study of logistics. The essays on Jesup's campaigns and the impact of the weather demonstrate this somewhat confusing field of specialization. Everyone is familiar with the old Napoleonic statement that the army moves on its stomach, but few realize just how true this observation is. Food for the men and the animals of the army was a major concern in Florida. The Seminoles and their allies were also very concerned with this aspect of war, but were masters at farming the most difficult of terrains. They amaze me to this day with their ability to adapt to radical changes in their habitat. From crop rotation and cattle penning in northern Florida to the cultivation of corn, squash, beans and other crops on the islands of the Everglades, these people are truly some of the most creative farmers in American history. Comparing the raising of crops and cattle by the Seminoles and Miccosukees with the problems presented to Thomas Jesup and the United States Army campaigning in the strange lands of Florida is shear fun for the researcher. Presenting the logistical problems inside of the operational planning of the army is a contribution I am very proud of, but there is still much to learn.

The personalities one finds in researching these wars are also a subject of fascination. Everyone relates to biography, and the Second Seminole War has a tremendous cast of characters to draw upon. From the pompous General Winfield Scott to the straight forward, sometimes abrasive William Jenkins Worth, the army supplies more than its share of the cast. Some of these men were almost obsessive in their desire to capture or defeat the Seminoles, particularly Colonel Thomas Childs in his quest to take Abiaka (Sam Jones). The cast of the Seminoles and Miccosukees is also varied and just as interesting. From the famed martyr Osceola to the bundle carrier and recognized leader Abiaka, few wars give us such a cast of Native American players. In these essays I have tried to incorporate them without going into extensive biographical information because of the scarcity on the side of the Seminoles and Miccosukees and the plethora of information regarding certain

xiv

army personnel, such as Zachary Taylor, Winfield Scott, Edmund P. Gaines and others. What I have found however, is the lack of good biography for many of these leaders and especially for Worth, Jesup, Walker Armistead and more. True, Chester Kieffer's biography of Jesup is very good, but there is enough information now available to justify an updated work. The biography of Worth, done in the 1950s does not emphasize his Florida campaigns and is mostly incorrect on what is reported. I have not found a useful biography of Armistead and would encourage those with an interest to get to work. Herbert J. Doherty's work on Richard Keith Call is long overdue for an updating since many new sources are now available that were not open when Doherty did his work

I have also included in this volume a number of essays on fortifications and the life of the soldiers within them. Fort Drane was the first serious study I made of the Seminole Wars, and I did it at the behest of a wonderful and determined friend, the late Alyce Tincher. Alyce was trying to save the site she believed to be Fort Drane from being mined for kitty litter clay. I was encouraged by my then boss, Bobby Jack White, to help her and thus I began my first serious work on the Seminole Wars. It was a challenge that nearly cost two of my colleagues in Tallahassee their jobs when political pressures were applied at the Department of State. It was not a pleasant experience for us and we lost the fight. But it was now clear to me that much more needed to be done to preserve Florida's Seminole War heritage. This led to my contacts with Frank Laumer, Canter Brown, Jr., and a host of others. It also led to my joining the Seminole Wars Historical Foundation and the Council on America's Military Past. It is with the hope that the publication of the following essays and articles will encourage others to look into these wars that I have offered this volume. It is not meant to be an all conclusive and exhaustive history but a series of essays that will provoke thought, discussion and further research into the Seminole Wars. With these goals in mind I trust the reader will support the efforts to preserve the heritage of these wars and what they mean to us today.

# ACKNOWLEDGMENTS

First, I happily acknowledge my wonderful wife of thirty years, Linda. Her time and effort in allowing me the freedom to research, read and travel has been invaluable. A special thank you is extended to John Missall, Frank Laumer, and Mary Lou Missall for their excellent editing skills and advice, and to Jackson Walker for the wonderful artwork and time spent on the dustcover. Those who encouraged me but are no longer living and not noted in the Introduction are Jim Covington, Billy Cypress, Lou Ellen Groh, Carol Raney, Barbara Rainey, and Art and Kari Rice. Among those with whom I am frequently in touch and who have worked steadily with me on various projects involving the Seminole Wars are Dr. Irvin Winsboro, Dr. Jim Cusick, John and Mary Lou Missall, the Laumer family, the entire staff of the State Library and Archives in Tallahassee, Bill Howell, Pamela Gibson of the Manatee County Library, Arva M. Parks, Dr. Roger Landers, Tom Jennings, Dr. Sara Warner, Dr. Canter Brown, Jr., Dr. Larry Rivers, Dr. James Michael Denham, Dr. Ed Keuchel, Alan Aimone of the West Point Library, Jerry Casale of Bethesda, Maryland, Deborah and Al Poppell, Dr. Dan Shafer of the University of North Florida, Dr. Brian Rucker of Pensacola Junior College, Paul Camp of the University of South Florida, Patsy West of the Seminole/Miccosukee Photo Archives in Fort Lauderdale, Rodney Dillon and Barbara Poleo of Past Perfect Florida History, Inc., Dr. Cecile-Marie Sastre and Dr. William Adams of St. Augustine, Dr. Susan Parker and Charles Tingley of the St. Augustine Historical Society, Taryn Rodriguez-Boette, Kyle VanLandingham (formerly the editor of the *Sunland Tribune*), Suzanne Heddy and her staff at the Halifax Historical Society, Harold and Pricilla Cardwell, Mr. Don Gaby, Becky Smith and Dawn Hugh of the Museum of South Florida History in Miami, Dr. Mark Kramer, Sarah Nell Gran and Larry Wiggins of the Hendry family, Dr. Nick and Debra Wynne of the Florida Historical Society, Kathy T. Thompson, Liz Dunham and Rodney Kite-Powell of the Tampa Bay History Center, Jim Schnur, Tom Bowen, Bob Hurst of the Historical Society of Bay County, Evonne Cline of the Dixie County Historical Society, the Kavanaugh family of Fernandina Beach, Ron Kurtz, Sidney Johnston of Deland, Bill Steele, Sybil Bray, Pam Vojnovski, Marion Smith, Marion Almy and her staff at Archaeological Consultants, Inc. in Sarasota, Lindsey and Cona Williams of Punta Gorda, Jerry and Mary Lou Wilkinson of the Historical Preservation Society of the Upper Keys, Tom Hambright of the Monroe County Archives in Key West, William and Claire Crawford of Fort Lauderdale and the Broward Historical Commission, John and Eleanor Thrasher, Dr. Ron and Diana Cohen, Tom Brady, and the membership of the Micanopy Historical Society, Jim and Toni Collins of Levy County, Earl and Bettie DeBary of Ocala, Chris Kimball, Kevin Hooper, Dr. Nick Reynolds and Dr. Heidi Weber of the *Journal of America's Military Past* who have so patiently edited my articles for their publication and Joan Shelton formerly of Fort White, Florida. I would be remiss in my duty to an old friend if I did not include Brenda Elliot, now of Rochester, New Hampshire, but formerly of Kissimmee, Florida, for her many hours of research and the discussion of the many findings we made. A final note should be added to include Don Ivey, formerly of Pinellas County, who helped me with co-writing articles and investigating many facets of Florida's history along with Ellen Babb and the other staff at Heritage Park.

Articles that appear in this volume came from a number of publications including the following: *The Sunland Tribune* (Tampa Historical Society), *El Escribano* (St. Augustine Historical Society), *The Broward Legacy* (Broward County Historical Commission), *The Journal of America's Military Past* (Council on America's Military Past), *The Halifax Herald* (Halifax Historical

xviii

Society), *At Home* (The Citrus County Historical Society), *Connections* (Boca Grande Historical Society), *Apalachee* (Tallahassee Historical Society), *Florida Keys Sea Heritage Journal* (Key West Maritime Historical Society), and *Past Times* (the Journal of the Historic Ocala and Marion County Genealogical Society).

No doubt I have missed a number of people who helped me get this far in the production of the essays and articles. Since my last book, *Faces on the Frontier: Florida's Surveyors and Developers in the 19th Century* was published without an acknowledgement page, I feel obliged to make it up to some of those left out of that volume but who helped me learn more about the Seminole Wars. Lastly I must thank Jessica Dalton who patiently scanned all of the articles and essays onto the CD that aided in producing the final manuscript. There will be a few errors in the text somewhere; there always is, and this is my responsibility. I am also responsible for the views expressed in this volume and no one else should be blamed for any faults found therein.

Lastly, I thank the Seminole Wars Foundation for their support in publishing this addition to their growing list of important Seminole Wars material.

# Fear and Anxiety
# On the Florida Frontier

# Expansion of the Southern Cattle Industry and Its Impact on the Seminoles

Cattle and Native Americans are not often spoken of in the same sentence as an introduction to the causes of warfare on the Southern frontier, yet the drive for more range land and the increased pressure for Indian removal cannot be separated. The adoption of European methods of farming and ranching by the tribes of the South made for some interesting contrasts in the success of their operations compared to their neighbors in Alabama, Georgia and northern Florida. Cattle ranching was introduced in the South by Spanish ranchers in the Sixteenth Century and allowed the Creeks, Choctaws, Cherokees and others to learn the fundamentals of care and control of the herds. By the Seventeenth Century large Spanish ranches had been established in central Florida with success, most notably the famed Lachua ranch near modern Gainesville, Florida. The exact dating of the introduction of cattle ranching into the Southeast is open to question and needs much more research to approximate a timeline with any accuracy. However, what is very certain is the Southeastern Indian groups noted above had become very reliant upon beef cattle as a source of protein by the beginning of the Eighteenth Century.[1] This growing reliance upon beef would lead to conflict over ownership and pasture land.

Recent scholarship has tended to be focused upon the issue of slavery and slave retrieval as the cause of the conflicts referred to as the Seminole Wars in Florida. Led by the works of Kenneth Porter, George Klos and Larry Rivers, scholars have correctly indicated the importance of this source of conflict as one of the major causes of these devastating wars. Unfortunately there has been a tendency to be very monocausationist in referencing this source of the conflicts. That the drive for additional pasture land and the increasing herds of Seminole cattle are also causes for these conflicts has often been overlooked or ignored.

The natural increase in the population of the Creeks and other Southeastern Indians after 1750 has been well documented. The rapid decline in deer and other game in the region is blamed upon this cause along with the increased pressure to provide hides for trade with the English firm of Panton & Leslie and others. These two reasons, for our purposes, demonstrate why the natives of the Southeast needed to adopt the cattle raising culture of their English and Spanish neighbors. The work of Anthony Paredes and Kenneth J. Plante clearly points out that the "rather dramatic growth in Creek population exacerbated the other changes and served as an important catalyst for the Creek War ..."[2] As the deer herds disappeared in the Southeast, cattle became even more important for dietary and trade purposes.

Historian J. Leitch Wright, Jr. emphasized the growing importance of cattle when he observed that, "Almost all village factors had cow pens in addition to truck houses. Cattle and swine ran wild, fed on the abundant grass and mast, and were rounded up once or more a year. A few were slaughtered for local consumption, but most were driven to markets in Saint Augustine, Savannah, Pensacola, and Mobile."[3] Indeed, by the late Eighteenth Century, the cattle herds of the Creeks and Seminoles had become very impressive to almost every Anglo visitor to their territories. The intrepid commentator William Bartram visited Florida in the mid Eighteenth Century and made the following literary report: "At the same time are seen innumerable droves of cattle; the lordly bull, lowing cow and sleek capricious heifer ... The cattle were as large and fat as those of the rich grazing pastures of Moyomensing in Pennsylvania." He gives us dramatic proof of the size of the herds of the Seminole leader, Cowkeeper, noting that they numbered from 7,000 to 10,000 across Paynes Prairie.[4] In his *A Tour Through the Southern and Western Territories of the United States of North America* (1792) John Pope described the cattle herds of Alexander McGillivray as "large stocks" requiring two or three white men to supervise their well being.[5] Another famous headman, William McIntosh, possessed eight hundred head, mostly steers, at the time of his murder.[6] The famed Indian Agent Benjamin Hawkins observed that the main reason the Seminoles left the Creek Confederation for Florida was the plentitude of game there and the "abundance of food for cattle and horses." Hawkins' often cited account of his visit to the Creeks in 1798-1799 has an almost regular litany of how many cattle were penned in each village, the style of the home of the headman and what crops were stored. He also observed how many cattle were sold that year by some of the villages. All the herding activities noted by these and other travelers required extensive grazing land, especially when the lands in the immediate vicinity of the village had been overgrazed.[7] Examples from the contemporary literature are consistent in their notations of the Indian cattle and making the main point perfectly clear: by the end of the Eighteenth Century the Creeks and Seminoles must be considered very impressive herdsmen and a force to be reckoned with in the future contest over grazing lands.

The large numbers in the Creek and Seminole herds required a large territory for grazing purposes. Because of the desolation caused by the overgrazing near the villages, land extending outward from these locations was brought into play. As these lands were further and further away from the center of the settlement it meant that herding techniques learned from the Spanish and others were also refined and adapted to the circumstances. As the new settlers in the "Wire Grass" of Georgia needed more land for very similar reasons, the two cultures were set upon a direct collision course. Two populations wanting and needing the same land at the same time could only lead to war.

Long before the American Revolution, Creeks and Georgians were already attacking each other along the extended frontier. Governor Peter Chester of West Florida had to promise his Native wards that he would expel any English settler who attempted to settle upon recognized Indian lands or who committed an act of violence upon any Native. Chester's 1771 threat did little to prevent the increasing violence along the frontier and within a short time of the edict reports reached the Governor informing him of an attack by members of the Lower Creeks upon white settlements in Georgia and that the Indians had raided the plantations for cattle and other plunder.[8] With the outbreak of the Revolution, however, British policy changed and these same raids were now encouraged by the British governments of East and West Florida.

The American Revolution on the remote Southern frontier was brutal, savage and devastating to those who inhabited the region. Encouraged by the British government, Creeks, Seminoles, Choctaws, and others became soldiers without uniforms against the expanding frontiers of Georgia and Alabama. Slaves, cattle and other plunder were the rewards along with British assurances of continued support. The British trading regime had penetrated the interior Southeast in a fashion the Spanish could not compete with successfully. Traders did not question religion or attempt to convert the native populations into something they were not. Nor did they attempt to force them into laboring relationships that required a sacrifice of time and effort for the benefit of some foreign crown. British goods were superior to those offered by the Spanish or French and became the staple European goods found in most Southeastern settlements. Traders from the colonies of Georgia and South Carolina could no longer compete with Panton & Leslie and other British trading firms since the war precluded any trade with England or the continent. The British found these frontier warriors useful allies against the rebellious colonies.[9]

The peace did not bring calm to the frontier and many issues remained unsettled. The Southeastern tribes who had sided with the British were exasperated and somewhat confused by the peace. They were never totally informed about their role in the war and did not understand completely the stakes being played out on the international scene. The weakness of the new government of the new country, the United States, did not aid the settlement of any questions either. With its inherent distaste for large standing armies, the new government intentionally kept the military force small and relied upon state militias to enforce peace. American weakness was apparent all along the frontier, and it must be remembered that it took the defeats of Harmer and St. Claire before General Anthony Wayne's Legion could win a decisive battle on August 20, 1794, at the Battle of Fallen Timbers in the Northwest Territory.[10] This reliance upon state militia units, coupled with an immature logistical system, a commissary unit that was almost worthless, and many other such problems precluded any real enforcement of peace along the frontier. With British intrigue continuing and weapons being readily supplied through the pliant government of Spanish Florida, the volatile frontier was almost ready for an explosion.

Into this mix must be added the constant pressure of the rapidly increasing population of Georgia and the Carolinas. The constant pressure applied by the Georgians upon the neighboring Creeks and Cherokees forced these tribes into some difficult situations. The Georgians acted as if the United States government had no jurisdiction in the matter and attempted to force the Creeks into a series of treaties that can only be described as fraud. Only a minority of Creek leaders were approached and obliged to sign the treaties of Galphinton and Shoulderbone which were based upon total misrepresentations by the negotiators for Georgia. The Federal Government finally stepped in and negotiated the Treaty of New York which gave the Georgians some of their demands. Only the latter treaty had the semblance of being submitted to a tribal council, the only body capable of obligating others to follow its dictates. In this case, too, the ego of the half-blood Alexander McGillivray was played upon, and he was awarded a medal and a rank in the American army. Indeed, many of the "leaders" of the Creeks were of mixed blood which gave them an advantage over their more pure-blood relatives and kinsmen. A class system based upon individually owned property began to arise in the Creeks, which started a division amongst the members that would have important consequences, including the murder of William McIntosh, one of the greatest accumulators. Two of the most important status symbols in this newly arisen class system were cattle and land, the very things the Georgians wanted too, by treaty or otherwise.[11]

Georgia was looking to expand westward into the Creek territory and later did receive additional concessions (in 1802 and

5

1804). But Florida was now back in the infirm hands of Spain. The Crown had signed the Treaty of San Lorenzo, which historian Sir Jack Holmes once observed, "Whatever its utility to Spain in Europe, this treaty marked the beginning of the end for Spain's North American empire by yielding control over the Mississippi and by surrendering the strategic posts north of the thirty-first parallel and east of the Mississippi."[12] Additionally it brought to the fore the problem of running a new boundary between Spanish Florida and the fledgling United States without any regard for the rights of the Creeks or Seminoles. No consent was sought directly with either of these tribes and because it would deprive them of hunting and grazing rights freely held for generations, they were bound to resist the attempt to run the line. When Andrew Ellicott and his Spanish cohorts attempted to run the line beyond the Chattahoochee River in 1799, they were met with stiff resistance and forced to abandon the task. Because the line represented a threat to their assumed rights, the Creeks and Seminoles threatened to resist.[13]

In Europe the French Revolution had erupted and the young Napoleon was soon to take power. Spanish attention was drawn away from its American colonies and what treasure it had left was being used to prepare the defense of the homeland. Florida, being one of the least productive colonies, was a total backwater and an assignment that Spanish troops hated to receive. Like their English counterparts, the average Spanish soldier viewed Florida as a death trap. Florida was sparsely settled, offered little economic or social advancement and had few amenities. Although no serious threats to the few settlements came from the Indians or Georgians, there was a constant battle along the frontier that the Spanish could not stop, nor did they have the inclination to do so, as it would have endangered their own well-being. A brief period of prosperity did exist in the pre-1812 era because of the American embargo of English goods. Spanish ports, especially Fernandina and settlements along the St. Mary's River, were havens for smugglers and slavers. The outbreak of the War of 1812 ended this respite and quickly plunged the Spanish, Americans, the Seminoles and Creeks, into a new round of severe border warfare.

The scarcity of Spanish settlements and the low population of East Florida led to continual border warfare along the St. Marys River further inland. The United States began fomenting revolution in East Florida through the auspices of former Georgia Governor George Matthews. So dangerous was this frontier that Surveyor General George J. F. Clark refused to order his surveyors any more than fifteen miles outside of the settled areas of St. Augustine, Cowford and Fernandina. Attempts to colonize East Florida by Bunker Harris and others led to almost continual conflict. Acting Governor Juan José de Estrada had more than he could handle with his negligible forces. The result was an undeclared war between the Georgians, Seminoles and others, who lived in the vicinity of Lake Miccosukee, northeast of Tallahassee.[14] One of the main goals of these adventurers in East Florida was to establish large cattle ranches in the Alachua area and use the resources described by Bartram and others for personal benefit.[15] East Florida was a tempting target for exploitation, and many found it too tempting to resist.

The drive for increased cattle lands by the Georgians and others was the crux of the complaint filed by the Seminole leader Bowlegs with Indian Agent Benjamin Hawkins in 1815. In his complaint, Bowlegs noted the raids on his lands, the destruction of his settlements and the stealing of his numerous cattle.[16] Bowlegs retaliated to the invasion by destroying the attempted settlement of Bunker Harris and driving the survivors out of the territory.[17] Whether the destruction of this settlement was directed by the Spanish or not is open to question. Horatio Dexter, an old Indian trader and Florida pioneer, reported that a scalp and letterbook were delivered to the governor in the presence of José de la Maza de Arredondo (Spanish Indian Agent) and his son. The letterbook contained a map of the Harris settlement which was later used, according to Dexter, as the basis for the famed Arredondo Grant in central Florida.[18] This was taking place at the same time that Colonel Nicholls and Captain Woodbine were supplying arms and ammunition to the Creeks and Seminoles and their black allies along the Apalachicola River. The 1816 destruction of the Negro Fort at Prospect Bluff set off a chain reaction that led to the so-called First Seminole War.[19]

The First Seminole War is hardly a real war but more like a large scale reconnaissance in force. Only two "battles" between whites and natives took place and in both cases the Seminoles and Miccosukees recognized their numerical inferiority and fled with few casualties. The largest engagement took place near the Fenholloway River, near modern Perry, Florida, and was between the forces led by McIntosh and a rear-guard of Miccosukee warriors. In reading the accounts of the battles filed by Colonel Robert Butler, Jackson's Adjutant, the fact that a detailed account was kept of the cattle and horses captured indicates the nature of the conflict. Slaves, of course, were recaptured and some returned to their owners, while others were given to the Creek forces under McIntosh. The actions of General Andrew Jackson's combined forces had one very important consequence: they were a real threat to Spanish control of Florida. This threat was skillfully used by John Quincy Adams in negotiating the treaty which transferred Florida to the United States.[20]

The acquisition of Florida by the United States opened up the northern section to immediate settlement by Anglos. Land speculation was rampant and Jackson's "cronies", as some are called, led the way along with those from Virginia and Georgia. In 1823 the Seminoles and Miccosukees were summoned to Moultrie Creek in modern St. Johns County, for a treaty session. This treaty confined the tribes to lands much further south in Florida, which was soon found to be nearly barren, with poor soil, few good hammocks and frequently covered with water during the rainy season. Florida Governor William Pope Duval, also acting as the Indian Agent, Colonel James Gadsden, Captain John Bell and Horatio Dexter all wrote reports about the poor land given to the Seminoles and Miccosukees. Almost all of them argued for an extension northward of the boundary so as to include good cattle land.[21] One of the best contemporary descriptions of the new conditions under which the tribes were forced to live comes from the U. S. Deputy Surveyor, Leroy May, another old Jackson hand. Visiting the village of John Hicks, the pliable headman of the Seminole group in the area, May noted, "I was in several of their houses and saw nothing except two or three pounds of venison, a briar root soup and bread. I am confident of Hicks' statement being true with respect to their starving

8

situation."[22] Trade in hides and slaves sometimes carried on along the coast by Spanish fishermen and traders was also denied to the Indians by the treaty, which caused some hardship among the displaced Seminoles and Miccosukees. Poor land, denied trade and the constant encroachments of the whites moving south forced the Seminoles and Miccosukees into new areas and new situations. The marginal lands upon which they were forced to live were utilized to their fullest and new methods were rapidly developed that enabled them to endure the long struggles ahead.

The constant push by the whites moving south forced two other treaties upon the Native population. The Treaty of Payne's Landing (on the Ocklawaha River) and the more infamous Treaty of Fort Gibson set the dates and times for the evacuation of Florida by the tribes. Among the most notable stipulations of the move was the requirement that all of their cattle and horses should be turned over to the agents and sold at auction with the money being placed in an account for them to draw on when they reached their new western homelands. The well documented corruption of the Indian Bureau need not be discussed but the denial of beef protein to the tribes during their voyage west is well known. After enticing the tribes to hunt the deer to near exhaustion, forcing them to adopt beef cattle as the most likely protein substitute and the constant adaption of white material culture to their daily lives, this denial and forced sale of their cattle was a cruel blow to the émigrés. There can be little wonder that the white settlers were constantly complaining to the government about the cattle thefts by the Indians (and not mentioning their own purloining of Indian cattle).[23]

Just how important cattle were in the Seminole culture is best shown by the fact that slaves (especially women) were rated in the number of cattle they were worth. Edward Wanton, the trader centered in Micanopy, Florida, swore that Reading Blunt sold a Negro woman, named Sarah, to a member of Bowleg's family for forty head of cattle. According to the testimony, "At that period it was usual for the Indians to rate all Negroes on sale at this rate of forty head of beef cattle, and that the size and value of the cattle was made to correspond with the size, age and sex, and value of the slave. That the largest beef cattle then rated at twenty dollars per head."[24] This indication of the importance of cattle in the

Seminole and Miccosukee culture of the day was little understood by the negotiators of the treaties. The lack of understanding, intentional or not, was to be a cause of the conflict we know as the Second Seminole War, America's most costly Indian war in money and lives lost. Although cattle and range lands were not the only cause of the conflict, their role as a causal factor should not and cannot be ignored if a true understanding of the Seminole Wars is to be obtained.

*Glassell's Spring*
*Glassell's Spring & Creek and Ocllawaha River.*
*With three Base lines. Surveyed and drafted by Peter Mitchel Esqr of Flda.*
*Scale. one inch to 2400 yds.*
*Compass variation 6°10' East*
*Course from Glassell Spring to Ocllawaha mouth N. 48° E.*

**Glassell's Spring**
(National Archives,
*Record Group 94*)

# The Establishment of the Indian Agency at Fort King

The establishment of the Indian Agency and later Fort King were not easily done. The Agency location, as is made clear in the following documents, was made central to the populations of both white and Indian settlers in the area. The Coffee Map of the vicinity (see above) shows clearly how this location came to be. The large number of Indian villages in the surrounding area, the main trading paths and the proximity to Silver Springs and the Ocklawaha River made this location important. The Indians had been forced to move south into the area from homes further north by the Treaty of Moultrie Creek. Some of the Indian groups, especially John Hicks', were in a desperate condition, without food or proper shelter. The tension was very high and scattered raids and outbreaks of violence had already occurred. Thus, it was determined that there was an immediate need for the establishment of an Indian Agency and in 1827 a military post.

For the military, however, the problems of the Florida frontier ranked low in priority, and the Quartermaster General's Office continually insisted that the establishment of a fort must be temporary, not permanent. This would preclude such things as planked flooring, gardens, bricked or lime-rocked chimneys or anything that would indicate a continued presence. Even the ordering of a boat for use by the post and agency were resisted by Washington. The problems of the frontier seemed too expensive. In one letter, found in the Territorial Papers, Major Thomas Cross,

12

Acting Quartermaster General, wrote to Major James M. Glassell, then commanding officer at Camp King, "... it is not the intention of the Government, to retain your command in its present position; and hence, any further measures in relation to the construction of quarters are uncalled for, as the work already bestowed on that object is now to be regretted."[25] As this letter was written on May 25, 1827, two years after the establishment of the Indian Agency and one year after a major round of violence between Indian and white settlers, the attitude of the army bordered on intransigence.

The army was well aware of the needs of the Agency, for in June of 1825 the Indian Agent, Gad Humphreys, had warned of the distress in which the Indian population found itself because of the drought. Early the next year, Governor William P. Duval transmitted an estimate to the War Department for the cost of clearing the Ocklawaha and Silver Springs for the purpose of supplying the Agency. Humphreys, in conjunction with the Governor, had already written asking for permission to clear out the river and stream. As he noted to Acting Governor George Walton, "I have written to the Department of War, for authority to remove at the Public expense, the obstructions in a Stream heading near the Agency & communicating with the St. John's River, by way of the Okelewaha, for the purpose of opening a navigation, that will enable me to procure the necessary supplies for the Station, upon infinitely better terms for the Government than it has hitherto been possible for me to do; the very great expense of transportation to which we have unavoidable been subjected, will hereafter, if the arrangement proposed is effected, be, I am convinced more than one half saved; the costs of labor & others incident to the undertaking, will not exceed; it is confidently believed $300. Treble this amount it is probable would be annually saved in transportation alone."[26] In October 1825, Thomas Ledwith examined the run and the river and indicated that it would take thirty days for ten men to clear out these water bodies for navigation. Yet, on May 16, 1827, Lieutenant Francis Newcomb made a report on the need of clearing out the run and river for the transportation of supplies to Camp King and the Agency. This project, he observed, would begin the next month and would render the streams suitable for large boats and barges. He further stated that, in order for the camp to be made comfortable for winter quarters, there was a need for window glass, bricks and lime, nails, iron and steel, and planking for floors.[27]

Colonel Duncan L. Clinch, on June 8, 1827, notified his superiors that, in conformity to orders, he had caused a new camp to be established at, "a Site Selected near the Florida Agency." The name given, according to Clinch, was Cantonment King. In Clinch's view, "I consider this post of more importance, in Controlling the Indians, and in giving protection and Security to the inhabitants of Florida, than any other post in the Territory, as it is in the immediate vicinity of the largest number of the Florida Indians, and between them and the white inhabitants." He also argued that the post should be manned by two companies until such time as the Indians were quietly settled in their new limits.[28] Yet, even with this strong representation of the situation, the War Department still considered the cantonment a "new temporary position."[29] Indeed, even when Major Glassell had recommended the more permanent fixtures, Major Cross wrote, on July 7, 1827, "... it must never be lost sight of, that the position is temporary, and that the accommodations should be of a corresponding character."[30] Finally, only after more disturbances were reported and an actual threat of more serious warfare was in the air, did Cantonment King become the permanent post, Fort King. Even then, it was abandoned shortly after the Dade Massacre and the killing of Wiley Thompson in December of 1835, when the troops were ordered to Clinch's Lang Syne Plantation, also known as Fort Drane.

It was during the struggle with the Washington bureaucracy that the survey of the site selected for the Indian Agency took place. Joshua A. Coffee was selected to do this work. He later assisted in establishing the line for the Indian territory in Florida and was familiar with the lands. These lands, he reported, were not sufficient to support the Indian population. As he bluntly put it, "There is no good land embraced in the line north of Big Swamp, except small detached hammocks." He also observed that the Indians had not accepted the Ocklawaha River as part of their boundary, as stipulated by treaty. This, he forewarned, would only lead to further trouble.[31] The plat for the Agency and the lands selected for its site by Humphreys and Coffee were in the northern end of the new Indian territory and on some of the finest lands embraced by the boundary.

Most importantly, it was on the, "direct line of communication between the Indians & White populations of the Territory; thus giving it to an extensive degree the power to regulate and control the intercourse between them, ..." This was most important in that: "There are already numerous petty dealers in Whiskey & other articles, settled near our borders, ..."[32] These elements could only spell trouble for Indian, soldier and settler alike. It was the duty of the Indian Agent to mitigate between these groups for the benefit of all. This would not be an easy or, in the end, a successful task.

# Benjamin A. Putnam and the Battle
## Of Dunlawton: A Reappraisal

The Battle of Dunlawton was one of the most important engagements of the Second Seminole War. The reasons for this assessment include the fact that the Seminole Indians and their Black allies almost eliminated an important force of Florida militia under the command of Benjamin Alexander Putnam. The Florida militia commanders had underestimated the strength and power of their adversaries. The entire East coast of Florida south of St. Augustine was almost entirely abandoned with no immediate hope of security. The thriving economy of East Florida, with its large plantations and growing wealth, was now in shambles, and would remain so for many years to come. The self-assured, overly confident Florida militia now realized that they had a hard struggle ahead of them and that they could not win the war without outside help. As historian John Mahon has noted, the Battle of Dunlawton, "wakened many volunteers to the fact that they were playing with death."[33] For these reasons and more, the Battle of Dunlawton was an early turning point in the Second Seminole War.

In the context of the larger war, the Battle of Dunlawton took place less than a month after the destruction of Major Francis L. Dade's command, one of the largest Federal forces then assembled in Florida. On the same day as the Dade Massacre, as this battle has come to be called, forces under the personal command of Osceola eliminated the Federal Indian Agent, Wiley Thompson, and the sutler's establishment within a few hundred yards of Fort King. Settlements in the immediate area of Micanopy, including those of

16

Gad Humphreys, Moses E. Levy and Gabriel Priest were burned and much property destroyed. Captain John McLemore's forces had been attacked near Suwannee Old Town and Captain Jacob Summerlin's command had seen battle near Newnansville. On the lower East coast, William Cooley's home on New River had been attacked and his wife, children and their tutor killed. General Clinch's Battle of the Withlacoochee had taken place, an event in which a large force of regulars and militia had been fought to a standstill. Closer to the East coast, New Smyrna was reported burned, while Hunter's, Depeyster's, Dunham's, Herriot's, Cruger's, Williams' and Anderson's plantations were all rumored to have been torched. Indeed, the entire Tomoka region, one of Florida's most productive, was deserted and charred. All of these losses had happened before Major Putnam's forces had found their way to the Dunlawton plantation.

Major Benjamin Putnam, the leader of the forces sent to secure the southern frontier, had just finished his first session in the Territorial Legislative Council, and had served as an alderman in the City of St. Augustine, Justice of the Peace for St. Johns County and other minor posts. His Florida military career had begun with his election as Orderly Sergeant of the Florida Rangers, the local militia unit of St. Augustine, in 1826.[34] His marriage to Judge Joseph Lee Smith's sister-in-law, Helen Kirby of Litchfield, Connecticut, helped to solidify his political career and brought him much happiness throughout his life.[35] At the time of the outbreak of the Seminole War, Benjamin Putnam's multifaceted career was on a definite upward swing.

Major Putnam's career, both military and political, were soon thereafter greatly affected when he was re-elected Major of the second brigade of the Florida Militia, under the command of General Joseph Hernandez. Colonel Joseph S. Sanchez, who commanded the second regiment, was Putnam's immediate superior.[36] By early December, the Second Regiment of the Second Brigade was ordered to duty by General Hernandez. The dreaded Indian War had broken out.[37] On December 17, 1835, because of the reports of the burning of many plantations along the Tomoka and the St. Johns Rivers, General Hernandez ordered this force, consisting of Company A of the St. Augustine Guards, Companies B and C of the mounted units and Company D, the infantry quota. A detachment of mounted volunteers, under the command of Mathew Solano also went south to protect the frontier.[38] On the 18th of December, Putnam's small force had reached Mala Compra and St. Joseph's, two of the plantations of General Hernandez. Putnam's force remained at the latter place, which became the supply depot for the southern operations of the militia, until December 20th, when the march was taken for Rozetta plantation, the former home of the Marquis de Fongueres, on the Tomoka River. This spot was to be the assigned post for the Second regiment, although the Major was unsure of its safety.[39]

Putnam had good reason to be nervous and wrote to Hernandez on January 4, 1836:

On or about the 22nd of Dec. Mr Sheldon and his wife both of whom were residing at Smyrna came up to my post representing that before they left, the dwelling house of Mr. Dunham had been burnt and that the Indians in considerable force somewhat exceeding a hundred were Spreading ravage and destruction around them. ... he also reported the destruction of property between Rosetta and Smyrna, and that Depeysters negroes, with some the Indians, paint on their faces, and Heriotts negroes had gone over to the Indians, and there was reason to believe that a combined operation, and attack would be made upon my small force at Rosetta. Capt. Solano whose habits of intercourse with the Indians had rendered him familiar with their Character and mode of operation expressed a decided opinion that the position of Rosetta could not be maintained by our forces against any number of Indians. ... Between that and Bulow's plantation a continued thicket lining the road would enable the enemy to cut us off from any communication to the north ...

Putnam, with this information in hand, called a counsel of war with his commanders and it was decided "unhesitatingly" to abandon this post.[40]

As reports began to filter in that the other plantations in the area were being destroyed and that New Smyrna had been torched,

Putnam's position at Rozetta did indeed seem endangered. By December 26 or 27, 1835, it had been ascertained that a mixed band of Uchees, Negroes and Seminoles had invaded the New Smyrna area and committed depredations on the local property. The Dunham house, near the inlet, was looted and burned, and John Shelton reported that Indians were dancing around the flames as the house went up in smoke. The Dummett plantation, across the Halifax River, soon was attacked and the house set on fire (although it only burned a hole in the floor initially). The homes of William de Peyster and Henry Cruger were quickly destroyed by the marauding bands. John Hunter had a narrow escape from death when he refused to answer the lures of the Negro John Ceasar and fled under the cover of darkness. The Anderson's plantation, Dunlawton, soon felt the wrath of the enemy and was heavily looted, although not burned. Samuel Williams' house was burned, but the remainder of the plantation was intact. Benjamin Heriot lost everything, except the corn house, when the raiders visited his domicile. The Tomoka area situation was, already, looking very bleak.[41]

The news was no better from the St. Johns River. There, the valuable plantation at Spring Garden, one of the showplaces of East Florida, was a near total loss. The *East Florida Herald* described the situation as follows:

> **Spring Garden burnt** - This valuable Plantation belonged to an enterprising citizen from the state of South Carolina. It is situated on Spring Garden Creek, which empties itself into the St. Johns about 12 miles above Lake George. The settlement was made at great expense, and labor, and under the active and judicious management of Mr. Forrester, had advanced to great value. Besides cotton, corn and other articles of provision, which the place had yielded in very great abundance the present season the proprietor reasonably calculated on upwards to one hundred hogsheads of sugar. The settlement is in the way of an old and constantly used crossing place of the Indians, and as a frontier position, a station might have been formed here which would have been advantageous to the public service, and it is the opinion of many, that if the government had afforded the means of

stationing twenty men there, and at two or three other points on the St. Johns, it would have afforded complete protection to all the settlements east of the St. Johns. The estimated loss of Col. Rees, is from $130,000 to $150,000.

Included in this loss was the taking, voluntary or otherwise, of nearly 160 Negro slaves, and all the horses and mules on the plantation.[42] The killing of "Llenvar", a twenty-three year old worker on Mr. Baya's plantation, added to the gloom of the reports from that sector.[43]

What may have made Putnam's predicament more dangerous was the reported numbers of the enemy in the area committing these depredations. John Shelton, noted above, reported as many as one hundred Indians at the burning of the Dunham house. Eighty to one-hundred and twenty were allegedly observed in the destruction at New Smyrna.[44] A later report, taken from a slave of de Peyster named Peter, stated that only thirteen took part in the destruction of the plantations on the Tomoka and that they killed only one man, an old Negro named Castello.[45] This was questioned in the Charleston *Courier* of January 12, 1836, which reported that, "DePeyster's negroes were traitors, and they must have been in league with the Indians; they assisted them with a boat to cross over to Dummett's."[46] As very large numbers of Blacks were reported being either captured, disappearing or joining voluntarily the Indian warriors, the potential number of opponents to Putnam's small force must have become somewhat unnerving to the all-volunteer militia.

Putnam also had more to worry about than just the potential enemy. His force of men, made up of units from the St. Augustine Guards and the local "Mosquito Roarers", was not a highly disciplined group. Alice Strickland, in her valuable work, *The Valiant Pioneers*, quotes James Ormond as noting that this force was, "undisciplined rabble, under no command of their officers."[47] Part of the reason for this was the lack of consistent organization of the Florida Militia and the confusing laws governing it. In the first eleven years of the Territory's existence, eight such laws were passed, requiring from one to four company musters per year, many allowing substitutes to be hired, occasional drafts of men, and no formal enactments allowing for standardized armaments. There was a general contempt for militia service, and the laws were generally ignored in most areas, including St. Augustine. "Volunteer Corps", such as the Mosquito Roarers, were often even less organized. As historian George Bittle has noted, "Volunteer corps frequently evolved when a few interested men gathered in a tavern and decided to form a local military company. Many units of this nature were formed in periods of national crisis and were short lived, but others existed over long periods." These units elected their own officers, wrote their own by-laws and generally set their own agenda within the loose framework of the existing militia laws. There was also no standard size for the organization of the companies, brigades, regiments, etc. In Florida, volunteer companies could run between twenty and one-hundred men. William Pope Duval, as governor of the Territory, encouraged a company of twenty-five men, including officers.[48] With this relatively chaotic lack of organization and discipline, Putnam's task as a commander was made difficult at best.

General Hernandez was very much aware of the weakness of the force under Putnam and was trying his best to secure assistance from the regular army, then commanded by General Abraham Eustis. Writing to that veteran warrior on January 7th, Hernandez stated, "The principal and most effective portion of my Brigade lies in the Country of Duval & Nassau - which are north of the River St. John and which constitute the 4th Regiment, and in the counties of Alachua, Columbia and Hillsborough, which is at present the seat of war, ..." He continued, "... that portion of my command which lies in the Counties of St. Johns and Mosquito is wholly insufficient for the protection of this City, and of the settlements which lie East of the river St. John and South of this." The general further noted that the Indians had stocked up on the bountiful harvest of the preceding year and were well supplied with foodstuffs. In his most telling representation, General Hernandez notified Eustis, "The State of things has produced Such a panic in this place as to render it impossible to calculate on the execution of a Single order", Hernandez realized the situation was on the verge of collapse and appealed to Eustis to provide troops enough to cover the St. Johns River from Spring Garden to Picolata. Such a move, he assured the officer, would boost the confidence of the residents and provide some actual security for the inhabitants.[49]

Meanwhile, Putnam also had difficulty overcoming the dull routine of camp life, something for which the citizen soldiers had little tolerance. In early January of 1836, while at Bulowville, [Rozetta having been abandoned on December 28, 1835] Putnam received a petition from twenty-two of his soldiers "begging permission to go home." Some began to ask for discharges as individuals. As historian Michael Schene has written, "With great anxiety he [Putnam] wrote General Hernandez that he had endeavored to put them off, 'but how long I shall be able to do so is doubtful; as there are so many I should find it impossible to prevent them by coercive measures.'" Rather than have the troops desert or disband voluntarily, Hernandez ordered Putnam to use the troops to attempt to recover some of the property already lost to the Indians.[50] Activity made the troops feel needed and useful and less likely to leave the Major without a command.

Some of the troops were sent out on patrol in an attempt to locate the Indian enemy or find the missing property, while others were busy fortifying Bulowville. This plantation, which had been quite literally confiscated from its reluctant owner, was more strategically situated and closer to the supply depot at St. Joseph's. John J. Bulow, Jr., the owner of the property, was not pleased with the troops being in his area as he had had a close working relationship with the Seminoles. As Major Putnam stated it, "I recollect that Mr. Bulow, was much dissatisfied by the presence of the troops at his place, and was very uncivil. When, afterwards, it became necessary to occupy his plantation, I did so, without consulting him on the subject. His dwelling-house was used for quarters, and he was literally dispossessed of his premises."[51] Captain John S. Williams put the situation even more bluntly: "Major Putnam placed him under arrest, and had him confined in an out-house on his own premises."[52] Putnam also had his flat-boats and canoes pressed into duty hauling men and supplies, along with picketing his plantation house and strengthening many of the out-buildings. These activities kept the troops better occupied than routine camp life and drill. It was from Bulowville that the expedition to Dunlawton went forth.

It should be remembered that the object of the expedition to the south of St. Augustine was the protection of property, not, specifically, the subjugation of the Indian enemy. Putnam's force, four uneven companies and Solano's mounted volunteers, was quite spread out among the plantations. In addition to sending a force to Spring Garden (on January 6th), the troops directly under Putnam also occupied, at various times prior to the Battle of Dunlawton, Rozetta, Bulowville, Carrickfergus, St. Joseph's, Dunlawton and Harford plantations.[53] At no time in January of 1836 did Benjamin Putnam have his entire force in one spot, or concentrated for the defense of any one of these homes. Also, it should be noted, that none of these locations were close enough to afford reinforcement should any of them be attacked by a concentrated force of the Indians. This wide dispersing of the troops meant that any concentration by the enemy would give them the advantage over the undisciplined forces under Major Putnam's command.

James Ormond, serving as a volunteer from Charleston, sent back a letter to the Charleston *Courier* which gives an idea as to the movements of Putnam's command in attempting to fulfill its difficult mission.

BULOWVILLE, (FL) JAN. 14. I am now stationed, with the company, at this place, to patrol between this and the 20 mile creek every other day, until further orders, with the hope of being ordered into the interior as soon as troops arrive in sufficient numbers to warrant such a measure. We have seen nothing of the Indians yet, and I suppose will not until we are able to go after them. Maj. Putnam's company leave here for Carickfergus tomorrow, from there they go down river to bring up all the provisions they can find on the different plantations. Keogh's company is expected up today with provisions from Hernandez's; they will be stationed at Dummett's.[54]

Earlier reports had noted that Putnam's force was at Bulowville and that, "Solano's troop (in which are the Smyrna men, under Dummett), amounting to 35, are stationed at JAMES WILLIAM'S, Matanzas."[55] The mission, to protect the property of the planters and to prevent the Indians from accumulating the crops and stores available at the unmolested plantations for their own purposes, appears to have been carried out to the best of the ability of the available troops, given all their shortcomings.

With his troops spread out among the plantations, mass desertion avoided for the time being, and supplies arriving from St. Joseph's, Putnam's forces were probably feeling more sanguine about the coming days. Surely, the people of St. Augustine were expecting good news: "Major Putnam, with his command, was posted at Mr. Bulow's at the last accounts; but probably on Friday or Saturday last sent forward to reconnoitre the country, and to endeavor to overtake the Indians, who are reported as being a few miles below Tomoka, rioting in the excess of drunkenness upon their spoils. We hope that a good account will be given of them, and that these *few* Indians will no longer be suffered to remain a terror to our citizens."[56] This attitude, that there were only a few Indians to be dealt with and that they, presumably could be easily handled by militia, demonstrates another problem: overconfidence and a low opinion of the enemy. It may be argued that this attitude is what allowed the wide dispersement of forces and led to the vulnerability of Putnam's force in the face of superior numbers.

While in the process of obtaining the supplies from the neighboring plantations, Putnam detailed a Sergeant Cooper, along with five privates, to guard some flats that were bringing away some corn. Putnam's and Dummett's men were to follow shortly thereafter and further scout the area south of Bulowville. According to the report published in the *East Florida Herald*, action soon followed:

Maj. Putnam had proceeded but a short distance when he discovered a heavy smoke south of him, and shortly afterwards was met by a Negro with information that Mrs. Anderson's house had been fired by the Indians. On their arrival at that plantation, at night, they discovered the house nearly consumed. Major Putnam posted his command in two Negro houses on each side of the road near a cattle pen, filled with cattle evidently driven in by the Indians, and waited until daylight on the 18th. Early next morning, two Indians were seen approaching them and were fired upon, one of them fell dead and the other wounded, supposed mortally. A short time afterwards, a party of Indians made their appearance, and were warmly received by our troops, and from this time a general battle ensued, which lasted nearly an hour. The enemy were reinforced during the action from time to time until they amounted to as near as could be calculated, about 120 Indians and Negroes. Our troops kept their posts until they were nearly surrounded, when they were forced to retreat, which they did in good order, to their boats, being hotly pursued by the enemy. Much praise is due to the gallant youths composing our forces in the engagement, and to the officers for the courage and bravery displayed during the action. ... Major Putnam reports that the Indians are increasing in numbers and daring, and from the disabled condition of his men he is unable to maintain his position, or even protect themselves, should an attack be made upon him, without reinforcements. The whole number in the action, was less than fifty & a majority of them were less than 25 years of age.[57]

A letter written by one of the men in the St. Augustine Guards gives a slightly more colorful account:

About daylight there were two Indians coming up the road: according to orders we fired upon them; killed one dead on the spot, and severely wounded the other, which no doubt caused his death. We then scalped him and took his ears and I have his beads. ... we beheld a party of Indians, about sixty in number approaching us; we retreated to the burnt building which we thought would answer for a fort, ... we fired away upon them for an hour not one our men being wounded we kept on firing until an alarm of a reinforcement compelled us to retreat. We went as far as the boats when they all rushed upon us, we ran back then, as we saw that if we did attempt to get into the boat we would certainly be massacred. We kept on fighting when a party of about fifty on horses compelled us to retreat, for they had almost surrounded us, we then retreated in reality but owing to our false retreat at first they would not dare to come upon us until we were shoving off and then every man that attempted to shove off the boat got a ball either through his cap, coat or got wounded. It was very distressing to stand and see the men fall in the manner in which they did. When I got into the boat I saw Ben Wiggins fall, then the Major got hold of his oar, and fell; then Domingo Martinelly, he also fell, Reynolds, he also fell, ... in the boat the Indians took, there was Marks and Gould and two negroes. One Negro and Marks and Gould swam across the river on to Pelican Island. Gould gave out and stopped on the Island, Marks continued swimming on for the beach shore he got there safe ... when I consider of the danger we were in and the number of Indians, I wonder how we made our escape - it was through the will of the almighty God that we did escape.[58]

One final account by an eyewitness to the Battle of Dunlawton should fill in the picture more completely. This last account is from a letter published in the Charleston *Courier* and sent by James Ormond on January 20th. Since other historians have relied heavily upon the "Reminiscences of the Life of James Ormond of Atlanta", written many years after the battle, it is instructive to see how his perspective changed over the years. In his later accounting of the battle, Ormond tells of the horrible mutilation of the dead Indian's body, the rallying of the militia to stand and fight by the "old Negro guide" [Ben Wiggins, a mulatto] and the battle lasting only one half an hour. He notes the allegedly pell-mell nature of the retreat where every gun was rendered useless by getting wet and the defiant gesture of Lieutenant William H. Williams exposing his posterior to the enemy and receiving a shot in the "sitting down place." He ends his later account with the glib, "So ended the fight of Dunlawton, in which we were completely whipped by the Indians."[59] Ormond's account, written just two days after the battle, leaves out some of these interesting details.

BULOWVILLE, Jan. 20. About day light two Indians came within gun shot, when they were fired on, and one killed on the spot - the other escaped, but badly wounded as he left his rifle. The Company was then extended to receive any attack, and we did not have to wait long; they advanced boldly, in a large body. As we had a thick scrub behind us, we were ordered to retire slowly to the buildings in our rear, and then await them, as the only place where they could not completely surround them. In about 15 minutes they came down, 45 were counted on the Canal bank, and we thought we could stand them very well, so commenced firing. Presently another party re-enforced them, and we were ordered to retreat to our boats. Only a few had got in, when we were told to come back - I say *we*, but for my part I had not got to the boat; however, we did not stand much longer, for a large party coming down our right, some on horseback, the Major thought we would be cut off from the boat, therefore ordered a retreat. This, as the boats were aground, was no easy matter; and while doing so, we were finely peppered. We brought away one scalp and are pretty certain of having killed five or six, as many were seen to fall, and were dragged off by their companions. I have four wounds, two slight, on my right arm and shoulder, one entering my left thigh, and passing up about an inch and a half from the back bone - and one just above my left ear - the ball struck my head and fell off, but it bled very profusely. I would have written you before this, but could not set up. I do not think any of my bones are broken, as I can now move my leg.[60]

Comparing the two accounts given by Ormond demonstrates how our perspectives change with time and the caution which must be used in selecting source material.

Putnam's wounded and battered force retreated for Bulowville. The command was also plagued by the lack of provisions, for, as Putnam wrote to Hernandez on January 18th, "I omitted to state that all our company provisions, being on the flats were necessarily abandoned by us to the enemy, we not being able in a condition or able to bring any part of it away, much of our cartrage powder was damaged by getting wet."[61] General Hernandez, realizing the danger of that position, attempted to send immediate reinforcements. He found, however, that the militia would not go beyond the head of the Matanzas. The newspapers added something more: "We learn that on the arrival of the United States troops at St. Augustine, the militia under Gen. Hernandez, were dispatched to afford assistance to Maj. Putnam, to bring in the wounded, &c. but fears were entertained that the Indians might get between the troops of Major Putnam and St. Augustine, and cut them off."[62]  The loss to the militia forces was reported as one dead [a Negro slave] and seventeen wounded, some severely.  Solano's force soon joined Putnam at Bulowville and assisted in getting them prepared to go back to St. Augustine.  The house of John Bulow was used for a hospital for the many wounded. Cotton bales were stacked up, in addition to the previous picketing, to act as a breastwork around some of the out-buildings.  Putnam estimated that the Indian force opposing him at Dunlawton was about fourfold his own troops, which numbered thirty-eight.  With the addition of Solano's troops, total force at Bulowville was fifty-five.[63] General Hernandez, realizing the dangerous position of Putnam's force, decided to order the abandonment of Bulowville and ordered Putnam to return to St. Joseph's, which he did on January 23, 1836. On the 28th of January, being wounded and having many in need of additional medical attention, Major Putnam returned to St. Augustine.[64]

The return of Putnam's forces and the state of his troops did not lighten the mood of his fellow citizens in St. Augustine.  As reported, the scene was one of mixed joy and tears:

> The men who were wounded in the battle at Dunn-Lawton arrived in town on Saturday evening last.  It was a melancholy sight to see the relations of these noble spirits, flocking to the boats to receive them, and the mingled feelings of joy and grief with which they were greeted, caused many a sympathetic tear to flow, from the otherwise uninterested bystanders.  One of them, Charles Flora died last night; he received a wound in his arm and one in the groin, and was otherwise much cut up with balls.  During the action he acted with the utmost coolness and courage amounting to sang froid.[65]

Domingo Martinelly died shortly after his return home from his wounds suffered in the battle.[66]

One of the interesting questions not answered by any of the published accounts of the battle is the fate of young Edward Gould, who was last seen alive by his colleagues on Pelican Island. It was presumed at the time that the lad had perished at the hands of the Seminoles, which was the case. In a letter widely reported in the press, Gould's father, Judge E. B. Gould, paid tribute to his son and his colleagues and noted, "I have been a great loser in the action at Dunlawton," echoing the sentiments of all parents who have lost a son in war.[67] However, the fate of the young Gould was not reported until January of the following year, 1837. Two Negroes were captured by General Jesup's forces about that time, and they relayed the fate of the young soldier:

> ... The Negroes state that he was taken off the island after the battle was over. He was wounded in the thigh, and they bound up his wound, and otherwise treated him kindly. At sunset they stripped him of his clothing, and told him to go, that he was too young to kill, and they would not harm him. He started from the camp, and had proceeded about fifty yards, when at a preconcerted signal, he fell before their treacherous rifles; twelve balls were lodged in his body, and he died without a groan. Poor Fellow! His fate was a hard one; he deserved better. He had just entered the 22d year of his age. ...[68]

Thus, the family of the unfortunate young man had to begin anew the grieving process.

With the Battle of Dunlawton and its aftermath, the entire frontier south of St. Augustine lay open to depredation. The Indians were not slow to take advantage of this. By early February, the Florida militia had abandoned any more attempts at saving the plantations of the eastern coast of Florida. What lay ahead was six more years of bloody, horrible war which totally devastated the economy of the once thriving region. The battle taught some severe lessons to the inhabitants of the Territory.

For Benjamin Alexander Putnam, the war did not end with this defeat. In July of 1836, Governor Richard K. Call appointed Putnam head of the new military district east of the St. Johns River.[69] In this capacity he helped to raise three companies, two mounted and one infantry, for the defense of East Florida and saw to the feeding of the men and horses.[70] He held this position until the end of those troops' enlistment. Putnam was then placed upon the staff of General Call as Adjutant General, a post he held until December of 1836. Yet, even though he was recognized and rewarded for his part in attempting to defend the frontier, Putnam was to be haunted by the battle for the rest of his political life. Whenever he ran for public office after that time, his political opponents were quick to remind the public, REMEMBER DUNLAWTON, BOYS. And, sometimes, they did.

**Portion of Macomb's Map 1837**
(*State of Florida Library*)

# Continually In Apprehension:
# Tampa Bay in Early 1836

On January 4, 1836, the young Second Lieutenant Benjamin Alvord of the Fourth Infantry wrote to the Quartermaster General of the United States Army, General Thomas Jesup, that the Schooner *Motto* had just left Fort Brooke for New Orleans. Its mission was to obtain ammunition for the recently arrived pair of twelve-pound cannon and the small arms then at the post. Alvord then added the telling portion, "... being continually in apprehension of an attack from the Indians the commanding officer decides that these materials Furniture &c of Motto cannot be turned over (as no officer can properly leave his command) ..."[71] Three days prior to this the new commander of the post, Captain Francis S. Belton of Maryland, commented that the defenses of Fort Brooke were recently extended and strengthened and that the original cantonment had been entirely abandoned. The widows and children of the casualties of Dade's recent battle had been shipped off to New Orleans. Brevet Major John Mountfort, another recent arrival, noted the improvement of the defensive works which now included a trench, new pickets and blockhouses. The total regular force available to defend the new works and the remains of the nearby village were one hundred and eighty men and officers plus a party of citizen rangers numbering about thirty. One hundred friendly Indians were encamped outside of the works and declared their readiness to fight their brethren.[72] Quoting a letter from "a gentleman attached to Major Mountfort's command," the *National Intelligencer* allowed the author to

32

declare, "Through the interposition of Providence, I am now alive to let you know it. We are really in the theater of war of the most horrible kind." This same writer was one of the lucky ones scheduled to ride out and overtake Dade's command and join in the march to Fort King. His group was delayed long enough to meet the three survivors, "horribly mangled" who gave them the news of Dade's demise.[73]

Fort Brooke, on that terrible day, was totally isolated and without means of defense against a massed attack by the Seminoles and their allies. The December 28, 1835, battle had cost the command at Fort Brooke one hundred and eight men and left only the sparse garrison described above. The fort had been strengthened but the outlying buildings of the nascent village had been destroyed, "in order to afford no cover by which the approach of the foe might be facilitated." Like their colleagues in Key West, they had cleared a field of fire that gave the enemy no chance of surprise attack.[74] The news did not improve with the knowledge of the defeat of the force under General Duncan L. Clinch at the Withlacoochee River on December 31. There would be no immediate relief by land.

What brought on this isolation, fear and imminent threat of death? One of the major causes of the Second Seminole War (1835-1842) was the constant and consistent lack of understanding between two differing cultures: one European, the other Native American. Ignoring the advice of those who knew the Native American culture best, the government of the United States insisted upon discussing issues and signing treaties with "the chief" of the tribe. Government negotiators failed to understand that the Creek, Seminole and Miccosukee culture relied upon a tribal council in which no individual chief had any power to conduct negotiations and enter into treaties without the approval of said council. When a government agent did not get the answers or lands demanded, he often recommended that the government ignore the "chief" they were dealing with and find someone more pliable. That new person would then be recognized as the "chief" and new negotiations would be conducted until the desired result was reached. The tribal council was totally ignored. The clan system upon which much of the political power within the Native cultures worked was brushed aside as so much poppycock. The government and its agents were ethno-centric to the extreme. Within this very simplified scheme, no meaningful treaty could ever be agreed to and understood.

The Second Seminole War was, in many ways, a continuation of the First Seminole War and the internecine warfare that followed. The final Indian Agent before the war, Wiley Thompson, continued the government's policies and attempted to get the Seminoles to emigrate from Florida to Indian Territory west of the Mississippi River. Thompson's manner was haughty and insulting. He continually addressed the Seminole negotiators as if they were the President's children or court appointed wards. After Thompson was killed, on the same day as Dade's force was eliminated, Alligator declared that the warriors danced around his hung scalp and mocked his language and mannerisms. He would no longer insult anyone.[75]

Without belaboring the complex origins of this most brutal war, it is worth noting that the white lust for land, cattle and other property was a major driving force toward war. Recent work by historian Ronald Satz indicates the constant problems that arose with the initiation of the Indian Removal Act and the bureaucracy it created. The lack of staff in Washington to oversee the Indian Agents, who were often corrupt political appointees, the insufficient funding of the removal by Congress, the parsimonious allotments for the military establishment assigned to carry out this policy, and the overall planning deficiencies of the government all helped to create an impossible situation. Many of these difficulties began long before Andrew Jackson became president but they did not improve with his, and subsequent, administrations.[76] From the initial confusion over supplying the Indians in Florida through the contract with Benjamin Chaires, to the insensitive administration of Wiley Thompson, the policy of removal in Florida was replete with errors, confusion and corruption. The final outbreak of war was not a surprise to anyone in Florida.

In 1823, the Treaty of Moultrie Creek decided the ultimate fate of the Seminoles and the other Native Americans living in Florida. The ultimate solution was intended to be removal, but from the beginning of the United States occupation of Florida, a reservation was decided upon and surveyed by James Gadsden. This army of-

34

ficer had earlier recommended the Tampa Bay area as an ideal position from which to control any possible foreign influences upon the Seminoles and their cohorts.[77] Tampa Bay was ideal from Gadsden's point of view because, as he wrote, "The Indians have long been in the habit of keeping up an intercourse and active trade with the Cuban fishermen, and to this cause, principally, has been ascribed the encouragement hitherto given to absconding negroes, and the savage depredations committed on cattle, estates, &c."[78] This constant theme of interdicting trade between the Cuban fishermen on the Florida coast and the Seminoles plays an important role in why Tampa Bay was chosen for the location of Fort Brooke. This letter also introduces the problem of the escaped slaves that has been the center of academic discussions concerning the Seminole Wars. There can be no disputing the fact that this facet of Southern society was a major trigger for this war. With the founding of Fort Brooke in 1824 and the arrival of the agent for dispersing the rations to the Seminoles, the stage was set for the events of 1836.[79]

As noted above, the situation of Captain Belton and the garrison at Fort Brooke was desperate. The Florida militia would be of little assistance in the defense of the area, so help could not be expected from this quarter either. By 1835, the militia situation in Florida was, at best, pathetic. Although Governor William P. Duval had requested 240 muskets and 250 rifles for this force in 1832, Florida had received only 198 obsolete firearms from the Federal Government. Assuming that the arms supplied to the militia was a guarantee of effective use was beyond reality. The reality was that the militia of Florida, even with the arms provided by the government or from personal ownership, was neither large enough to handle the situation at hand nor well trained in the basic elements of military drill, use of firearms or tactics. At the outbreak of the war, there was not one registered gunsmith in the entire Territory.[80] Belton could not and did not expect any help from this source.

After learning of the fate of Dade's command, Captain Belton had to quickly assemble a resourceful defense. On January 2, 1836, he took the friendly Indians camped outside of the stockade into the service of the United States. This force numbered about ninety to one hundred men and would be used to threaten or attack the rear of the enemy. As it was impossible for emigration of the Indians to take place under the circumstances, the Captain felt these friendly Indians would be of "infinite service" to the post.[81] Three days later, Belton wrote to W. C. Bolton, then commanding at Pensacola, "This place is now invested by all the Florida Indians in the Field with a large force of Negroes, particularly from the plantations of Tomoka & Smyrna, as appears from the examination of a prisoner just taken." The Captain continued, "The fleet of transports ... are of course, in alarm, & without arms & subject to an attack, & as far as I can judge, from the flanking movements of the Indians, down the bay, they intend an attack on the island between the Transports & this post, where the friendly Indians families are posted, till they can be shipped." Belton concluded his letter declaring, "We have no communication with any post in Florida & I am of the opinion that 7500 men could not force it at present." He then requested of Bolton all the arms and men he could spare for the defense of Fort Brooke.[82] In a second letter to Bolton, Belton stated, "We are prepared for the most desperate assault they can make, inspirited as they are by the action at Withlacoochee on the 28th."[83] While Belton was worried about facing the entire Seminole nation and its allies at Tampa, Governor John Eaton and General Richard K. Call were writing out their notes on recent events. Eaton addressed his letter to Secretary of War Lewis Cass on the 7th of January: "Our troops & the Indians (400 in number) have had a fight on the bank of the Amaxura River [Withlacoochee's old name]. The loss of the Indians is about fifty – no prisoners. The battle lasted for an hour, Gen'l Clinchs regulars are the principal sufferers. Fifty or sixty are wounded & five or six killed." The Governor then erroneously stated that Wiley Thompson had died in this battle, demonstrating the problems of communication in war on the frontier.[84] Call wrote to Eaton on the same day noting, "The precise strength of the enemy has not been ascertained. It is variously estimated by men of intelligence to be from 1200 to 2000." The General continued, "... all the Plantations South of Tampa were destroyed. ... They have raised the Tomahawk in despair, they are waging a war of extermination and the Safety of our fellow citizens requires that not a moment should be lost in carrying the war into their own country." Call also observed that the country favored the Indians' style of warfare and that an army of 2,500 to 3,000 should be immediately sent to the field.[85] Captain Belton, from his isolation in Tampa, could do nothing to prevent the destruction of the plantations south of his position.

Governor Eaton, on the 9th of January, wrote again to Cass hoping for more rapid action from that quarter. He once more related the necessity of disbanding the Spanish fishing ranchos in southern Florida who, he charged, "no doubt aid & encourage the Indians, under their fishing pretext."[86] Yet, Captain Belton says little at this juncture about Spanish assistance to the Indians. He did not, however, remain idle and penned up in his stockade. On the 12th of January, he led a command out of the post and toward the end of the day made the capture of one Indian. This prisoner was from the Peace River encampment and provided Belton with some information he hitherto had not possessed. The Indian informed the Captain that there had been an additional battle fought between the Miccosukees and the militia on the Alachua prairie (Paynes' Prairie) and that the whites had fled the field [which was substantially correct]. He also opined that another engagement had taken place on the Santa Fe River but offered no specifics. The same prisoner also declared that the Miccosukees were supposed to have attacked Fort Brooke the previous evening, but did not. Belton then informed the Adjutant General of the Army (Roger Jones) that he was affixing bayonets to poles stuck in the ground and covered with twigs and leaves in the hopes of breaking up any direct assault on the fort.[87] The Captain was taking no chances and doing the best job possible under trying circumstances.

Over in Havana harbor, Commodore A. J. Dallas also heard the news. As commander of the United States West Indies Squadron he had the responsibility for any demands made upon him for the defense of the country. He immediately went into action and headed toward Key West in his flagship, the *Constellation,* after ordering all the marines he could spare from the fleet to Tampa Bay and a detachment of seamen from the fleet to look after the lighthouse at Cape Florida.[88] By the 17th of January the marines were on the way to Fort Brooke where they would assist the army until August of 1836.[89] The immediate need was not just for the fleet vessels of the Squadron but also shallow draught vessels of the Revenue Service to reach closer to land and penetrate up Florida's shallow waterways. At the behest of Governor Eaton and Territorial Delegate Joseph White, the Treasury Department was prevailed upon to order its valuable cutters to aid in the military effort. The cutters *Dexter, Washington* and *Dallas* were soon doing yeoman's service and providing much needed relief to coastal inhabitants and the army.[90] Again, one of the missions of the cutters was to intercept any trade between the Spanish fishermen, Cuba and the Indians.[91] Belton was much appreciative of the sending of the marines and the arrival of the cutters because he had discovered a plan to attack the fort by the combined forces of Micanopy, Osceola, and Little Cloud. The arrival of the marines may have been the deciding factor in why this attack did not materialize.[92]

Governor Eaton was also seeking reinforcements for the beleaguered station and had even suggested that the army begin a campaign from Tampa moving down the western side of the peninsula. At the same time he offered the concept of sending troops to Charlotte Harbor and rescuing the inhabitants there and sending an additional force up the Peace or Myakka Rivers in a sort of pincer movement to cut off the Indians in that area. In addition to the inhabitants of the fisheries in Charlotte Harbor, Dr. Crews, the customs collector, with his family was stationed there. Dr. Crews had already been a few years on the job at the time of the outbreak and knew most of the local Indian and Spanish fishermen. So far removed from any type of military force, he was in immediate danger and even more isolated than Tampa Bay. Eaton's suggested plan of operations was intended to accomplish crushing the Indians on the west coast and saving the inhabitants and collector at the same time.[93]

The arrival of the marines under Lieutenant N. S. Waldron was one of the more important events in forestalling an attack by the Seminoles and their allies. With detachments from the *Constellation* and the *St Louis* it was an obvious signal that other troops were on the way. Arriving aboard the *Vandalia* and the other transports this force greatly augmented the numbers visible to spies. The *Vandalia* remained in the harbor, which added an imposing spectacle for the attackers to contemplate.[94]  With the almost daily arrival of supplies from the numerous transports, the Seminole leadership was quick to realize that other troops and ships would soon be in the area.  The obvious build up of material and men could only mean one thing to this enlightened group: it was time to rethink their strategy.

The obvious landing of the forces of General Edmund P. Gaines at Fort Brooke in February probably signified the end of any real danger to Fort Brooke and nearby settlers.  However, his landing almost did away with the post!  In a letter to Captain Thomas Webb, commander of the *Vandalia*, Gaines outlined his immediate plans.  In this letter of February 10, 1836, Gaines proposed using the marines and crews of the navy to transfer the men, inhabitants and Indians from the post to the empty transport ships in the harbor for better security.  He asked the Captain if he would allow this measure to take place under the protecting guns of his proud ship.  Gaines was contemplating using the entire garrison force, including the marines, to go to the relief of the forces at Fort Drane (Clinch's partially fortified plantation home in northern Marion County).[95]  Gaines was still thinking of abandoning the post on the 13th of February when Captain Webb notified Dallas of the proposal.  With the arrival of the Louisiana Volunteers under General Persifor Smith, the need for the garrison troops was lessened and it may be presumed that this arrival saved the fort for the time being.[96]

As word of the Seminole attacks in Florida reached the rest of the nation, the people of the neighboring and other southern states began to volunteer for service in Florida.  These fresh troops were under few illusions as to the nature of the enemy.  In its January 29, 1836 edition, the prominent *National Intelligencer* noted the tenacity of the Seminoles and their allies: "The Indians themselves, heretofore a conquered people, and from whose energy no danger was apprehended, have been profiting from the false security of the whites.  Gaining experience from past defeats, and putting into exercise their whole skill and resources, have on a sudden started up a courageous and determined host."  The paper continued in noting the tactics of the Seminoles: "Nor have these rude sons of the forest displayed any want of skill or foresight; on the contrary, they have manifested a wary dissimulation, celerity of movement, courage in attacking and a skill in retreating, subversive of all our military plans."[97] This wily enemy of white civilization lay in wait for the volunteers from South Carolina, Tennessee, Alabama, Georgia and the District of Columbia. The nation was also getting ready to send in one of its finest generals, Winfield Scott, a true hero of the War of 1812.

Gaines' force soon left Tampa Bay and headed toward the Withlacoochee where they would meet with great difficulty and be rescued by the very forces they had come to relieve. At the same time, Winfield Scott was amassing a large force of regulars and volunteers for a push from the eastern portion of the Territory in an elaborate plan to entrap the Seminoles in a three-pronged pincer movement. In early March, Colonel William Lindsay, Second Artillery, arrived at Ft. Brooke and proceeded to organize for the coming campaign. Sent by Scott to move his troops, the marines and a large contingent of Alabama volunteers northward toward the Cove of the Withlacoochee, Lindsay had difficulty from the beginning. By the 13th of March, the column had begun to move out toward the final staging area, Chocachatti (near modern Brooksville). On the way, Lindsay decided to construct a post closer to their line of march and ordered the building of Fort Alabama (later site of Fort Foster). Arriving too late and wasting time and energy firing guns and scouting the area, the force never made its rendezvous and turned around and headed back to Tampa on the 31st of March. They fought one major skirmish along the way, but accomplished very little except an almost continual quarrelling among the volunteers and Colonel Lindsay. This was indicative of what would happen to other grand plans during this war.[98]

By mid-March 1836, the forces of the United States Army and Navy were working to expand their knowledge of the area and sent out several reconnaissance missions. One of the earliest was led by U. S. Naval Lieutenant Levin M. Powell, who led a detachment of twenty-five men to the shores of the Manatee River. The mission discovered no Indians at the alleged camp but did see signs of recent activity including a large number of footprints and cattle tracks. All were headed toward the area of Sarasota Bay or further south.[99] By the end of the month, the command at Tampa Bay was confident enough to send Lieutenant Powell with a force from the *Vandalia* northward to the Anclote River after reexamining the Manatee River to the head of boat navigation. Most of the islands between the Manatee River and the Anclote River were explored for recent signs, but again nothing was found. Powell attributed the lack of signs on the Anclote Islands to their distance from the mainland, which made them difficult to access.[100] The Seminoles and their allies had apparently fled inland to await their next battle.

Charlotte Harbor was examined by the U. S. Revenue Cutter *Washington* under the command of Captain Ezekiel Jones at the end of March. The command fell in with a number of Indians camped at the mouth of the Myakka River. About twenty-two Indians were seen in one body by the boat under Lieutenant Smith and numerous fires were seen in the distance. The two guides, both from Bunce's fishing ranchos, proceeded ahead of the main body of men and met with three of the "hostile" party. They soon recognized each other and entered into a parley. The two intrepid guides could not, however, ascertain the numbers or size of the other encampments without giving themselves away as enemy spies.[101] On April 2nd, Lieutenant Powell left the *Vandalia* and proceeded to some of the islands in Charlotte Harbor. Here Powell, "found the inhabitants flying in every direction to escape the fury of the Indians." Upon examination of the collector's house, he found it burnt to the ground and no sign of Dr. Crews or his family. Sailing Master Stephen C. Rowan was then dispatched to the nearest mainland and came upon some of those responsible for the destruction. Rowan immediately attacked this band and reported killing two and taking one captive. The others escaped into the nearby woods where Rowan's small force dared not to go.[102] The report filed by Lieutenant Powell indicates that the inhabitants of "Josepa" Island were those he helped to rescue from the clutches of Wy-ho-kee and his band.[103]

Captain M. P. Mix of the U.S.S. *Concord* wrote on the 30th of April that there were still some inhabitants left at Charlotte Harbor and that little protection could be offered them as the closest units were thirty miles away. He also wrote to A. J. Dallas that, "The Indians are assembling in all directions with a determination, as they threaten, to destroy all of the fisheries in the Bay and to burn the Transports at anchor in Hillsboro Harbor, or such of them as may remain after the departure of the volunteers." Mix was concerned that the troop strength and the condition of the stockade made it possible, in his opinion, for the Indians to succeed. Mix also noted that General Scott had requested that the *Concord* remain at anchor in the harbor and that Lieutenant Waldron's marines also stay put. He declared that a "state of anxiety" existed at Tampa Bay for want of knowledge of the next moves by the Seminoles and their allies. Such a state of anxiety was probably unfounded but it is very understandable given the successes of the Indians in resisting the United States' best generalship.

The high tensions at Tampa Bay were likely to be increased as the news from two other borders reached the area. In Texas the revolution for independence was drawing much of the national press interest and there was daily discussion as to the role of the United States in that conflict. Many were in favor of sending regular troops into the foray and committing the navy to a full time blockade of Mexico. Regular voyages were undertaken by the navy to gather information and keep a watchful eye on the developments there. Most of these sailings came from the West Indies Squadron thus drawing away needed naval strength from the Florida coasts. In the north, the revolt in Upper Canada also drew away some of the military attention and forces to guard against any problems arising there. This further depleted the military strength available to fight the Seminoles in Florida. As the total military might of the United States numbered less than ten thousand men at this time, any venture away from the center of action had possible dire consequences.

Even after the scouts of the Manatee River by the forces under Lieutenant Powell, rumors still persisted about a large force of "Indian negroes" on that waterway. According to the St. Augustine *Florida Herald* for April 23, 1836, "Three days ago two Indian negroes were taken – from one of whom information was obtained of a negro fort on the Manatee River, about 15 miles south of Tampa Bay. Gen. Eustis had taken up the line of march to attack. It was not known how many negroes are in the fort, but the negro stated there was a large number." Such gossip spread among

42

the Territorial newspapers like a wild fire and added greatly to the anxieties of the population.

In mid-April, General Persifor Smith of the Louisiana Volunteers and Captain Ross of the U. S. Marines came on board the *Dallas* to discuss the coming short campaign up the Myakka River where the enemy had been reported previously. From April 12th to April 17th the men from the *Vandalia, Dallas,* and other smaller vessels prepared for their adventure. For a while there was some hope that the enemy would be found but after the troop's departure on the 18th of April, little could be expected. Dr. Crews' body, and that of his assistant, had been found and it was presumed that most of those responsible had already left the area. This was confirmed when General Smith and his forces returned with nothing much to show for their extended efforts. According to the *Florida Herald* for May 12, 1836, "… there seems to be an opinion that the Indian captured by Lieut. Powell committed the outrage on Dr. Crews, as he was employed in the boat of Dr. C. and was heard to make threats to that effect previously."[104]

By the end of April, Fort Brooke was beginning to take on a familiar appearance. According to one writer, stationed at "Shelton Camp, (16 miles from Tampa Bay)," the fort was a breath of fresh air: "Tampa is a beautiful place, with orange and pride of India trees in blossom, the sight of which was reviving to us thirsty travelers in the desert. The air acted on my lungs like exhilarating gas."[105] John Erwin of the Tennessee volunteers also observed that, "Fort Brooke situated on Tampa Bay was a military post of considerable importance as it was situated within the hollow of a curve in the bay. It was three parts out of the four surrounded by water, its watch towers and sentinel could be seen a mile before reaching it, our camp was one mile north of the fort." Erwin also raved about the abundance of oysters nearby which claimed made his men "better and fatter immediately."[106] These observations differ significantly from those recorded by earlier visitors prior to the change in location. The old fort at the time of the earliest expeditions against the Seminoles was described by W. F. Rowles, Surgeon for the Creek Volunteers. Writing in the *Southern* magazine in 1841, the doctor recalled, "The appearance of Fort Brooke during the stay of the Creeks was singularly animating. The Barracks and store houses are built facing the bay and the river Hillsboro, and present long rows of low combustible *shanties*, some of them whitewashed and neatly paled in with old staves of barrels, tierces, &c. It was amusing," he continued, "to see the taste and ingenuity of our officers exerted in such a place, with such means, to make their quarters comfortable. The post was guarded by a circle of sentinels. The underbrush cut down for some rods towards the forest and beyond the Hillsboro." He too noted the watch towers and added that many of the tents were lining the old streets among the orange trees. Numerous cannon were to be seen pointing "ominously toward all the approaches."[107] Alexander B. Meek noted in his journal the existence of the famed Live Oak trees and the numerous orange trees on the grounds. He compared it favorably to "an ornamental college green" and declared the post impregnable against any possible Indian attack.[108] It should be remembered that most of the small settlement had been destroyed to create an open field of fire for the garrison. The settlement contained about thirty or forty families all of whom were considered quite poor.[109]

The beginning of May brought on sickness and it was reported that Fort Brooke was no exception. According to the *National Intelligencer* for May 6, 1836, "There was 400 sick at Tampa Bay, and the climate was getting worse and worse for the Army." This report came on the heels of the Battle of Thonotosassa. Here the forces sent back to Fort Alabama to remove the materials and equipment were fired upon by the Seminoles while attempting to cross Thonotosassa Creek. It was the hardest fighting General Scott's forces faced in their time in Florida. Members of the Fourth Infantry and the Second Artillery were joined by the Alabama Volunteers under Colonel William Chisolm in a very spirited battle in which two whites were killed and twenty-five wounded (the majority of them from the volunteer ranks). The loss to the Seminoles and their allies is unknown. The fight lasted about an hour and ended with a charge with fixed bayonets by the Regulars and Volunteers. The battle also featured the use of cannon to some effect, an unusual occurrence in this war. The Indians had chosen their position well. It was on a curve in the creek lined with dense hammocks. The first fire, as is common in such battles, caused the most damage to the U. S. forces. The men then retired to Fort Brooke to recoup and refurbish themselves.[110]

May not only brought on the onset of the "rainy season" in 1836 but it also saw the beginning of the agitation to remove the marines back to Pensacola and other naval assignments. Major Henry Wilson, then commanding the fort refused to release Waldron's marine detachment for other duties. He felt strongly that the security of the post would be compromised if the marines left at this juncture. Captain Mix of the *Concord* disagreed with this assessment. Mix noted that there was a relative lull in activity for the marines and that much of their time was spent guarding William Bunce's rancho at the mouth of the bay. Wilson was waiting for either reinforcements or replacements for Lieutenant Waldron's valuable force. Until such time as either of these alternatives arrived, the Major was not about to release the marines. [They did not leave until August of 1836.][111]

One of the more humanitarian gestures found in this period of activity involved the removal of the families around Sarasota Bay, known locally as the Caldes Rancho. On May 8th Lieutenant Charles P. Childs of the revenue cutter *Washington* was ordered to sail to Sarasota Bay and confer with "Old Caldes" or his son. He was to convey to them the danger in which they existed and advise them to move to either Tampa or to Bunce's Rancho where they could be afforded protection. The settlers were not eager to leave their homes and were afraid that the army would separate the families because many of the wives were Indian. Many in the settlement had already departed when Childs arrived, though he did observe about twenty individuals living there at that time. All were busy loading canoes which were filled to capacity and rode low in the water. The only thing preventing the final departure was the weather.[112]

Early June found the army clearing out the ever growing shrubs and weeds from the open area around Fort Brooke. Making the post more inhabitable by larger numbers was also on the agenda of the officers. Gardens which had been neglected had to be tended and some of the early crops harvested. In addition, three advanced redoubts were constructed at this time. Colonel Lindsay and his force were ordered on to Mobile and his departure was approved by many in camp, especially the remaining troops from Alabama. The only Indian activity reported in early June was that of a few raiding parties who stole a number of cattle during night raids. But it was the sickness that worried Major Wilson and he observed that the post had only one assistant surgeon, Dr. Reynolds. If this one medical officer should become ill, the remainder of the post would suffer. Like other shortages in the officer corps, the lack of medical officers was a severe handicap for the army serving in remote areas. Wilson requested a second medical officer for the post, but did not receive one while the Major was in command.[113]

The usual diseases of the Florida summer hit the troops hard. The various fevers, "bilious", "black vomit", and intermittent played havoc on the health of the army and navy. The volunteers also suffered from the climate. Colonel John Warren commanded the Second Military District for the Florida Militia and reported, on June 9th, an outbreak of the "measles" among his troops.[114] This is not a serious disease in this day and age, but it was deadly to the frontier settlers and military personnel. Mumps too made their appearance in this time but did not make their way to Tampa Bay. The army, because of the fevers' appearance in the summer months and the deadly effects it had on the troops seldom campaigned in the "rainy season" in Florida. Not until Colonel William J. Worth took command in 1841 did Florida see a summer campaign.

The rainy season did bring on new administrative tasks for the commander and garrison at Fort Brooke. Money for the emigration of the Seminoles of Black Dirt's band and others had to be accounted for and rations distributed. Funding and rations for the "suffering inhabitants" also had to be allotted to the settlers seeking refuge in the area. One of the more emotionally difficult tasks remained to be accomplished: the selling of the effects of the soldiers killed in Dade's last battle, and settling the debts of the officers, like Captain G. W. Gardiner. The proceeds from the sale of the effects usually went into the company fund handled by the company commander but receipted through the Paymaster General of the army.[115] Such tasks were not welcomed by anyone in the company.

Fort Brooke and the settlements near Tampa Bay were relatively safe from the attacks of the Seminoles and their allies at the end of the first campaigns. The war had already seen the defeats of armies under Generals Clinch, Call, Gaines and Scott. Waiting in the future were the terms of Generals Thomas Jesup, Zachary Taylor, Walker Armistead and William Jenkins Worth. Six more years of guerilla warfare remained ahead for the army, navy, marines and volunteers. The Second Seminole War was to be the longest continually fought and most expensive of all of the United States' wars with its Native Americans. This war brought glory to none of the political or military leaders and played a role in the increasing agitation against slavery, just then beginning in the northern portion of the country. The panic and terror of the first six months of the war in Tampa Bay subsided into a near routine of shuffling the troops into and out of the Territory and seeing to the emigration of most of the Seminoles, blacks and Miccosukees to the west. Those who survived those first months of the war never forgot them. It was a time to try the souls of all men, women and children of all sides.

# The Upper Florida Keys at the
# Outbreak of War in 1836

*D*uring Florida's Territorial Period (1821-1845), Indian Key was one of the most controversial settlements in the Territory. The major reason for this was Jacob Housman. The ambitions of Jacob Housman are well established in the island's history, from his seeking status for it as a port of entry, and to making it the county seat of the newly created Dade County in 1836. Housman, as historian Michael Schene has noted, went so far as to construct a courthouse on the island with his own funds. Also documented is the erstwhile Housman's conviction for embezzling goods taken from the *Ajax*, which had grounded on Carysfort Reef in 1836. Schene has also recorded the fact that most of the appointed officers for the newly formed County of Dade were friends and associates of the notorious wrecker.[116]    Yet, the exploits of Jacob Housman are not the only story of the famous Key in 1836.

As early as April 24, 1835, Major Francis L. Dade received orders to patrol between Cape Florida and Charlotte Harbor, "to examine the Country lying between the above-mentioned points, and to order and compel to return to their boundary line, all the Indians that may be found without it."[117]    The report of Indians moving outside of their assigned area raised a few apprehensions, but did not appear to greatly disturb most of the residents. A routine report of a message found in a bottle captured the attention of the Jacksonville *Courier* on August 6, 1835, but little else was reported. By August 20th, the same paper confidently reported, "There can be no doubt now, but that the Seminole Indians will commence their emigration

48

on the 1st day of November next." Little wonder Mr. Spencer began advertising his health resort on Indian Key and noting his, "... very commodious buildings, sufficient to accommodate any number of persons who may favor him with a call, with separate rooms fitted expressly for families."[118] Although there were occasional notices of Indians in the area, no one seemed too alarmed.

Being isolated from the mainland and Key West, it took some time for the news of "Dade's Massacre" and the killing of Indian Agent Wiley Thompson to reach Indian Key. A disaster closer to home was soon learned of, when the family of Captain William Cooley was slaughtered at New River, just eight days after the Dade debacle. On January 11, 1836, William Whitehead, the collector of customs at Key West, notified Commodore Alexander Dallas of the immediate situation: "Dear Sir: Most painful intelligence has been received today from the Main land, of the massacre of two Companies U. S. Troops, with all their officers, while marching from Tampa Bay to Fort King. - Intelligence has also been received that the Indians in the Vicinity of Cape Florida have likewise massacred a family on the Coast, and that the inhabitants of all Settlements in that vicinity are removing down towards Key West."[119] What Whitehead failed to realize was that most of the settlers had already reached Indian Key by this time and were in a state of shock and disbelief. Commodore Dallas acted as quickly as feasible and sent fifty men towards Cape Florida, the Miami River, New River and the various Keys hoping to assist anyone fleeing from the Indians. Reports also noted that the lighthouse at Cape Florida had been out and that crews were on the way to reinstall the light for the passage of ships.[120] Strange as it may seem to modern eyes, two days after this last report, on January 23, 1836, the Key West *Inquirer* stated that the Indians had not gone any further than the Cape. "It has been satisfactorily ascertained," the paper reported, "that they had not a few days back yet visited Cape Florida, although their fires had been observed at no great distance in the interior. Four canoes of friendly Indians or those accustomed to trading at Indian Key were in that vicinity a few days since, but it is said they received warning not to land and soon afterward disappeared." After regretting that the Indians were not allowed to land and be detained, the newspaper then detailed the situation on the key, "Considerable alarm still prevails at

Indian Key, and we think not without reason, as the force they can muster for its defense does not amount to more than 15 men - and as parties of Indians have been in the habit of visiting it for the purpose of traffic, they are consequently acquainted with the resources of the Island, the value of the property there &c."[121] The account appearing in the Charleston *Courier* for January 23, 1836, from Indian Key on 15th January, noted the Indians were trying to trade for powder and shot. The writer believed these to be the same as those responsible for the Cooley Massacre. A further report, dated the 17th January, declared the Indians were massing at Cape Sable and New River. If the *Inquirer's* report be true, the defense of the Key was almost impossible.

However, in the midst of the beginnings of war, the confusion and the trauma of the refugees, Housman, Lemuel Otis, Joseph Tift, Silas Fletcher, Thomas Greene, James L. Spencer, and a host of others, totaling one hundred and three signatures, petitioned Congress to maintain the division of Monroe County, as passed in the Legislature of the Territory. In this action they were opposed by the leadership of Key West, notably Asa Tift, William Marvin, J. B. Browne, Stephen R. Mallory, and others.[122] Politics as usual continued in the face of the enemy.

Commodore Dallas' forces were soon patrolling the area and searching for the enemy. The Commodore reported to the Secretary of the Navy, Mahlon Dickerson, on February 5th, that Lieutenant Bache had taken marines and others to Cape Florida and restored the light. So confident was the Commodore, he notified the Secretary, "There being no immediate danger to be apprehended for the safety of this, or any adjoining Keys, I shall leave here [Key West] tomorrow morning, accompanied by the *St. Louis,* for Pensacola."[123] To ease the fears of the inhabitants of the Keys, the Revenue Cutter *Jefferson* remained in the area cruising the Keys. As reported in the *Army and Navy Chronicle* for March 17th, "Captain Jackson of the Revenue Cutter *Jefferson* has been ordered from the St. Johns, to cruise among the Keys near New River, for the protection of that part of the Territory. Capt. Jackson, though a short time among us, by his kind, officer-like, and gentlemanly deportment, gained the good will and esteem of all who shared his acquaintance. His arrival among us first gave the inhabitants of the River a feeling of greater security."

50

Unfortunately for the "inhabitants of the River," most of whom had fled to the security of St. Augustine or Indian Key (depending on the river), their homes and plantations had been destroyed by the Indian raiders.

The inhabitants of the Keys should have felt even more secure because of the efficiency of the local militia unit under the command of Major Thomas Eastin and Captain Jacob Housman. Yet, there appears to have been some problems with the unit allegedly formed by Captain Housman. According to a Congressional report, Housman's unit was supposed to have served between January 9, through June 9, and again from June 9, through August 24, 1836. However, although Housman submitted bills totaling $5,219.82 to the Committee on Claims, none of the necessary papers were ever "authenticated" by proper authorities. It appears that no one ever officially mustered the troops into service at thirty cents per day, with fifteen cents per day offered for rations. No one ever certified that the unit was actually mustered in nor that they ever served one day on their assigned task, which was to patrol the Keys and islands to prevent the escape of Indians and "disaffected negroes" to the West Indies. No one from Indian Key, if they were ever in this unit, was paid for any service performed in the early days of 1836.[124]

However, wrecking continued to occupy the attention of everyone on the Key. In a report published in the *Army and Navy Chronicle* for April 7, 1836, the strong currents along the Keys were the major culprit in causing an unusually large number of wrecks along the Florida Reef. The speed of the current was estimated at three to three and a half miles per hour and when vessels got caught in it and on the coral reefs, it was nearly impossible to free them from their doom. According to this report, "vast amounts" of cargo were saved by the "bold and enterprising men who follow wrecking on this coast." The fact that the war, itself, had increased the traffic is not commented upon, yet this played a major role in the rise of wrecking revenues at Key West in Judge Webb's court.

All was not quiet on Indian Key and immediate danger was sensed by all. As early as March, two Indians and "one Spaniard" were detained on the Key and thought by all to be spies. These individuals verified that a large number of Indians had amassed at Cape Sable. Regardless of the presence of the *Jefferson*, the inhabitants complained of no Federal forces in area. As one writer put it, "We are certainly in danger of an attack, and it astonishes me that of the force now in Florida none is sent round here, but they are driving the Indians directly upon us. Shocking indeed would be the result if they should come down upon us." Another echoed this complaint and stated, "It is of great importance that a force should be immediately sent to this part of Florida. This place as well as Key West is much exposed, but I have no doubt this will be the first to receive an attack; we have no protection, there is not even one Revenue Cutter now on the Coast."[125] Although this was not strictly true, the sense of alarm is apparent and clearly represents the fear felt by most residents of Indian Key.

On May 28, 1836, the Key West *Inquirer* reported that the Cape Florida Light House had been abandoned by Captain Griffin after he spotted six Indian canoes, filled with warriors, headed toward New River and passing within two or three miles of the Light House. He met his replacement on the way there and the latter could not be deterred from fulfilling his duty. The report, which undoubtedly was known in Indian Key before being reported further south, again increased the tensions on the island. As the report noted, "Emboldened by being left in entire possession of the coast, they no doubt will make occasional incursions along the Keys and Islands, and the citizens will be subject to depredations from them continually." The newspaper went on to attack the government for not stationing troops along the coast, especially at Cape Florida. This position, close to the coontie grounds at New River, was supposed to have been occupied early in the year, but was not at that time. The citizens were obviously feeling the pressure of the continued Indian presence.

In June, the residents of the Keys, under the leadership of William Marvin, petitioned Commodore Dallas, declaring, " ... the Inhabitants on the Southern Coast of Florida, particularly at Indian Key, consider themselves dangerously exposed to the incursions of the Indians. It is ascertained without doubt, that a large body of Indians are collecting in the neighborhood of Cape Sable, but twenty miles from Indian Key. Their fires are seen from that Island." These citizens noted the constantly observed traffic of the Indians along the coast and among the islands. They also stated that the Light House was about to be abandoned. In a note of final desperation, the petitioners informed the Commodore that the two Indians captured along with the Spaniard had escaped by jumping overboard from the *Dexter*, and, although one was supposed wounded, the others escaped unharmed. They respectfully asked that a cutter be assigned to the area permanently.[126]

On June 18, 1836, the reports came that every day Indians were seen in the vicinity of the Cape Florida Light House and that it would soon have to be abandoned. Indian Key was again noted as being under scrutiny by the Indians and that it could be attacked at almost any time. As the report noted, "The island being so situated that the Indians can reconnoiter at any time and see what vessels are in harbor, they will undoubtedly, (if they attack at all) do so in the absence of an armed vessel." Again, the call came for a permanent establishment of cutter patrols and the stationing of armed troops in the area. The Indians, it was feared, could attack at any time, and, under the circumstances, without reprisal.[127] A little over a month later, on July 23, 1836, the Cape Florida Light House was attacked and all the buildings burned. The keeper, Mr. Thompson, survived the attack, but his man, Carter, did not.[128] The news of this action pushed the fear to a higher level.

Aside from the occasional stops of the revenue cutters and other naval vessels, no large contingent of troops was stationed on Indian Key. This situation changed in late July when the Schooner *Motto* left Key West with a detachment of marines specifically for the protection of Indian Key.[129] On August 18, 1836, Lieutenant Thomas J. Leib, in command of the detachment, described what he found at Indian Key.

> ... I proceeded to Key West in the *Motto*, landed the mules, ammunition, and field piece, and with all possible dispatch proceeded to Indian Key; arrived there on the 16th July, and called on Capt. Housman, the proprietor of the Key, to obey that part of my orders relative to powder. He assured me that he had not any more than sufficient to protect the place. He had on the Key, at that time, two six-pounders, and every man there has either a rifle or musket, consequently requires powder for the use of them. He has since then received two

more six-pounders for the defense of the place. He has also three double-barreled guns for his own use. ... the inhabitants were in a great state of alarm, Indians having been seen the day previous to our arrival in their canoes, within a short distance of the Key; and but a few days previous, two Indians, who had been made prisoners, escaped from the place, and had threatened to attack the Key, and murder every inhabitant.[130]

The troops did not stay long, most being ordered to duty on the mainland and the Key was soon left, again, to its own devices.

Shortly after the departure of these troops, an article appeared in the Charleston *Courier* which indicates the essential weakness of the defenses. Quoting the Tallahassee *Floridian*, the Charleston newspaper stated, "The Floridian says that a gentleman arrived in Tallahassee from Key West who states that a vessel recently touched at Indian Key, commanded by a Spaniard and an American, laden with negroes supposed to have been procured from the Seminoles in exchange for ammunition. There was not sufficient inhabitants at Indian Key to detain the vessel."[131] The veracity of this statement is questionable, especially when we learn that the U. S. Cutter *Dexter* had been stationed there for six to eight weeks, during which time this incident allegedly took place. Captain Rudolph of the *Dexter* also noted in his report that the number of Indians near the Keys was "greatly overrated" and did not number one or two hundred.[132] While the exact situation on Indian Key during this limited time period may not be known, the anxiety level of those on the Key was undoubtedly very high.

This situation was not improved when news came of the destructtion of Captain Whalton's [spelled Whatton in the report] garden on Key Largo, chopping down his fruit trees and digging up his potatoes and vegetables. On October 8, 1836, the Indians attacked the Schooner *Mary* (a small fifteen ton vessel out of Key Vacca) while it was anchored in Tavenier Creek. The crew of five men made their escape "amidst a shower of bullets" in the life boat and made their way to Indian Key at eight o'clock the following morning. For several days thereafter, the Indians encamped on Key Largo and their smoky fires were constantly seen by the inhabitants.

Soon, a detachment of one hundred and seventy men, under Lieutenant L. Powell, arrived from the ship *Vandalia* and proceeded to drive the Indians into hiding.[133] About the same time, Territorial Governor Richard Keith Call was writing to Commodore Dallas about a combined attack by Florida militia and the U. S. Marines to drive the Indians from the area of Cape Florida and the Upper Keys.[134]

By the end of the year, operations were being planned and the troops put in motion that would soon lead to the establishment of a series of fortifications along the Florida coast. Yet the majority of the action and troops remained in northern Florida, leaving Indian Key's inhabitants anxious and poorer. With travel becoming more dangerous and Indians lurking along the coasts, much of the normal activity of the settlers was curtailed. Coontie gathering and flour manufacturing fell sharply with the loss of the coontie grounds along New River and other spots. Fishing and turtle gathering were greatly reduced and one report noted, "In consequence of the Indians being among several of the Keys, it is impossible to get a Turtle here at this time for any price."[135] Only wrecking brought in any usable income to the denizens of the Upper Keys. In the following year came the death of Captain John Whalton and the crew of the Carysfort Reef Lightship and other disasters. Not until General Thomas Jesup's 1837-38 campaign were more permanent fortifications established and the Indians less likely to attack the Key.[136] However, Indian Key was always vulnerable and each of its inhabitants were aware of the constant danger. That so many chose to stay and risk their lives and families says much about the spirit of these pioneers of the Keys. In this first year of the Second Seminole War, this spirit had been mightily tested.

First Delegate to Congress from the Territory, and Brigadier General of the Militia of Florida.

Published in New-York City by Geo. Thurston.

**Joseph Hernandez**
*(St. Augustine Historical Society)*

# St. Augustine:
# A Time of Trouble and Need

The winter of 1835-36 was cold and wet. Freezes were common in northern Florida and the troops at Fort Marion, St. Francis Barracks, Key West, Fort Brooke and Fort King were bundled up and fighting the dampness and chill. All were anticipating the removal of the Seminole and Miccosukee Indians from the peninsula of Florida as per the Treaties of Moultrie Creek and Payne's Landing and subsequent agreements. But that event was not to be and troubled times lay ahead. Incidents in the Alachua region had indicated that some of the Native Americans were not ready to depart the land of their fathers. Raids had been conducted on local farmers and cattlemen and tensions were running high. With the reported death of Charlie Emathla, one of the pro-emigration leaders among the Seminoles, the Indian Agent for Florida, Wiley Thompson, issued a warning that, "The citizens are warned to consult their own safety by guarding against Indian depredations."[137] The dispute over forced emigration had just gotten much hotter and was about to boil over.

Even before the death of Charlie Emathla, General Joseph Hernandez, the head of the Florida Militia in East Florida, had warned Governor John Eaton and Secretary of War Lewis Cass that certain Seminoles were beginning to show resistance to emigration. He noted that, "It is generally believed that they will not move without being made to do so by actual force." The general proceeded to inform his correspondents that almost everyone in St. Augustine and Jacksonville were convinced that the Indians would resist any attempt to forcibly remove them and that the local press reports were overly optimistic. With the danger rising, Hernandez requested that two to three hundred muskets with their corresponding accoutrements be sent as quickly as possible for the protection of the inhabitants. He planned to have one hundred and fifty to two hundred men in the field, mounted and armed, within a very short time to guard the plantations from Spring Garden to Palatka and then westerly towards the Suwannee River. Such an action, he believed, would secure that portion of the frontier and act as a deterrent to any Seminole action.[138]

General Duncan L. Clinch was the commanding officer of the Federal troops stationed in Florida. By December he had realized that open resistance was only a matter of time. He quickly ordered Hernandez to call out whatever forces he commanded in East Florida and place them at the ready to move.[139] The primary reasons Clinch was allowed to call out the militia was the small number of federal forces available to him and the fact that President Andrew Jackson was impatient to get the job done. General Clinch had merely 536 men available in Florida and only 26 of these were officers. Jackson had even instructed Cass to allow Clinch to call on Georgia for additional troops to put down the sporadic outbreaks and depredations.[140] This force was assigned the task of removing upwards to 5,000 Indians with and estimated 1,500 of them capable of bearing arms in resistance. This number did not include the large aggregate of blacks, free and formerly slave, whose exact force was unknown. Clinch's force was not going to be adequate to the job, and he suspected as much.[141]

To man the frontier posts throughout the country, the U. S. Army had only 6,758 men and officers available for duty.[142] This small force was to cover 53 active posts spread from Minnesota to Florida to Maine. It also had to worry about an outbreak of hostilities among the western Indians, problems along the Maine border, rising tensions in Texas and defending the sea coasts from possible invasion by a foreign enemy. Because of the rush for internal improvements, few engineers, topographic or otherwise, had worked extensively in Florida, and there was a severe shortage of geographic knowledge about the interior of the Territory. As General Thomas Jesup put it, "We have possessed Florida sixteen years; during the whole of that period we have had a topographical corps on the register, and borne on the army returns; but the officers have been taken from their appropriate duties and employed upon those purely civil; the consequence is that we have, perhaps, as little knowledge of the interior of Florida as of the interior of China."[143] The fact that Florida was in the Inter Tropical Convergence Zone, with its definite wet and dry seasons and subtropical climate, was not well known to the military. The oppressive heat and humidity of the climate had seldom been experienced by the regular forces and the militia probably did not hold its drills during the summer months when the effects of the climate were at their worst. Locations of rivers, streams and swamps were unknown to most of the military, regular or militia, and the fords, depths, velocities and widths of these natural objects were anyone's guess. Flora and fauna were unfamiliar to most who took the fields against the Seminoles and their allies. Lack of sanitary practices added to the increased rate of disease among the troops and killed many. Florida's other unique "critters" added to the problems of the regulars and militia and often led to a significant lowering of morale amongst the troops. Before the war's end over 1,500 would perish because of disease and related problems, including a large number of suicides. The military was totally unprepared for the nature of this war.

The militia and the regulars were both handicapped by the nature of the troops available to them to fight the war. The regular forces were heavily laden with foreigners who often did not speak English at all or understood only the minimal amount to get by the recruiting officers. From the 1820s to the 1850s the number of soldiers of foreign birth increased from about a fourth of all troops to nearly two thirds. Illiteracy was a problem for many and written orders often had to be translated before being understood by the troops. Recruiters were given bonuses for the number of men they signed up and often turned a blind eye when interviewing these unfit men and boys. The doctors performing physical examinations often had questionable calls to make. They had to check to make sure the recruit could see, hear and had the use of all of his limbs. They also checked under the recruit's arms and on the hips for the letter "D" which was indicative of a deserter who was trying to get back into the force. Ulcers, lacerations and other defects were also noted, as were whipping scars. Captain George McCall once noted that one of the recruits had answered that he was born in New York but his accent gave him away as having another possible place of origin. When asked where he was born before he was "born in New York," the recruit, John O'Dougherty by name, declared, "County Tyrone, to be sure." Many of the new soldiers had never in their lives handled a gun and this increased the time needed for training.[144] Such was the state of the army at the beginning of the war.

"St. Augustine is entirely defenseless, and will remain so until the return of the *Dolphin*, the Captain of which has orders to take from Savannah 500 stand of arms."[145] This was not entirely true, in that the militia was supposedly on hand to take care of the situation. But was it ready for the field? General Hernandez, whose correspondence is often very candid, wrote to General Abraham Eustis that, "The principal and most effective portion of my Brigade lies in the Counties of Duval and Nassau which are north of the River St. Johns and which constituted the 4th Regiment … That portion of my command which lies in the Counties of St. Johns and Mosquito is wholly insufficient for the protection of the city, and of the settlements which lie East of the river St. John and South of this."[146] As noted earlier, these units were in want of arms and often went into the field with their fowling pieces. One observer noted a gathering of Hernandez's crack unit: "Sunday Dec. 6, 1835 …There was a grand muster today of the militia to see how many men they can turn out. There were a little over a hundred & a sorry figure they made of it without arms & marching in single rank divisions to the music of several fifes & a broken drum. I saw in the ranks one man with a club foot & another with his foot injured so he had to wear it over his shoe. They expect arms by the return of the *Dolphin*, sometime this week." On December 11, 1836, this same observer noted the arrival of the arms and ammunition, at Picolata, and an escort of twenty-five men had to be sent to bring them into town. "Such a motley set I never saw before. I saw a drill on the square of the officers & non commissioned officers of the militia. They do very well for recruits." Surely the rain of six straight hours did little to make a more favorable impression.

60

The arms and ammunition arrived the next day but not without the carts breaking down five miles outside of town and some of the muskets missing from the boxes. It took another two days to get the ammunition and remaining arms into old Fort Marion for safe storage.[147] Such were the home-grown defenders of St. Augustine.

As the dangers grew in the area, the militia had to be called out prior to official authorization from any federal authority. General Hernandez did not hesitate to use his powers of discretion to take hold of that responsibility firmly and order Colonel John Warren into the interior with about 250 men of the militia.[148] A second group from St. Augustine was sent south of the city to protect the plantations along the Tomoka and other rivers and was led by Major Benjamin Alexander Putnam. Stationed first at Rosetta Plantation, he was soon joined in late December by Lieutenant Solano and was rapidly receiving information that the plantations near New Smyrna were in flames and a large body of Indians were in the area. In conversation with Solano, who was familiar with the Native Americans of the vicinity, he decided to abandon the post at Rosetta and retreat back toward St. Augustine and take the command to Bulow's plantation, a much better defensive position.[149] Putnam and his column had arrived too late to save Henry Woodruff but did assist in rescuing Joseph Woodruff and a Mr. Forrester from Spring Garden. These men were immediately sent back to St. Augustine and joined the ever increasing numbers of "suffering inhabitants" who would remain, in some form, throughout the seven years of war.[150]

Putnam's men were not the best trained or most disciplined group in Florida. In fact they were almost on the verge of mutiny a couple of times during their relatively short stay at Bulow and later Dunlawton plantations. According to Putnam they were restless, anxious to go home and protect their own families and willing to sign a petition requesting leave to do just that. As the beleaguered major put it, "... the object is to inform you that the majority, say two thirds have become very impatient at being continued any longer from their homes and businesses, and today a petition signed by twenty two was sent onto me begging permission to go home. I have endeavoured to put them off, but how long I shall be able to do so is doubtful; as there are so many I should find it impossible to prevent them by coercive measures." Putnam did have compassion for their cause, however he felt it would be a shame on the force if they abandoned to the torches of the Indian foe the property they had protected. Many of the troops began to resist and resent doing even the most necessary though menial tasks. Even faced with this semi-rebellion Major Putnam continued to construct a blockhouse and an "avenue of pickets" leading to the dwelling house so that a small force could maintain the position against a larger body of Indians.[151] Putnam's luck would not last and the construction activity was soon to be for naught.

On the 15th of January, General Hernandez ordered a mounted company headed by Captain Douglas Dummitt to join Putnam and then proceed southward to take provisions from some of the large plantations that had been abandoned. Dummitt's force had been delayed in the juncture by unknown causes but the combined militia companies soon headed south to carry out the order. On the 18th of January they reached Dunlawton and began to take off the provisions. However, as Sergeant Cooper and five men began their work, under the smoke of the burning plantation house of Mrs. Anderson, Indians were alleged to be approaching. Putnam divided his force into two groups, one in the pine barren and the other in the Negro houses along the road leading to the sugar house of the plantation. About midnight two Indians with rifles were seen approaching. The force waited until they were close at hand, then fired instantly, killing the lead man and severely wounding the second, who proceeded to escape into the darkness. Soon after the remainder of the band approached the troops and proved to be a fairly large and well armed force. Major Putnam immediately sensed that his current position was not secure and ordered a withdrawal to the bank of the river where the troops back would be to the river and their scows. Putnam later estimated that the force opposing his numbered about one hundred and twenty braves against just over fifty men. The fighting lasted nearly two hours when the ammunition of Putnam's small force began to give out and he ordered a retreat to the boats. Unfortunately the tide had gone out and left a large area of muck and low water to wade through to affect their escape. This action cost the St. Augustine Guards and Mosquito Roarers three dead and sixteen wounded.

The loss to the Seminoles and their allies was estimated at eight dead and several wounded.[152]

The Battle of Dunlawton forced Hernandez to order Putnam and the other scattered forces south of St. Augustine home to re-group. This action inevitably left the entire East Coast of Florida open to depredation and attack and the Seminoles and their allies soon took full advantage. The battle was also very demoralizing to the citizens of the Ancient City. As reported in the Charleston *Courier* on February 2, 1836, "The men who were wounded in the battle at Dunn-Lawton arrived in town on Saturday evening last. It was a melancholy sight to see the relations of these noble spirits, flocking to the boats to receive them, and the mingled feelings of joy and grief with which they were greeted caused many a sympathetic tear to flow, from the otherwise uninterested bystanders. One of them, Charles Flora, died last night; he received a wound in the arm and one in the groin, and was otherwise much cut up with balls. During the action he acted with the utmost coolness and courage mounting to sang froid." Militia historian Robert Hawk noted that, "Although the militia fought well under difficult cir-cumstances, they withdrew from the field ..."[153] General Hernan-dez did not have enough force at hand to deal with the situation, just as he had foretold. He tried to get Colonel John Warren to send fifty mounted men to the south to aid Putnam but Warren could not spare them at that time. The general had no choice but to abandon the richest area in East Florida to destruction and devas-tation.[154]

While Putnam was away from St. Augustine defending the southern frontier, news arrived of the attack on Colonel Warren's baggage train with the loss of some supplies and the wounding of a number of men. Even more discouraging was the additional tidbit that noted Dr. McLemore, leader of the reinforcements at that ac-tion, wanted to make a charge into the hammock but only twelve of his men responded. The doctor had two horses shot out from under him and the tip of his sword and the guard shot off as well.[155] Unknown in St. Augustine until January 25th, the com-mand of Major Francis L. Dade had been attacked on the road from Fort Brooke to Fort King, near today's Bushnell, and all but three of the command of one hundred and eight men died in the ensuing battle.[156] On the same day, Osceola led a smaller group to attack and kill Indian Agent Wiley Thompson and Lieutenant Constantine Smith as they walked towards the Agency building near the sutler's store. The sutler, Erastus Rogers and his staff were also killed by this band and the store set afire. The garrison of Fort King, a mere six hundred yards away, could do little to revenge the killings as they were out-numbered and out-gunned by the Seminoles and their allies. Most of the garrison had been drawn away to man the new post of Fort Drane, which occupied the plantation of General Duncan L. Clinch.[157] Clinch at the time was preparing, at the urging of General Richard K. Call of the Florida Militia, to attack the supposed stronghold of the Seminoles in the Cove of the Withlacoochee River.

Call had arrived at Fort Drane on Christmas Eve of 1835 and had with him a force of 560 mounted volunteers. Clinch had nearly 250 regulars on hand and these were formed into a battalion under the command of Lieutenant Colonel Alexander Fanning. They began their movement toward the Withlacoochee on December 29, 1835 and had not yet learned of the fate of Dade or Thompson. Unfortunately, the lack of specific geographical/topographical information and poor guides led this force of over 750 men into the swamps along the north bank of the river without finding the supposed ford. Instead, they found a swift, deep river nearly fifty yards across and no way of crossing without exposing the troops to possible ambush. It had taken three days for this column to reach the river and if there were ever any chance of surprise it was already lost when they reached that point. On the last day of 1835, Clinch ordered the troops to cross the river in a canoe found along the bank, and the regulars crossed first, bailing the leaking craft as they went. Very few of Call's volunteer force had an opportunity to cross when the Indians opened fire, a nearly perfect ambush. The Battle of the Withlacoochee was another defeat and retreat for the white forces and further demoralized and divided the Territory.[158]

The news of this defeat reached St. Augustine on the 5th of January and was confirmed by the arrival of Captain Gustavus Drane and Lieutenant Francis L. Dancy who were at the scene. But St. Augustine was not sitting idle waiting for events to unfold.

The citizens did take measures into their own hands in preparation for what they thought might be an attack upon the city. Samuel P. Heintzelman, assigned quartermaster duties because of his poor health, observed the preparations first hand and has left us something of an account of the citizens' actions. On December 30, 1835, they moved two six-pounders from the old fort to more usable locations. The first one was placed at the bridge across the St. Sebastian Creek and the other about a half mile or more where the North River and St. Sebastian approach each other forming a near peninsula. The young officer noted that the city was well situated for defense.[159] By January 7, 1836, with the large number of slaves coming into town with their masters from the threatened plantations, the city council ordered all slaves out of town for fear of slave rebellion or illegal supplying of the Indians. Six hundred dollars was subscribed by the people to clear out the old ditch leading from the fort to the St. Sebastian and this was palisaded. A blockhouse was constructed at the other bridge site over this same river.[160] On January 24th Captain Porter added a picket to the bridge defenses across the St. Sebastian.[161] The town may have been under the threat of attack and sometimes appeared in a panic mode but it stuck together in time to shore up its defenses until help could arrive in the form of the army and volunteer units from South Carolina.

General Abraham Eustis was the commanding officer in Charleston and was assigned the duty of bringing as many regular troops into Florida as possible along with the arms and ammunition needed by the army and the volunteers. He left Charleston on the 12th of February 1836 and headed to St. Augustine in the Steamboat *Dolphin*.[162] By this time the citizens of Charleston were well aware of St. Augustine's predicament and that three to four hundred women and children had fled there to escape the horrors of the Indian attacks. That these innocents were starving and in a destitute state was common knowledge.[163] On January 21st the citizens of Charleston were meeting to decide what to do to assist St. Augustine. At this meeting Robert Hayne reported that $4,000 had already been expended by the committee of citizens and General James Hamilton announced that substantial loans had been made available to the government to support the efforts. This meeting produced the resolutions that sent the South Carolina Volunteers to the defense of St. Augustine.

By the 24th of January enough men of the 4th Brigade had been organized that some were almost ready to leave for the beleaguered city.[164] The 26th saw some of the first troops embark on the Steamboat *Santee* and sail away by nine in the morning for St. Augustine. Following an order issued by Eustis, Captain William Henry Timrod commanded a detachment of the German Fusiliers numbering fifty-one men and boarded the steamer along with thirty members of the Hamburg Rifles. This group landed in St. Augustine around 11:00 a.m. on the 28th. Timrod's narrative of the events speaks for itself: "The Citizens were overjoyed at our arrival, in proportion to the extreme state of terror from which we relieved them. They all expressed it as their firm conviction that had we not made our appearance that day, the town would have been attacked in the night. The only troops that occupied the garrison for a week before our arrival consisted of a company of Regulars under Capt. Porter and they by constant service every night at the outposts were completely exhausted." The Captain of the Fusiliers continued, "Occupied in the usual details of Garrison duty we spent a very pleasant time, until relieved by the regular levies on whose arrival, my company & the Hamburg volunteers embarked for home in the Steamer *James Boatwright*, Capt. Chase." He was quite satisfied with his accomplishments and was assured that, "One thing is certain, the object to effect which we left our homes & families was completely answered. Our arrival in Augustine saved that city, which otherwise would have afforded an easy prey to the savage foe. This is all I had in view and having effected it, I am more than satisfied."[165]

M. M. Cohen's more famous and detailed account of the "saving" of St. Augustine has a similar ring to it. Arriving two days later than Timrod, Cohen's Washington Volunteers and Washington Light Infantry were also greeted enthusiastically by the denizens of St. Augustine. Cohen waxed more poetic about the scene of arrival: "Yes, here we are, and received with the most cheering welcome; men, women and children all crowd to see us; doors are thrown open and sashes up. We read our welcome 'in a people's eyes;' some of which eyes are sparkling with joy and gratitude;

66

from the same causes, others shine yet lovelier with tears, as the sun beam is more beautiful when seen through the rain drop." Like Timrod he noted, "Our arrival creates a sense of security in the minds of the inhabitants, to which they had long been strangers, and brings 'rest to their feet, and slumber to their lids'." Cohen's forces were put up at Allen's boarding house while the Fusiliers and Hamburg Volunteers were stationed at the Government House. Cohen also tells us that twenty of his force took up post that evening just beyond the city gates and another ten were stationed at the St. Sebastian Bridge with a field piece. Knowing that the Seminoles were prowling in the area, the troops had to keep a sharp eye out for any movement. The accommodations for the troops did not match the warm and friendly greetings and by February 2, 1836, the South Carolinians were complaining in good soldierly manner.[166]

Letters pouring into the Charleston *Courier* all through February of 1836 show that the destruction of East Florida continued unabated. Letters dated the 20th of February from Hernandez's Plantation discuss in detail the ruins of the General's sugar mills and the total destruction of the Williams plantation, where all dwelling houses and other buildings had been burned to the ground. Surprisingly the horses and cattle on the Hernandez plantation had not been run off or killed and many of the main buildings had been looted but not burned. Because the Irish Volunteers were the first on the scene after some reported burning and destruction, it was assumed that the Indians felt comfortable enough to hold off on their scorched earth policy and maybe enjoy some of the fruits of their victories. The writer of the letters also noted that the first thing he searched for in the Hernandez house was the lead which he found intact. This indicated to him that the enemy had not returned after their initial attack. The General was one lucky man compared to his neighbors.[167]

With the arrival of General Eustis the tenor of the military operations changed drastically. Regular military operations were now the norm and fewer of the "chase the fox" games were played by the Indians and militia. Eustis was also under the command of General Winfield Scott, who had been ordered into Florida to take command from Clinch. President Jackson was not happy with the turn of events in Florida and although he did not personally like "Old Fuss and Feathers," he respected his military abilities and normally diplomatic manners. Scott took his time about assembling the forces to defeat the Seminoles and their allies. Only after he had everything in place, including his band and traveling library, did he intend to take the field. Events, however, did not let him take such a leisurely approach. His erstwhile rival, General Edmund P. Gaines, had ignored orders to stop in Pensacola and proceeded to Florida in an attempt to "rescue" Clinch and the Florida militia. This unplanned move forced Scott to move his timetable up and, accordingly, Gaines got the blame for upsetting what would have been a victorious plan, if Scott can be taken at his word.

Eustis' role in Scott's grand strategy was to take the South Carolina volunteers and the regulars under his direct command and perform a long swing southward towards Volusia and then across the country to near the headwaters of the Ocklawaha River, cross that river and destroy the Indian town of Pilalakaha and then proceed to join up with Scott and Colonel William Lindsay's force of regulars and Alabama militia coming northward from Tampa. The object was to catch the Seminoles in a three-pronged vice in the Cove of the Withlacoochee. Poor discipline among the forces under Lindsay, Scott's slow movement and the distance to be covered by Eustis (along with the lack of any topographical knowledge of the interior) and illness in the troops destroyed this plan before accomplishing anything of note except Eustis's remarkable march and the burning of Pilalakaha. The sickness was so bad along this march that 300 of Colonel Brisbane's regiment of 700 could not make it across the St. Johns at Volusia. Measles was the major culprit in slowing this operation down.[168]

With the large armies now taking the field against them, the Seminoles made a conscious change in overall strategy. They now took to more isolated attacks upon farms, small settlements and the occasional harassment of cities and military installations. In August of 1836, for example, the Seminoles and their allies struck at the mill of William Travers near the present town of Mayport.[169] Eustis was reported spending most of the summer chasing the Indians around the countryside from Picolata to Volusia to St. Joseph plantation and back to Julington Creek and wearing down the forces of the First Artillery. Sickness became more and more of a problem as the summer wore on and cost the army the splendid services of Major Julius Heileman, who died at Fort Drane. Companies E and D of this regiment arrived in St. Augustine with only two officers, Captain Justin Dimick and Lieutenant Irwin, both of whom became sick within a week. Company E went from forty-three effectives ready for duty to thirteen in less than two weeks.[170] The wearing down of the enemy was also part of the Seminole/Miccosukee strategy and it was the surest way of leveling the playing field during the next campaign season.

Historian George Buker has noted that from about the beginning of 1837 until the end of the Second Seminole War in 1842, St. Augustine's role was that of staging area and a base for rest and recreation. As the war moved southward the importance of the town diminished because the harbor was difficult and there were few roads leading to it from the center of the action. As General Thomas Jesup began planning for his grand adventure in the 1837-38 campaign season, he all but ignored St. Augustine and concentrated on getting steamboats and barges up the St. Johns River, troops over to Tampa for Colonel Zachary Taylor's move down the Kissimmee River and getting enough vessels to Colonel Persifor Smith for his sojourn up the Caloosahatchee River. The only real involvement of St. Augustine was in that portion of the campaign assigned to General Hernandez taking his mounted forces down the peninsula between the St. Johns and Indian Rivers. The role of the Ancient City had become secondary to the actual movements of troops to the seat(s) of war.[171]

St. Augustine and the surrounding territory were not totally left alone to bask in the sun in peace. The capture of Osceola, Coacoochee and others under the white flag sent these famous leaders into the cells of old Fort Marion. Coacoochee and eighteen others, including two women, soon escaped from the fortress much to the dismay of General Jesup. The infamous raid on the traveling theater group also spiced up the life of the town as did the raid on Jenkes plantation on North River. However, overall, the city did not experience any further major traumas after the 1837-38 campaign season. Most of the attention was drawn away from the war and began to be concentrated on the battle over the proposed constitution and the coming of statehood. The possibility of a division of the Territory also gained some attention as did the constant appeal for more money for internal improvements. All of these diversions took the attention away from the numerous soldiers who entered and left the city on "R & R" weekends and the slow beat of the too frequent death dirges played as the soldiers were laid to rest after their battles with disease. Only toward the end of 1842 did the attention turn briefly back to the terrible days at the beginning of the war when the remains of Dade's command were brought back to rest under the pyramids at the military cemetery. This single, sobering event truly brought back the memories and sacrifices of so many in keeping the Indian menace away from the Ancient City. That event and the large number of suffering inhabitants still receiving rations from the government were the most notable reminders of what was St. Augustine's time of trouble and need.

# Charlotte Harbor In The
# Second Seminole War

It must have seemed an idyllic location, sitting high on the bluff of Caldez Island (Useppa today) overlooking the tranquil waters of Charlotte Harbor. Coming from the red hills country of Jackson County, filled with cotton plantations, crude farms and heavy red clay, this must have resembled paradise. Dr. H. B. Crews, customs collector, was indeed a lucky man. His only responsibilities were to oversee the fishing ranchos, collect the taxes and duties due and send the money back to Key West. Most of the Indian population in the area had relatives working with the Spanish fishermen and often intermarried with them. Sure, there must have been some renegades in the area but these could easily be deterred by the others and the sometimes large number of fishermen, Indian families and others who gathered on the islands for fishing, celebrations and other occasions. Situated on the bluff, he had little to fear as he could see any potential enemy coming for miles before they reached his piece of heaven on earth. What had the good doctor to fear?[172]

This scene of beauty and tranquility would soon be broken by the war cry of the Seminoles and their allies. Dr. Crews' Spanish neighbors had been in the area for over two hundred years prior to this time. Few of them had ever ventured into the interior of the country surrounding Charlotte Harbor for more than ten or fifteen miles. Although trade with the native population was common and intermarriage took place, the interior lands beyond the harbor were little known to white men. Some of the earlier Indians inhabiting the area were probably not of Seminole or Creek descent and may have been the remnants of the Caloosa or other groups. Over time, these Indians became known as the Spanish Indians, although this is still a debating point among the scholars of the region. As pressure from white migration forced the Creeks and others southward into North Florida, several groups entered into the realm of the Spanish and some made it to the Tampa Bay area. According to the most recent study by archaeologist Maranda Almy, however, none of these appear to have made it to Charlotte Harbor.[173] The Seminoles, also forced southward from the pressure of white migration and constant border warfare soon settled in the interior and around Charlotte Harbor. The general consensus is that most of the Indians at work on the ranchos during the time of Dr. Crews were of Seminole origin. Thus, when the war cry was heard in this southern outpost it was one known to most of the Indian inhabitants, who may have warned Dr. Crews of impending trouble. Crews had no way of knowing just when or from where a strike against the ranchos might come.

After the cession of Florida to the United States, the ranchos had continued in business and the trade with Cuba flourished. Fish were the mainstay of this trade and Charlotte Harbor was legendary for its great abundance of this food source. The United States exercised its jurisdiction in the area by means of a customs inspector. Elections were held there too, and voting seems to have been active. An election notice in the May 14, 1829 Key West *Register* notes that three inspectors for the election were appointed to meet, "at the house of Caldees: Inspectors – Wm. Frean, Antonio Giraldo, and Ede Van Evour." The same newspaper noted the clearing of the schooner *San Fernandez*, Yanez captain, for Charlotte Harbor with a load of merchandise.[174]

Richard Keith Call, twice governor of the Territory, described the area to Commissioner Elijah Hayward, of the General Land Office as follows: "On the western margin there are two excellent Ports: the Bay of Tampa and Charlotte Harbor, at each of which settlements have been formed. The latter is a place of rendezvous for the Spanish fishermen of Cuba, who keep up a regular intercourse between that place and Havana. It is important that the lands along the margin of the Gulph should be disposed of as early as possible."[175] The value of the fisheries was duly recognized by the Territorial Legislature which authorized the appointment of commissioners to protect them and Territorial Governor William P. Duval appointed one George Willis to protect the fisheries at Charlotte Harbor in February of 1832.[176] By the time scheduled for the removal of the Seminoles from Florida (1835), Charlotte Harbor was already getting some of the trappings of a full fledged settlement, complete with political activity and economic growth based upon the Spanish fisheries and trade with Cuba.

As further illustration of the trade that was growing in Charlotte Harbor, it is interesting to note the names of the vessels and captains that traded in the area as reported in the Key West newspapers. On October 13, 1831, the Key West *Gazette* noted that the sloop *William Stewart*, Cushman commanding, had cleared port for Charlotte Harbor. In its October 26th number, the same paper reported that the Spanish schooner *Segunda* had just arrived from Charlotte Harbor with news that Captain Stover of the Schooner *Ploughboy* had run aground off of Anclote Key and that help had arrived to bring the unfortunate man into port. The *Segunda* was frequently employed by Peter J. Fontane, a well known merchant of Key West, for transporting goods to and from Charlotte Harbor and Havana, Cuba.[177] The February 2, 1832 issue of this paper listed three vessels, all of which came from Boca Grande (the Schooners *Pizarro* and *Florida* and the Sloop *Cuba*) as arriving in port. The captains of these vessels were Hoxie, Rooke and Sawyer (no first names available). Dry goods dealer J. Cottrell & Company of Key West also traded actively with Charlotte Harbor and the *Gazette* noted that the Sloop *Azelia* had cleared port on March 7, 1832.[178] Fourteen days later the paper reported that the Sloops *Dread* and *Florida* had arrived in port from Boca Grande.[179] With a bit more flare, the Schooner *Josefa* arrived in port on April 11, 1832 carrying the survivors of the wrecked Schooner *William & Frederic* which had grounded off of Sanibel. The crew was aided by three men who procured the assistance of Captain Caldez and his above named schooner. The *William & Frederic* was carrying a load of lumber from Apalachicola to Key West.[180]

William A. Whitehead, the Collector of Customs for the Key West district, gave us a true picture of the growing importance of the Charlotte Harbor fisheries when he wrote a letter to accompany the bill for the protection of the fisheries then making its way through Congress. The entire letter is reprinted in the *Gazette* for May 30, 1832. The collector noted that the duties paid by the Spanish ranchos in Charlotte Harbor aggregated a total of $4,717.53 for the period from 1829-31. The total value of their exports to Cuba was put at $18,000, mostly from salted fish, fish roe, fish oil and American manufactures. Much of the salt purchased for packing the fish came from the Salt Ponds at Key West, thus helping that town's economy. For that day and age this was a substantial economic contribution to the Territory of Florida.

Whitehead's description of the community of the four ranchos in Charlotte Harbor is of great interest to the understanding of the area's growing importance. It is worth quoting at length:

Sir, I know not whether the Government has been informed by the former collectors of this port of the existence of four Spanish fishing establishments on the western shore of the peninsula of Florida, at Charlotte's Harbor. Since I have held the office, I have deferred stating their situation until an opportunity should offer for a personal inspection of them. I have lately made them a visit, and am now able to state to the Department what fell under my observation. They appear to have been occupied by the Spanish for a number of years prior to the cession of Florida to the United States as fishing places for the supply of the Havana market, the head fisherman himself at one of them for forty seven years. At the change of flags, it was the intention of this individual to have become an American citizen, but, through ignorance of the language, and other causes, he neglected doing so, but has continued to reside at Charlotte's Harbor, carrying on the business to this time, under the impression, it appears, that the act allowing Spanish vessels to enter the port of Pensacola, and of St. Augustine, on the same footing as American vessels, for twelve years, contained in the clause giving them, also, the right to fish on the coast for the same period. At the four establishments, there may be 130 men, half of which number probably are Indians, and about 30 Indian women, with from 50 to 100 children. They live in palmetto huts, and in the most simple manner, their chief articles of food being the fish they catch. They salt and send to Havana (each establishment having a small schooner for the purpose) from 6 to 8,000 quintals annually, the usual price being from 3 to 4 dollars per quintal. Charlotte's Harbor being within this district, their vessels regularly enter and clear at this port, paying their tonnage duty, and the duties on the supplies they may bring from Havana. The salt, with which they cure their fish, is also regularly imported.

I conceive it important that the fisheries of the United States should be protected for its own citizens, but, in this instance, there is no intrusion upon the established fishing ground of any American. There is no settlement nearer than the Cantonment at Tampa Bay, which is 70 miles distant, and the inhabitants have uniformly acknowledged themselves as amenable to the laws of the Territory. That they have among them many Florida Indians, and that their settlements may draw others beyond the Indian boundary, is the only thing at present materially against them.

I have thought it my duty to make this representation, understanding it is probable application will be made to have them dispossessed of the privileges they now enjoy, in order that the Government might be aware of the condition of the people.

With remarkable insight into the motives of the act and the probable results, Whitehead clearly gives us one of the best pictures of Charlotte Harbor on the eve of the Second Seminole War. Unfortunately, as he expected, there was a campaign to undermine the position of the Spanish ranchos there and anywhere else along the coast of Florida, especially at Manatee and Tampa Bay.[181]

As the war clouds began looming over the Charlotte Harbor area, so did storm clouds of another sort: Mother Nature's. In January of 1835, news was reported of a major storm hitting the shores of southern Florida. The Key West *Enquirer* for January 24th wrote of it as follows: "On Saturday last about 9 o'clock P.M. a rumbling noise was heard in a W.N.W. direction from this place, and in a short time a violent rush of wind followed which continued near ten minutes, with greater force than had been felt here for many years." After noting the grounding of some ships in the immediate area the paper also advised, "To leeward the gale was equally severe--the sloop *Felix* was blown ashore in Charlotte Bay, and several houses blown down on Sanybal Island." Several people were reported drowned by the storm but only Dr. H. S. Waterman and son near Indian Key were reported by name. This can easily be known as the storm before the storm.[182]

By early 1835 it was becoming obvious that not all of the Seminoles were willing to emigrate to the West under the removal plan of Andrew Jackson. The Seminoles firmly believed that they had not agreed to the Treaty of Moultrie Creek, Paynes Landing or any removal plan put forth to their representatives who went west to inspect the proposed new homeland. The reasoning behind this lies in the form of government established by the Seminoles and most other North American tribal units. Government of the Indian "nations" belonged in the hands of the tribal council, not any individual chief or leader. Unless an agreement was made by this council, there could be no treaty signing that had any status with the Indians. No treaty was ever submitted to the tribal council of the Seminole Nation for approval in this era. What did happen was a number of individual "chiefs" (often easily manipulated) were designated by the United States government as recognized leaders of the tribe who could sign on behalf of the entire unit. Even though the United States government knew of the powers of the tribal council, it deliberately chose to ignore the facts. Those leaders, like Charlie Emathala, who were willing to take their villages or families out west were soon eliminated or intimidated into submission by the war party led by Osceola, Tiger Tail, Coacoochee and Alligator. Behind the Miccosukee tribe was the power of Abiaka (Sam Jones) who defiantly refused to allow emigration and actually threatened death to those willing to leave. With these leaders, there would be no smooth transition or emigration west. The stage was soon set for tragedy.

As the Indian raids in Florida increased, especially in the Alachua area, tension grew within the Territory. On April 24, 1835, the defense of the Charlotte Harbor area was assigned to Major Francis L. Dade, then commanding at Key West. The purpose for this move was to have Dade take patrols to the area and force those Indians found without of the designated boundary of their Territory and force them to return. Dade does not appear to have been able to carry out these instructions for on August 14, 1835, he was writing the Quartermaster General of the Army, Thomas Jesup, telling him that transportation via the *Motto* to Charlotte Harbor was not possible since the ship was on duty in Nassau. Dade asked for some assistance from the Postal Department to arrange transportation for his troops.[183] Dade's transportation problems were the subject of a letter from General Duncan L. Clinch, then in charge of the Territory, which asked for the assistance of the Revenue Cutters. According to Clinch, "A small armed vessel of that class would, in my opinion, aid our operations very much, & could be placed on that kind of duty for a short time without the least injury to the revenue service…" The object for the Revenue Cutters was to assist Dade in capturing Indians and bringing them to Tampa for transport west. It was indeed an "arduous, disagreeable & perplexing" assignment.[184]

The October 8, 1835 letter referenced above was followed by one dated October 29, 1835 and addressed to Commander Alexander J. Dallas, commanding the West Indies Squadron of the United States Navy at Pensacola. Dallas was requested by the Secretary of the Navy, Mahlon Dickerson, to send one of the ships of war under his command to assist General Clinch's forces in "collecting and embarking" the Seminoles about to be shipped West. Dallas did as ordered and put on notice some of his command to help with the movement of the Indians. The navy's role in the early months of the war was to prove crucial to the survival of hundreds of citizens and the maintaining of Fort Brooke at Tampa.[185]

One of the figures that played a large role in the drama at Charlotte Harbor and elsewhere was the rancho operator, William Bunce. Bunce had had a checkered career in Florida and had lived in Key West for a number of years. In 1829 he signed a petition asking for the creation of a mail route between that city and

Charleston, South Carolina.[186]  By the end of that year, he had lost a lawsuit to shipper Antonio Giraldo and his wife Catalina, and lost everything in a Marshal's sale, which included four houses and lots in Key West.[187]  At this time, he moved his family and fortunes to the Manatee River area and was appointed Justice of the Peace by Governor Duval on January 25, 1834.[188]  In Tampa he was the friend of Judge Augustus Steele and often visited him.

Bunce's operation at the mouth of the Manatee River was extensive and employed ten Spaniards and twenty Indians.  All of the Spaniards had married Indian wives, and had children and grandchildren living at the rancho.  In a letter to Indian Agent Wiley Thompson, Bunce noted the Charlotte Harbor ranchos at Caldez Island, Cayo Pelow, Punta Rassa and Estero Bay.  He also noted that only these and his own rancho had worked that season because of the low demand for fish in Havana.[189]  Judge Steele added in his letter that none of the Indians employed on the ranchos were "claimed by the Seminoles."  The reason for this was that each of them had been on the ranchos for so long that they spoke Spanish, many had been baptized in Havana and considered themselves as Spanish, even though descended from the Seminoles.  As further evidence of the non-Indian nature of these people, the Judge also noted that two of the boys from the Bunce rancho were employed by the Revenue Service in Key West and one on his own revenue crew.[190]  Regardless of the friendship and data provided by Judge Steele, the inhabitants of Bunce's and the other ranchos were to share a common and unpleasant fate.

On December 28, 1835, the command of Major Francis L. Dade, numbering 108 men and officers, was ambushed near the current city of Bushnell, Florida.  All but three privates of this ill-fated command were killed on the spot.  The three men survived long enough to make it back to Tampa with the horrible and embarrassing news that the regular army had been reduced in numbers by this attack.  On the same day, while walking outside of Fort King (Ocala) with Lieutenant Constantine Smith, Agent Thompson and the lieutenant were gunned down by the Seminoles under the immediate command of Osceola.  Sutler Erastus Rogers and his staff at the sutler's store suffered a similar fate.  The Second Seminole War had begun in earnest.  For all practical purposes, the garrison at Fort King was imprisoned in their own fortification. Fort Brooke on Tampa Bay was daily expecting a strong attack and lived in constant fear.[191] News soon came of the destruction of the forces of the Florida militia under Major Benjamin Putnam at the Battle of Dunlawton and the burning of almost every plantation south of St. Augustine.[192] Florida was aflame and little relief was in sight.

The situation in Charlotte Harbor was tense and speculation was rampant, yet life went on as usual. It was not to remain that way for long. The army and the navy were concerned for the lives of those on the frontier. Their problem was the lack of manpower and materials. Nationwide, the number of effective troops available for duty at the time of the outbreak of the war was less than 4,000.[193] This force was to cover the entire frontier from Minnesota to Maine. A significant number of those available for service were assigned to permanent fortifications and could not be transferred to Florida. The call for volunteers went out to most of the southern States and was quickly responded to by most. The problem of getting these volunteer units into Florida was a logistical nightmare. The army had no vessels of its own other than a few transports and therefore had to rent or order the construction of all the crafts it would need.

The news of the Battle of the Withlacoochee, fought on December 31, 1835 and January 1, 1836, was not encouraging even though the official report called it a victory. From February 27th to March 6th, General Edmund P. Gaines' relief column was pinned down on the banks of the Withlacoochee River and stuck there until reinforcements arrived under the command of General Clinch. General Winfield Scott's masterful plan, the three-pronged pincer movement through uncharted territory with no means of communication began in late February and ended by April 30th, with little to show for the grand effort. Scott wrote to Adjutant General Roger Jones on April 30, 1836 and informed him that it would take at least 3,000 regulars (not volunteers) to control the situation above Charlotte Harbor. "For the country below," the beleaguered General noted, "additional means will be wanted, viz. 2 or 3 steamers of a light draft of water and 50 or 60 barges of different sizes, capable of carrying from 10 to 50 men each." Emory

Upton, in his evaluation of the historical situation declared, "The lack of arms at so critical a junction, can only be ascribed to the shortsighted economy which ever prompts Congress to defer preparations for war, till hostilities are actually begun." For the year 1836, 24,500 men (mostly volunteers) were called into service alone, most spending some time in Florida. By the time this conflict ended in 1842, 41,122 men served in the military in Florida, by far the largest Indian war ever fought east of the Mississippi River.[194]

By March of 1836, the navy was very active along the coast and was beginning the necessary exploration of the coast line of Florida. It should be noted here that very few maps were available to either the army or the navy at this time. Even the Alafia River, less than thirty miles south of Tampa had not been explored or mapped. The navy's immediate attention was drawn to the East Coast of Florida because of the heavier settlement in the area. The attack on the family of William Cooley at New River (Fort Lauderdale) led to an exodus of the settlers from there and the area around Cape Florida. Most of the Revenue Cutters and smaller vessels were attempting to rescue the stragglers from this area and the Key Biscayne Light House. The upper Keys were in turmoil too, and Indian Key settlers were fleeing to Key West, which cleared two hundred yards of vegetation from the northern area of the city and was appealing for additional troops, which soon arrived under Lieutenant Benjamin Alvord. Supplying the garrison and manning the early forts established along the road from Fort Brooke to Fort King also took man power from the naval units in Florida. The home base of the West Indies fleet was inundated with requests for arms and men to be sent up the Blackwater River and as far away as Marianna. The navy did its level best to comply with these requests and sent a schooner to Milton on the Blackwater River and nearly one hundred stand of arms to Marianna. By mid March, the navy was just getting enough marines and sailors into the Tampa area to begin exploring the Manatee River basin and north of the Anclote Keys. Charlotte Harbor would have to wait.[195]

Ships of the line, including the *Constellation* and the *Vandalia* were depleted of their marines to protect the garrison at Fort Brooke and at Indian Key. On March 28, 1836, a short expedition was sent up the Manatee River to search for Indians, with none being found. However, the U.S. Revenue Cutter *Washington* continued down the coastline and soon fell in with Indians at the mouth of the Myakka River. Commander Ezekial Jones reported that Lieutenant Smith counted twenty-two Indians in the encampment and saw may fires in the distance. Two friendly Indians, acting as guides, were sent ashore and encountered three hostiles. A fight might have broken out had not one of the latter recognized one of the friendly Indians as an acquaintance. Little information was obtained in the interview.[196]

On the second of April, Lieutenant Levin M. Powell's force from the *Vandalia* encountered a more worrisome scene. "Lieutenant Powell arrived with his force at Charlotte Harbor on the 2nd Inst. & found the inhabitants flying in every direction to escape the fury of the Indians. The Collector's is burnt to the ground and himself supposed to be murdered as he had not been heard of. Acting Sailing Master Rowan was immediately dispatched with a party of men in pursuit of the enemy, with whom he came up with about daylight attacked them, and succeeded in killing two and capturing one, the rest took to the woods, and his force was too limited to pursue them."[197] Powell's description of the terror includes the picking up of two "periougues" of the fugitives from Josepa Island who reported that the attack on them was led by a chief Wy-ho-kee. Twenty-five Indians were alleged to be in his band of warriors. Lieutenant Powell also noted picking up a third boat loaded with fleeing residents whom he sent back to find the women and children hidden in the woods. He claims to have restored them to their homes before sending Master Rowan on his mission.[198]

The worst fears for the life of the Collector were soon realized. On April 30th the Key West *Enquirer* reported that news brought to port by the Sloop *Eden* was not good and that Mr. Patterson, who was to replace Dr. Crews, had seen that the house had been burnt and the place abandoned. The next issue of the paper noted the gruesome news that the body of the Collector, along with that of an Indian guide and a Spaniard, were found. Crews' body had been badly mutilated by his attackers. The bodies were probably interred somewhere on the small island where they were found. It was reported that the three men had gone hunting.

On the 4th of April, the Revenue Cutter *Dallas* joined Powell's force. According to its logbook, Dr. Crews was sent flying from the Indians as they approached the island and set his home on fire and that those hostiles had pursued him for some distance before being lost to sight by the friendly Indian observers. A small boat under the command of Lieutenant Renfort was sent from the cutter with thirteen men to assist Powell. As they approached the rendezvous area shots were heard. Someone had mistaken a Spanish Indian fisherman for one of the hostiles as he approached the rancho and fired upon him. The situation was very tense. The crew from the *Dallas* soon joined Powell's command as they attempted to surprise an Indian encampment at the mouth of the Myakka River. The area was too shallow for the cutter and head winds picked up so much as to thwart much of the planned attack. After sailing eighteen miles up the river, they found it was too shallow for further exploration. The cutter's crew supplied Lieutenant Powell with all the ammunition he requested before sailing towards the old rancho, now nothing but a smoking ruin. Before reaching the mouth of Charlotte Harbor, the cutter was joined by the *Vandalia* which was transporting the troops, recently arrived from Louisiana, under the command of Colonel Persifor Smith. Arrangements were made to try and procure a guide from the Spaniards or the Indians to take this command, along with that of Lieutenant Powell, up the Myakka.

Finding a guide under the circumstances was a difficult proposition. After searching two other ranchos in the area and finding both abandoned and in ruins, the cutter's whale boat, under Lieutenant Gatewood, found a Spaniard who was willing to undertake the task. They found this willing soul six miles up the Caloosahatchee River. At 4:00 P.M. on the 18th of April, the transports with the Louisiana volunteers and a squad of marines under Captain Ross were ready to undertake the adventure up the Myakka. Gatewood assisted the transports to the mouth of the river. Seventeen men from the *Dallas* and some from the *Vandalia* joined the expedition up the river. Soon after they departed gunshots were heard and Lieutenant Renfort led some men in boats to the spot to assist the troopers. It proved to be another false alarm.[199]

The expedition up the Myakka River went by water as far as the boats could go and Powell's force was then incorporated into that of Smith's. They marched up both banks of the river looking for signs of the Indians but found only recent signs of a small band leaving the area and headed south, towards the Everglades. One abandoned village was found but, again, no signs that the enemy had been there recently or in any great numbers, as had been rumored in Tampa. Colonel Smith soon determined that any further effort here would be a waste of time and ordered the expedition to return to Tampa. Powell did so too, and was accompanied by nearly one hundred of the rancho inhabitants, who soon settled in with Bunce's group on Mullet Key. Charlotte Harbor was abandoned to the whims of the enemy.[200]

As the rainy season and sickness were soon upon the troops, all operations were brought to a standstill. The troops were sent into their summer quarters, the volunteers sent back to their respective states and the navy resumed its normal cruises in the Caribbean. Little could be done for the inhabitants of Charlotte Harbor but to put them with the other fishermen under Captain Bunce. Unfortunately, this was to spell their doom. Bunce was greatly distrusted by the new commander in Florida, General Thomas Jesup. Jesup had been warned by many, including Governor Call and others that Bunce had been supplying the Seminoles and their allies with guns and other stores. When a captured Indian told the same story to the General, Jesup was furious and ordered the removal of the Spanish Indians and the fishermen to the West with the rest of the Seminoles.

Bunce and others protested most loudly against this treatment, but it did them little good. Jesup had the support of the Secretary of War, Joel Poinsett, and other powerful figures in Washington. The General considered Bunce and the Indians with him to be traitors and ordered their deportation to the West. By mid-May 1837, the former inhabitants of Charlotte Harbor were planning their brief farewell. But Jesup was approached by many who had been friends with Bunce and the Captain himself made many representations about the Indians employed by him. Jesup demurred

until he was persuaded by Micanopy, Holatoochee and other Seminole leaders that they would not come in or consider surrender if
these people were allowed to remain. Others swore to Jesup that
Bunce's band had provided them with aid. The General, con-
fronted with these allegations and some undisclosed proof decided
the final fate for these forlorn people must be emigration to the
West. On April 22, 1838, he wrote to Secretary Poinsett of his decision. The final fate of the rancho fishermen and their families
had been decided.[201]

# A Brief Moment of Fame In The Whirlwind of War: Fort Drane, 1836-1837

In 1835-36 the climate of Florida was still basically unknown to the United States Army. It did not fully realize that the Territory was on the edge of an Inter Tropical Convergence Zone where the dry and wet periods are distinct and related to the Hadley cells and Trade Winds. The vegetation of its swampy areas held abundant moisture that made travel in the interior difficult and uncertain. The heat and moisture of the summers were ideal for breeding disease-transmitting organisms that brought with them malaria, typhoid fever, a wide variety of diarrhea-like ailments and numerous other illnesses not understood by the medical staff of the day. Heat and moisture stressed the body and reduced its immune system. The climate ate into the psyche of the troops causing many to desert. It made for difficult campaigning.

The geography of the Territory was equally obscure. There were few maps of the interior and most of these totally unreliable. The placement of rivers upon the maps that were produced showed numerous errors and little information about the size, velocity, depth, volume or gradient relationships. Fording places were not labeled and bridges non-existent over most rivers and streams. The impact of the karst topography of Florida was unknown to the military and the majority of the inhabitants. The timing of the yearly freshets was uncertain. Few guides, white, Indian or black, were available to the army and most were unreliable. Readily available, potable water sources were equally unknown and the sulphur water of the area was distasteful to all. This general ignorance of the topography was to be a major factor in many of the unsuccessful attempts to attack and capture the Seminoles and their allies.[202]

This was just part of the situation facing General Duncan L. Clinch in late 1835 as he attempted to get ready to enforce the removal of the Seminoles from Florida to new homes in the west. As early as January of that year he had recommended an increase in the forces available for this task at Fort Brooke (Tampa) and Fort King (today's Ocala). On 17 October 1835 he reminded the Adjutant General, Roger Jones, of this request and admitted, "I may have rather under estimated the means necessary to carry into effect the views and plans of the Government." He then noted that he had assured the Adjutant General that his forces were sufficient if the Seminoles were concentrated in a single area. However, he warned, "But when scattered over a large extent of Country, composed of marshes & swamps that are almost impenetrable to the white man, it is entirely inadequate to give that protection and quiet to the frontier inhabitants which they expect." Clinch also transmitted the news that nearly one hundred of the force then at Fort King were sick and could not be relied upon for active duty. Finally, he revealed that he had no staff assistance at all. The only officer who offered any assistance, Lieutenant R. P. Smith, had been transferred to the west. Clinch had, "not even a confidential private to Copy my letters and orders."[203] By 3 November he was suffering personal losses to raiding Indians with the destruction of his operation at Silver Glen Springs, off of Lake George on the St. Johns River.[204]

While the General was beginning to see the storm overtaking him, the Secretary of War, Lewis Cass, was assuring General Joseph M. Hernandez of the Florida militia that Clinch would soon have seven hundred troops available and that an armed vessel was at Tampa to offer additional aid in removing the Indians. This, the confident Secretary wrote, "will be sufficient to induce the Indians to remove peaceably, agreeably to their treaty stipulations." He also informed the anxious citizen soldier that there was no appropriation available for the calling of the militia and that President

86

Jackson did not see the need to request such a measure, "until the reasons for it appear more decided than they now do."[205] The commanding officer at Fort King, Lieutenant Colonel Alexander C. W. Fanning, could not have disagreed more with the Washington "wait and see" attitude. As this able and brave soldier observed, "We have fallen into the error committed at the Commencement of every Indian War: The display of too little force--the attempt to do too much with inadequate means."[206] Receiving messages and intelligence almost daily, Fanning was in a much better position to see the events unfold, and what he was seeing was not pleasant.

The number of regular troops stated to be available was alleged to be seven hundred, however the actual number capable of duty was five hundred and thirty-five. Of this group a number of them were scattered over the Territory of Florida from St. Augustine to Key West to Pensacola. Muskets ordered for the militia by General Hernandez had not reached Florida by the time of the war's outbreak. Of the total force available in Florida only twenty-six were officers of the line. This force constituted eleven companies of troops to handle an estimated five thousand Seminoles and Miccosukees, which included about twelve hundred warriors. The number of blacks among the Indians was not specifically known but many were recognized for their leadership and advisory roles in council. By December an additional four companies had been transferred to Florida, bringing the total to fifteen.[207] On 28 December 1835 this force was reduced by one fifth with the destruction of Major Francis L. Dade's command. The killing of Indian agent Wiley Thompson and Lieutenant Constantine Smith at Fort King on the same day marked the "official" outbreak of war.

Fort King had been reduced greatly by the movement of Clinch's force to his personal plantation, Lang Syne, situated in northern Marion County. Construction of a fortification enclosing the main house and other buildings was in the hands of Captain Gustavus Drane, a ranker known for his flamboyance. Drane oversaw the construction of a fortification one hundred and fifty yards long by eighty yards wide and pickets twelve feet high above the ground. According to hospital steward John Bemrose, the whole was loop-holed and a blockhouse erected at the eastern end. From this high perch the howitzer would lob shells into the nearby woods. This work was given the name of Fort Drane in honor of its builder. The fort was constructed in the latter part of November of 1835 and occupied soon thereafter by most of the garrison of Fort King.[208]

Not everyone was pleased with the construction of Fort Drane. Some questioned the motives of the commanding officer, General Duncan L. Clinch. Morris S. Miller, then serving as a Lieutenant at Fort King, expressed his displeasure to his brother on 29 January 1836: "The main body of the troops are at Genl. Clinch's plantation which he has dignified by the name Fort Drane. I cannot think that he has acted for the good of the service in this measure. He has five companies of regulars at his own plantation and one at McIntosh's his *brother-in-law*. This, to me, smacks of self too much for a true patriot." Morris further noted that the stations were not within the confines of the Indian "nations" and relatively out of harm's way. Fort King, from his perspective, was in the heart of the hostile territory and no one felt safe leaving the confines of the fort for fear of losing their scalp.[209]

Clinch felt that his new fortification was justified as the new center of his planned advance on the Cove of the Withlacoochee River, the alleged center of the Seminole settlements. This post would be closer to the mysterious area and would be able to protect the communication lines between Micanopy and Fort King, which had already experienced attacks on settlers and army alike. Additionally, the abundant crops grown by Clinch and McIntosh could be used to supply the army in case the ordered rations and forage did not arrive as scheduled. This move was both prudent and profitable for the general. By 12 December, General Richard Keith Call and the Florida mounted forces from Middle Florida arrived at Fort Drane well armed and mounted. The build up to remove the Seminoles had already begun by the time Dade's command met its fate on the flat, palmetto and pine fields near modern Bushnell.[210]

Clinch, who had informed Washington of the assassination of the friendly leader Charley Emathla and the numerous attacks on outlying plantations, was anxious about the growing situation over which he could exercise little effective control. Other officers, too, attempted to inform the Secretary of War and the Adjutant General of the growing tensions and incidents. Captain Francis Belton, commanding at Fort Brooke, wrote to the Adjutant General on 12 December 1835 informing him of the attacks on sutler Saunders' store thirty miles from the fort and the burning and plundering of Mr. Simmons plantation earlier that week. Lieutenant Colonel Fanning urged Clinch to immediately leave St. Augustine and head to Fort King because the Indians were gathering in Big and Long Swamps southwest of his position. Each commander felt an immediate threat to their fortifications and the people housed therein for protection. By mid-December Clinch was writing that he still did not have sufficient troops to man the situation and pleaded for more to be sent to Florida.

General Call and Colonel John Warren each responded with volunteer units and by 16 December were moving toward Fort Drane and a unification with General Clinch. Warren's force was attacked south of the Alachua Prairie at Black Point and suffered some casualties. Call's mounted force of about two hundred and fifty men reached Micanopy on the 22nd of December and found a small party of Indians burning a house near a hammock. The advance guard attacked this group and a small, sharp skirmish ensued in which four Indians were reported killed and four militia wounded, one feared mortally. The total volunteer force numbered about five hundred at Fort Drane with nearly three hundred and twenty regular troops ready for duty. Excitement was high at the fort as this sizable force was about to take the field. At that moment the news of the killing of Thompson and Smith reached them. They could only wonder at the fate of Dade's command knowing that it had left Tampa a few days earlier.[211] At eight o'clock on the morning of the 28th of December, the troops left Fort Drane for the Cove of the Withlacoochee.

Bemrose tells us that the mood was business like and the troops were well provisioned. Immediately the terrain and weather began their work on the column. The wagons had particular difficulty, sinking into the bogs and morasses up to their axle-trees. The unevenness of the roads slowed the progress down precipitously. Some of the marshes crossed were over one half mile across and waist deep. The first days march netted only twelve miles. Making coffee or tea proved difficult because the water from the ponds, the only usable source nearby, had been muddied by the horses and infantry marching through them. Worries about alligators and snakes went through the minds of the men, many of them strangers to this new environment. Numerous thickets and dense hammocks dotted the way toward the river. On the second day the column reached the pine barrens, with its dust and sun beating in their faces. The heat sapped their strength. Luckily, Bemrose continued, the march was performed during the dry winter months. Such was the country through which Clinch's combined forces marched on their way to the Withlacoochee River.[212]

The troops themselves were a motley crew. This is not surprising in an age where over one fourth of the army was foreign born. Dade's command of one hundred-eight, for example, showed forty-six of the dead were not natives to the land they fought and died for. Until 1833 recruiting officers (a form of detached service that depleted the ranks of on-duty officers) received two dollars for every recruit they enlisted. Frequently the examining doctors split this fee and allowed some very suspicious candidates to pass muster--until they reached their units, where their unfitness became immediately obvious.[213] Desertion was common on the frontier and in 1831 was reported to be nearly one quarter of the entire enlisted strength of the army. Drunkenness was also a major player with the frontier army, especially with militia forces. No leader of this type of army could be sure of the reliability of his troops under fire in such an inhospitable environment.[214] Bemrose gives us a wonderful word-picture of this group on its way to the river: "What a medley our little army consisted of. There were Georgian and Floridian crackers (country farmers) with their nasal twang in answer to queries; Indians exclaiming with their 'Inclemas cha' (good) and 'olewarguses' (bad). The Yankees with their 'I reckon so.' Many Germans spluttering in high and low Dutch. A sprinkling of Frenchmen. Irish were predominant, swearing by the Holy Spoon and all the patron saints, St. Patrick taking the lead. ..." All of them, the hospital steward maintained, were in a mood to fight and thought the next day would bring woe to the Indian foe.[215]

The "Battle of the Withlacoochee" was fought on 31 December 1835 and was a disaster for Clinch and his force. Attempting to ford the deep and wide river was out of the question. No preparations had been made for such an eventuality. A single canoe was spotted on the opposite shore and one of the brave privates stripped down and swam across the rapid river and retrieved the vessel. Only five men could fit in this craft and Clinch made the decision to attempt a crossing. According to his biographer, Clinch had nearly seven hundred regulars and militia with him and surely no Indian force could stand up to this sizable force.

Clinch's disdain for the Seminoles and their allies' fighting abilities and valor were to cost him any chance at glory on this day. With less than half of the force across the river, the Indians attacked with full furor. What happened next created a debate that has lasted to the present time. After crossing most of the regulars Clinch alleged that most of the militia refused to come across and aid the troops under fire. General Call disputed this allegation and wrote numerous protests about the sad treatment he and his men faced in the press of the country and in the official reports. Clinch's biographer, Rembert Patrick, summed up the battle this way: "In his one relatively large battle during almost twenty-eight years of military service, the General had taken a chance, and as generals so often do in war, he had made the wrong decision. By underestimating the fighting ability of the Seminoles in the protection of their forests and swamps and by dividing his forces, he had suffered a minor defeat."[216] In this summation Patrick is incorrect. This was a major defeat. Coming on the heels of Dade's battle and the loss of Thompson and Smith, the Battle of the Withlacoochee had a profound negative impact on the mental and emotional outlook of the army, the government and the people of Florida. This feeling was compounded by the defeat of the Florida Militia forces under Major Benjamin A. Putnam at the Battle of Dunlawton, which exposed the entire east coast of Florida south of St. Augustine to depredations and raids that destroyed much of East Florida's wealth.[217]

The bravery and tenacity of Clinch, Captain William M. Graham, Lieutenant T. P. Ridgely and Colonels Mills and Warren of the Florida Militia can not be denied. However, as the troops limped back to Fort Drane they could not help but wonder as to the meaning of this battle. The Seminoles and their allies had inflicted numerous casualties including four dead and fifty-four wounded. The Indians had retreated into the fastness of the Cove and did not offer further resistance at that time. According to Halpatter-Tustennuggee (Alligator) the Seminole losses were three killed and five wounded, including Osceola Two blacks, alleged slaves of Micanopy, were also killed in the battle, which led that hereditary leader to forbid his slaves from further participation in battles. This angered the other leaders and lessened his voice in council.[218]

Bemrose described the scene as they approached Fort Drane: "To see the cavalcade of wounded and hear their groans and cries for water was heart-rending. Each man was brought on a blanket stretched across two pine saplings and carried by two horses. In this mode they brought about 50 poor fellows who were danger-ously wounded." Many were stunned by their first combat whose "eyes were starting out of their sockets" and looking cadaverous. Most stared straight ahead and did not vary their gaze. Many had musket balls pass through their clothing and caps. Bemrose's English friend, Mackay from Qundle, Lincolnshire, had his can-teen shot through. Many of the minor wounds were not reported but treated on the spot or waited for further attention until after their comrades had been attended to. The dead were buried at the campsite of the previous evening in shallow graves (later discov-ered and desecrated) without markers.[219]

Clinch returned to Fort Drane and drafted his reports. His esti-mation of the Indian dead is of interest in comparison with that of Alligator. "Owing to the thickness of the scrub & swamp," the general noted, "and the abduction of their wounded & many of their slain it was almost impossible to discover the precise number. Sufficient evidence however was produced to justify the assertion that their loss in killed and wounded must have been near one hun-dred."[220] This "estimate" of the opposition dead is an exaggeration that needs no further comment. Clinch isolated himself and his command at Fort Drane, particularly after Call and the militia forces left at the end of their enlistment. He complained to the Adjutant General that he had heard nothing from Commodore A. J. Dallas on the coast and had no news of troops arriving from Forts

Pike and Wood. Yet, even in the thick of the Florida wilderness he was able to get enough news to argue that the newspapers had made, "thousands false & malicious statements" concerning his conduct of the war. The general even confided that President Andrew Jackson had done him an injury by announcing that fourteen companies had been placed at his disposal, which was surely unintentional on the President's part. People were expecting too much from him and the limited resources at his command.[221]

General Clinch was soon getting more forces at his disposal, including Colonel Richard C. Parish's three companies of mounted militia from Middle Florida, and Lieutenant Henry Prince also arrived with a unit of the Fourth Infantry and some broken down wagons. Prince notes in his diary for the 15th of January, "Marched 25 miles encumbered with 15 waggons – Arrived at the Lang Syne picketification – Assigned to duty with (D) compy. 4th Inf. The Capt. Wounded – Jno Graham commanding." Prince also notes that on the 21st the command received the news of Dade's fate.[222]

Clinch kept his garrison force busy repairing the buildings and scouting the surrounding vicinity. On 13 January, Colonel Parish's force came under fire near the burning home of a Mr. Curry. Lieutenant Bannerman and Captain Bellamy immediately took action and dismounted their troops and rushed the hammock where the Indians had fled. As Parish and the other troops advanced to the scene they were fired upon on both flanks by the unseen enemy who fled immediately after the first discharge of their weapons. The skirmish lasted until darkness ended the firing. According to Colonel R. C. Parish's report he suffered three men wounded while the Indians had six killed and "considerable" wounded. During the fighting Major Sam Reid conducted himself in a most gallant manner, according to the commanding officer. Reid was one of the most knowledgeable men on the frontier at this time, having guided the Naval units searching for live oak trees along the coast in 1830-31. He would participate in other scouts sent during this enlistment and rise to the rank of colonel of the militia.[223]

Colonel Parish would soon participate in the highly controversial killing of one of his own officers. The mounted volunteers were camped outside of Fort Drane when Lieutenant William

Ward refused to perform a duty when ordered to, even though it was not his scheduled turn. Parish ordered Ward arrested and confined to quarters. On Sunday, 31 January, Ward was ordered to be moved or brought to the guardhouse, but he refused to go and allegedly armed himself with three pistols. Parish approached Ward and some words were exchanged. Ward made a move that Parish thought was a movement to shoot at him, whereupon he unloaded a full load of buckshot into the belly of Ward, who died fifteen minutes later. Ward's brother soon arrived with Call's reinforcements and Parish thought it wise to remove himself inside the pickets of Fort Drane.[224] The upshot of this incident, in which Parish was exonerated by his peers, was a duel in Tallahassee between Parish's commander, Colonel Austin Alston and George T. Ward, the brother of the dead officer.[225] This duel led to another cycle of familial/political duels in the Territorial capitol. It is also representative of some of the problems regulars often observed among volunteer units and one of the reasons for the constant distrust and dislike between the militia and regulars. It also helps to explain why Clinch wrote to Secretary Cass to send regular troops and rescind the requisition of volunteer units from Georgia and South Carolina.[226]

Clinch was becoming disgusted with the criticism of his command but he did not have long to wait before he was replaced as commanding officer in Florida. On 29 January Congress had passed legislation increasing by $500,000 the funds for the promulgation of the war. Since the first appropriation was for a paltry $80,000 this was a substantial increase and recognition by Congress of the seriousness of the situation. General Abraham Eustis was called upon to take every troop that could be spared to Florida from his base in Charleston, South Carolina. He was to report to Clinch but by the time he arrived in Florida that officer had been supplanted by Major General Winfield Scott. Scott was given broad authority to call upon the governors of Georgia, South Carolina, Alabama and Florida for all the volunteers that could be spared. Clinch was now under Scott and ready to turn over command.[227]

There was one major problem with giving Scott this command and that involved the rights of Edmund P. Gaines to command a portion of this army in Florida. These two very bitter rivals could never work in the same field together. Their rivalry for position and prestige dated back over twenty years prior to this most recent outbreak. During the last Indian uprising, the Black Hawk War, Gaines, in whose district this mostly took place, was bypassed by the president in favor of Scott. Gaines did not take this decision lightly. Florida, for administrative purposes only, was divided in two with a western and eastern half each controlled by of one of these two gentlemen. When the war broke out and Gaines had heard of the distress in Florida, he immediately assumed he would be playing a major role. Cass could mollify the disgruntled Clinch but Major General Gaines was a totally different person. Issuing orders to Lieutenant Colonel David Twiggs, Gaines immediately prepared to swoop down on Florida and take the field as soon as humanly possible. Cass took action too and sent a command to Pensacola to intercept Gaines and direct him to the Texas border, where trouble was also stirring. Gaines, with advice from staff and others, decided to ignore the order (which did not include a copy of Scott's appointment) and proceeded to Florida post-haste.[228]

Gaines was all action upon his arrival in Tampa on 9 February 1836. He immediately began organizing for a march to relieve Clinch, from whom he had heard nothing. He was joined in Tampa by Florida General Leigh Read and his force. Gaines toyed with the idea of abandoning Fort Brooke and marching the garrison, friendly Indians and all, along with him to what he perceived would be the rescue of Clinch. Happily a squadron of marines on loan from the navy, under Lieutenant Waldron, arrived on the scene and the plan for abandoning Tampa was laid aside.[229] Four days after his arrival, Gaines led his troops on the road to Fort King where he understood Scott had ordered numerous rations to be placed for his campaign. Being short of rations and other necessities of war did not deter Gaines's force, which stopped to bury Dade's command along the way. To their chagrin there were no rations available at Fort King upon their arrival. He quickly decided to send a pack train to Fort Drane to get what he could from Clinch, who was awaiting the arrival of Scott within days. Gaines got only enough to avoid starvation. He then headed back to Fort Brooke and took the route Clinch had recently pioneered. As the cagey veteran realized, he might get a shot at the Seminoles lodged in the Cove as a bonus.[230]

Writing from Picolata on the St. Johns River, Lt. Henry Prince noted in his diary for 17 February 1836 that General Scott was expected there at any time.[231] Scott had taken the time to visit the governors of South Carolina and Georgia on his way to Florida for both military and diplomatic reasons. Always the meticulous planner, Scott envisioned a campaign of three prongs aimed at the Cove of the Withlacoochee; one starting from Tampa and moving north, a second starting from Picolata or St. Augustine and approaching the area from the south and east via the Indian town of Palatlakaha and a third starting at Fort Drane and taking the route used by Clinch (and Gaines). This was grand strategy straight from the textbooks of Jomini and other students of Napoleonic warfare. The only difference was the relatively secure knowledge of the terrain and weather patterns in Europe verses the nearly unknown wilds and swamps of Florida. Scott also did not anticipate Gaines' predicament and the impact it would have on his own grandiose plan.

By 27 February Gaines' force had reached the bank of the Withlacoochee River and proceeded to search for a ford said by friendly Indians to be in the area. While the search continued the Seminoles and their allies opened fire on the command. After an hour's skirmish the fighting ended and the army encamped. The guides now told Gaines that the ford was further up the river, about three miles, and the ford would be easy to find. The next morning the command moved out in the direction indicated but, upon reaching the designated spot, the river was found too deep and rapid to ford. Lieutenant James F. Izard attempted to discover the fording place but was mortally wounded by fire from the opposite bank. Gaines decided to build a small field work and send to Clinch for assistance. The help desired was provisions, ammunition and a movement about ten miles further up the river to encircle the enemy and crush them between their combined forces. The command constructed "Camp Izard" and while waiting for Clinch, they amused themselves by taunting the Indians to fight in the open. Clinch did not come.

96

An assault by the Seminoles and their allies on 1 March inflicted some casualties and forced Gaines to strictly ration his materials. The looked-for reinforcements were not in sight and the rations were running very low. Horse meat became the order of the day. After several days of assaults and intermittent firing into the camp, Gaines' force was beginning to weaken. On 5 March a voice came from the forest and proved to be that of Caesar, an "old Negro" known to many of the whites, who declared that the Seminoles were tired of fighting and wished to parley. Gaines was in the midst of bargaining with them when the advance of Clinch's force arrived and began firing, thus scaring the Indian negotiators to the other side of the river and effectively ending the talks. Gaines was actually very lucky in this instance because, if Sprague is correct, he was opposed by a superior force of over 900 Indian and black warriors.[232]

What happened next is the stuff of legend. Gaines went back to Fort Drane with Clinch. The flamboyant general basically announced that the war was now over and that he was turning over command to Clinch who would wait until, "the officer charged with the diplomatic arrangements of the War Department" should arrive. Earlier than Gaines expected, Scott arrived at Fort Drane on 13 March and took command.[233] According to Bemrose there were now 3,354 troops at Fort Drane, the largest single concentration during the entire war. Almost all of these troops were encamped outside of the pickets of the fort. The usual camp noises were broken the sound of Scott's choice regimental band. The contrast between the two men could not have been different. Scott with band, traveling library, fine wines and three wagon loads of fine furniture clashed in style with the Spartan Gaines. As the steward carefully observed, "Gen. Gaines and his ambitious rival met occasionally in this out-of-the-world place, and I noticed a cold situation passed between them. There was no companionship and evidently there existed a distaste, a repelling power proving that when interests clash two of a trade seldom agree." This is a classic understatement.[234]

Gaines departed the next day for his assigned duties on the western frontier. He left behind nearly eighty wounded and sick soldiers to be taken care of by Scott's command. To accommodate this extra load, a number of axmen and skilled carpenters were put to work, and within three days they transformed the appearance of the fort by adding a new two story building of pine, complete with shingles, clapboards, supports and rafters. The wounded and sick were now housed in relative comfort by the construction of this sturdy building.[235]

Scott's grand design began to take shape while he remained at Fort Drane and orders were issued to put it into effect. From the beginning the plan was doomed. Materials he ordered to the front did not arrive. The clash between Colonel William Lindsay and Leigh Read created an atmosphere of distrust and disorganization. Lieutenant Colonel Crabbe of the Alabama volunteers ordered all of the Seminole scouts taken into custody when one of them was injured by firing allegedly done by his troops. Lindsey went into a rage and never regained control of the situation. That wing of the plan had to be abandoned before reaching its assigned zone of attack. Because of poor guides and a lack of accurate maps, General Eustis was slowed down on his advance and did not reach the assigned area in time to hear the signals from Scott's column. Eustis did have some success and killed a number of Seminoles and their allies, most notably Yahadjo and Yuchi Billy (or so they thought – he was captured a year later very much alive). They also burned the Indian settlement of Palatlakaha near modern Bushnell. Scott's column had less military success, unless one includes good marching order and two flatboats wheeled to the Withlacoochee to facilitate the crossing. Two small skirmishes were the only tangible results. The Seminoles and their allies melted away as the army advanced and did not offer a full battle again until Christmas Day of 1837 at the Battle of Lake Okeechobee. As the historian of this war, John Mahon, has correctly noted, "This was very neat, too neat to work well."[236]

The major problems were related to the climate and terrain of Florida. Few maps existed that were of use to the army and reliance upon scouts proved to be tenuous at best. Getting transportation was a difficult task as both wagons and boats were in very short supply.[237] Florida was significantly lacking in roads, forcing the military to construct most of the roads that extended beyond the immediate range of the larger villages and towns. Just a few days after their return to Fort Drane, members of the Fourth Artillery had to assist in constructing a road to the Withlacoochee River, and young Lieutenant Benjamin Alvord supervised the fifty-plus men in this task.[238]   As warmer weather approached, the sick list grew and many places were abandoned because they were deemed unhealthy by the medical staff.   Provisioning the troops and finding usable forage for the horses and mules also proved difficult and expensive.   By May, Lieutenant Colonel James Bankhead was complaining of the new recruits to the Dragoons, who had few suitable mounts, little equipment and less training.   This gallant officer also noted that another blockhouse, pickets and barracks had to be constructed to house these men under the watchful and deadly eye of the enemy.   The hammocks and depressions that covered the area around Fort Drane made concealment of the enemy forces relatively easy and increased the risk to work parties.[239]

April of 1836 saw the campaign in full swing, and the Seminoles had returned to what Mahon calls their "peripheral strategy" of attacking isolated columns, small villages and other remote and vulnerable targets.   The strategy of avoiding a large direct battle with the army was strictly followed.   Fort Drane, on 14 April, suffered an attack on its defenses at about two in the morning.   Bemrose writes that this attack was little more than a diversion to draw attention away from the fact that one party of Seminoles was racing in to steal some horses.[240]   Six days later another night attack ensued in an attempt to destroy the reduced garrison before Clinch could return.   The garrison was able to handle the task at hand and Clinch's arrival on the 24th found the fort intact.[241]   In a recent book on frontier warfare and policy, historian John Buchanan argues persuasively that the Native American's inability to take fortified positions was one of the main weaknesses in their defense of their homelands.   The failure of the Seminoles and their allies to attempt very many such sieges and the failure of those they did attempt would seem to support Buchanan's theory.[242]

May brought with it the beginnings of the "sickly season" in Florida.   Bankhead and his subordinates at Fort Drane began an agitation for the abandonment of Fort King.   Their reasoning was twofold, to get the garrison transferred to Fort Drane which was, "the most exposed frontier post" and to lessen the distance for the transfer of supplies. Fort King, they argued, was not in the center of operations and was difficult to approach. As of 1 May there were only 86 troops stationed at Fort King while Fort Drane had 213 in camp and at its dependencies (especially Oakland, the plantation of John McIntosh). Too many people riding between these posts and that at Micanopy were being shot at and some were killed on this route. Better to abandon Fort King than to risk any more lives.[243]

Yet lives were lost at Fort Drane on a shockingly regular basis. Many of these losses came at the hands of the Seminoles and their allies as they ambushed supply trains and messengers between the posts. The poor supply situation made life inside Fort Drane and other posts more difficult. Food became scarce at Drane in late May of 1836. On 26 May Bankhead wrote to Captain R. B. Lee at Micanopy that he would not be able to assist him in feeding the citizens and their families there because the supply train had not arrived and, "the quantity of provisions here will barely suffice to sustain the troops on this frontier until the wagons can be sent …"[244] Bankhead soon left Fort Drane and his place was assumed by Captain Lemuel Gates on 29 May 1836.

Shortly after Gates took command at Fort Drane, Governor Richard K. Call replaced Scott as commander of the forces in Florida. Just prior to this, however, Fort Drane's garrison was forced to witness the destruction of General Clinch's fine sugar house by the Seminoles. Major Julius Heileman, commanding at Micanopy, wrote to Scott to inform him of the situation in his area, including the destruction of the sugar works and, "that his negroes have revolted & the commanding officer has them in close confinement."[245] This was an element of this particular war that has drawn significant attention of late. It was important throughout the war but more especially in the beginning stages of the conflict. The revolt of Clinch's slaves was indicative of the unrest over which the army had little control. Call, a slave holder and intimate of Jackson in his early career, was to now assume a more difficult and complex role, that of General of combined volunteer forces and regular army. A militia general commanding regulars was bound to produce as much volatility as a slave revolt under these circumstances.

100

Shortly after Call assumed command he was stricken with fever. Exactly which type of fever is unknown. The news that a large contingent of Tennessee volunteers was under way to Florida surely lifted his ailing spirits. Any uplifting was short lived as the same disease that incapacitated him quickly killed his beloved wife. Assuming military command of the entire Territory and suffering the emotional trauma of losing one's spouse made Call at times unsteady in balance and behavior. Some, especially the Tennessee volunteers, reported that he was a drunkard, which was surely not the case. Call's campaign was planned in a fashion similar to Scott's, but it was poorly supplied. General Read did not accomplish the task assigned to him, as the steamer *Izard,* commanded by a young lieutenant named Raphael Semmes, sank in the mouth of the Withlacoochee and did not clear the way for the barges sent to supply Call's force as it reached the river. If something could go wrong with a campaign, it did for Call. Five days after taking charge he had the melancholy task of informing Cass of the death of Major Heileman at Fort Drane from the fever.[246] By the end of July Call was writing Adjutant General Jones about the unhealthy situation at Fort Drane and recommending its abandonment.[247] With the garrison enfeebled by disease and the loss of such a fine commander, Call felt compelled to close the fort even if it meant giving no protection to settlers in the area. Those within the fort were forced to relocate.

Drane was abandoned officially in July of 1836 but because of a lack of support troops the sick and wounded could not be evacuated until 7 August. The first attempt to bring wagons to the fort for the evacuation resulted in an attack in force upon the train commanded by Captain William S. Maitland. The "Battle of Welika Pond" saw a desperate fight that included some of the sick from Fort Micanopy joining in the charge which finally dispersed the foe. Five men lost their lives in this battle and six more were wounded. The fort was finally evacuated and now stood alone in the wilderness. Unfortunately for posterity, the Seminoles under Osceola soon destroyed the fort, Clinch's plantation house and all of the out-buildings on the property.[248]

Fort Drane did not disappear from the minds of the army. With the sickly season in full force, the fort at Micanopy was ordered closed. Call was furious with Lieutenant Colonel Ichabod Crane for ordering this move, but he did not reinstate that post immediately. Crane sent Major Benjamin K. Pierce to do the honors of closing this important post and while approaching the area he learned that a large number of Seminoles under Osceola, reported as sick with the fever, were encamped near Fort Drane. With little hesitation Pierce ordered every animal that could be ridden, including mules, to be mounted and ride with him to the fort. The object was surprise and Pierce achieved this most valued of military goals with great élan. With some of his command hanging on to the manes of their mounts and others shouting to the heavens, Pierce caught the Indians in the open and forced them to head to the hammocks. The foe did this with great alacrity and began a heavy fire on the troops. The fight lasted an hour before the firing let up and the Indians faded into the shade of the approaching night. Pierce did not order a charge on the hammocks, not knowing the strength of the enemy. He soon withdrew back to Micanopy and safety, having lost one killed and sixteen wounded for his efforts. Call and others hailed this as a major victory and lauded Pierce for his valiant effort. Although it was not a battle with large forces and casualties inflicted it was a bright spot on a very dim horizon. It was the first clear cut victory for the army in this most frustrating war.[249]

Call's campaign visited the site of Fort Drane too many times for the Tennessee volunteers, who were tiring of being shot at, charging hammocks to find the enemy gone and not having any supplies where the governor said they were supposed to be. John Erwin, serving with the first regiment of Tennessee volunteers, constantly assailed Call for his lack of provisioning the troops. He noted during one of his command's stops at Fort Drane that the resting of the troops while waiting for supplies gave the enemy ample time to evade the troops or prepare to give them battle. Erwin also found that green beef was not to his liking. On another stop at the fort he witnessed the arrival of nearly six hundred Creek volunteers under Colonel John Lane. Fighting alongside of the Creeks was nothing new for troops from Tennessee.[250] Henry Hollingsworth left an account about the charge of the Tennessee troops on the grounds of Fort Drane where the Indians were said to be encamped. Troops taking all angles of attack surprised the alleged camp only to find it abandoned. It is Hollingsworth that gives us a vivid description of the completeness with which Fort Drane was destroyed by the Seminoles. The October foray into the old wilderness fortification by the boys from Tennessee produced very little except exhausted horses and men.[251]

No discussion of Fort Drane would be complete without mention of one of the war's many tragic events, the suicide of Colonel John Lane. Call made the official report to the Adjutant General on 22 October 1836. "With the most painful regret I have to inform you that within a very few hours after the arrival of the Regiment, its gallant Commander Colo. Lane, in a paroxysm of insanity produced by a fever of the brain occasioned by excessive fatigue and anxiety on the march committed suicide by introducing the point of his sword above the right eye, and forcing almost through his head."[252] W. P. Rowles, the surgeon for the Creek volunteers, described Lane's condition prior to the gruesome death: "While uttering these astounding facts, his manner, as it had done for several days, indicated a high state of excitement. His face was flushed, gestures rapid, voice stridulous and eyes restless." Twenty minutes later Rowles was called to Lane's side.[253] Many of the Tennessee volunteers mention this strange death in their memoirs of the campaign. Theodore Rodenbough, in his history of the Second Dragoons, disputes the suicide and claims it was "accidental" noting that some observers stated that Lane was jovial and laughing just prior to retiring to his tent. Which ever theory may be believed, the sad fact was the loss of someone so promising. As Rodenbough quotes in his volume; "But seldom has thy trophied car, O Death! Conveyed in triumph to thy dark domain a richer spoil."[254]

Fort Drane limped along through the remainder of October until its disbanding in January of 1837. Some scouts were sent out from the post but the numbers of troops stationed there continued to fall. November's Post Returns show only 103 men present for duty at the fort. The commanding officer in its last days was Lieutenant John H. Winder of the First Artillery. Writing on 30 November 1836 he noted the escape of an Indian prisoner from the confines of the fort. The reason he states for this escape was that he was the only commissioned officer present and he had only one sergeant for duty. The guard had to be entrusted to a corporal who had little control over the lax sentinels who allowed this escape. He even hinted that someone may have helped the Indian to escape, because the means of jumping the picket was a strategically placed barrel up against the wall.[255] If security was so poor and the post without officers again, it was time to close the post.

The actual reason for the ending of the life of this post was simple. The troops were needed elsewhere and the center of the conflict, if such it had, went further south on the peninsula. But the real end of Fort Drane waited until late in the twentieth century. In late 1987 the author received a telephone call from Alyce Tincher, then president of the Marion County Historical Society. She wanted assistance to try and save an old Seminole War fort called Drane. Her drive and tenacity worked wonders in inspiring research but they were not enough to save the site of this valued fort. After getting depositions from men engaged in removing the clay soil lying under the old fort (to be used for kitty litter) and seeing two men take away what appeared to be Indian artifacts and human remains, Ms. Tincher approached the State's Attorney for Marion County. He flatly refused to consider the case. The State Archaeologist had his hands tied by behind-the-scenes politics. There was no saving this site. Today, if you want to see the remains of Fort Drane and all that it stood for, look no further than your cat's litterbox.

# Fort Micanopy

The history of the Second Seminole War in Florida does not begin with the battle known as the "Dade Massacre" but with a number of smaller skirmishes between whites and Indians in and around Alachua County. Prior to the "Dade Massacre," the citizens of Alachua had petitioned the government for the stationing of at least four companies of troops in Micanopy and reported depredations of their cattle and other livestock.[256] This petition, and others that followed, reflected a long-standing duel between the races over land, cattle and runaway slaves.[257] The heat of conflict became unbearable in early December of 1835 and Governor John Eaton called out the militia and asked General Duncan L. Clinch for regular troops to quell the potential disturbance. Clinch requested the militia, under Colonel Warren, to meet his supply train and guard it on its way to Lang Syne Plantation, the future site of Fort Drane and Clinch's designated headquarters. This task accomplished, Florida Militia General Richard K. Call arrived on the scene and took personal command of the militia on December 19, 1835, nine days before the Dade battle.[258]

As Call recalled, "... the troops of Middle Florida, under my command, had been assembled, organized, had performed a march of two hundred miles, and had attacked and destroyed a party of the enemy, discovered plundering and burning a house within half a mile of Micanopy. ... on my arrival I found the whole country overrun, and in the possession of the enemy. Every house had been abandoned."[259]    Call does not tell us the names of some of the victims of these Indian raids. However, some of the names of those putting in claims with the Federal government for compensation indicate that the plantation owners of the Micanopy area were very hard hit. Moses Levy's "pilgrimage" plantation was one of those destroyed, as was that of Malachi Hagan (or Hogan), whose home, like Levy's and McIntosh's, was burned to the ground.[260] Levy had his overseer, James Verhain, took his moveable property to Micanopy for safety, to a place occupied by Charles Waldron and soon picketed by United States troops. Levy and others estimated the value of his moveable property at $1,200 while Hagan believed his property to be worth about $300. No mention is made of Levy's slaves or the value of his plantation property, but it was probably very high by the standard of the day.[261]

Another large loser in the immediate area was former Indian agent Gad Humphpreys, whose "Defiance" plantation was made the military post for the region, Fort Defiance. Not only did Humphreys lose his house and some of the out buildings, but twenty-eight slaves were left without direct protection and were soon captured and removed by the Indians. Humphreys valued the lost slaves at $650 apiece and the property at $3,294. When this fortification was abandoned and destroyed by United States troops to keep it from falling into Indian hands, Humphreys was left in a financial hole.[262] He later removed to St. Augustine and received aid from the government under an act to aid the sufferers of Indian depredations in Florida. He never received compensation for his financial loss from the United States government.[263]

John McIntosh, an important planter and plantation owner related to the powerful Houston family of Georgia, and, through them, his neighbor, Duncan L. Clinch, also lost his "Oakland" plantation to the Indians. In his indemnity plea, he estimated the loss of this substantial plantation at $44,000, all property included. The Committee of Claims for the United States Senate reduced this evaluation to $20,000, feeling that only the buildings could be paid for if the bill were to be reported favorably. The Committee of Claims, listening to all the evidence in early 1839, was not satisfied that all of the proper documents had been submitted and asked to be discharged from further consideration of McIntosh's claim.[264] McIntosh did not seek any redress for the use of his property as a military post by the United States Army. Thus, the financial loss and personal suffering, as evidenced by the previous examples, was substantial immediately prior to and after the official outbreak of hostilities between the Indians and white settlers.

Reports of the depredations of the Indians literally flew into St. Augustine and Jacksonville. On December 17, 1835, Gabriel Priest reported having moved his family and others from the Wacahoota settlement into Hogtown on December 6th. Upon returning the next day, December 7th, with fourteen or fifteen men, they came to a scrub hammock where they were fired upon, with the result that one man was killed and another, Priest's son, wounded. The entire settlement at Wacahoota was burned by this party of about fifty Indians.[265] Colonel Warren had a skirmish with the Indians south of the Kanapaha Prairie on the way to Micanopy. The battle, which became known as the Battle of Black Point, cost the lives of eight of the militia, and some of the remnants of the command, who had been in the vanguard, were in Micanopy when the fighting at the baggage train erupted.[266] Nearly everywhere on the Alachua frontier fighting had broken out prior to the Dade battle and the beginning of "official hostilities." Micanopy was in the center of the major action and was one of the main outposts, with nearly five hundred men in and around the settlement by the end of 1835.[267]

"Total ruin" was the dire prediction of many concerning the fate of Alachua County during the first hectic months of activity. With Fort Drane established at Clinch's plantation and Fort Defiance at Micanopy, the immediate neighborhood would have appeared to be well protected, however, this was not the case. Within four miles of Fort Drane, Wiley Brooks' home was burnt to the ground. Horses and cattle were stolen from Gad Humphreys' plantation, the site of Fort Defiance, before the month of April was through. The utter boldness and willfulness of the Indian adversary insured that no place would be completely safe for many years to come. Indeed, it was predicted that because signs pointed to the Indians splitting into small groups, the war would be fairly prolonged and certainly not over within the first year.[268]

Because it appeared that Fort Defiance and the many settlements around Micanopy would be some of the first targets of the Indians, the army and militia moved rapidly to build up the defenses. Lieutenant Francis L. Dancy, later a Colonel in the Florida militia,

Surveyor General and State Engineer, and Lieutenant M. M. Clarke were the Assistant Quartermaster Generals at Micanopy. In January of 1836 they received many letters from the Office of the Quartermaster General giving them money to draw on in Savannah for the supplies needed by troops in central Florida, including Fort Brooke (Tampa). All along the chain of command in the Quartermaster General's Office, letters were sent to inform them of the amount of funds available and to whom to report every detail of supply.[269] General Clinch was informed of all of these arrangements on January 19, 1836, at the same time as the orders were issued to the officers of the Quartermaster General's Office. Major Thomas Hunt, the acting Quartermaster General at the outbreak of hostilities, also noted to Clinch that he had not heard from his command in some time and had, on his own, remitted the funds to Savannah for the use of the above named officers.[270]

On the next day, Hunt wrote to Brig. Gen. Abraham Eustis, at Charleston, requesting that Lieutenant S. B. Dusenbery of the Adjutant General's Office be stationed somewhere on the St. Johns River to facilitate the movement of supplies inland. He also noted that 30,000 rations had been sent to St. Augustine and "A large supply of Subsistence stores" had been ordered to Fort King.[271] It is worth noting that Hunt realized the relative inconvenience of shipping supplies to Fort King and St. Augustine and the need for a more direct route for supplies into central Florida. The army later settled on Garey's Ferry on Black Creek (Middleburg) and the old Spanish fort site of Picolata as the main points for shipment into the interior of Florida. The latter post had the advantage of being the old route to Alachua and thus had an established road bed over which to ship supplies. Many of the supplies ordered for the army in Florida came from New York, Baltimore and Charleston so there was a premium on good transportation. The severe lack of roads and other transportation routes in early Florida, therefore, greatly hampered military operations.

One of the key factors in transportation in early Florida was construction of boats. To haul materials down the St. Johns, or the Ocklawaha, or even Orange Creek, boats of many types and sizes were needed. However, there was a serious lack of such craft in Florida at the outbreak of the Seminole War. Supplies could not be shipped from Savannah for the same reason, the lack of suitable craft. In exasperation, Hunt wrote to Lieutenant Charles Dimmock on April 12, 1836, "I have received your letter of the 3rd instant and regret extremely that the boats called for were not furnished. Why could they not have been obtained--were there not workmen--no materials in Savannah? If the materials were growing in the woods, and you could find no other workmen than raw soldiers or plantation negroes, the boats should have been built and furnished. It is perhaps now too late to render them available; but they must be furnished cost what they may." Hunt went on to explain that during the War of 1812, he had seen sixteen oared boats constructed in four days and sailed across Lake Erie, so he knew that boats could be quickly furnished. Thus, there was a reason for his tone of remonstrance and exasperation.[272]

Fort Defiance, meanwhile, was becoming the center of much activity, even though Fort Drane was the launching point for most of the early expeditions against the Seminoles. Micanopy was considered a healthy spot by the military and some type of hospital facilities were set up under the direction of Dr. Richard Weightman. Convoys of sick and wounded made their way from the battlefields and Fort Drane to Micanopy for further attention. On June 16, 1836, one of these convoys was attacked with the loss of two men and an additional ten wounded.[273] When Fort Drane was ordered abandoned on June 24, 1836, the troops were ordered removed to Micanopy. The scene reported by John Bemrose is not very pleasant and he noted that he would always recall, "those poor desolate men [who] clung about and around me." He also recorded that he was invited to dine with his colleague and friend, Dr. Weightman, and was shown into his marquee by his personal servant, who offered him much needed refreshment.[274] Things on the frontier were not always as tough as we sometimes imagine.

During June and July of 1836, Fort Defiance was occupied by elements of the 3rd Artillery, commanded, when well, by Captain R. B. Lee, but more frequently by Lieutenant Martin Burke. According to the Post Returns, 114 men (in aggregate) were stationed at Fort Defiance during these two months with numerous other "unassigned officers and men," most of whom were listed as sick. Captain Lemuel Gates took command in July and filed the Post Return for that month, showing 110 men on duty. His returns indicate a large number of wounded, including Dr. Weightman, Brevet Captain R. B. Lee, and Captain J. A. Ashby. These officers, and many men, were wounded in actions, the most notable being the "Battle of Micanopy."[275]

Because the battle is important to the story, I will quote Major J. F. Heileman's report in full:

Micanopy, June 10th 1836.

General:

I have the honor to report that yesterday morning a party of Indians, estimated at one hundred and fifty or two hundred, made their appearance in front of this place, at a distance of about three quarters of a mile. Their object was evidently to draw us out; and not having any disposition to balk their views, I instructed Capt. Lee to take his company, and skirt a hammock to the right of this post, and gain the left of the enemy. At the same time I directed Lieutenant Wheelock to mount with his dragoons, and make a corresponding movement on the left, and Lieut. Humphreys, with a detachment of D and E companies of 2d U.S. Artillery, to move across a field in front, holding a six pounder with a few men in reserve.

The promptitude with which my orders were complied with brought the three detachments immediately in contact with the enemy. Seeing the heavy fire of the enemy, I became at once satisfied they were treble our numbers, and immediately moved forward with the six-pounder. The horses not being well borke, I was obliged to cast loose the prolonge. I had hardly done this, and while waiting a flank movement of Lieutenant Wheelock to unmask the six-pounder, when I received a message that the Indians were coming on the rear of the place. Having left a few teamsters and citizens in charge of the work, I deemed it proper to move back with the gun, and gave directions accordingly. Taking myself a shorter route across the field, I arrived a few moments before the gun; and finding the report to be untrue, I directed Lieut. Talcott 3d Artillery, to report to the field at full speed, while with a few men I reconnoitered the rear of our position.

After an hour and twenty minutes of hard fighting under a broiling sun, our troops returned, having driven the enemy two miles into their strong holds. The gallantry and good conduct of both officers and men is beyond all commendation I am able to bestow; and it is with deep regret that I report Capt. Lee, 3rd Artillery, severely but not dangerously wounded. He was shot early in the action yet directed his men to push forward, which they did manfully. I enclose Dr. Maffit's report; and let me express my acknowledgements to Mr. Center, a resident of this place, for his unremitting kindness and attention to our wounded men and ourselves generally. ...

Another report in the same edition of the *Army and Navy Chronicle* noted that because of this action, Fort Gates (Oakland) was ordered to be abandoned and the forces consolidated with those at Fort Drane. General Eustis ordered all available troops to follow up this apparent victory.[276] The unfortunate Major Julius Heileman died shortly thereafter, at Fort Drane, on June 27th, allegedly from exposure and over exertion during the Battle of Micanopy. His death left a widow and six children who, because he did not die directly in battle or from wounds sustained in battle, could not collect his pension and were left on "the charity of the world." Another of the major players in the battle, Lieutenant Wheelock, took his own life as a result of the engagement. "His exposure," it was noted, "brought on a fever, and in a moment of delirium he shot himself with a pistol."[277] Thus, though the battle casualty list did not reflect it, the number of dead from the Battle of Micanopy included some important individuals.

The sickness at Fort Drane, as noted earlier, forced the abandonment of that post on June 24, 1836. The sick and wounded went immediately to Fort Defiance and arrived, in total, on July 7th. Because the state of medical knowledge was relatively elementary, the infections and disease spread among the troops stationed at Micanopy rapidly and the men were soon ordered to leave. Although it had been predicted for early to mid-June, the final abandonment did not come, however, until August 24th. The order to abandon Fort Defiance included instructions to destroy the fort lest it fall into the hands of the enemy. This job was done efficiently and thoroughly, for as one observer noted on October 5, 1836, " ... passed Fort Micanopy which is at present in a most perfect state of destruction - passed many farms once in fine condition but now desolate and deserted."[278]

Before the post was totally abandoned, however, another skirmish took place, which is known as the Battle of We-li-ka in the Post Returns. This battle took place on the 19th of July and involved an alleged 300 Indians. Major Ashby was severely wounded in the neck and, as noted earlier, Dr. Weightman was also wounded in the thigh. Ashby's men had been on escort duty when the action occurred and as soon as the first volleys rang out, the entire garrison of Fort Defiance went to the rescue. The battle took more than an hour and resulted in 12 soldiers being wounded and many horses killed. Many of the 150 sick lying in beds at the fort took part in the battle, though "in a feeble and debilitated state." Several of the men, it was later reported, were mortally wounded in the battle. The number of Indian casualties were not listed except to note that the U.S. troops had won the day and many Indians were observed to fall on the field.[279]

In his accounting of the Battle of We-li-ka, Lieutenant W. S. Maitland wrote to Governor Call that Ashby was escorting twenty-two wagons of commissary stores and provisions to Fort Defiance in final preparation for the abandonment of Fort Drane. The first volley from the Indians came within a mile of Micanopy in the direction of the We-li-ka Pond. After a brief charge into the hammock bordering the pond, Captain Ashby found the enemy removed from the area. Yet, after a short respite, and within a quarter mile of the fort, a second volley of fire hit the column. This time the garrison and Ashby's men combined to attack the hammock area and drove the Indians from the field. Maitland's recording of the event differs in two important areas, the first is that the Indian force is estimated to be 250, a decrease from the original 300, and secondly, he makes no mention of the assistance rendered by George Center, or any other civilian. He gives the total killed as two soldiers and nine wounded, three seriously.[280]

While in preparations for the final abandonment, Major Benjamin K. Pierce, brother of future President Franklin Pierce, learned of the enemy lurking about Fort Drane. With 110 men and a Mr. Jackson, a wagon master familiar with the area, as a guide, Pierce took one field piece and the troops to Fort Drane, where the Indians, " ... it appears, had erected a village," and were living with their families. Pierce claims that 300 Indians were in the immediate vicinity and were led by Osceola (he calls him Powell). His troops had the element of surprise on their side and they were able to drive the Indians into a neighboring hammock, leaving, Pierce observed, 10 dead on the field. Because they were outnumbered three to one and the Indians now had the advantage of the covering hammock, Pierce broke off the engagement with 1 killed and 16 wounded. He brought these men back to Micanopy to recover and mend. The Battle of Fort Drane, as it has been called, was fought on August 11, 1836, thirteen days before the final abandonment of Fort Defiance.[281]

When Major Pierce left Fort Defiance, he took with him 390 men. The post at Micanopy was re-established, under the name of Fort Micanopy, on April 30, 1836, by companies B, H and I of the 4th Artillery under the command of Brevet Major L. Whiting. An aggregate of 141 men were assigned to this post with 125 on actual duty when re-establishment took place. According to the Post Returns, the 4th Artillery marched to Fort Micanopy via Forts Armstrong, King and Drane. This route was nearly opposite that of Major Pierce's when his command left and reported to Garey's Ferry, soon renamed Fort Heileman.[282]

Fort Micanopy did not experience the direct assaults of battle as its predecessor had. No pitched battles were ever fought at this post. However, this does not diminish the importance of the fort as an institution of safety for the surrounding territory. Throughout its life, it was garrisoned regularly with U.S. troops, most often of the 4th Artillery and 7th Infantry. It served as a hospital base for the "Micanopy Square" in the time of Zachary Taylor's command of Florida's forces. During the overall command of General Thomas Jesup, the fort served as a major supply depot for all of the surrounding forts, which reported to the commanding officer of Fort Micanopy. The garrisons of the fort performed many duties of importance and were more often than not on active patrol through the hammocks and swamps of the surrounding vicinity.

In its daily life, the garrison of the fort often performed useful duties that later assisted the development of the area. For example, garrisons were often assigned to construct and maintain military roads in their neighborhood. To quote one such order: "The Colonel Commanding understanding that the most direct route from Fort Russel to Fort Micanopy is to cross the Orange Creek at the former point, directs that you construct a bridge at that place so soon as praticable, employing in that service the whole of the disposable force of your command. You can procure from the Quarter Master General at Pilatka any tools you may require to enable you to comply with these instructions."[283] By a law of 1819, all garrisons were required to raise their own crops, whenever possible, for the benefit of the entire force. These gardens and the crops grown therein often formed the basis for later settlements and alerted potential settlers to the type of vegetables, fruits, and forage crops that could be produced in a given region. Most garrisons also raised their own cattle and hogs, whenever possible, to reduce the costs of maintaining the soldiers in a given area, like Florida, where the expense of almost any necessity of life was relatively high. Again, this knowledge could be used by potential settlers for their own benefit.

Fort Micanopy, like many major posts on the frontier, also had its problems with those selling whiskey and other strong drink to the soldiers and profiteering to the detriment of the morale of the garrison. On October 2, 1840, Assistant Adjutant General W. W. L. Bliss wrote the following: "It having been represented to the Commanding General that the presence at Micanopy of a resident named Hosea[?] Merry is prejudicial to the public interest, you are authorized by him to order the said Merry from the post if in your judgment the interest of the service requires such a measure." The exact nature of Merry's indiscretion is not disclosed, but given the complaints about the large number of grog shops in the area, one can speculate as to the nature of the indiscretion.[284]

A letter of January 20, 1841, is much more explicit in its condemnation of a local resident. "Sir, This post has long been annoyed by a great number of grog shops and tippling houses. In

September last while Capt. Bonneville was in command, one of the worst of them, kept by Francis Bray; a discharged soldier; had his liquor destroyed and his family removed from the post. This act has met my approbation as one indispensably necessary to the discipline and efficiency of the garrison."[285] Alcoholism was very much a part of the frontier, no matter what part of the country, and it did have an impact on the efficiency of the army. One soldier, Private Justice Wright of E Company, 3rd Artillery, was known as a "beastly drunkard" whose commanding officer wrote on January 8, 1841, "I have been in command of him for nearly five weeks and have not been able to get a single tour of duty from him during the whole of that time, and at the same time that he renders no service he is a great encumbrance to the rest of the Company."[286] There can be little wonder at the serious thought given to the problems of alcohol by the commanding officers, especially in a military situation where each must do his duty and depend on others to do theirs.

The healthy climate prevailing at Micanopy, as noted earlier, made it appear ideal for a hospital station. On March 5, 1840, the garrison learned that the Commanding General, " ... designs having a general hospital erected at Micanopy." Because Lt. Col. Whistler's garrison had enough to do chasing down marauding Indians in the hammocks of the area, local persons would be allowed to be hired to construct the hospital building. The order added the following description: "It will of course be built of logs covered with clapboards, and floored with puncheons."[287] What is lacking in this brief order is the covering for the building. It cannot be assumed that the roof for this hospital was made of native cypress or cedar shingle because many of the forts of the period used tarpaulins for covering. Regardless of the type of covering, the fact remains, that for civilians and soldiers alike, Fort Micanopy had medical attention available for those injured by the many raiding parties that roamed over Alachua and surrounding counties.

The violent nature of the war and its impact on those fighting in it is reflected in the unique diary of Bartholomew M. Lynch, edited as "The Squaw Kissing War." In this raw record, he noted, "My company gone to Micanopy, got a 3 months furlough from Col. Twiggs, arrived at Micanopy on 1st June. Capt. Fowler did not grant furlough. Duty light at Micanopy, only hunting parties. Two dgs [dragoons] flogged here and one citizen without any form of trial, in consequence of taking some liberties with a notorious whore whom the officers knew to be such. Brigadier General Taylor was here at the time. Lt. Blake was provost martial at the whipping and when the last Dgrs. was whipped says give him 10 more for me. ..." He noted later in the diary that Captain Fowler struck him with a rifle for no reason at all. Lynch then reports, "I went to Gen. Taylor with my blood flowing. He laughed at me. It is no use to sue a devil if the Court be held in hell."[288] Lynch was not the only one to witness or suffer violence at Fort Micanopy. A letter dated January 19, 1842, tersely sums up another type of violence all too well known in our own day: "Sir, Private James Steck [?] of C Compy 7th Infty murdered his wife on the 11th Inst. for which crime he has been turned over to the civil authority. I have to request that he be discharged [from] the service. Very Respectfully, Your Obt. Servt. Wm. Whistler, Lieut. Col. 7th Infty."[289] The violence of the frontier, the boredom of garrison duty, the alcoholism, etc. all contributed to make any post a potentially dangerous place for those both inside and outside its pickets.

Fort Micanopy shared many traits with other installations throughout Florida, however it was an important supply depot, a hospital and rallying point for many expeditions against the Seminoles and their allies. What has been presented above is simply an overview of the fort's history and its place in the overall scheme of the Second Seminole War. It is by no means a complete history of the installation nor is it a view through a microscope. The information presented above is meant to be an introduction to the history of this fascinating fortification and the people involved in its evolution. There is much more to be explored, discovered and explained about the life of this post and those surrounding posts that depended upon it and its garrisons for security and assistance. This paper is also a challenge to search even deeper into the realms and reams of military documents to discover the true story of the events which occurred here in that most frustrating of conflicts, The Second Seminole War. It is also, in a fashion, a plea to you to search farther afield than just the records and diaries located locally or even within the confines of this state. The final picture can only be drawn with the artistic stroke of pure historical research, wherever that may take you.

**Richard K. Call**
*(Florida State Archives)*

# Tallahassee:
# From the Diaries of Captain
# Samuel P. Heintzelman

In the eyes of history, Samuel P. Heintzelman is known primarily as a Major General of Union Volunteers during the Civil War. His service to the country at Bull Run (where he was wounded), the defenses of Washington, the battles of the Peninsula Campaign, the Battles of Fair Oaks, Malvern Hill, and the Second Manassas are all well known and documented. However, like most of the over three hundred generals who served in that war (on both sides) he also had a turn of service in the wars against the Seminoles in the swamps of Florida. The Manheim, Pennsylvania native, born in 1805, graduated from West Point in time to serve as a ranking officer in the Second Seminole War. Most of his time was spent on Quartermaster's duty at Tallahassee and St. Marks/ Port Leon. His observations about this area are hitherto unreported in the historical writings of that war and add a sharp contrast to the currently accepted view of some of the era's key events.

The outbreak of the Second Seminole War came with the slaughter of the command of Major Francis L. Dade near the modern city of Bushnell. On the same day, Indian Agent Wiley Thompson and Lieutenant Constantine Smith were assassinated about six hundred yards from the gate of Fort King, near modern Ocala. At that time, Lieutenant Sam Heintzelman was serving in St. Augustine and had a first hand view of the results of the Battle of Dunlawton, fought by Florida Militia under the command of

Major Benjamin A. Putnam. The results favored the Seminoles and their allies and left the entire eastern coast of Florida open to depredations. He was on hand to hear from participants about the inconclusive Battle of the Withlacoochee and the frustrations of the army campaigning under General Winfield Scott. In early 1836, the young Lieutenant was shipped off to Columbus, Georgia to act as base Quartermaster for the Creek campaign under General Thomas Jesup.

Heintzelman left Columbus on November 13, 1838 and arrived in Tallahassee on the 21$^{st}$ of the same month. In hand were letters of introduction to Colonel Austin Alston and Colonel Sam Reid, the former's son-in-law. Upon arrival he took a room in Brown's Hotel that he described as "rather indifferent." He quickly made a connection with Captain John Rogers Vinton, then temporarily stationed in Tallahassee before heading north. On the very first night they took a ride around the town. "We took a ride on horse-back towards evening by the Racetrack & grave yard. We passed through the principal part of the town. It does not make much show." The impressionable lieutenant then described the large amount of Spanish moss hanging from the trees which he noted, "indicates an unhealthy climate. If other evidence were wanted, the number of new made graves would be sufficient." He also had complaints about his lodgings, and that they served bad coffee with no milk. The beds were uncomfortable and, "The rooms are small & poor attendance from the servants – prices enormous." It was not an auspicious beginning for a general in the making.

On the 22$^{nd}$ of November, Heintzelman took the railroad to St. Marks, the major supply depot for the army in Middle Florida. His description of this trip bears repeating: "The distance to St. Marks is 22 miles & a wretched rail road. We had a horse to pull us along. We were nearly three hours in getting there, including the detention in getting past some farther cars. The road is so much out of repair they cannot run the Locomotive." St. Marks did not fair better in his estimation. "St. Marks is a miserable, small town, coming up to my idea of a mean fishing town. We rambled all over Old Fort St. Marks. It is an irregular work, apparently two sections connected by a curtain & all falling to ruin." The first impression of the old village probably lay behind his ultimate moving of the depot to the new town of Port Leon in 1840.

Tallahassee was not without its redeeming values and interesting people. Captain Vinton was not the only military man in town and some were old acquaintances from previous duties, like Captain John Graham, twice wounded at the Battle of the Withlacoochee, and now residing in Tallahassee with his bride, the former Mrs. Black, sister-in-law of Lieutenant Francis L. Dancy of St. Augustine. Both Graham and Dancy were the sons-in-law of Judge (later governor) Robert Raymond Reid. One of the first women he had the pleasure of meeting was Mrs. Thomas Eppes, whom he considered and called a lady. He was soon calling on Colonel Richard Green, who was living in Governor Call's house while he was on campaign. Not long after, he widened his circle of acquaintances to include Governor Richard K. Call and his aide, David Walker. Another way to make acquaintances was to take your meals at the local restaurant, LeBeaus, where nearly everybody showed up at one time or another. As his circle widened so did his experiences and prejudices.

Another means of meeting the local population was to attend the churches of the town. On November 25th he attended his first meeting at the Presbyterian Church. There he heard an indifferent sermon delivered to a small congregation. The building was small and neat inside and relatively plain on the outside. His impressions of the Episcopal church were somewhat better. "Went to the Episcopal church in the morning with Col. Green. Heard the new minister, Mr. Lee, preach. This is a good preacher." He noted with contentment, "The church was not very full & no singers. They have a good organ & gave us music on that. The church is very neat on the exterior though not so good inside." The natural born critic was never totally pleased with anything he found in the Territorial capital.

His circle of acquaintances soon grew to include both Drs. Randolph, the Eppes family, the Gambles and Bradens, the Alstons, Mrs. Achille Murat, and numerous others of all classes. He also became enthralled with Mrs. Veitch, the sister of Mrs. Eppes. Throughout the diary young Heintzelman notes his growing feelings toward this fair lass, recently widowed. Although he is very interested and constantly decries his bachelorhood, he never makes the big leap and proposes to her. Yet, at nearly every opportunity, he walks her home from church, takes her to picnics at San Luis, rides in the country with her or spends many evenings listening to her singing. He is always on the brink, but never over the edge.

His duties as Quartermaster for the army in Middle Florida gave him many inroads into the community. Often, the results seemed to have surprised him. On his fifth day in town, Mr. Eppes called upon him to see about some accounts left over from his predecessor and invite the Lieutenant to dinner with the family. Heintzelman notes that he was in Columbus nearly six months on similar duty before anyone called upon him for business or social reasons. Invitations to dine were frequent occurrences in town and he seldom lacked for company. His first meeting with Dr. James Randolph came over a dinner and a game of cards. Chess games with the master of the house were always noted in the diaries. The Gambles were good enough to invite him for Christmas dinner, after which he noted that he had gained fifteen pounds since coming to Tallahassee and then weighed a whopping one hundred and forty seven and a half pounds. The dinners were obviously well attended by the young man.

The round of parties thrown in the small, indifferent town is surprising and the young Lieutenant was a constant attendee. On the 19th of December, 1838, Heintzelman noted that he had been invited to Gambles and that there would be a "cotillion party" that evening. He at first doubted whether he would go to this event, however, he soon relented and became one of the guests. "The party commenced about 8 P.M." he notes, "with nine ladies, all told, two of them married. I succeeded in dancing twice during the whole evening. There was not a single lady could be styled handsome. It did not break up until one in the morning." The 25th of January 1839 found the adventurer at a dancing party hosted by the Randolph brothers, James and Arthur. The party was thrown in honor of their cousin, William who had recently gotten married. "The room was crowded & quite a number of ladies considering the bad weather." He also observed that it was very warm in the early evening. "We had an excellent supper," he continued, "& it

122

did not break up until one A. M. I danced but once. There were too many gentlemen & I did not care much about it." When there wasn't a major party to attend, the evenings were often passed playing cards, chess or some other game with other borders at the hotel or in his private room. Sam Heintzelman was always very social and ready to mix with anyone willing to have a good time.

This all sounds like the army was here to party and grow fat, but this was war time and many of the diary entries concern the war news. Much of this news came from the local area and records the numerous killings of men, women and children by the hostile foe. It notes the nearly constant flow of troops into and out of the area attempting to suppress the implacable enemy. Sometimes he makes note of the local militia, such as when he wrote, "Saw the Tallahassee Guards parade about, 18 dressed in gray frock coats," or the time when he observed their drills at San Luis and picnicked with them afterward. As his job was to supply these troops and those of the regular army, he was constantly trying to balance his accounts, order supplies and forage and take care of the needs of the nearby fortifications.

In supplying these posts with forage, food and other supplies, Heintzelman had to travel over the entire area of Middle Florida. His descriptions of the places he visited in the line of duty make for very interesting reading. One of his many visits took him to Camp Wacissa. Unlike the typical picture many have of these frontier installations, Camp Wacissa is simply described as, "a cluster of houses, not arranged for defense & no pickets." Fort Lawson, as yet unnamed at the time, [29 March 1839] is described as a camp six miles from St. Marks with "four fine log buildings" and no pickets. Fort Robert Gamble was noted as being a fortified residence and no picketification. Other posts were more in the traditions of the frontier and had pickets with blockhouses. There are few mentions of artillery pieces at any of these stations. One telling visit to Middle Florida made the lieutenant declare that almost all of the plantations passed were abandoned by their owners because of the Indian threat. Also, like all regular army officers, he held the militia in contempt and invariably described their posts as "rowdy" or "filthy".

The reality of frontier warfare often hit the Tallahassee area and made the people impatient with the army. The constant reporting of deaths among the neighbors made everyone feel uneasy. Entries in the diaries note, "Indians had killed a man & his wife & two children & burned his house near the head of the Waculla & 10 or a dozen miles from town." On December 20, 1839, he recorded that an express rider informed the town that, " a train of wagons from Camp Gamble four miles beyond the Ocilla was attacked by the Indians & one teamster killed & another wounded. This occurred on the road troops travelled but a day or two ago." Reports of murders and mutilations were common fodder for the diarist and the local newspapers. Such treatments went both ways however, and Heintzelman did describe one such scene. He noted, " ... an Indian had been killed by a man named Estler about five miles from town near Dr. Tradewell's. ... Mr. White saw him & thinks it is a Uchee creek Indian ... His whole scalp was taken off & his right hand & otherwise mutilated." The war had its brutalities on both sides of the ledger.

In the midst of the carnage and gore of war, the townspeople of the area combined with their country cousins and participated in a number of activities. The most frequent combining of these people was in the best of southern tradition, the camp meeting. The day of 23 September 1839 found the newly anointed Captain Heintzelman ready to attend such an affair. After crossing numerous streams and indifferent roads, he arrived at a field of about eighteen acres near the village of Miccosukee. "There were near 2000 persons at the encampment." he observed, "It is a beautiful situation; about 18 acres in a pine grove with a good shed and fine tents. Many of them consisting of several rooms & chimneys. Much better than any I saw in Georgia." He continues; "There were a great many young men from Tallahassee & not very well behaved. I felt quite unwell the night I got there & all day & yesterday. The preaching was quite indifferent (the best was Smith, the presiding Elder), ..." Finally, he notes, "Several of the tents were well supplied with liquor & made very little secret of it." He concluded his discussion of this meeting by saying he got well acquainted with the Alston and Parrish families and observing that Mrs. & Miss Wirt were also there.

Mention of the Alstons brings to the fore a famous duel and murder. According to the story given by the diaries kept by Heintzelman, Gen. Leigh Read had written a very vicious letter in the newspapers concerning Col. Alston's actions while on frontier duty under his command. The Colonel did not take this lying down. Not only did Alston make threatening gestures in public towards Read, but he also insulted his kinsman and friend, James Branch. By December of 1839, the situation had deteriorated well beyond the point of no return. Heintzelman noted in his diary for the 17th of December that Read had killed the old Colonel in a duel. By January 6th of 1840, Willis Alston had arrived back in Tallahassee from Texas. No one was under any illusions as to his intent. Heintzelman personally tried to entice Willis to return to Texas through the offices of his friend Dr. Waddel, but the offer was refused. Read was in a panic and feared greatly for his life. He had Dr. James Randolph and Mr. Gilliard brought up on charges of aiding in the threats against his life, but these were proven groundless. Alston did shoot and wound Read while the latter was sitting in Brown's Hotel. Read returned fire, wounding Alston in the arm. Alston also cut him with a Bowie knife across the chest as he was escaping from the scene. The General then went into hiding and his supporters tried to get the troops involved. This was refused by Captain Bullock. Read then left town and stayed in the residence of his brother-in-law. For nearly eight months the drama continued until Willis stepped from the shadows of Michael Ledwith's house on Park Street and put an end to Read's life with both barrels of his shotgun.

What has not been reported before is that Leigh Read tried to hire someone to assassinate Willis Alston after the affair at Brown's. To quote Heintzelman, "Gen. Read has been reported to have been lately at Gov. Branches near Tallahassee. They say he is afraid to show himself after the attempt he made to hire an as-sassin, to poison or make away with Willis Allston. A fine man he to command troops in the U. States Service--to be a Brig. Gen'l. The Vols ought to compell him to resign." Alston gave himself up to the authorities and was put in charge of a guard. Heintzelman declared that this was the result he had long anticipated and he hoped it would now quiet the community. As for Read, "His course has been such he can only blame himself for his violent end." Future Governor John Branch accused many others for their role in this affair, including Governor Call and Major Hayward. Alston later made bail on the charge and was soon back in Texas. In Texas he met a violent end when, after stabbing another man, he was taken by a mob and killed.

Sam Heintzelman, as the Quartermaster in charge, was also responsible for the moving of the army depot from St. Marks to the new town of Port Leon. Port Leon, across the St. Marks River and about three miles further south, was founded in 1839 by Sam Reid and others. By 1840, the town was taking shape and lots had been sold, warehouses and wharves built and shipping beginning to stop on a regular basis. St. Marks had never impressed Heintzelman and was prone to periodic flooding. This hampered military operations and made life very difficult for those trying to supply the army. When he was approached on the subject, Heintzelman almost jumped at the chance to relocate. The principles in the deal were Governor Call, David Walker and Sam Reid. It took some gentle persuading by Captain Heintzelman to get the Quartermaster General to approve the move, but when given the pluses and minuses, the deal was done. Also, the railroad had been extended to the new town and this appeared to make it the best location for all concerned.

Another reason for Heintzelman's moving was the inability to find suitable help to man the stores at St. Marks. The lack of labor or an educated work force hampered the operations of the Quartermaster corps throughout the nation. Wages were higher in such a remote area and the Congress kept a close eye on profiteering in the supplying of the military. Storage fees were also higher because of the lack of suitable buildings and other capital improvements. Shipping costs to the southern ports on the Gulf were very high because of insurance rates and the lack of useable vessels for the shallow waters of the region. Heintzelman's labor problems began almost from his first day on the job. His first hire was an alcoholic and could not be kept on the job. The second person proved to be a minor embezzler and made off with a small amount of funds which the Captain had to make good. The attraction of a new town with its possibilities made Port Leon a likely place to find qualified and trustworthy help.

Heintzelman's gossipy diary contains over five hundred pages of hand written material that burst forth with all the vigor expected of a man of action. He left Tallahassee in late 1840 but returned to settle the militia claims in late 1841-42. After his sojourn in the southern climes, Captain Heintzelman headed northward to Buffalo, New York for a two-year stint. He served with distinction in the Mexican War and then was shipped to the West, serving in southern California and Arizona against the Yuma Indians. While there, he invested in and was the president of the Sonora Exploring and Mining Company. He later was with the Defiance Mining Company in New York. We have already noted his distinguished Civil War career and should note that he was retired from the army in 1869 with the rank of Major General. He served on the Board of the Mutual Guarantee Life Insurance Company and with the Emigration Company of Washington D. C. He passed from this life on May 1, 1880 still living in the city he so gallantly defended during the early days of the Civil War.

# "Airy and Comfortable"
## Or Life in the Forts

The life in the frontier fortifications around the United States has never been portrayed as glamorous or luxurious. This is especially true of those located within the current boundaries of the State of Florida. Here the insects, vermin, alternate cold and hot and the nearly constant dampness caused untold miseries among the United States forces stationed in the territory. Added to these natural difficulties were the continual tensions between men living in close quarters, brought on by the complexity of an unnatural society of men forced to live with other soldiers of very different political persuasions, religions, nationalities and languages. Include the constant scouts and skirmishes with the Indian foe, and the trauma becomes more understandable. Finally, there were the routines of garrison life, the drudgery, the brutality of the officers and the occasional violence, frequently caused by bad whiskey. Under such circumstances, the misery of frontier life became almost too stark and bleak to bear. For many it simply was too much, and suicide became a viable alternative to such a life.

Exactly what were these frontier outposts and how were they outfitted? In simple terms, there was no particular pattern to these posts and much was left to the ingenuity of the individual engineers assigned to construct these wilderness bastions of frontier defense. The most common construction was the fortification, rectangular or square, with two blockhouses at opposite corners, which also became the symbol for such places on the early maps. Some fortifications had a single, tall (three-storied) blockhouse in the center of an

128

enclosed area, for example, Fort Mellon, in the area of modern day Sanford, Florida.[290] Others, like Fort Pierce, were relatively open affairs, with an officers' quarters measuring 124' x 18' covered with boards etc., with three 30' x 15' tarpaulin covered log enclosures for the enlisted men and a hospital 28' x 16'.[291] The outside of such open affairs were guarded by rough-hewn pickets loosely spaced and a protective blockhouse for the artillery piece(s) to fire from, and lower rooms for storage. Still other sites, such as Fort Drane, simply took existing buildings, incorporated them into the picketification and used the buildings for the main housing of troops and officers.[292] Historian Albert Manucy has described how such forts were constructed:

> To build such a fort, you simply obtain a few hundred trees, cut them in 18-foot lengths, and split them up the middle. Then you set them into the ground side by side like a fence, fasten them together with timbers, cut loopholes eight feet from the ground and build firing steps under the loopholes for the riflemen. Outside you dig a ditch that served as a kind of moat. You hung a strong gate, and your fort was practically finished.[293]

Michael G. Schene, in his discussion of the construction of Fort Foster, on the Hillsborough River, notes that troops had to be sent out to discover the trees suitable for the construction, preferably straight, and then to cut them, drag them back to camp, split and sharpen the logs into a point and then place them into the ground so that ten to fourteen feet were left above ground. They were fastened together with scrap lumber nailed to the flat side of the split logs (which faced inward) at the appropriate points and loopholes cut for the firing line, usually six to eight feet apart.[294] Obviously, a great number of trees were required to create these frontier fortifications, not to mention the vast energy expended by the troops in cutting and splitting them, and erecting the walls and blockhouses.

The army, however, was never satisfied that all costs were being watched carefully and instructed the officers to keep costs down whenever possible. "As quarters have been erected at nearly all the stations," one letter noted, "it is scarcely requisite to prescribe the kind of buildings to be put up. They should be made airy and comfortable of logs of pine [?] covered with clapboards and flored with puncheons, a few nails &c. being all that the Qr Mrs. Dept need furnish for their construction."[295]  Another letter chastised an officer at Palatka for the large amount of people employed in building that post. Only those "indespensable" to the operation of the fort should be used in the construction, e.g. certain mechanics and laborers. Under no circumstances were costly buildings to be erected, especially on private property.  "Huts of rough and cheap construction for supplies should alone be erected," it stated that most forts should be temporary, and built by the troops themselves.[296]  It almost appears as if the army tried to run the war in Florida cheaply, but the army being the army, it could not resist the temptation of tearing one side of a post down with its troops while building the other side of the same post with hired labor, just to fulfill a contract. Cut, cut, cut, may have been the tone of the orders, but the business as usual attitude prevailed in the field.

Probably the largest problem in maintaining a fortification in the wilderness of northern Florida was the acquisition of supplies. This logistical problem was fraught with difficulties because of the lack of roads, cleared rivers, canals or other means of getting the supplies to the posts. Even the most basic of transportation needs, wagons and boats, were difficult, and sometimes impossible to obtain in the territory. On January 26, 1836, the acting Quartermaster General, Major Thomas Hunt, wrote to his operatives in Charleston and Savannah, "You will also purchase and ship about ten wagons, good and strong, if they can be procured without detention, suitable for Florida roads, with harness for six horses each. If you can get the wagons and harness conveniently, you are authorized to purchase fifteen."[297]  By April, this same officer was writing in extreme frustration to Lieutenant Charles Dimmock, the Assistant Quarter Master at Savannah over the lack of boats:

I have received your letter of the 3rd instant and regret extremely that the boats called for were not furnished. Why could they not have been obtained--were there no workmen-- no materials in Savannah? If the materials were growing in the woods, and you could find no other workmen than raw

130

soldiers or plantation negores, the boats should have been built and furnished. It is perhaps too late to render them available; but they must be furnished cost what they may. You will therefore cause them to be built, if they cannot be purchased, and send them on immediately. During the last war, I took the materials from the woods where they were growing, and in less than four days had a sixteen oared boat completed and launched, which afterwards crossed Lake Erie. I therefore know that it was possible to have furnished the boats called for; and that which can be accomplished by human means should not be left undone by a Department, on which, more than any other depends the efficient operation of the Army.[298]

Wagons and boats depend on roads and waterways to get the supplies through and this, too, presented major problems. During Florida's dry seasons, even such large rivers as the Apalachicola and Chattahoochee dry to such low levels as to not allow normal passage of steamers or other large vessels. Of course, Indians themselves offer a menace to communication. "Information has reached here," wrote Major Hunt, "that the Creek Indians are in open hostility and are in such force on the Chattahoochie as to interrupt the communication up that river, consequently large supplies of Subsistence Ordinance and other stores will, from necessity, have to be sent by way of Augusta, Georgia, to Fort Mitchell and its neighborhood. You will therefore furnish transportation for all Subsistence, Ordinance, and other stores."[299] Simply to supply the existing posts, therefore, was not an easy proposition and points to the importance of logistical planning in any military operation.

Because of the lack of provisions in the territory, many of the supplies needed to fight the war had to be purchased from outside the area. A letter of December 10, 1841, written by Quartermaster General Thomas Jesup, will serve as an example of this point:

I herewith transmit a statement showing the quantity of Forage shipped to several depots in Florida since the 26th ultimo. Captain Crossman reports that his is now loading a vessel with Hay at Boston destined for Tampa which will

131

carry 700 Bales, and one for Savannah which will carry 800. Captain Tompkins is loading a vessel at Philadelphia with Forage which will carry from six to seven hundred bales of hay and from 6 to 8 thousand bushels of grain. Captain Dusenbery has taken up a vessel for the same depot which will carry about 7000 bushels of grain and will sail in a few days; and Captain Hetzel is now loading a vessel at Alexandria for Saint Marks which will carry about 8000 Bushels of grain and is expected to sail on the 12th instant.[300]

Cargoes from nearly every major port in North America were sent to Florida to fight the Seminole War, owing to the lack of provisions in the territory and their relatively high prices. One example of the latter should suffice: "Hay advertised at Port Leon will cost not less than $1.50 per hundred, corn 88 cents and oats 58 cents per bushel."[301] Because of the relatively undeveloped nature of Territorial Florida, higher prices, because of the lack of sufficient supply, would be the norm and transportation costs were correspondingly high for the very same reasons. It was economically cheaper to ship the forage and other supplies into Florida than attempt to purchase them within the territory, where they did not exist in numbers great enough to sustain a war effort.

When the army did attempt to procure supplies from the territory, it was constantly dogged by poor quality and unscrupulous suppliers who did not hesitate to defraud the government. One of the more interesting series of letters in the Quartermaster General's records involved a trio of men whom General Jesup accused of fraudulently selling and shipping "bad bacon" to posts in and around Tallahassee. John Ledgerwood, J. W. Powers and M. Scott allegedly sold bad bacon to the army and signed each other's vouchers for the costs of shipment in their wagons and teams. According to Jesup's letter of December 16, 1840, Powers worked in the Quartermaster General's Tallahassee office, but did not have the power to sign receipts, while Ledgerwood declared that his name had been forged on false vouchers and used without his consent. However, he did admit to signing accounts for the other two so they could receive their pay. Jesup, correctly, refused to pay these accounts because the entire transaction was fraudulent.[302] Jesup, in a follow-up letter of

December 29, 1840, noted that he had contacted District Attorney C. S. Sibley to press for criminal charges, but was advised that because of the "peculiar circumstances" of the country, prosecution was ill-advised.[303] Jesup allowed the charges to be dropped.

Another of the constant complaints heard concerning the Florida operation was the use of public monies for private gain. It makes for remarkable reading to see the large number of claims for compensation that appear in the official records from the citizens of Florida. Most of the claims are for lost plantation property, including slaves, dead or requisitioned horses and mules, compensation for work performed or payment for some depredation by either Indians or soldiers. James Riz and George Colee, for example, wanted the government to pay them for wood stolen from their property for the construction of some military installation. However, it was known that Doctor Tripler and others in the vicinity, "had wood cut in that neighborhood for sale to Steam Boats, it is apprehended that the wood here charged for was cut for that purpose."[304] More spectacular is the report filed on October 8, 1841, about the malfeasance of certain officials at Palatka:

A person by the name of Eaton, who served under the orders of Captain Waite as a Wagon Master, called at the office to day and informed me that a person by the name of Bell, who has charge of public property at Palatka, frequently applies public labor to private objects. He says that negroes hired at high wages are employed in making rails, and public trams employed in hauling them, to fence a field belonging to Bell, and that a person employed at forty dollars a month, (one Hunt, sometimes called Knickerbocker) oversees them. Eaton says that an Englishman by the name of John Dix, Clerk to Paymaster Brown, is allowed by the Quarter Master's Department a house for his mistress.

He mentioned one instance of Bell having taken a man from the train, a teamster, who was a tailor by trade, to make clothes for him, his family, or friends. He charged Bell with numerous speculations and informed me that Mr. Cole, the Sutler, could give information as to his improper conduct.

I will thank you to cause the most rigid investigation to be made, and if there has been very improper conduct on the part of Bell, to discharge him immediately. And no abuse like that stated in the case of Dix must be tolerated for a moment.[305]

That such behavior as reported of Mr. Dix was not unknown in Florida's frontier posts is reinforced by the knowledge that General Jesup once banned the use of hospital wagons because of the transportation into forts of very dainty soldiers (ladies of the evening) and their leaving the said forts with equally dainty officers.[306] All in all, Florida's war was notorious in northern circles as one which went to enrich the local population at the expense of the nation. However, though a few instances do appear on the record, the Seminole War is little different from any other war fought by U. S. troops.

The use of Black slaves during the conflict was also noted in the official records and is the subject of many claims. Not only were these people subject to hard labor, but often they were forced or asked to perform the dangerous duty of guide or spy for the troops in the field. The cases of Titus and Primus are two well known such individuals who gave much needed guidance to U. S. troops who would otherwise be lost in the Florida wilderness. Road duty was also an important function of Black slave labor during the war, as Florida was ill-equipped to facilitate heavy military or commercial traffic. One of the more notable facets of the use of slave labor was reported in the letter of March 25, 1841, concerning the direct payments to slaves for extra labor performed. In this case, S. J. Sequi, of St. Augustine's well-known Sequi family, hired out some of his slave labor to work on projects in the Palatka area and signed for all of the wages earned, but turned over $10 to the slave for his extra time. Sequi informed Colonel F. L. Dancy, Florida Militia, of this transaction who, in turned, informed the Quartermaster General's Office at Palatka. General Jesup, when informed of this transaction, questioned the direct payments to slaves and pointed to the uproar which occurred at Old Point Comfort under similar circumstances. Jesup, though acknowledging the need for slave labor at the southern posts, ordered the practice stopped on grounds

134

that Congress would be upset and would question any payments made to slaves. Payments could only be made to owners and no sub-payments to slaves were to be allowed.[307] Slaves as road crew, hired skilled labor, guides or servants were important to the war effort and Jesup was quite correct in stating that slave labor was a necessity at most southern posts.

Of course, if a slave or any other person took sick the medical practice of the day would be of little assistance, except to hurry them to the next life. And even though military posts were required by law to maintain gardens for the growing of fresh vegetables, little of the benefits would seem to have helped those incapacitated by illness or wounds. Amputation was a way of life in the medical corps and was the most common answer to any infected area or wounded limb. Dr. Samuel Forry, recalling to a colleague an operation he performed at Micanopy, noted that the patient had accidentally discharged his gun and blew off two digits, smashed his thigh and had the ball finally lodge in his left wrist. He amputated the leg and the two digits and watched the patient die within three hours, probably from shock.[308] Any reader of *Reminiscences of the Second Seminole War* by John Bemrose, ed. by John Mahan, gets an immediate sense of the lack of scientific knowledge held by even the best of doctors on the Florida frontier. Bemrose, himself, when sick with "country fever" asked Dr. Leavensworth to bleed him as a form of curing this dreaded disease. So common became the death of a soldier or other unfortunate that this fine man became, in his own words, callous to nature of humankind and careless in his duties.[309] Even when progressive ideas, such as the ordering of ice for the benefit of the hospitalized, were proposed, the bureaucratic mind precluded positive action:

> I have received your letter of the 17th ulitmo, covering one from Assistant Surgeon Hammond, recommending the erection of an ice house at Palatka and the filling it with ice for the use of the sick at the different posts on the St. Johns river. There is no appropriation within the control of the Quarter Master's Department from which payment for ice could be made. By a liberal construction of the regulations, an ice house might be built as an appendage to the Hospital;

but the Medical Department alone can supply the ice, if indeed any Department can legally do so. So much of your letter as refers to the supply of ice has been referred to the Surgeon General.[310]

With a Surgeon General as unprogressive as Thomas Lawson, little came of this request and the positive benefits that might have aided the sick and dying in Florida. The main fears of the doctors in Florida were the fevers, miasma, swamp gases and infections, which they knew were beyond their powers to cure. The task of being a doctor in the United States Army under the command of Surgeon General Thomas Lawson, with little formal preparation and only a kind heart to guide them could only lead to frustration and, as Bemrose noted, a callousness toward the sick and dying that could cost the remaining humanity most had within themselves.

A few years ago, a Florida State University graduate student, Felix P. McGaughy, Jr. edited the diary of one Bartholomew Lynch, a common soldier during the Second Seminole War. What this fascinating diary portrays is the uncommonly brutal nature of the officer class, with one exception all West Pointers, in their command of the raw recruits and common soldiers of the United States Army. Lynch describes brutal, almost barbaric, beatings, the constant drunkenness of the officers, and the savage orders to inflict uncalled for punishments for the least offense. A good example comes from his own experience: "Captain Fowler struck me with a rifle and cut me without reason. I went to Gen. Taylor with my blood flowing. He laughed at me. It is no use to sue a devil if the Court be held in hell."[311] Some have wondered whether Lynch was exaggerating or embellishing on his stories. I believe that he was not and offer the case of Captain M. L. Howe, 2nd Dragoons, whose commanding general regretted learning that he, "should have so severely punished one of his men as to have caused his death," and thought that it should be handled only by the civil authorities.[312] The U. S. District Court handled the case in its fall term of 1840 and the witnesses were not called together until October of that year.[313] The charges against Captain Howe bring to light the severity of the crime.

Specification 1. In this that he the said Captain M. L. Howe 2 Dragoons did by beating, kicking, dragging on the ground a considerable distance, and having carried on a barrow or litter his head hanging down Pvt. James Jones of G Company 2nd Dragoons cause <u>congestion</u> of the <u>Brain</u> in him the said Jones thereby tending to the <u>death</u> of the said Pvt. James Jones this on a march from St. Augustine to Picolata, E.F. on or about the sixth day of December 1839. Specification 2. In this that he the said Captain M. L. Howe 2nd Dragoons did beat with a large stick, kick, have dragged on the ground, had placed in the stocks, and while in the Stocks, have water thrown down on the said Pvt James Jones G Company 2 Dragoons all of which treatment caused the body of the deceased Pvt James Jones immediately after death to have the appearance of <u>putrid</u> and spoiled flesh ...Specification 3. In this that the said Cap M. L. Howe 2 Drag's did when Pvt James Jones "G" Company 2nd Drag's was nearly exhausted and unable to stand have him the said Pvt James Jones put in the stocks and then have water thrown on him and that he the said Cap M. L. Howe did say in reply to a request made by the said Pvt James Jones to be killed and so get rid of his Captain Howes cruelty "damn you I have a grave ready to bury you in" or words to that effect, this on the march from St. Augustine to Picolata E Florida on or about the sixth day of December 1839.

Howe was additionally charged in the General Court Martial with conduct unbecoming of an officer in slandering the reputation of Captain T. Dade, cousin of the slain Major Francis L. Dade.[314] The obvious brutality exhibited by these charges indicates the level of primitive violence sometimes practiced by the officer class toward the enlisted men of the U. S. Army and gives more credence to the charges found throughout the Lynch diary.

The officer class could be equally petty and vindictive against members of their own group. In one of the more uniquely insipid incidents of the war, Major T. Fauntleroy attempted to bring charges against Colonel Thomas Hunt and Captain R. E. Clary, the former for not yielding his quarters to the Major who, at the post, was the

Colonel's temporary superior, and the latter for disobeying his direct orders to oust the Colonel, primarily because he obeyed the orders of the Colonel. The correspondence in this relatively silly melodrama shows the worst side of the officer class. The end result being that a Colonel does outrank a Major and the Captain was correct in following his superior's direction. Major Fauntleroy had to wait until the Colonel transferred out of the area to obtain the prized quarters.[315]

Some of the problems which appeared in the frontier fortresses came as the result of alcohol abuse. Of course, to call some of these liquid libations whiskey is to glorify the reality with a dignity unbecoming a good liquor. However, much of the correspondence found in the Letters Received by the Office of the Adjutant General does center on the ready availability of whiskey and other spirituous liquors. At Micanopy, one man and his family were expelled from the vicinity, without any sympathy from the commanding officer, for selling whiskey to the soldiers of that post.[316] General Walker Armistead complained to Secretary of War Joel Poinsett that, "Black Creek without possessing one of the advantages of a Town labors under its worst disadvantage, abounding in Grog Shops, and a riotous population, its civil jurisdiction is in constant conflict with the military authority & subversive of it, ..."[317] Armistead, again, on June 22, 1840, put forth the proposition that, "... at several of our most important posts, a set of persons have taken up their residence, who are destitute of character, and who are in the habit of selling whiskey and other liquors to the troops, ..." He also accused these same disreputable characters with selling whiskey and ammunition to the Indians.[318] However, of this last charge, selling liquor to the Indians, the army itself was not totally innocent. On November 10, 1840, we read, "It is the direction of the Commanding General that three Barrels of whiskey be sent by the first opportunity to the Commissary at this post [Fort King] for issue to the Indians."[319] The dispersement of liquor to the Indians, obviously, served as an inducement for treaty making, which justified its distribution to the enemy.

More importantly for the future development of the State of Florida, were the normal duties of soldiers found in the frontier posts. Road building was one of the most important contributions made by

138

the United States Army to the development of the territory. The road from Fort Frank Brooke [not to be confused with Fort Brooke at Tampa] to the falls of the Steinhatchee River was completed by the garrison at this post in early 1841.[320] Indeed, most of the roads connecting the outposts of defense were maintained or constructed by the garrisons of the nearest fortifications. This was routine duty, but, for the development of the future State of Florida, it was anything but routine. At the beginning of the war, few roads existed to aid in settlement; by the end of seven long years of warfare, the territory was partially blessed with a network of usable roads that could not have been constructed without the aid of the federal government and an influx of outside labor. For citizens of northern Florida, it should not be forgotten that the famed "Bellamy Road" was constructed by Captain D. Burch, under contract from Colonel William Bellamy, after the good Captain had constructed most of the road connecting Pensacola to Tallahassee.

The requirement, by a law of 1819, that each garrison should supply as much of its own forage, vegetables, fruits, etc. as possible, particularly in the form of a fort garden, had an external benefit which many have not recognized. The "experiments" with various agricultural crops by the frontier posts often gave clues to the incoming settlers as to what type and variety of crops could be grown in a given location. For families coming into a new territory with a unique climate, like that of Florida's, this type of information could mean the difference between life and death. The frontier gardens of these isolated outposts proved to be of immense value to the new immigrants, especially during the period of the Armed Occupation Act of 1842.

Finally, no discussion of the life of soldiers in the frontier forts would be complete without acknowledging why they were established in the first place, to provide protection. The almost daily routine of cooking, gardening, latrine duty, and caring for the livestock pales in importance to this function. Daily scouts went forth from these bastions in the wilderness to face an unseen and frequently uncatchable foe. The constant marauding by the Indians, unpredictable and fast, left the soldiers, unfamiliar with the territory and disdainful of local militia assistance, constantly in fear of what lurked behind the next bush. Throughout the territory, from northern

Florida to Cape Sable, the Indians were on the move. The daily reports of cattle, hogs or horses lost to Indian depredations and theft almost befuddled the regular forces and many militia units with their cunning, daring and audacity. Few would ever forget the numerous feints against the fortifications which only served to tie down the garrison while its cattle and horses were stolen. The sheer frustration of these brilliant tactics sometimes led to brutal reprisals on the part of the soldiers. However, the fact remains that the daily duty of scouting, scouring the country for Indian signs and the frequent burning of Indian villages, pumpkin fields, etc. was the main duty of the garrisons stationed in Florida. Next to this duty, all other problems or benefits pale.

I end this brief discussion of life in the frontier forts with a note on what I have left out. I did not mention the role of women in these fortifications, although many died from disease, Indian attack or other causes. I have not deeply explored the role played by Black slaves or Free Negroes in these isolated outposts. Nor have I discussed the Indian perspective, nor the grand strategy of the various commanders, like Zachary Taylor, Winfield Scott, Walker Armistead or William Worth nor have I taken note of garrison life's impact on the careers of the nearly one hundred Civil War generals who served at some stage of the conflict in Florida. All of these topics, and many more, do need further exploration and examination. (Yet, I have not intentionally left these topics out of the discussion.)

Roll of Suffering Inhabitants of Florida drawing rations at Jacksonville E. F. on the 1 day of June 1842

| # | Names | Whites | | Blacks | | Remarks |
|---|-------|------|------|------|------|---------|
| | | Over 14 Years | Under 14 Years | Over 14 Years | Under 14 Years | |
| 1 | Sarah Davis | " | " | 1 | " | Free — Cripple |
| 2 | Ellen Woodlin | 1 | 2 | " | " | Widow + 2 children |
| 3 | Susanna Saunders | 1 | 6 | " | " | Widow — Husband died in service |
| 4 | James McCormick | " | 3 | " | " | Permanently lame; draws for children |
| 5 | Henry Sweeny | 1 | 3 | " | " | Widow + 3 children, no means of support |
| 6 | Sarah Davis | 1 | " | " | " | Widow — no means of support |
| 7 | Lucy Richards | " | " | 2 | " | Free — Widow draws for 2 children |
| 8 | Hester Lowther | 1 | 3 | " | " | Widow + 3 children — no means of support |
| 9 | Ephraim Tyner | 1 | 4 | " | " | Orphans — No means of support |
| 10 | Sarah Bandy | " | 4 | " | " | Widow — draws for 4 children |
| 11 | John Beasley | 2 | 3 | " | " | Widow + 4 children — Husband killed by |
| 12 | Elizabeth McKee | " | 2 | " | " | Widow — Husband killed in service |
| 13 | Nancy Simpson | 1 | 1 | " | " | Widow — draws for 2 children |
| 14 | Mary Hogan | 2 | " | " | " | Widow — no means of support |
| 15 | Jenny Dees | 2 | 1 | " | " | Old + infirm couple, + grandchild |
| 16 | Vrecy Oslen | 1 | 6 | " | " | Widow + 6 children — Husband killed by Indians |
| 17 | Jane Murray | " | 1 | " | " | Orphan — no means of support |
| 18 | Catharine Flynn | " | 4 | " | " | Orphans; no means of support |
| 19 | Elizabeth Roberts | " | 1 | | | |
| | Carried Forward | 14 | | | | |

# Jacksonville
## 1835-1842

The Territory of Florida was a largely unexplored geographical feature to the United States Army in 1835. Very little of the peninsula had been thoroughly explored or mapped. South of modern Ocala was the reservation that had been agreed to in 1823 at the Treaty of Moultrie Creek. It too had seen little examination and only the external boundary had been delineated. General Duncan L. Clinch commanded the few regular army troops then in Florida and these numbered less than five hundred and fifty effectives. The estimated Seminole population, including the various bands of Miccosukees, Tallahassees, Euchees, Creeks, etc. was given at nearly five thousand. Of this number an estimated fifteen hundred were classed as warriors. Should the Seminoles and their allies determine upon resistance, the reality of immediate removal would be a false hope.

The army was aware that Florida contained numerous lakes, swamps, rivers and bayous. They did not know the depths, velocity or widths of most of these water bodies. The locations of fords, bridges or other means of crossing these obstacles was unknown. The climate of Florida was new to the army and it was not completely aware of the definite wet and dry seasons of subtropical southern Florida. The oppressive heat of the summers was something experienced by only a few of the regulars. The sapping effect on health, endurance and morale was as strange as the climate that caused these problems. The flora and fauna were also new to the troops, many of whom were newly immigrated to this country

142

from Ireland, Germany, the Netherlands and England. The fevers caused by germ-carrying mosquitoes and other insects, added to poor sanitary conditions, would take a vicious toll on these new Americans. By the end of the war over fifteen hundred men would die chasing the elusive Seminoles and their allies.[321]

By the time the Second Seminole War was declared over, the government had spent over twenty million dollars on the army alone, had used approximately ten thousand regular troops and about thirty thousand militia or other citizen soldiers. It became, in the words of historians Allan R. Millett and Peter Maslowski, "the Army's longest, most costly Indian conflict."[322] Few conflicts have ever engendered so much controversy as the Seminole War. The fact that it represents one of the largest, if not the largest, slave revolt in American history made white southerners very concerned about its outcome. The use of dogs to hunt other human beings, savages though they may have been called in the press of the day, was disgusting to those who were no longer in danger and far from the frontier. Finally, the capture of many prominent leaders of the Seminoles under the alleged protection of the white flag of truce was a violation of American honor that many could not tolerate. The northern abolitionists who were just beginning their long crusade to end slavery had a political field day with this embarrassing conflict. The cost in lives lost on the frontier has never been totaled.

The citizens of the small town of Jacksonville were settled down in the summer mode of living with its daily hot, sunny mornings and frequent afternoon showers. The local newspaper, the *Courier*, was reminding everyone to carry with them an umbrella to ward off the sun and the rain. The paper for 20 August of 1835 noted that the Seminoles were getting ready to meet their obligations of the Treaty of Payne's Landing and emigrate to the west by November. By the time the 3 September edition reached the streets, the tone had changed. The people were being informed of the death of a mail carrier riding between Fort King (Ocala) and Fort Brooke (Tampa), while the *Courier* chided its St. Augustine rival that this did not look like anyone was removing "peaceably and quietly" from Florida. The end of the month saw the offices of the newspaper flooded and out of commission for two weeks with the wicked weather to blame for the halting press. On 22 October the *Courier* announced the pending sale of Indian cattle as per stipulations in the treaty and the advertisement was signed by the Indian Agent Wiley Thompson.

General Joseph Hernandez, the commanding officer of the Florida militia in East Florida, was not as optimistic as the editors. On 26 October the General was writing to both Governor John Eaton and Secretary of War Lewis Cass that the Seminoles were beginning to resist emigration. He declared, "It is generally believed that they will not move without being made to do so by actual force." Hernandez proceeded to inform these gentlemen that nearly everyone in St. Augustine and Jacksonville was convinced of the impending danger of an Indian uprising and asked for from two to three hundred muskets with "corresponding accoutrements" for the protection of these and other nearby communities. He planned to have one hundred and fifty to two hundred mounted volunteers in the field and stationed from Spring Garden northward to Palatka and thence westerly toward the Suwannee River. This could cordon off the major eastern settlements from possible attack.[323] The General had reason to be less optimistic than the local press.

The *Courier* soon reported on the rising toll of death and destruction in Alachua County. By its 3 December 1835 edition the newspaper boldly stated, "By the news from Alachua, it appears that the Seminole Indians have openly shown their opposition to the measures of the Government for their removal, by commencing hostilities upon the inhabitants residing near them. Their first act was the murder of Charles O'Mathla, a chief of the Mickasuky tribe, who was in favor of a removal." The editor then quoted Colonel John McIntosh, who resided near Orange Lake (Micanopy), as saying that the frontier near him was defenseless and open to all sorts of agitation. On a happier note, McIntosh expressed confidence in General Clinch, his brother-in-law, to handle the situation and maintain peace along the frontier.

One week later the paper declared "Indian War" as its headline and proceeded to note the preparations of the inhabitants of Jacksonville for the coming campaign. Colonel John Warren, who commanded the militia from Duval and Nassau Counties, immedi-

144

ately left Jacksonville with a regiment of men for the Alachua frontier. The editor also observed the lack of muskets and rifles among the militia, stating that many left with their fowling pieces across their saddles.[324] Hernandez considered Warren's Fourth Regiment of the Florida Militia to be, "The principal and most effective portion of my Brigade ..."[325] By the 17 December edition "Indian Hostilities" was the banner headline and many details were given of Indian shootings and burnings. The loggers of the lumber firm of Palmer & Farris had its employees move downstream to Picolata and noted that all of the plantations and other works south of there had been abandoned. Near the plantation of Zephaniah Kingsley some of these loggers were fired upon by Indians. Farther afield, near Wacahoota and the plantation of Captain Gabriel Priest, the Indians began firing upon local groups and Captain Priest was forced to move his family to the fortification then being built at Hogtown (Fort Clark, southwest of modern Gainesville). The war was on even before the terrible events of 28 December had been played out.

Colonel Warren did not fair well on his first venture into the hostile land. As reported in the 24 December edition of the *Courier* his baggage train was ambushed on its way to Wacahoota and a number of troops killed and wounded. One of the mortally wounded was a Mr. Weeks of the Mandarin settlement. The baggage train contained all of the paper work, medical supplies and ammunition for the Florida troops and all was lost to the Seminoles. The shooting did attract the other column who hurried back to help their comrades but were too late to prevent the catastrophe. The arrival of General Richard Keith Call and the Middle Florida militia helped to ease the situation temporarily. These were the militia that would join General Clinch and the regulars in their ill-fated march to the Withlacoochee, which resulted in the defeat of this force by the combined forces of Seminoles, Miccosukees and blacks. Warren's men were in the thick of the fighting and were not the majority of militia, who were accused of not being willing to cross the river during the Battle of the Withlacoochee.

One of the more interesting orders given during this tense period of the first full month of the war was that ordering a captain and twenty five men to establish a post in Jacksonville. Posts were

also to be established at Mandarin and Whitesville with a lieutenant and twelve soldiers as temporary garrison.  Colonel W. J. Mills
was put in charge of making these places safe and was additionally
ordered to mount a regular guard in each place.  Additionally, the
captain commanding was to, "take into custody all slaves and free
persons of color, except they are in the actual service and presence
of their owners, overseers or employers…"  Weekly reports were
to be filed with Major Issiah D. Hart who would remain in Jacksonville and oversee the entire command.[326]  From this order alone
one can begin to measure the actual fear of the slave revolt felt by
most whites in these settlements.  It is also from this order that the
origins of the blockhouse at the northeast corner of Ocean and
Monroe Streets came.  As Jacksonville historian T. Frederick
Davis described it: "It was a structure of logs – a large square room
raised high above the ground on a pedestal-like base.  It was entered through a door in the floor, by means of a ladder.  In the
event of an Indian attack, the ladder could be drawn up and the
opening closed."[327]

As if the defeat at the Battle of the Withlacoochee were not
enough, the entire east coast of Florida was exposed after the defeat of the Florida militia at the Battle of Dunlawton, fought on 11
January 1836.  Here Major Benjamin A. Putnam suffered relatively
few casualties but was forced to retreat by an overwhelming force
of Indians and blacks.  Putnam's force was the last sizable group
south of St. Augustine and the removal of these troops left the destruction of the great plantations of East Florida to the whim of the
enemy.  East Florida would soon be in ruins and the economy
shattered.  It was a devastating loss.[328]

While all of the above was reported and the build-ups to the
Battle of the Withlacoochee and the Battle of Dunlawton were being played out, the army was dealt a huge blow to its prestige and
its effective force in Florida.  Clinch had called upon all of the
regular forces in Florida and the southeast to prepare for a forced
removal.  He ordered the command of Brevet Major Francis L.
Dade, an old Florida hand, to report to Tampa from its base in Key
West and then proceed to Fort King as a show of force to the recal-
citrant Seminoles.  While on its way to Fort King, the detachment
under of Major Dade was annihilated by the Seminoles and blacks

under the command of Micanopy, Alligator, Jumper, Abraham and others. At the same time, Agent Thompson and Lieutenant Constantine Smith were gunned down by Osceola and his band within six hundred yards of Fort King. The sutler and his associates were also killed at this time, adding insult to injury. The result of these actions was the loss of nearly one fifth of the entire regular force in Florida. It meant that the garrison at Fort King was reduced to a simple occupation of that post, with too few men to even make a regular scout or patrol. Most of Clinch's force was at his old homestead at Lang Syne Plantation, now called Fort Drane. Fort Brooke at Tampa was daily waiting to be besieged by the surrounding Seminoles and their allies, and the commander, Major Belton, could only pray that the marines would land, which they did. There was a real and strongly felt fear in the inhabitants of Jacksonville and St. Augustine, now left to their own devices.[329]

As troops from other states arrived to assist the regular army in attempting to subdue the Seminoles, Jacksonville became the headquarters for the Fourth Regiment of Florida Militia, and this unit was actively engaged in scouting the immediate area for signs of the enemy. On 19 January 1836 Colonel Warren reported to Hernandez that Lieutenant Colonel Mills was out scouring the vicinity between the St. Johns River and Julington Creek and was to take up a temporary post at the latter position. Major Hart had been sent to Whitesville, on Black Creek, to scout in that area and try and persuade the inhabitants to stay at their homes. This unit also established posts at Jacksonville, St. Johns Bluff and on the St. Mary's River. Daily guards were given to the mail carriers between Pablo Creek and North River and the carrier between Durbin Creek and Twelve Mile Swamp. The Colonel also reported that, "… most of the houses are even abandoned between Julington and the Cowford, and nearly all have abandoned Black Creek. I am therefore unable at this time to detach the force you call for, 50 mounted men to go south, as it is impossible to raise sufficient horses."[330] The next day Colonel Warren had to inform General Hernandez that half of the people of Nassau County had moved over the St. Mary's River into southern Georgia. Such was the panic in this section of the Florida Territory.[331]

Even the far away Charleston *Courier* reported on the panic in East Florida. In its 18 January 1836 edition, the newspaper reported that Captain Willey was sent up river from Jacksonville to procure the schooner *Motion* on behalf of it owner, who feared it would be destroyed by the Indians. Upon arriving at Mandarin, where it was docked, Willey found the *Motion* filled with men, women and children, white and black, looking for safety from attack. These wretched people pleaded with Captain Willey to leave her there until they could build a blockhouse for their own protection. Willey reported the number of people on board the vessel to be about one hundred and thirty. Further on in the newspaper of that day, a letter was published from someone at Fort George (Z. Kingsley) who reported the inhabitants rushing toward the mouth of the St. Johns River and to Amelia Island to escape the ravages of the savages. All had abandoned their property to fate and thought only of saving their lives. The 30 January edition of this paper also reported the cheering news that the Savannah Phoenix Rifles (120 strong) were leaving that day to take up posts at Jacksonville, Picolata and other posts further up the river. Volunteers and regulars were now pouring into Florida, and just in the nick of time.

Skirmishes with the Seminoles and their allies were a frequent occurrence around Jacksonville, and most of the outlying region was destitute and abandoned. Many of those who fled the onslaught came to Jacksonville for protection and security. Delegate Joseph White fought hard in Congress to achieve some form of funding or aid for the victims of the war. Writing to the Secretary of War concerning the fate of these unfortunates, White noted, "The indifference which has been manifested in Congress to the appeal which has been made on behalf of the distressed inhabitants of East Florida, who have suffered by Indian depredations, in the desolating war now going on, requires that I, as their representative, should lose no opportunity of obtaining for them a just indemnification for the injuries which they have sustained, from causes over which they had no control, and of the existence of which they were entirely ignorant. The pretext for receiving with coolness and indifference an application founded on justice & humanity, is, that the Government is not responsible for acts done in

148

open war. I deny that this insurrection of ruthless barbarians is to be put upon a footing with nations whose conflicts are preceded by declarations of hostility, to whom the international code can be made to apply."[332]   White did not get the indemnity he sought for the inhabitants, however he did achieve a form of aid that allowed "suffering inhabitants" to receive rations from the military posts. These rations saved the lives of countless members of the community and gave hope that when the war ended they could possibly return to their homes.

While all of the confusion of the beginnings of the war was taking place, the clashing of monumental personalities could be heard above the din of battle.   Clinch was the nominal commander in Florida and after the Battle of the Withlacoochee he was almost put in disgrace by President Andrew Jackson, who could see no reason why the Indians he had so handily whipped in 1818 could not be removed.   The fact that he had three times as many men in addition to Indian allies than Clinch was totally lost on the President, as was the fact that the Indians were not fools and retreated in the face of overwhelming force.   Clinch did not have any such force at his side and the Indians were concentrated in a highly defensible position with the army stuck on the other side of the river with no knowledge of any fording place that was safe.

Jackson turned to General Winfield Scott to handle the situation, not knowing that General Edmund P. Gaines was already on the move from New Orleans with troops to relieve Clinch.   Florida, it turns out, was divided as to command responsibilities with East Florida falling under Scott and West Florida under Gaines.   With little direction from the General of the Army, Alexander Macomb, this confusion led to Gaines heading to Florida with an undersupplied force to relieve Clinch while Scott was leisurely heading to Florida recruiting State volunteers from the neighboring States to fight the same enemy.   As these two were intense rivals, with over twenty years of nearly open personal warfare between them, the Florida stage was being set for a colossal showdown that hardly included the Seminoles or their allies.

The results were a disaster that only increased the personal hatred between the generals, showed the army up as a quarreling group of stogy old men haggling over the glory supposed to have been won in 1812 and did nothing to lessen the danger of the Florida frontier. Gaines was ignominiously trapped near the same crossing spot as Clinch and had to be rescued by that officer. Scott planned a beautiful three pronged attack on the Cove of the Withlacoochee only to find that this was not Europe and he was not Napoleon and the Seminoles were not going to stand pat and fight line against line. Clinch, nursing the wounds of the president's slights, resigned his commission. This left Governor Richard K. Call, a former aide to Jackson who had never led a large force against any enemy, to lead the defense of the Florida frontier.

Call's campaign was fairly well thought out and very poorly executed. Most of the blame, if such it is, can be laid on the door of the Territory and the cunningness and skill of the elusive enemy. Call, a militia general, had command of all forces in Florida, regular and militia. The regulars were resentful of this promotion of someone not one of their own and lacked enthusiasm for the cause. The volunteers from Tennessee and Alabama were distrustful of Call and when supplies failed to materialize, they accused the ill, grief ridden (his wife had just passed away) governor of alcoholism, which was certainly not the case. The lack of communication with General Leigh Read and other forces, the dire need of adequate transportation (which was simply not to be had), and the unruly behavior of undisciplined volunteers who were not expecting to do stationary duty made Call's task all but impossible. He was soon replaced by General Thomas Jesup, the Quartermaster General of the Army. All of this confusion and disorganization left the few settlements remaining almost unprotected and vulnerable to attack.

Perhaps General Jesup's greatest skill was his ability to organize the war effort. A born leader and skillful soldier Jesup had risen from the ranks of the young officers in the War of 1812 and had distinguished himself on the front lines along with Gaines, Scott, Macomb and others. On 3 August 1837 he received orders from the new Secretary of War, Joel Poinsett, to establish a number of posts, depots and other installations that were convenient for sailing vessels to land and provide assistance or provisions for the suffering inhabitants. The system that had been in place up to that point had been a direct dole from the military supplies at various garrisons, like Fort Heileman, Jacksonville, Newnansville and Fort Brooke. Jesup was now ordered to assemble the people at Jacksonville, Tampa or Charlotte Harbor and get them assistance through assigned agents and no longer keep military personnel and materials tied up feeding this segment of the population.[333] This task proved impossible to implement and the military continued the task until the end of the war. Jacksonville was now an official military post with an assigned garrison of about fifty men serving mostly under the Commissary Department. They worked out of the warehouse constructed along the water front and were under the orders of the commanding officer at Fort Heileman on Black Creek. It was this unit that maintained the suffering inhabitants in Jacksonville until the end of the war.[334]

The Florida troops kept up their constant vigil around the Jacksonville area and as far south as Mandarin, the most exposed of the communities in Duval County. Moses Curry, one of the commanding officers at the post at Mandarin, noted in mid 1836 that he was not familiar with all of the army Regulations required of post commanders and therefore requested a copy of these for his use. He also noted that he was not sure to what department he should make his various requisitions and also asked for guidance on this important subject.[335] Curry's requests show the lack of training and knowledge of the regular functions of post commanders found in most militia units, which was a weakness in this system of national defense. In September, Curry's commander, Colonel Warren engaged the enemy near the home of Joseph Sanchez at San Felasco Hammock (Alachua County) and drove the enemy from the field with the help of Captain David Thompkins of the First Artillery, United States Army and a 24 pounder howitzer. This engagement followed an attack on the wagons of one John Stanley on the Picolata Road to Alachua.[336] Warren, with the assistance of regulars, did his job well and appears to have been learning his job well by this time. All of these skirmishes, scouts, filling forms and other duties were being performed by the militia basically for the first time under fire. It was a steep and rapid learning curve for most.

One of the saddest stories of the war was the destruction of the settlement at Mandarin. From early in the war the settlement knew of its exposed position and requested a post be established there. This was granted and Moses Curry and others commanded a small guard post of one officer and twelve men for a number of years. However, as the war appeared to move southward, the post was abandoned by the army and requests by Governor Robert Raymond Reid to General Zachary Taylor for a post at North River and Mandarin were ignored.[337] Even though the James family on Julington Creek had their home destroyed in late 1839 by an attacking band of Indians, the army still would not concede that danger lurked in the swamps of northeastern Florida.[338] Governor Reid's appeals to General Walker Armistead, who replaced Taylor in command in Florida, had little effect either. Finally, on the evening of 20 December 1841 a band of twenty-one Indians under Halleck Tustenuggee, after questioning a local slave belonging to William Hartley, opened a surprise attack on the unprotected settlement and the house of William Hartley was the first assailed. Mrs. Hartley and Domingo Acosta were the first to fall in the fusillade and William Molpus was mortally wounded. Mrs. Hartley's infant son was killed later after the band returned from burning other buildings.[339] The community immediately appealed to the new commanding officer in Florida, Colonel William Jenkins Worth, who responded quickly and personally to their plea. Worth ordered Lt. Colonel Bennett Riley to have a force sent to Mandarin and to construct a blockhouse for its defense.[340] These measures were too late and too little to save some of the settlers who moved from the town never to return. The Hartley clan resolved to move to Jacksonville until the end of the war and there they received rations under the program to aid the suffering inhabitants.

Jacksonville's depot cost the government over sixty-two thousand dollars to construct and maintain through 1839.[341] Additional costs were added later as the vouchers became available. The largest portion of the costs was for lumber and other building materials. Labor costs totaled $22,716 for the period covered in the report and it was noted that the price of labor, "seems to have been proportioned to the high charges made for everything else." This same report included the observation that on several occasions a charge of five dollars a day was made for supervising the labor getting the lumber. This should not be surprising in that the woods were still filled with the enemy and an element of danger was encountered in every expedition outside the town limits.[342]

Jacksonville did not receive flattering notice by the troops who sailed by or were given time to roam the village streets. Hospital steward John Bemrose mentions going by the town and camping near Twelve Mile Swamp but left us no description of the village itself.[343] Lieutenant Henry Prince noted, "In coming down the river today we met two pretty steam boats going like the wind. We passed Jacksonville on the left bank of the river, a little town growing up under the auspices of the war. It is rather smaller than Key West Town."[344] Probably the least flattering description of the town came from the pen of Dr. Jacob Rhett Mott. In his memoir of the campaign in Florida he stated the following: "We reached Jacksonville by 1 o'clock at night; where we slept until morning, for the purpose of taking on wood. I had time enough to walk through this miserable little place with a brother officer, while the operation of wooding was going on; but saw nothing worthy of commemoration in its dozen scattered houses and sandy streets."[345] The town in this era was not impressive but, as Prince observed correctly, it was growing under the auspices of the war. The thriving lumber industry spurred by the construction of fortifications, government offices and wharves did provide some impetus to economic recovery. After the terrible destruction of the surrounding communities and the great plantations of East Florida, this was a needed shot in the arm. With the improving of the river that the war effort demanded, the growth of the town through construction and expenditures and the leadership of men like John Warren, Issiah Hart, Dr. Baldwin and others the town was on the verge of emerging as an important center of trade and commerce. The Second Seminole War was an important chapter in the growth of the city and Duval County.

154

# The Fort Brooke to Fort Mellon Road

The author of the following document, Lieutenant Colonel Alexander Cummings, was a proud veteran of the War of 1812 who began his long and illustrious military career in 1808 as a Second Lieutenant of the "Light Dragoons." Prior to the War of 1812, he had received two promotions (First Lieutenant and Captain), which was a difficult task in the days of the small army. A native of Ireland, he worked hard during the war and was rewarded with a transfer to the 4th Regiment of Infantry in 1815. Within four short years, he had risen to the rank of Major of the 8th Regiment of Infantry, transferring to the 7th Regiment of Infantry in 1823. In 1828, Cummings received a promotion to the rank of Lieutenant Colonel of the 2nd Regiment of Infantry. Assigned to Florida duty in November of 1838, as he notes below, he immediately set out for his post at Fort Brooke, Tampa Bay. The uncertainty of travel on Florida waters during the Second Seminole War (1835-1842) is well illustrated in the following document. After the completion of the road, from Fort Brooke to Fort Mellon, Cummings returned to Fort Brooke and was rewarded for his diligent attention to duty with a full Colonel's rank in December of 1839. He did not have the pleasure of enjoying this rank for too long. Alexander Cummings passed from this earth on January 31, 1842.[346]

The route depicted on the map includes a number of place names which currently exist on the map of Florida, including the city of Maitland. However, some of the other spots are foreign to our current experience. Forts Sullivan, Cummings, Gatlin, and Mellon no longer exist. Luckily, historian Canter Brown Jr., in his award-winning volume, *Florida's Peace River Frontier* has identified these places for us. The old Indian town of Itchepuckesassa/Fort Sullivan is today's Plant City; Fort Cummings is known to all today as Lake Alford; and Fort Davenport gave its name to the community of Davenport in Northeastern Polk County.[347] Fort Gatlin is reputed to be the original home of today's Orlando, while at the eastern end of the road, Fort Mellon became the nucleus for the city of Sanford. This wartime road became an important route for the early settlers of the area and greatly facilitated communication between the settlements, which relied heavily upon the troops stationed at Fort Brooke for protection from the occasional marauding bands of younger Seminoles presumed to be in the vicinity once the war had ended. An important part of the route is still in use as State Road No. 92, connecting Lake Alford with Davenport and Kissimmee.

In the document that follows, the reader will see the rough frontier of Florida in its most raw form. The road was constructed in essentially virgin territory (as the army and white population understood the term). The low, boggy and muddy wetlands were a major impediment to road construction. The men labored nearly as long constructing some of the bridges and causeways as they did in building Forts Sullivan and Cummings. What is more remarkable about the document is that this construction took place at the beginning of what was the rainy season in South Florida. The lack of mention of weather is a good indication that this year was one of the few dry years during that long and tragic war. Additionally, it should be kept in mind while reading this report that the entire enterprise was done under the watchful eyes of the Seminoles and their allies. Just because the army officers make little or no mention of their immediate presence does not mean they were unobserved. The fact that recent horse tracks were noticed headed toward the Big Cypress clearly indicates their presence. The tenacity and bravery of the men of Cummings' command cannot be doubted under these telling circumstances.

Head quarters,

Eastern District of Florida,
Fort Heileman, June 10, 1839.

Sir,

In obedience to a circular dated Head quarters, Army of the south, Fort Brooke 23d May 1839, requiring a report of my operations in Florida from the commencement of the campaign last Fall to the present time, giving as far as practicable the movements of the several detachments, under my command, the number and extent of bridges, causeways, Blockhouses built &c. I have the honour to state, that I arrived in Florida on the 8th of November last at Garey's Ferry, and was informed that Genl. Taylor had left directions that I should repair to Fort Brooke on the 12th of Nov. I set out with my staff for Fort White [on the Sante Fe River], where I expected to find a steam boat for Tampa Bay. In this however, I was disappointed, and after remaining there four days with a hope that a boat would reach the place, I retraced my steps to Newnansville, & from thence to Micanopy & continued on to Fort Clinch [on the Withlacoochee River] where I met with Genl. Taylor who was on his way to the Suwannee & Middle Florida. From Genl. Taylor I received an order for my Government in obedience to which, I proceeded on to Fort Brooke, being accompanied as far as the Anuttelaga Hammock by Captain Garrett of the 1st Inf, with his company, who was directed to establish a post at this point. I reached Fort Brooke on the 8th of December, where I found about 260 Indians & negroes assembled for emigration. Captain Abercrombie had not returned from the Sanybal [Caloosahatchee River], to which he had been sent by Genl. Taylor with a view to prevail on the hostile Indians to come in. The command at Fort Brooke being small I was desirous that the Captain should return with his company before I should set out on the duties assigned me by the General. I deemed it hardly safe to leave the post without a sufficient force for its protection while there was so large a number of Indians & negroes, some of whom, it was believed, were not too well disposed towards us.

Major McClintock with four companies of the 3d Regt. of Artillery, arrived at Tampa Bay about the middle of Dec. which with the three companies of Infantry, made the command appear large on paper, it must be understood, however, in speaking of companies,

157

that none of them were complete; the Artillery averaging about forty, & the Infantry a little over fifty men to a company.

On the 7th of January 1839, three companies of Arty & two of Inf. marched out in the direction of Hitchpucksassa with Brevt. Major Wilcox & I joined them in the evening, the train consisted of thirty four wagons loaded with provisions & forage, the road was accurately measured & marked by Lieut. Ketchum, Actg. Topographical Engineer.

8th. The troops were under way at daylight & left the Peace creek road 11 miles from Tampa Bay, two miles farther we came to the Plantation of Mr. Simmons, which had been abandoned soon after the commencement of the war. The Indians had destroyed all the buildings fences &c &c. from this place the road was opened as we advanced, at the distance of 15 miles we came to a small stream with muddy bottom over which was thrown a bridge of rough logs, two miles farther brought us to Buzzard creek [Baker Creek], which empties into the Thono de sassa lake, the stream was deep & muddy on each side, here we made a substantial bridge about 200 feet in length with a causeway on each side which enabled us to pass the wagons over in safety. Encamp at this creek where we were engaged two days in building the bridge.

10th. Pass through low grounds & swamps, the pioneers had heavy work in opening the road, progress about 5 miles.

11th. Made an early start & after passing over & through swamps & Hammocks arrive at the old settlement of Hitchpucksassa, where we commenced building a Fort 110 feet square, with two Block houses & two Store Houses.

12th. This morning I made an excursion in the direction of the Sand Hills, with the mounted company, passed over a high ridge with a lake on each side, this was the commencement of the Sand Hills, after riding about 15 miles returned to camp in the evening, where the troops had been busily employed at the work & had made considerable progress.

13th. Returned to Fort Brooke in company with Adjt. Clendenin intending to come out again in a few days.

23d. In conformity with previous intentions I set out this morning with a small escort of Dragoons, the post at Hitchpucksassa was completed & was named Fort Sullivan, Captain Garner with his company 3d. Arty were left as a Garrison to the Fort. The work was in fine order, the block houses were used as quarters for the soldiers in which they were very comfortable & two good & substantial Store houses were put up for the preservation of the public property.

24th. Leave Fort Sullivan at an early hour, having dismissed my escort of Dragoons, & continued my journey in company with Lieut. Hoffman. In passing the Sand Hills we are most of the time in view of a large pond or Lake, the water of which is very good & they abound in fish of various kinds. About the middle of the day I came to the camp where I found Major Wilcox busily employed, the Fort was pretty well advanced, the Block houses & store houses nearly completed. This post is situated on the point of the ridge, with a Lake on each side and a beautiful sheet of Water in front covering about 300 acres, abounding in fine fish & turtle.

Between the lake which lies on the north side of this post & that in front, there is a stream which connects the two, about 200 yards in length with a dense Hammock through which a road was cut & a strong bridge built between 200 & 300 feet in length which required great labour, this is 46 1/2 miles from Fort Brooke, the country in advance is unknown to us & to our guides, no white man had yet passed through it.

26th. Set out with the intention of ascertaining the situation of Fort Gatlin, from the best information I could obtain it was about 23 miles S. W. of Fort Mellon, I had with me Lieut. Anderson of the 2d Infy. & 30 mounted men with a negro Interpreter & an Indian guide, neither of whom know anything of the country nor (apparently) of anything else. Our course at first was about N. E. & continued so bearing a little to the north all day, passed two streams within the first 4 miles & two others at the distance of 15 & 20 miles all of which would require bridging.

27th. At 12 Oclock struck Genl. Jesup's road which passes down to To-hop-ke-laga, on which we traveled four of five miles after leaving this road discovered a large trail of mounted men who had recently passed in the direction of the Big Cypress.

Owing to the ignorance of the guide we were led out of our way & passed on the north side of lake Ahapopka, on discovering this mistake, I concluded to go on to Fort Mellon, the Hammock which leads off from the north end of the lake, is about a mile wide, in passing through which we crossed two small streams of clear running water. Encamp on the bank of a handsome creek about 30 feet wide which our guide said was the outlet of Ahapopka Lake.

28th. Pass through several Hammocks some of which are wet & boggy, about noon came to a handsome stream about 25 yards wide with a thick Hammock on each side, which was difficult to penetrate owning to large vines & cypress knees. The ground also, was deep & boggy, this stream rises or rather issues from a spring a short distance above the crossing. Arrive at Fort Mellon at Sundown. I only remained at this post one night, it did not strike me as a favourable location for health, the place being low & the country immediately round it wet & muddy.

29th. Set out on my return taking the south side of Lake Ahapopka, to Fort Maitland 14 miles the direction is nearly south, here we left the road & took a course West, South West, without a trail. In camp at a pond of bad water.

30th. About two & half miles, brought us to Genl. Jesup's road, which we struck at the South end of Lake Ahapopka, continued our course about two miles farther when we came to our trail outwards, about 8 miles farther encamp between two ponds which afforded protection to our front & rear, on a handsome knoll of land, and only required a Sentinel on each flank.

31st. Arrived at Camp where Major Wilcox had completed the Fort which he named Fort Cummings. Leaving one Company of Artillery at this post under the command of Lieut. Bragg, I directed Major Wilcox to proceed in the direction of Fort Maitland & establish another post between twenty & thirty miles in advance of Ft. Cummings & to build bridges over the Streams which he has done, the station is named Fort Davenport.

Each of these three posts viz. Fort Sullivan 26, Ft. Cummings 46 1/2, & Fort Davenport 66 1/2 miles from Fort Brooke is Garrisoned by one company of Artillery (3d. Regt.) & is commanded respecttively by Capt. Garner, Lieut. Bragg & Lieut. Wyse & have so far proved healthy.

Between Fort Brooke & Fort Davenport there has been six strong bridges build besides causeways.

The distance from the Gulf to the St. Johns by this route is 120 miles over a sandy pine barren most of the way, the numerous lakes gives the country a picturesque appearance, along the borders of these lakes & on the small streams, there are thick Hammocks, some of which afford good land for cultivation but I should think it impossible that anything like a dense settlement can ever be formed on this route.

Since my return to Fort Brooke I have remained in command of the district which embraces the three posts above named as well as Fort Cross 45 miles N. W. of Tampa Bay. The troops at the different posts within the district have been engaged so far as their means would enable them in scouring the country in their vicinity.

Respectfully Submitted
Alex. Cummings
Lt. Col. 2d. Infy.

Brigr. Genl. Z. Taylor
Comg. Army of the South
Tampa Bay
E. F.

# All His Wants Should Be
# Promptly Supplied:
# Persifor F. Smith on the Caloosahatchee

Writing on December 28, 1837, the "Maligned General", Thomas Sidney Jesup, ordered Major I. B. Brant, Quarter Master at Tampa to take every measure possible to keep the Louisiana Volunteers in good supply. In his order he noted:

> General Smith reports that he will have eight hundred men in the field, and will not have transportation for more than half his force. His operations, from his proximity to Holatoochee, will be more important upon the results of the campaign, perhaps, than those of any other commander: All his wants should be promptly supplied. The failure of his column from want of transportation, or from any other cause, would be most disastrous, and might lead to the failure of every other column.[348]

In Jesup's plan of operation, access to the west coast of Florida and the area approaching the Big Cypress Swamp had to be denied to the Seminoles and their allies. It was the job of General Smith and his command to stop the Indians from reaching these destinations. It was a crucial role in the complex operations of the United States Army against the Indians of Florida and one that Smith was quite capable of performing to Jesup's satisfaction.

Persifor Frazer Smith was born in Philadelphia, Pennsylvania in 1798 and later graduated from the College of New Jersey (now Princeton) in 1815. He took up the study of law while at school and moved to New Orleans in 1819. Smith quickly made his mark in the rough and tumble town and rose rapidly in its politics.[349] He married into the family of the prominent Francois Bureau, taking Bureau's daughter, Francis Jeanette, as his wife. He also became very active in local militia matters, rising to command of a battalion in a few short years. In 1834, his strong political ally, Edward Douglass White, became Louisiana's first Whig governor and appointed Smith to the post of adjutant general in the following year. With his political and military connections in place, Smith soon received the news of the outbreak of hostilities in Florida and was in a position to come to the aid of the Territory when General Edmund P. Gaines requested such in early 1836.[350]

Dr. Canter Brown, Jr. has recently shown the importance of Smith's role in the 1836 campaign. Brown has also noted the difficulties that Smith encountered in raising the first force of volunteers, including getting White to help gather the funds for the thirty dollar per man bounty. The internal politics of this command, well documented by Brown, show the tense situation in New Orleans. These included having White turn down a request by his rival for governor, Major General John B. Dawson, to lead the volunteers in Florida. The governor got around the seniority of Dawson by politely noting that the call for troops from General Gaines was for a colonel's command, eight companies, and as Dawson insisted upon maintaining his rank, the request was denied in favor of Smith, whose administrative office of Adjutant General was translated to a field rank of Colonel. Soon thereafter, Persifor Smith led the volunteers upon the perilous voyage to Tampa to begin their service.[351]

Smith's troops served with valor and distinction during their tenure in Florida. They suffered many of the hardships of army life on the frontier, including bad food, mosquitoes, worn out clothes and shoes and an impossible country for campaigning. Their Peace River expedition was difficult and without many positive results, except the exploration of about fifty-two miles of new territory, before the food ran out and they were forced to return to Charlotte Harbor. The volunteers returned to Fort Brooke on April 25, 1836, where they were greeted by orders for their departure back to Louisiana, thus ending their brief, but difficult service.[352]

The performance of the Louisiana volunteers under Smith's leadership was outstanding and widely recognized in the ranks of the regular army, something highly unusual in a war where volunteers were normally considered second-rate soldiers at best. In late July of the following year, Smith again offered to lead Louisiana's volunteers into the field in Florida. This time the command of the regular army was in the hands of Major General Jesup, who had replaced Richard K. Call, and was familiar with Smith's capabilities. As he noted to Secretary of War Joel Poinsett:

> Sir: I enclose a copy of a letter received today from General P. F. Smith, of Louisiana. The general commanded a regiment under General Scott and General Gaines in the first campaign, not only with credit, but with distinction. If he could bring a regiment of infantry into the field - and I have no doubt of his ability to do so - the service would be greatly benefited. By adding to his regiment a small body of regular troops he would be able, with naval co-operation, to commence his operations at Charlotte Harbor, or further south, and destroy or drive out the parties of Indians in the southern portion of the peninsula. ... I consider it of the utmost importance that a regiment should be obtained from Louisiana, and of equal importance that General Smith should command it.[353]

This time the terms of the service would have to be different. As Smith noted in his letter of July 30, 1837, to Jesup: "The regiment I commanded in 1836 left the service of the United States highly and justly discontented with it. They had served the whole time faithfully; indeed, had passed it nearly two weeks, had been the whole time in constant activity, and when they arrived here, in rags and poverty, found not the slightest preparation on the part of the government to pay them off, notwithstanding the most positive orders on the part of General Scott." The governor of the Louisiana, Smith reminded Jesup, actually had to borrow money to pay the

164

command.  The army paymaster, who was supposed to have reimbursed the men for expenses, was, in one last bit of frustration for the volunteers, remanded to Alabama and was not on hand in time to perform the required duty.  Yet, Smith stated hopefully, a year had passed since this ugly incident and it was probable that he could raise the troops Jesup needed for his Florida campaign.[354]

Two of the major reasons for Jesup's enthusiasm for Smith's Louisiana volunteers were their proximity, compared to Kentucky or Tennessee, and the fact they came from an area with a similar climate.[355]   Another factor which weighed heavily upon the reasoning of Secretary Poinsett was the very cumbersome arrangements necessary to properly staff a volunteer unit, especially under an inexperienced commanding officer.  Smith, having proven himself an able and willing administrator, would be able to avoid most of the petty grievances frequently voiced by elected volunteer leaders.  Also, the expense and time spent in gathering a new force would be greatly reduced with Smith in charge of the operation.[356]  Taken altogether, Persifor Smith was the ideal candidate to lead a major volunteer force when combined with regular troops against the stubborn foe.

After looking into business affairs in Philadelphia during most of September, Smith returned to New Orleans where his junior officers were already raising the required force.[357]  By November 2, 1837, Persifor Smith and the Louisiana volunteers had left New Orleans, bound for Tampa.  There he was supposed to meet with five companies of Philadelphia troops and units of the 2nd Infantry to outfit and get supplies for their trip to the Caloosahatchee country.  The force from Louisiana was about two hundred and fifty men.[358]  The Philadelphia force raised was to be about five hundred men, as noted earlier, meant that when Smith was ready to embark from Tampa, his force would number about eight hundred men.[359]

Smith's force was to be but one element in a much larger, more elaborate plan than any yet attempted in Florida.  Jesup's plan was very involved and set into motion as many as nine different columns at one time.[360]  The main thrust of the plan, however, involved four columns, each entering the southern end of the peninsula from different routes, driving the Indians into the center of the Everglades and isolating them from any chance for outside assistance.  Through constant campaigning and pressure on the food supply, Jesup hoped to end the war by March or April of 1838. To do this effectively would require that his forces would be in the field by no later than October. This hope was not to be. As the master planner stated:

> I had desired to commence operations on the 1st of October, because, at that time, the St. Johns is navigable a greater distance that at a later period; and I could avail myself of more than two months of the services of the Florida troops, whose term of service expired in December. The regular troops, however, did not begin to arrive until near the last of October, and they continued to come in until December. The principal volunteer force arrived about the 1st of December.[361]

The late arrivals of the various forces meant that the campaign started later in the dry season and would have to end before the beginning of the rainy season. Operating in the rainy season meant sickness, death and impossible conditions for a campaign against the Indians.

While Jesup led forces down the St. Johns River from Fort Mellon, General Joseph Hernandez and his Florida militia would scour the area between the St. Johns and the Atlantic coast. As the distance between these two forces narrowed, the Alabama and Tennessee volunteers and others joined with Hernandez's column and attempted to push the enemy further into the Everglades and deny them the coast. The movement of these troops led to the foundation of a number of establishments, namely Forts Pierce, Jupiter, Lauderdale, Christmas and Bankhead on Key Biscayne.[362]

Just as important to the overall success of the campaign were the western columns, outfitted and embarking from Tampa. As Jesup described the first of these: "General Taylor was directed to proceed from Tampa Bay, open a road in nearly an eastern direction into the heart of the country, establish a post on the head of Peas creek, another on the Kissimmee, and attack the enemy in that quarter."[363] This he did with his actions culminating in the Battle of Lake Okeechobee, fought on Christmas Day 1837. The other column, was to rendezvous in Tampa and enter the field through the

Caloosahatchee River. The operations of this column covered the whole country from Fisheating Creek, which enters Lake Okeechobee from the west, to Cape Sable, where forces under Colonel Thomas Lawson established Fort Poinsett. This column's activities resulted in the establishment of Forts Deynaud, Center and Keais (pronounced Keys) and the eventual capture of two hundred and forty three prisoners.[364]

Each of these two columns had specific assignments. Smith's mission was to deny the enemy access to the coast and the Big Cypress Swamp, the former because of the potential for gaining arms and supplies, and the latter because it was known to be an impossible area in which to successfully campaign. Also of importance was the need to keep the Indians south of the settlements and away from their brethren further north. Taylor's troops were to swing around to the east of the big lake and, after establishing Forts Basinger and McCrea, close off any communication with the north via the Kissimmee River valley or the reaches of the upper St. Johns River. With the constant movement of troops from the coastal forts (Lauderdale, Poinsett, Dallas and Jupiter), attacks on the Seminoles and their allies on the "islands" of the Everglades, and by denying the enemy access to the "coontie" grounds in southeastern Florida, Jesup felt confident that his campaign would have very positive results in ending the war.[365] The total force at his command, by January of 1838, was 8,993; 4,637 regulars, 4,078 volunteers, 109 seamen and 178 Indians.[366] All of this depended not only on the valor of the troops, but the reliable delivery of supplies and arms.

The supply problem for such a large undertaking as this campaign was enormous. The proper boats had to be ordered from Philadelphia and New York; specially designed steamboats had to be constructed to accommodate Florida's shallow waters; pontooniers had to be organized and assembled; boat builders had to be on hand for special needs; great quantities of forage and food had to be advanced to the fighting stations; articles for the construction of the frontier fortifications had to be obtained and forwarded to the troops; necessary animals had to be procured for the mounted troops and wagon masters; huge numbers of rations had to be prepared in advance; medical supplies had to be assembled, along with obtaining the medical officers, regular and volunteer, to use them properly;

tents, shovels, canteens, belts, caps, etc. all had to be ordered, assembled, shipped and forwarded to the front lines of four major columns. The tasks were daunting and complicated in the extreme.

In a lengthy memorandum to Major Collins, Jesup listed the articles needed for an "advanced Depot": 400 blankets for pack-saddles, 6 crosscut saws, 200 pounds of spikes, 2,000 horseshoes with nails, 400 cast steel axes, 20 froes, 20 Broad axes, 3 complete sets of blacksmith's tools, 20 coils of rope for packing, 800 packing bags, 2,000 pounds of iron, pitch for boats, and many other "essential" items.[367]  The logistics of this campaign in the swamps of Florida were difficult, complex and, in the end, highly frustrating to the clever general.

As noted earlier, Smith's departure from Tampa was delayed by the fact that he had little in the way of transportation to get him and his command to southern Florida.  Jesup, whose office as Quartermaster General of the Army was responsible for getting supplies to the armies in the field, fumed at the constant delays his command suffered during the early part of the campaign.  The commander's correspondence throughout this campaign is filled with urgent requests for supplies: "Sir, Send forward to this place [Fort Lane] without delay, the boats which I directed some time ago. I mean barges or flats of the second size. The movement of the troops will be greatly embarrassed if they should not arrive, had they been sent up when I requested them they could have been sent forward with forage yesterday."[368]  Basic necessities, such as shoes and other articles of clothing were often lacking or not forwarded to the frontier soon enough.  In one notable incident, the lack of shoes greatly delayed the posting of nearly four hundred troops because the saw palmetto had disabled some of the men and the General refused to move them further south until the articles needed were supplied.[369] Always aware of the men's morale, Jesup found it intolerable that other consumables were lacking or of such poor quality that they were unfit for use, even by the regular troops: "Greatly to my surprise," he wrote on December 29, 1837, "on my return to this post yesterday, I ascertained that there was neither sugar or coffee here for the troops.  This is a most unpardonable neglect of some officer of the Commissary Department.  Report, without delay, the cause of this neglect. ... The Beans sent to the Army are utterly unfit for issue, if you send any of them send those that are fresh."[370] Delays in troop movement, improperly packaged supplies, not enough equipment for the forward posts, lack of transportation facilities and a myriad amount of other factors caused Jesup great worry and may be one of the more important reasons for the failure of the campaign.

Jesup did, however, have some ability to adapt and adjust, as when he advised Colonel Taylor to improvise in constructing boats needed to explore the Kissimmee chain of lakes. As Jesup advised:

> I am induced [illegible word] from information received from the Indians and others, that the chain of Lakes extending from Tohopkaliga to Pahai Okee may be navigated by macinac boats, if not by those of larger size. Should we find this to be the fact, supplies may be taken from Tampa to the eastern side of the Okee chobee. (It is doubtful whether wagons or even packhorses can be taken to that point from this side.) I will thank you to cause a reconnaissance of those lakes to be made as far at least as the last named, and if you find them navigable, cause boats to be built, or brought from Tampa, to be employed as transport on them. Boat builders might be taken out to Fort Gardner and the boats constructed there. Canoes of Cypress enlarged by sawing them through the center from end to end, and widening them by inserting timber between the parts, in the manner of the fishing boats used on our bay, would be well adapted to the service we shall have to perform. If the Lakes are navigable, and boats can either be built on them or brought from Tampa, the war may be certainly closed this winter.[371]

The innovation to be noted is, "in the manner of the fishing boats used on our bay." Here Jesup is describing the "Chesapeake Bay Log Canoe" which was constructed in just the manner described by the General. Jesup was very familiar with the craft, having been in Washington D.C. for many years. The beauty of this vessel is its great carrying capacity with a light draught of water. By extending the craft outward, as described above, the displacement becomes such that the canoe can navigate in very shallow waters. This, of course, was perfect for the streams and some lakes of the Kissimmee chain and other areas covered by this campaign. Jesup's long career in the army, in numerous frontier assignments and in many important theaters of war, made him aware of the need for such adaptation.[372]

While Jesup was making his way down the east side of the peninsula, Persifor Smith and his force were working their way up the Caloosahatchee River. His mission, as noted above, was to prevent the Indians from attaining refuge in the Big Cypress Swamp or from obtaining supplies from outside along the west coast. Jesup was optimistic about the possibility of ensnaring the enemy in the heart of the Everglades. Writing to Colonel Taylor in early 1838, he noted, "If Colonel Smith can prevent the enemy from passing to the West, or if he can place a few boats on the Okee Chobee, to unite with yours, or prevent the Indians from occupying the Islands and Cypress Swamps to the south of the Lake, I shall entertain no doubt of a sweep."[373] On the same day of this letter, January 18, 1838, the General learned of Colonel Smith's capturing Holatoochee and forty of his people, who, along with eighty other prisoners, were sent immediately to Tampa and thence to New Orleans.[374] This capture made some national news because it coincided with the surrender of Jumper and his band to Colonel Taylor. Smith's position was reported as "still westward of Col. Taylor."[375]

To assist Smith and Taylor in holding the Indians in the Everglades, a series of fortifications was established around the lake and along the coasts of Florida. From Smith's forces came the establishment of Fort Center, on Fisheating Creek, Fort Deynaud, on the Caloosahatchee River, Fort Keais, on the northern edge of the Big Cypress Swamp, and Fort Poinsett, on Cape Sable, which was commanded by Colonel Thomas Lawson, best known as the Surgeon General of the Army. In regards to the latter post, Jesup declared, "A post at or near Cape Sable would hold the Indians in Check, and perhaps compel them to retrace their steps."[376] The overall strategy of surrounding the Seminoles and their allies in the Everglades, destroying their crops, cutting off all possible outside supplies and forcing a final confrontation or surrender was well thought out and articulated. However, because of the problems of supplies and the elusiveness of Sam Jones' and other bands, the concept failed in actual application.

Jesup also had to maneuver in conjunction with negotiations headed by a delegation of Cherokee Indians, whose presence in Florida was an additional burden on the commander. Yet, though he appears to have had little faith in the results of the negotiations, General Jesup did participate in the attempted diplomacy. As he reported in late 1837, he had met with the Cherokee delegation, arranged a meeting with Micanopy and other Seminole leaders, held a conference where surrenders were agreed to and seems to have acted in good faith with the government's policy. But he had no faith in the Seminole leadership which, he believed, had little or no influence over most of the warring faction.[377] Also, he insisted on getting his forces in the desired positions and having the supplies forwarded to them, in case the negotiations failed. In a letter to Secretary of War Poinsett, Jesup stated, "General Hernandez will turn Indian River with his mounted men, and pass the foot and supplies across. I shall not allow his operations, nor those of Colonel Taylor or General Smith, to be checked for a moment by the Seminole councils; and the delay of this column will be more than counterbalanced by the increased efficiency of its means."[378] After a year of experience and frustration when negotiating with the enemy, the cautious General was not going to be lulled into complacency.

Aside from the capture of Holatoochee and his band and the surrender of Jumper to Taylor, Jesup did not have the war wrapped up as he had planned. Many factors appeared to mitigate against a successful conclusion in early 1838. In a moment of frustration, he wrote:

Providence seems to have taken the Seminoles under its special protection. I have learnt since I wrote to you, that a vessel loaded with Rice has lately wrecked near New River, and that the Indians had secured a great part of the Cargo, this will give them subsistence for some months to come. ... Act as you may think best for the service; and should approach Colo. Smith's command give him such instructions as from your knowledge of the country and the enemy, you may consider proper, or unite his force with yours if in your opinion any important object can be obtained by it.[379]

Smith soon was ordered to report to Taylor at Ft. Bassinger to discuss his further operations. Indian cattle, too, proved to be something of a problem for the army, in that special attention was given to their capture or purchase. If the wide-ranging cattle could be captured, killed or bought, the war would end sooner. The reports given throughout the campaign indicate that there were still substantial numbers of these food animals within procurement distance of the enemy at any time. As the General noted to Colonel Taylor, "It is of the utmost importance that all the Indian Cattle be taken from them, purchase all you can from the Indians and Negroes who come in."[380] Keeping supplies with which to carry on the war out of reach of the Indian enemy proved to be a difficult, if not impossible, task for Jesup's forces. The very nature of the fertile Everglades, the free roaming cattle and hogs, the comparative plentitude of game and the occasional ship wreck all worked against the general's scheme of depriving the enemy of supplies.

The plans of the army were also frustrated by the constant barrage of intelligence, most of it rumor or reports from "escapees" and captives. The frequent references to reports of Indian locations and numbers, all differing from each other, shows how difficult it was to accurately pinpoint the enemy's camps. Reports like, "Alligator is on the west side of the Okee Chobee not more than one or two days march from Fort Deynaud, so says an Indian whom I have sent with a message to [illegible, although probably Halotoochee] urging him to go into the Fort."[381] Or, "An Indian Negro who came into camp on the evening of the 9th informed me that several small parties of Indians had crossed the Okee Chobee in boats to the south west side, the same place, perhaps, where Captain Munroe destroyed the Canoes."[382] Again: "An Indian who went to the head of New River for his family returned last evening, he reports that the Indians, where he left them, were making their way to a Pine Island a few miles from the swamp at the head of the north branch of New River."[383] This constant stream of intelligence, though sometimes accurate, was often simple rumor and perhaps, even disinformation, to use the modern term. Good maps, too, were lacking. John Lee Williams was so uncertain of the exact location of Lake Okeechobee that he did not include this vast inland sea on his famous map of 1837. The army's lack of knowledge in this area was also well known. As Jesup explained to the secretary of war, "... the greater portion of their country was unexplored wilderness, of the interior of which we were as ignorant as of the interior of China. We exhibit, in our present contest, the first instance, perhaps, since the commencement of authentic history, of a nation employing an army to explore a country, (for we can do little more than explore it) or attempting to remove a band of savages from one unexplored wilderness to another."[384] This lack of accurate intelligence was another major factor in the final failure of Jesup's intricate plan of operation.

Colonel Smith's operations during this campaign were closely followed in the press and in the correspondence of the commander. On March 1, 1838, for example, Smith's forces were reported to have surrounded "a large body of Indians, men, women, and children," on an island in the Everglades and that, taken in conjunction with the surrender of a large force of Indians and Negroes at Tampa and General Nelson's success in central Florida, would soon lead to the close of the war.[385] On March 8, 1838, Smith was informed of the approval of his plan to head further south into the Everglades to campaign against the enemy supposed to be in that region.[386] Six days later, Jesup informed Taylor that Smith's medical officer, a Doctor Steincke, had left the command and that the Colonel had no other medical officer under his command. Jesup ordered Taylor to supply one if it were in his power to do so.[387] In nearly every report of the expedition of Taylor's force reported in the media, Smith's contingent was mentioned, with the exception of the debate over the Battle of Lake Okeechobee, in which Smith's forces did not participate.

In reporting the progress of his campaign, Persifor Smith stated that he had left Fort Deynaud and moved south on March 7th with a company of Second Dragoons, a battalion of Second Infantry, marines under Captain Dulany and his own Louisiana volunteers, with the exception of one company he had left to garrison Fort Center. On the edge of the Big Cypress Swamp, "I erected on this spot, which is about 35 miles S. by E. from Fort Deynaud a small work in which I placed 20 days rations & one compy of La. Volunteers, naming the work, until the General's pleasure is known, after one of the officers who fell with Major Dade [Keais]. This point is on the border of the great Cypress Swamp & within miles of the point where I found an Indian trail entering it, when I was here on the 26th Feby. Our wagons could not well approach it nearer." His men then took with them five days rations upon their backs and proceeded to enter the swamp. After "incredible labour & fatigue, being all day Knee deep in water and mud & on wet prairies where the slimy surface is still more difficult," he searched for five days trying to locate the enemy. He was rewarded by finding a woman and her child, who then negotiated with the others to come into Fort Keais or Fort Deynaud. Smith then led his men out of the swamp to await results. However, his description of the territory is worth noting to indicate the extreme difficulty of military operations in this region of Florida.

> "The difficulties of this march through this part of the country are beyond all belief. No doubt the late rains have increased them, but even in the best season, troops must operate without any baggage but what they can carry on their backs, and in case of sickness, wounds or accident such as snake bites, the sufferers must be carried on the men's shoulders, as we were obliged to do in the latter case, a litter could not be carried through some of the hammocks we passed. One prisoner said the large marsh we crossed was considered by the Indians impassable, and in fact we found no trail in that direction. But having never had any guide here we have got to be expert woodsmen. One prisoner was sent home by the route we came, on account of her children and the difficulties of the way.[388]

The whole area, the valiant Colonel stated, was under water during the rainy season, making it impossible for campaiging. As General Jesup observed, "Colonel Smith has had a most arduous service. His operations are a further proof that the Indians can be concentrated by peaceful means only. ..."[389]

By April 16, 1838, Colonel Smith's forces had had some relatively successful campaigning under their belts and he could report the gathering of one hundred and seven Indians for transport to Tampa and New Orleans. He noted in his report, "Some come in every day & a party of 25 or 30 are expected today or tomorrow."[390] By May, the number had increased to one hundred and twenty of the "Halvetochin tribe."[391]    Prior to his leaving the area, he was to receive more prisoners, most of whom came into him at Fort Keais and Fort Deynaud.  Once assembled, the prisoners were sent, via the Peace River to Tampa and thence to New Orleans to await final transfer to the Indian Territory.

Toward the end of March 1838, some of the troops under Smith's command were at the end of their enlistments.  This, of course, caused many adjustments in the plans of the high command, including the proposed abandonment of Fort Poinsett, on Cape Sable. Although this proposal was negated quickly, the fact of its planned abandonment gives an indication of how quickly adjustments had to be made because of the widespread use of volunteer forces with limited enlistment periods.  Smith had to see that all arrangements for their transportation and mustering out were in place and carried out. Some of the Philadelphia volunteers wanted to be discharged at Tampa, while others, particularly the Louisiana men, wished to be mustered out at New Orleans.  These administrative details took up much time and concentration of the Colonel commanding and relied on the good communications between posts for their success. Overall, Persifor Smith carried out all phases of command, including those of a bureaucratic nature, with ability and humanity.[392]

By the end of April, 1838, General Jesup was seeing the ultimate end of the Seminole War as something far removed from the actions of his troops.  He saw that the Seminoles would never leave Florida unless forced by circumstances and overwhelming white numbers. He proposed that the area of southern Florida be left in Indian hands for the immediate future because the costs of removal, in money and men lost, would be too great.  In essence, Jesup anticipated the actual course of events, including the reserving of lands in South Florida for Indian occupation.  He even predicted the eventual passage of the Armed Occupation Act of 1842 when he noted, "I think a corps of Rangers should be raised in Florida of about six companies, ... it should be raised for war, and each man should in addition to his pay and emoluments, be allowed a quarter section of land in receiving an honorable discharge after the termination of the war."[393]   He would later have the opportunity to help provide the provisions needed by the armed colonists.

Persifor Smith's troops had performed their duty well and honorably. Through the rugged terrain of southern Florida, they had trudged diligently and faithfully. No one could have asked for more from a volunteer force. In quoting the New Orleans *Commercial bulletin*, the *Army and Navy Chronicle* described Smith's return to Louisiana.

> **The Soldier's Return** - Our fellow citizen, Gen. Smith, after a rugged tour of duty through the swamps and savannahs of Florida, has returned to the bosom of his family, having reached our city on the night before last. [May 1, 1838] He appears in fine health, though somewhat reduced in flesh, from the fatigues of the campaign. The scene of his military operations was confined to the southern and western territories of Florida, below Charlotte's Harbor, whither he was sent with a detachment of three hundred men in pursuit of a body of Indians. He hemmed in and drove the enemy to the extremity of the Peninsula, till they could fly no farther and were glad at length to sue for peace. After a talk with the chiefs, the whole Indian camp, amounting to two hundred and twelve in number, came in and surrendered themselves as prisoners of war. Having thus finished the campaign and the term of their enlistment having expired, Gen. Smith disbanded his forces and returned home, where he is greeted with the cordial welcome and high commendations which his arduous services rendered to the State so richly merit.[394]

General Jesup had a less glowing account of the exploits of the Louisiana volunteer's contribution, although he noted a much higher figure of Indians taken prisoner: "His operations covered the whole country from that river [Caloosahatchee] south to Cape Sable. The results were one or two skirmishes, in which he lost a few men, probably killed some of the enemy, and took 243 prisoners."[395]

The Jesup campaign of 1837-38 was an elaborately planned affair which deserved better results. However, it was plagued from the very beginning with poor coordination by the Commissary's

176

Office, the almost total non-performance of certain suppliers, poor topographical information, the reliance upon large numbers of limited service volunteer forces, including Smith's, and an impossible task of bringing to an end a war against a capable, resourceful and determined foe. Jesup was fortunate in having many able men in his ranks, too, including Smith, Colonel James Bankhead, Colonel Zachary Taylor, General Joseph Hernandez and many others whose ranks were lower, but whose names appear on the pages of history in a more famous conflict of the 1860s.

Smith's career after this second tour of duty in Florida was one of exemplary service. He served with distinction on the benches of the city court of Lafayette and Jefferson Parish. His service in the Louisiana militia included a term of office as adjutant general during the administration of Andre B. Roman.[396] Smith's military service in the Mexican War brought him national attention and lasting fame. There, he again served under Zachary Taylor and Winfield Scott, taking an active roll in both generals' campaigns and winning a brevet to Brigadier General. He was distinguished for his bravery in the Battle of Contreras and at Mexico City. In 1848 he served as the military governor of Vera Cruz. Persifor Smith was promoted to the brevetted rank of Major General in 1849 and given the command of the Division of the Pacific. Later service included commands of the Department of St. Louis and the Department of Utah, where he was put in command of a force preparing to put down the Mormon disturbances. He was given the full rank of Brigadier General in 1856. While preparing to lead his men into Mormon territory, he died on May 17, 1858, at Fort Leavenworth, Kansas. Such was the man who led the Louisiana volunteers against the Seminoles of Florida from the army based at Fort Brooke, Tampa, Florida in 1837-38. He served us well.

# Jesup's Strategy and the Role of Lieutenant Colonel James Bankhead at Fort Lauderdale

The founding of Fort Lauderdale has always held fascination for the historians of Broward County. Dr. Cooper Kirk became so interested that he worked many years researching and writing the biography of Major William Lauderdale, which is still the standard work on the subject. Kenneth Hughes has written well on the campaigns that led to the founding of the fort(s) and added greatly to our knowledge of the episodes which culminated in the final expulsion of the Seminoles from southeastern Florida.[397] Yet there are some unknown factors in the founding of the fort on New River and confusion in the primary documents intensifies the mysteries. The following will attempt to penetrate some of these unknowns and bring to light some of the little known players in the drama of the founding of Fort Lauderdale, particularly Lieutenant Colonel James Bankhead.

The context of the founding of the forts along the Atlantic side of the state has been explored in depth by Kenneth Hughes in his earlier pieces on the Second Seminole War in South Florida. Briefly stated, Hughes argues that the fortifications were constructed as the troops of General Thomas Jesup moved south to attempt to capture the forces under Sam Jones and other Miccosukee and Seminole leaders. Hughes also correctly points out that the movements of Jesup coincided with the forces sent up the Caloosahatchee under Percifer Smith and those coming down the Kissimmee from Tampa, led by

Zachory Taylor. A fourth column of soldiers, mostly Florida militia and other volunteers, was led by General Joseph Hernandez and combed the grounds between the Atlantic Ocean and the St. Johns River.[398] These various columns were designed to entrap the Indians in southeastern Florida and prevent their attacking and raiding the settlements to the north. The movements of the troops and the posts established to provide their shelter and storage facilities give us the broad context for the establishment of the fort on New River.

An even more detailed look at the troops and the correspondence of the leaders show that the planning and execution of these movements was very intricate from the very first. General Jesup, as Quartermaster General for the U. S. Army, had devised the plan of attack and sought to bring it to fruition in the campaign of 1837-38. The success of the operation depended upon proper reinforcements, well executed tactical movements and timely deliveries of troops and supplies to the required destinations. In true Burnsian fashion, these plans often went awry. Instead of the steady, metered, rhythmic arrival of men and supplies, the General experienced the frustration of seeing his plans sink with the boats in the Jupiter Inlet, or the boats ordered specifically for this mission on the St. Johns arrive piecemeal, if at all. Forage for the animals lagged woefully behind schedule. And, to add further insult, the men suffered greatly for the want of shoes and could not march further south after the Battle of the Loxahatchee in pursuit of the enemy.[399] Few things could have frustrated a general of Jesup's caliber more thoroughly than the inability of the suppliers to get the goods to the front.

Problems with the specially built boats, ordered from Philadelphia and New York, arose almost as soon as the troops left Fort Mellon. Jesup wrote, "In relation to the boats at Fort Mellon, which you supposed were ready for service when the troops moved, General Eustis informed me this morning that Lieut. Collins had reported to him that not more than six of them were serviceable. Let the large Macinac boats be sent up--the bulwark boats. We shall have to rely on oars and poles for our supplies."[400] To understand the supply problem in some depth, it will be useful to explain what was entailed in establishing a forward depot for operations against the Indians of Florida. In a letter of January 2, 1838, the month prior to the founding of Fort Lauderdale, General Jesup wrote to

Lieutenant C. O. Collins, the Assistant Quartermaster operating in Florida at that time, detailing the needs of such a post:

> The accompanying list of Articles should be provided and kept at the advanced depot. I have order Major Brant to send one hundred and fifty packsaddles--this will leave two hundred and fifty to be provided for. ... Memorandum of articles required to be kept on hand at an advanced Depot, a copy sent to Major Whiting with the foregoing letter, viz; 400 Cast Steel Axes 2 dozen hand hatchets, 500 pounds double 10d nails, 2000 horse shoes, with nails, 20 iron wedges, 200 pounds of spikes, 20 Broad Axes, 20 Froes, 6 Crosscut saws, 6 dozen crosscut saw files, 3 sets of Black Smiths tools complete, 12 iron Wedges, 20 coils of Rope for packing, 2 dozen drawing Knives, 1" Grind Stones, half fine, half coarse, 800 packing Bags, 400 Blankets for Pack Saddles, 2 Dozen Nail Harnesses, 6" Gimlets assorted, [?] Handsaws, [number blurred], 100 [?] files, 1" Foot Adzes ...

And this listing reflects only half of the articles named. Other items of note included wood rasps, augers, 2000 pounds of iron, chisels, "2 Large Ferry Ropes", scythes, oakum, caulking irons, cane knives, "400 packsaddles", pitch for boats and, finally, "Tarpaulins to cover stores at all the temporary advanced posts."[401] The amount of planning and execution to get these materials to the front lines was considerable. Considering all of the possible hazards to travel and communication during the campaign, it is a tribute to the Quartermaster's Corps that any post was successfully established. If one considers that this campaign was designed to encircle the enemy in southern Florida by creating a number of posts out of which to operate, the enormity of the task becomes apparent.

The immediate reason for the establishment of Fort Lauderdale as an advanced post was the numerous reports of the alleged encampment of Abiaka (Sam Jones) at the headwaters of New River. Jesup related that another reason for the New River post was the murder of two soldiers on the river while there was a recognized truce. As he reported it, "Major Lauderdale had been detached with a company of the 3rd artillery, and two hundred Tennessee volunteers, to explore the country south, and to establish a post at New river. Previous to his arrival there, two of our people had been killed by some of Toskegee's warriors. We were then in the midst of a truce; the Indians were afterwards captured, and the property of the murdered men found upon them. Hearing from Indians who had come in, that Appiacca [Sam Jones] was in the everglades near New river, I ordered General Eustis to proceed to that point with additional force; but, in consequence of depredations committed by the Indians in Middle Florida, his destination was changed, and he was sent to the north frontier of the Territory; and Lieut. Colonel Bankhead, with a strong detachment of the 1st and 4th artillery, was ordered to New river."[402]   Jesup's report leaves out the detail that prior to the appointment of Lieutenant Colonel James Bankhead, Lieutenant Colonel Benjamin F. Pierce was to have set up the advance post south of Fort Jupiter.   However, Pierce was incapacitated at the time and Bankhead received the assignment.[403]

Lieutenant Colonel James Bankhead, the man who was to join Lauderdale on New River, was a very experienced officer with service dating back to June of 1808.  A native of Virginia, he saw extensive service in the War of 1812, rising to the rank of Colonel during that conflict. He was retained by the U. S. Army as a Captain of infantry but was soon breveted to Major of artillery on December 2, 1815.[404]  Bankhead was no stranger to Florida, however, and was in charge of United States forces at Amelia Island when a pirate named Aury was expelled.  He retained control over Fernandina until the end of U. S. occupation.  This command also engaged him in the defense of Lieutenant Frederick Griffith, who was sued for seizing slaves at Fernandina while under Bankhead's command.[405] Bankhead was promoted to Lieutenant Colonel on April 26, 1832, and was assigned to the 4th Artillery at that time.[406]  As noted in Jesup's report, cited above, it was while serving with the 4th Artillery that Bankhead was ordered to the command on New River.

There can be little doubt that the first official post established on New River was the camp founded by Major William Lauderdale. However, some confusion remains as to whether this was a "camp" or a "fort."  The diary of Captain Robert Anderson offers the best evidence as to the nature of the evolution of the position when he called the place "Fort Lauderdale" on March 6, 1838.  Yet, until the picketing was commenced on April 11th, every other reference is to "Camp Lauderdale."[407] Kenneth Hughes has noted that when Lieutenant Levin Powell's naval command joined with Lauderdale, he established "Camp Powell" on the south bank of the New River.[408] A letter from General Jesup to Major Lauderdale, dated March 3, 1838, indicates that the general considered whatever the major had established as an official post when he wrote, "I learn from Capt. Webster that a number of Indians, principally women and children, are in the vicinity of New River. I wish you to communicate with them, and require them to encamp near your post on the River."[409] As noted earlier, the official report filed by the general indicated that Major Lauderdale had been sent to New River with the intention of establishing an official post. But, on March 28th, Lieutenant Colonel Bankhead was ordered to cut off any direct use by the Indians of the old coontie and hunting grounds on New River by establishing his command further up the river, implying that the location of Lauderdale's camp was not satisfactory:

> Colonel,
> The Major General commanding has received your letter of the 25th instant reporting your operations against that party of Indians at the head of New River and in the Everglades. He directs me to say that he desires you will take a position with your command as high up the river as possible in order that as much as practicable to narrow their limits and prevent them from re-occupying the main land. If they can be kept to the glades and be prevented from hunting and the opportunity of makin Countee, it is hoped that the want of subsistence will soon drive them to listen to the terms prescribed them. The command will remain in the position which you may select until further orders, which will be duly communicated.[410]

The question that arises from this letter is: Did Bankhead establish a new post up river from that created by Lauderdale? Unfortunately, the Anderson diary, which contains a sketch of the fortification, describes the location as 1/8 mile above "Cooly's patch." This is the supposed site of the former homestead of pioneer

William Cooley, whose family was killed eight days after Major Dade's command was attacked near Bushnell. Anderson mentions no other post or encampment in his diary that may be construed as a different location for Fort Lauderdale.[411]

The final clue as to the location of the fort, however, can be had from the fact that the letter of March 28th preceded the replacement of Bankhead by Lieutenant Colonel William S. Harney by only three days. The Anderson diary indicates that Harney had arrived on April 2, 1838, and the letter directing Harney to Fort Lauderdale is dated March 31, 1838.[412] The difference can be allowed for by the time of travel and the moving of equipment. Anderson indicates no further movement of the camp from its original position and no letter from Harney has been found to signify a change of location from that first established by Major Lauderdale. Therefore, one can logically conclude that the position of Fort Lauderdale did not change from that established by the man for whom it is named.[413] Bankhead thus led his forces into the Everglades to tangle with the Indians in the Battle of Pine Island from the original site of the fort.

The "Skirmish at Pine Island" has been discussed and published in earlier editions of the *Broward Legacy*, by Dr. Cooper Kirk. However, returning to the overall strategy of General Jesup it has been seen that the purpose of getting Bankhead to establish his command higher up on the river was to cut off supplies of coontie and game to the Indians. When looked at in its broadest context, this is in keeping with the concept of entrapping the Indians within the confines of the Everglades. Once the ring of fortifications and depots was established, Jesup envisioned a general squeezing of the Indians from all fronts. Troops from Persifer Smith's column, established at Fort Center on Fisheating Creek and at Fort Keais near the Big Cypress would push the enemy south and east into the waiting arms of the troops from the southeast coast and guard the escape routes to the Big Cypress and other western South Florida haunts. Colonel Zachary Taylor's forces would push down the Kissimmee and control the northern and eastern shores of Lake Okeechobee from Fort Bassinger and Fort McRea. Any move of the enemy to the south would be intercepted by the troops under Lieutenant Colonel Lawson from his post on Cape Sable or by the troops stationed at Fort Dallas on the Miami River. Therefore, the little engagement at

Pine Island takes on a much more important aspect because it did force the Indians under Sam Jones to go away from the coast, where they could receive supplies, and deeper into the Everglades where the army thought it was establishing an entrapment.

Bankhead was well aware of his commander's concepts. On March 29, 1838, he wrote, "I enclose an important sketch of the country between the Hillsboro and Miami River. ... If the Indians driven from Pine Island have gone north west toward Okeechobee, it would be absolutely impossible to pursue them in that direction, but if they have gone south, which I shall soon ascertain, I will pursue them; and at the same time advise Lt. Col. Lawson at Cape Sable of it with the directions to him to move with his command northerly. I shall learn from Hallek Hadjo on his return in what direction they have gone."[414] This idea of pushing the Indians further into the Everglades and either starving them out or driving them into the arms of the awaiting troops from the surrounding posts was well communicated by Jesup to his subordinates and they attempted to carry this plan into full operation. Unfortunately for the general, the Indians were more adaptive to their situation than he anticipated and much more elusive than ever conceived. No matter how hard the commanders, such as Bankhead, Powell, Lauderdale, Smith, Taylor, etc. tried, they would never corner the Indian foe to a point where all resistance would be futile.

As early as March 30, 1838, Jesup was beginning to realize the futility of attempting to entrap the Indians in the Everglades. In one of the more telling letters in the Adjutant General's correspondence, Jesup wrote to Colonel W. I. Mills:

Colonel,
... The war will continue, how long is uncertain, but at all events, until the whole race of Seminoles be exterminated: for while a warrior remains we have him to fight. I do not believe the enemy can ever concentrate again, they are broken and dispersed, and if we can prevent all intercourse between them and the white population, or rather the blacks and the Spanish fishermen, and thus cut off their supplies of ammunition and clothing, they may ultimately be destroyed if we cannot pick them up.

I think a corps of Rangers should be raised in Florida of about six companies. They should be mounted and stationed at convenient distances from each other along the frontier. They should be kept in constant motion, never allowing the enemy to rest for a moment. This corps should be raised entirely in Florida and the southern counties of Georgia, it should be raised for the war, and each man should in addition to his pay and emoluments, be allowed a quarter section of land in receiving an honorable discharge after the termination of the war. I wish you would see your Delegate on this subject. I will write to him in a few days.[415]

The thinking reflected in the above statement can be readily identified with that shared by Senator Thomas Hart Benton and other expansionists who were to formulate the Armed Occupation Act of 1842. By 1842, Jesup was back in Washington while William J. Worth commanded the troops in Florida. The latter was busy recruiting forces to settle along the frontier in Florida. The "Delegate" referred to in the above quotation was none other than David Levy Yulee, whose work on behalf of the Armed Occupation Act has long been recognized.

Jesup's thinking about a possible war of extermination also reflected the reality of frontier Florida. The long, harsh and brutal Second Seminole War became the longest, most expensive in men lost and dollars spent of any Indian war in American history. The vicious nature of the war, the constant attacks, ambushes, ruthless killing of women and children by both sides, took a toll on the collective psyche. The push for the removal of the Seminoles and their allies continued into a Third Seminole War, which lasted an additional three years, 1855-1858.

One of the men lucky enough to escape the confines and brutality of Florida was Lieutenant Colonel Bankhead. Rising to the rank of full Colonel in July of 1838, he was cited for meritorious conduct in relation to his Florida service. Although passed over for promotion early in his career, being labeled, "An intelligent man, but not a good Officer",[416] he soon found himself on the southwestern frontier. By March of 1847 he had been promoted to Brigadier General and was cited for gallantry and meritorious service during General Winfield

Scott's campaigns of the Mexican War.[417]   During the Vera Cruz operation, Bankhead was part of Scott's "little cabinet" along with Colonel Joseph Totten, Lieutenant Colonel Ethan Allen Hitchcock and a young Captain of Engineers named Robert E. Lee.  Bankhead's service included administrative care of Cordoba and Vera Cruz where he distinguished himself as an able and very efficient administrator, whose fairness under wartime conditions even won praise from the Mexicans forced to endure the conquest.[418]   General James Bankhead did not have to endure the anguish experienced by many of his Mexican and Florida War compatriots, the American Civil War.  Bankhead died on November 11, 1856, widely respected and beloved by his fellow officers.[419]

# Clearing the Cove:
# Worth's 1841 Campaign

As summer approached with its heavy rains and the dangerous "miasma" rose from the unhealthy swamps, General Walker Keith Armistead readied his troops for summer quarters in Florida's more healthy encampments. Medical authorities had warned the army about the dangers of summer campaigns in such illness-prone areas as Florida. Yet the number of troops on the sick lists continued to rise. Armistead and other officers could offer no explanations. Encampments which caught the sea breezes, such as Fort Harrison at Clearwater harbor, were thought to be healthful alternatives to more inland locations. But still the sick lists grew.

Armistead did not remain in Florida long enough to see his troops transferred in large numbers to these safe havens. In May of 1841, he was replaced by Colonel William Jenkins Worth, the dynamoic protegé of General Winfield Scott. Worth did not believe that the idleness of garrison duty during the summer months was healthy for the troops. Worth informed the Adjutant General that, "It stands thus then; there is much & distressing sickness & many deaths; (people die every where) but the burden of the afflictions grows out of garrison service: the cause, absence of mental & physical excitement, heavy food in excess, & greater facilities for inordinate indulgence."[420] Worth was not going to allow his troops to remain idle in summer garrison duty. As he took command, he noted that as of April 30, 1841, there were 815 men on the sick lists and that the actual number approached 1,200. One of his first orders of business upon receiving command was to direct an all-out assault on the Cove of the Withlacoochee River and in a line across the Territory to the St. Johns River. In so doing, Worth hoped to eliminate the remnant of the Indians from the settlements and then concentrate on those in the southern portion of the Territory.[421]

The basic plan of operation was to have forces from Fort Clinch on the Withlacoochee River, Fort Harrison at Clearwater Harbor, and Fort King (today's Ocala) scour the Cove and converge at Fort Cooper. On his second day of command, Worth wrote to Lt. Colonel Gustavus Loomis, commanding at Fort Harrison, to search the area of the Pinellas Peninsula for cypress trees suitable for making up to sixty canoes, twenty-three feet in length and "the ordinary width." Instead of ordering these canoes from South Carolina or other areas, Worth's plan called for the troops in Florida to do the construction, thereby saving the army money.[422] The impetus for this move was a vast "retrenchment" movement in Congress which called upon the War Department to cut back on its expenditures. In keeping with this policy, Worth issued the above orders and implemented a series of cost-cutting measures, including letting many of the civilian laborers go and using regular army personnel whenever any need arose. For the forces converging on Fort Cooper, these measures had little effect, in that most of the posts providing provisions and forage were well stocked under General Armistead.

On June 16, 1841, Worth issued the orders to commence the movement into today's Citrus County, focusing on the Cove of the Withlacoochee. The Indians had been reported in the Cove and along the coast on the Crystal and Homosassa Rivers. The orders also read, "Each command will consist of 200 men to be organized so as to admit of not less than four detachments, and as many more if there be Officers, if necessary, not to go below 20 men, exclusive of mounted force; of which description each command will be accompanied. ... The troops will keep the field, until further orders, probably 20 or 25 days. ... All Invalids or feeble men will be excluded from this operation." His directions indicate that Lt. Colonel Clarke would take the Tampa to Fort King road to Fort Dade and launch canoes for a descent of the Withlacoochee from that base. Lt. Colonel Riley would take his troops from Fort King and converge toward Fort Cooper from the East, while Lt. Colonel Loomis would take the troops from Fort Harrison and head toward Fort Clinch via the "Annuteliga route" until he reached a point where he would "deflect" toward the river and follow its left bank to Fort Izard. In such a way, with the available healthy forces, Worth hoped to cover the Cove, the Withlacoochee and points in between, sweeping the remaining Indians from the area and opening it up for the return of settlers.[423]

By the end of June, the Indians had raided in the Micanopy area and had retreated back into the Cove. Troops from that sector, stationed at Micanopy, Wacahoota, Wacassassa and Wheelock attempted to pursue this group and added their forces to those already assigned to the assault.[424] As these troops reported to Lt. Colonel Riley, they supplemented his corps. On July 1st, Clarke's command was ordered to leave their temporary base at Fort Cooper and enter the Cove, "particularily examining the chain of lakes in the cove."[425] Simultaneously with this, Captain E. S. Sibley, at Cedar Key, was ordered into the field taking with him, "any means of transportation within your reach to throw ten days provisions for two hundred & fifty men and Ten days forage for Seventy five horses, upon the Crystal or Homossassa rivers, where Capt. Miller of the 1st Infty. is operating with a detachment of canoes, and where Lt. Col. Riley will arrive in the course of four or five days with almost 225 men horse & foot and with but six days rations inclusive of today."[426] Given the difficulty of the territory, this was a logistical problem of no small magnitude.

The swampy terrain caused considerable difficulty for the mounted troops. Lt. S. J. Johnson reported the following on July 3, 1841:

I arrived at the Withlacoochee nearly opposite the place known as the Orange Grove - about 2. O'Clock P.M. yesterday, and found the blaze of 1st Lt. Collinson R. Gates on a large Cypress tree. His command must have passed the point but an hour or two before my arrival. The trail from Fort Cooper to this point (three miles below the Panasoffkee Creek) is a little north of East and very practicable for Horse. On Entering the Hammock near Lt. Gates' landing the guide Tony discovered a fresh trail of Cattle & Hogs, being driven off by Indians. ... I pursued this trail on a full gallop for nearly five miles & until it crossed the Withlacoochee about two miles above the mouth of the Panasufekee - at a place called the "Boggy Hammock." I endeavored to cross my command but did not succeed, my Horses bogged, completely, at 20 yards from the River. Several of my men could not swim, and I was compelled to abandon the pursuit of the enemy.[427]

Lieutenant C. R. Gates, of the 8th Infantry, had nearly as much difficulty in boats launched near "Deer Foot Village," located about three miles from Fort Cooper. In this lake area he found a number of islands which had been inhabited at the beginning of the war, but also found seven corn cribs. He then found a recent trail leading toward the village through the saw grass. But, "I was not enabled with the canoes to get within three hundred yards of the Island's for the thick saw grass - the Grass extended for four or five miles East, and apparently opened into another Lake." The frustration of searching for the enemy under such circumstances is clearly indicated in the reports above.

Colonel Worth's forces were not without success, of sorts. On July 5, 1841, Worth reported that troops under his command, while descending the Withlacoochee, came across a large village of fifty lodges and extensive fields of pumpkins, squashes and beans, all of which they destroyed. Several Indians were captured by this group and sent to Tampa for shipment west. Forces under Lt. Colonel Riley, in canoes, penetrated "Charly-a-popka" [Tsala Apopka] and, "found the enemy's Island planting grounds, and destroyed extensive crops covering almost the entire surface of three of the largest."[428] That the Indians would have villages as large as fifty huts, extensive plantings along the river and heavy crops on three of the largest islands in Lake Tsala Apopka five years into the war is a remarkable statement, especially when the area was one of the first scouted and "scoured" by the army at the outset of the war in early 1836. The strategic importance of the Cove of the Withlacoochee and the surrounding area is clearly demonstrated by these reports and speaks volumes about the military intelligence of the Seminoles and their allies.

190

The campaign in the Withlacoochee and Cove continued on until the latter part of July and into August of 1841, at which time Colonel Worth assumed there was little more to be accomplished in that sector. Additionally, he had other problems with which to contend. On July 23, 1841, he reported that his wagons were breaking down, one being made totally useless. His provisions, especially the bacon, were so damaged as to be, "unfit for issue; which reduces my supply of meat to almost nothing." Luckily, just at the moment of this exhaustion of the meat supply, a wagon train under a Lieutenant Campbell arrived. This arrival did little, however, to lessen the ever increasing number of sick being placed on the lists, which the erstwhile Colonel feared would become, "another cause of embarrassment."[429] From this point on, Worth's attention was drawn toward the attacks taking place in Middle Florida (which drew critical comment from Governor Richard K. Call) and in driving the Indians south of Tampa further into the Everglades. His campaign in the Cove and on the Withlacoochee ended with little actually accomplished except to assure the army that few of the enemy still resided in these ancient haunts. Their numbers were considered so few as to be not worth another concerted campaign. With the final surrender of Tiger Tail's band toward the end of the year, little was to be feared from the once deadly Cove of the Withlacoochee.

# Into the Cove Again: The Gates
# Withlacoochee Expedition of 1841

The campaign designed by Colonel William Jenkins Worth to force the Seminoles and their allies from the Cove of the Withlacoochee called for a number of expeditions into the area from numerous directions. In classical pincer style, the various forces were to converge on the Cove, in the vicinity of Fort Cooper, and drive the remnants of the tribe out of the area, thus freeing the northern portion of the Florida Territory from the menace of sporadic attacks. As part of this operation, 1$^{st}$ Lieutenant Collinson R. Gates of the 8th Infantry was assigned the task of taking an expedition down the Withlacoochee River from Fort Dade and examining the area for possible entry points into the chain of lakes known as Tsala Apopka from the river. Given the nature of the terrain, this was to be a very difficult assignment.

Collinson R. Gates was born in New York State in 1816 and was appointed to the Military Academy in 1832. He was not at the top of his class when it graduated in 1836, finishing forty second in a class of forty nine. Upon graduation he was promoted into the regular army as a Brevet Second Lieutenant in the 4th Infantry Division and sent, almost immediately, into the foray in Florida. His unit saw action in the Battle of the Wahoo Swamp on November 21, 1836, and other skirmishes of that opening campaign. After a short tour on garrison duty at Fort Monroe, Virginia, he was back in Florida before the end of 1837. He was promoted to the rank of First Lieutenant of the 8th Infantry on July 7, 1838, and served with that unit shepherding the Cherokees on the infamous Trail of Tears. After this

192

tour, he was sent to New York to help guard the Canadian border during the Finian "uprising" and temporarily settled down to garrison duty in other New York posts. He was soon returned to Florida, participating in the campaign and the battles in the Big Cypress Swamp of southern Florida. After leaving Florida in 1843, he was sent west to guard the borders in Texas and, with the outbreak of the Mexican War, he saw extensive and important service in many of the major battles of that conflict. He participated in the Battles of Palo Alto, Resaca-De-Palma, Churubusco, Molino del Rey, Chapultepec and in the capture of Mexico City. For his bravery and gallant conduct, he was promoted to the rank of Captain and Brevet Major. Unfortunately, he was wounded at Resaca-De-Palma. Gates was then assigned to frontier duty at San Antonio, Texas and at Fredericksburg, Texas after the war and there contracted the disease that led to his death at Fredericksburg on June 28, 1849, at the young age of thirty-three years.[430]

Accompanying Gates on the expedition below were two notable men who were later to achieve some fame and fortune. Lieutenant John Rodgers of the United States Navy, rose to the rank of Rear Admiral, serving with distinction in the Civil War as the commander of the ironclad, *Galena*. His fifty-four year naval career, following that of his father, who was a commander during the Revolutionary War, made him one of the longest serving officers in naval history. The other notable was Lieutenant John T. Sprague, Worth's son-in-law, and the author of *The War in Florida, Its Origins, Progress and Conclusion*, the classic account of the Second Seminole War. As an Aide-de-Camp of General Alexander Macomb and Adjutant to Worth, Sprague had access to most of the important correspondence and scouting reports, which he admirably assembled into his now famous work. He also later served with distinction during the Civil War and was commander of Fort Clinch, Florida, during the immediate post-war period. He served as the acting military governor of the State during the Reconstruction period.[431] These men were the major leaders in support of the expedition as reported and transcribed in the following report of Gates to Lieutenant Colonel W. S. Clarke:[432]

Ft Cooper E. F.

193

July 3, 1841

Sir

In obedience to your instructions received on the twenty eighth ultimo, "to descend the Wythlacoochee from Fort Dade with a detachment of the Eighth Infantry below the Panee Sofekee to a point opposite Charlo-Popka Lake, and from thence enter the Lake and proceed to Fort Cooper; explore the country especially fords, and landing places, discover Indian signs, pursue, attack and destroy any Indians that may be found, cooperate with you whenever it was in my power, and rejoin you at Fort Cooper on or about the expiration of the fifth day": I accordingly embarked at Fort Dade on the morning of the twenty ninth Ultimo with fifty men of the Eighth Infantry, an Indian Interpreter, accompanied by Leiut. Rodgers of the Navy and Leiut. Sprague Adgt. Eighth Regiment arranged in eight canoes. The distance from Fort Dade by the Big Withlacoochee, the branch which I descended, to its junction with the Little Wythlacoochee I found to be Sixteen miles, very crooked in its course, varying W.S.W. N. N.N.W. N.N.E. This branch now unusually low, is from twenty five to thirty feet wide, and not averaging in depth more than three feet, in twelve places I found fords from one to two feet deep. The branch was much obstructed by fallen timber firmly embedded in the Stream, upon which the drift had been accumulating for years. Fish are to be found in this stream in great abundance. The character of the Country through which this branch winds its course is a low wet swamp of Cypress, and Oak, extending, I should judge, upon each side from four to five miles; occasionally the pine land approaches the Stream. At present the country could be traversed by horsemen, with some difficulty however, but at other seasons, from the indications upon the trees, the country must be submerged in water from two to four feet deep. I discovered heavy beaten Indian trails approaching the stream, not crossing it, which had not been traveled for some three months. A number of Indian fishing poles were found on the bank which appeared to have been cut about the same time. Two miles from the junction of the two forks of the Wythlacoochee I entered the main river, which I found to expand into a Lake about two miles in diameter, a number of Cypress and Willow Islands, surrounded by dense swamps of Cypress. On the left bank, as the Stream contracts

194

to its outlet, the pine timber approaches it were I landed and by marks found that Captain Beale,[433] with his troop had been there a few hours previous. This was the route of the column under your command; by land twelve miles from Fort Dade by water twenty miles. Again entering the narrow Stream the accumulation of floating timber and grass almost obstructed the passage. My command continued in boats until ten o'clock at night, unable amongst the numerous Willow and Cypress Islands to find any dry land sufficient to encamp upon. These Islands are made by the outlets from the Lake, many impassable, which after winding in various directions concentrate and again form the main Stream. I endeavoured to keep the left hand outlet in order to communicate with you and if possible find the points designated in my instructions. In this however, I was often defeated as many of the passes were impracticable. On the morning of the thirtieth I communicated with you, you having encamped one and a half miles from my encampment: distance by land from Fort Dade fifteen miles, by water twenty four miles. Three miles below this point I came to a bridge and causeway crossing the Wythlacoochee and a branch leading into the Wahoo Swamp, the bridges were impassable for horsemen. Here my Guide discovered an Indian track coming from the Wahoo, this I followed up with a party of men and lost it upon its intersection with your column which had passed over it the same day, its direction was toward the Cocochatee. The distance from the bridge to your trail was two miles. My route this day was in narrow passages winding in various directions through thick patches of pond lettice and high grass - bordered by Cypress Swamp, these passages led me into a Lake about four miles in diameter studded with Islands of Willows, three I explored and found them uninhabitable. The Lake was surrounded by Cypress swamp as far as could be seen from the tallest trees. Today I made seventeen miles. Soon after leaving my camp on the first instant with much difficulty I made my way through a small outlet into a Lake of clear water, in width, I suppose, two miles, bordered by Willow and Cypress swamp. At a point of dry land extending into the Lake I discovered an Indian corn and pumpkin field, some acres in extent, accessible only by water. I found there three lodges and strong evidences of recent occupation. While destroying the field my lookouts in the boat discovered an

Indian coming up the river in a canoe, pursuit was immediately given, but upon approaching him he abandoned his canoe and took to the Cypress swamp. My object was to cut him off and cause him to surrender, as soon as I came within hail I directed my interpreter to say that we were friends and would not hurt him. This he disregarded when I fired upon him but without effect. My command entered the Swamp for half a mile with great zeal but the water being from three to four feet deep, arms and ammunition wet, pursuit under so many disadvantages would have been fruitless. In this vicinity a canoe trail was discovered through the Willows. Taking with me thirty-four men accompanied by Leiuts. Rodgers and Sprague, leaving the remainder of my command to protect the boats, I entered it and after wading through water four feet deep three quarters of a mile I came to a deserted village of thirteen lodges, upon a small spot of dry land in the midst of a Cypress swamp. Following up the hard beaten trail leading from it I again entered a deep Cypress swamp of about one mile when I again struck dry land. Here I found another village of twelve lodges, deserted, and two extensive corn and pumpkin fields in a high state of cultivation, these I destroyed. The beaten track from this village led into a Cypress Swamp but from the depth of the water I was unable to follow it. I found many other canoe trails many months old, one, more fresh than the others I took, which led me to an old town of twelve lodges and fields of pumpkins. I caused everything to be destroyed, which could possibly be of use to the enemy. The approaches to these locations were very difficult, accessible only by boats through winding passages of thick willows, and were doubtless once the strong hold of a large body of Indians. These places having been recently inhabited only as the resort of a few straggling Indians who sought them for subsistence and protection. At two spots on the right bank of the river I destroyed Camps of three and four lodges which were the resorts for making coonty. After forcing my way through a narrow passage of the river I entered into a Lake of clear water one and a half miles in diameter, surrounded by swamps; on a point extending into the lake I destroyed a small pumpkin and corn field. There being no lodges about it, and a vast Swamp extending in its rear with a lake in front is a strong evidence that the Indians plant in one place and live in another. Today I made but eight and a half miles, my command being much fatigued from the heat of the day and wading in water. Upon my route down today, the Second instant, the river assumed a more decided character. The clear portion of the Stream was about ten yards wide, then came thick grass which bordered the dense Cypress swamps which line the bank from two to four miles in width. I found many Islands which in dry seasons were habitable. I explored them but found no traces whatever of habitation. A canoe was pulled up and turned over upon one, but from its decayed state it had been there months. I discovered two high bluffs upon which were many old Indian sheds which were doubtless once the resting places of Indians up and down the river. For the first time since my first day of starting I was enabled to find pine land. This was a point of the river where once had been an Indian village, many trails were leading from it, but all very old. The river from this point to Camp Izard is very rapid confining itself most of the way to one Stream. Below this point there are fordable rapids, Varying in depth from one to two feet which terminate three miles above Camp Izard, with Sandy bluffs and pine lands. Lieut. Callender[434] arrived the same evening which enabled me to rejoin you at Fort Cooper with my boats on the third instant. The distance from Fort Dade to Camp Izard by water is Seventy miles. In accomplishing this distance I endeavoured to comply with my instructions but from the inaccuracies in the map and the want of a guide acquainted with the country, I found great difficulty in finding any point or at any time knowing my position. I am satisfied there is no entrance from the Wythlacoochee into Charlo Popka. There are numerous fords on this river coming from the main land, crossing small streams and numerous Islands. The whole country bordering the river from Fort Dade to within twenty miles of Camp Izard is a continuation of Swamps, hammocks, Cypress and Willow Islands, and the whole route I did not find one acre of land which was habitable for a White man. This portion of the river if it can be called such, is but a succession of Lakes bearing North and North West. Below this point to Camp Izard it bears west and assumes the character of a river. Indains in large numbers have been in the vicinity within the last year, but at present there are but few, whose location cannot be found. I am greatly indebted for the services of Lt. Rogers & Lt. Sprague who voluntarily offered to accompany me on the expedition.

I have the honor to be
with great respect
Your obt Servt
C. R. Gates
1 Lt 8 Inf.

To:
Lt. Colonel W. S. Clarke
Comdg. Tampa District

# Winding Down the War In Southeast Florida: Fort Lauderdale in 1841

The summer of 1841 was hot and brutal. For the first time in the history of the Second Seminole War (1835-1842) the United States Army, under the command of Colonel William Jenkins Worth, had conducted a summer campaign against an evasive Indian foe. All other campaigns previous to this were conducted during the cooler, dryer periods from the late fall until the late spring. No one, not even the intrepid United States Deputy Surveyors, ventured into the swamps of Florida during the "sickly" season, when the tepid airs of the "miasma" rose from the wet ground to kill and incapacitate those who ventured inland from the coasts. The summer of 1841 was no different in that respect.

Colonel Worth was well aware of the effects of the weather upon his troops. Discounting the prevailing medical theories of the day and the advice of his own medical corps, this protegé of General Winfield Scott ordered the troops into the fields. He did this because he felt it necessary to end the war and was under heavy pressure to do so. He also felt that the losses would justify the expense, as he noted to the Adjutant General of the Army, Roger Jones:

> It stands thus then; there is much & distressing sickness and deaths, (people die every where) but the burden of the afflictions grows out of garrison service: The cause, absence

of mental & physical excitement, heavy food in excess & greater facilities for inordinate indulgence.

Putting the troops in the field would lessen the negative affects of garrison duty. It would also have the benefit of placing the enemy on notice that no season would be safe; that the army would and could capture and kill at any season. Carrying the war into the enemy's territory in the "sickly" season would add to the destruction of crops and disorient them. It would, in the humble opinion of Colonel Worth, shorten the war.[435] Ending the war was something his more illustrious predecessors could not do. Therefore, the health costs to the troops would be minimal when compared to ending the conflict, already in its sixth year.

Not every officer stationed in Florida agreed with Worth. After campaigning all summer in the stifling heat and dampness and not finding a single Indian, Captain John Rogers Vinton had his doubts, especially after facing his "enormous sick lists".[436] Vinton, a strong-willed, pious veteran of the Florida campaigns, noted the loss of troops, the frustrations of camp life, the tensions of daily campaigning and the lack of advancement as reasons for doubting the validity of hunting such an elusive enemy during the torrid Florida summers. The service during the summer of 1841 had already caused him to "suffer some relaxation" in his usual zeal for campaigning. As he prepared to move southward, in late fall of 1841, he could only reflect that he had the good fortune to be serving under Brevet Major Thomas Childs, a man whose fortunes had enjoyed a favorable turn during the summer campaign.[437]

Childs was another gritty veteran of the War of 1812 who had served many years on the northern frontier before his long stint in the Florida service. He had entered the U. S. Military Academy in 1813 and, with the immediate need for trained officers during the War of 1812, he was graduated after less than one year's classes. Childs was promoted into the army as a Third Lieutenant on March 11, 1814, and was directly ordered to the Niagara frontier, arriving in time to participate in the capture of Fort Erie. He also had a role in the Battle of Niagara (July 25, 1814) and was heavily involved in the defense of Fort Erie as a Second Lieutenant of the Corps of Artillery. After the war he remained in New York and received his promotion to First Lieutenant in 1818. Eight years later he received another promotion to Captain while on garrison duty at Fort Washington, Maryland. After an extended tour of duty on the Maine frontier, the Massachusetts born Captain was rushed to Florida in early 1836, in time to participate in the attack on Fort Drane and Osceola's band of Seminoles (in northern Marion County, Florida). For this action he received the rank of Brevet Major. With the exception of a short tour in the recruiting service, he spent almost the entire period of the Second Seminole War in Florida's heat, swamps and wet prairies.[438]

Vinton had noted Childs' "good fortune" in hunting the Seminoles and their allies during the summer campaign, but it was accomplished under great strain and persistent pursuit. Childs had been the officer responsible, under direct orders from General Walker Armistead, then commanding in Florida, for the capture of Coacoochee, his brother and the brother of King Philip, all under a flag of truce. For this act Childs received some condemnation in the national press, although most Floridians rejoiced at the news.[439] Childs failed to capture the rest of the band at that time, most fleeing to the adjacent Everglades. The Major then ordered portions of the Third Artillery, which he commanded in East Florida, into the Everglades. On the 25th of June, 1841, Captain Martin Burke received orders to lead his men, fifty-three in number, in boats, from Fort Dallas on a "search and destroy" mission to the "islands" of the Everglades. Burke's force failed to capture any of the enemy, however, it did destroy numerous fields of crops, recently abandoned. The mission also gave Worth and Childs intelligence that the Seminoles and their allies were on the move in the Everglades, in small, separated parties.[440] For the remainder of the summer, troops under Childs, in conjunction with the naval forces under Lieutenant John T. McLaughlin, of the famous "Mosquito Fleet," moved constantly across the Everglades from posts in southern Florida.[441] As Worth's Aide-de-Camp (and later son-in-law), Lieutenant John T. Sprague noted, "The past, however, taught one thing not to be mistaken, though painful and revolting - that the Indian's ally was the summer season."[442] This ally had to be overcome, along with the enemy's forces, if the war was to be brought to a conclusion. Hence, the need for the expeditions of Burke, McLaughlin and the others.

The corps of the Third Artillery was stationed with Childs at Fort Pierce as the fall campaign of 1841 began. Using a number of intelligence sources, Childs formulated a plan of attack along the eastern coast south of his position. The Major ordered Virginia-born Lieutenant Edward J. Steptoe south with fifty men in eight boats to explore the branches of the "Alleatsokee" River, going as far up these forks as possible with the boats.[443]   The Lieutenant did as ordered and also found that within five miles of the head of the "right" branch was General Eustis' trail, made during the Jesup campaign of 1837-38. Just prior to Steptoe's return, Childs received intelligence from the captain of the steamboat *Gaston* that this man had observed a vessel landing "two barrels of beef" which was quickly retrieved by twenty Indians on the beach. Captain Richard D. A. Wade 3rd Artillery, had been assigned to scout this area, but because he was still in the Everglades near Lake Okeechobee, he was not expected to reach this spot on the beach quickly enough to capture this band of warriors.[444]   Childs decided to take Steptoe's command and companies commanded by Lieutenants Edward O. C. Ord, Thomas W. Sherman and George Taylor southward in an attempt to seize this band of the enemy.[445]   The total command entering this expedition consisted of five officers and eighty enlisted men in thirteen boats. They left Fort Pierce on September 6, 1841.[446]

Childs' command went into the Atlantic at Jupiter Inlet and followed the coast southward for twenty miles, with a parallel company on land to look for the haulover into the "Hillsborough Lagoon." Much to the Major's surprise he found a freshwater lake thirteen miles long and one to two and a half miles wide [Lake Worth]. The southern outlet of this lake was covered in sawgrass and impassable for the boats. He estimated that this lake was fifteen miles from the actual Hillsborough Lagoon laid down on his inaccurate map. Using his field glasses he espied a number of small islands in the lake which, upon examination, contained only one dwelling and a corn field. However, on the sea coast side of the lake the Major's force discovered, "extensive fields of corn, pumpkins, potatoes, the Indian pea, melons, tobacco, rice & sugar cane in the highest state of cultivation." These the Major ordered destroyed. He described the entire coastal length as being a continuous field broken by sawgrass and bushes, but all connected by a trail. Form an observation tree, it was obvious that his command had been spotted coming down the coast. There were no Indians to be found. The Major's command spent five days on the lake destroying the "luxuriant fields," which he estimated would yield over two thousand bushels of potatoes and several hundred bushels of corn. It took eighty men two full days to destroy these crops. Childs felt that this was a heavy blow to the Indian's supply base.[447]

Within days of Childs' expedition, Captain Burke left Fort Dallas and repaired to Fort Lauderdale, assuming temporary command there. He reported leaving this post on September 3rd with one-hundred and seventeen men, six officers and two additional men brought along to fill out the boat companies. Following New River into the Everglades, the command soon spotted a new boat trail in the sawgrass leading to one of the numerous small islands. The Indians, Burke surmised, had spotted the command and fled into the adjacent swamp, leaving behind one rifle, two canoes, a small skiff, and most of their camp utensils, including numerous blankets. The tools for harvesting coontie and making it into starch were also abandoned in their haste and these were destroyed by the troops. Following their "squaw guide", the command continued on toward Lake Okeechobee. Noticing smoke in the distance, Captain Burke assumed the smoke was a warning to other Indians of their presence. The guide told them that it was a signal to gather the women and children, but not a warning. Discounting the guide's explanation, Burke ordered his troops further into the glades toward the smoke. Approaching the lake from its southern extremities, Burke's men soon spotted two Indians on the shore, calling upon them to land. The Captain was suspicious of such a call and told the interpreter to ask them to come forward under the assurance of safe conduct. They came and told Burke that they were the Indians on the island the day before. They had recently come from the Big Cypress [South of the Caloosahatchee River], via Fisheating Creek and had gone to all of the usual places and islands. These contained no food or other sustenance for the Indians themselves. They were in want of food and were willing to leave Florida, being tired of running and in constant fear of capture or death. When these "captives" were pressed for the whereabouts of Sam Jones, they remarked that the last they knew he had gone to the hunting grounds, south of Fort Dallas, Burke's point of departure.[448]

By the eighth of September, Burke's command was scouting the southern shore of Lake Okeechobee, arriving at an old palmetto fortification [Fort McRae]. After failing to meet the two warriors who had agreed to bring in their women and children, Burke ordered a scout of the southern rim of the lake, taking three days provisions to sustain the troops. They had not left the stockade more than four hours when the boats were hit by a quick moving storm from across the lake, rapidly driving the vessels ashore. Luckily, none of the provisions or men were lost in this storm. On advice from the squaw guide, Burke reasoned that they were at least five days from Fort Dallas. Judging the stores on hand to last at least eight days, Burke went south to find the outlet of "Incha-Hatchee" which led from the southern end of Lake Okeechobee into the Everglades. Failing, however, to find this outlet, the command was forced to find another way back to Fort Dallas. Finding another, easier, route with fewer haulovers, the entire command arrived back at Fort Lauderdale on the afternoon of September 16th, all provisions having been exhaustted. They returned the next day to Fort Dallas via the inland route through the Rio Ratones [Snake Creek]. Only one warrior returned with Burke, but he was "willing and anxious" to act as a guide for the troops.[449]

About the same time Burke was returning to Fort Dallas, a report reached Fort Lauderdale from a local wrecker who reported seeing two men, who looked like Indians, along the beach, south of New River Inlet. Captain Richard Wade, commanding at Fort Lauderdale, immediately sent a force under Lieutenant Francis O. Wyse, numbering twenty-five men in canoes, to the scene.[450] Wyse's men arrived too late to capture the enemy, but found a fresh trail which was followed for several miles. Signs left by the two men indicated to Wyse that they may return to the Inlet. Wyse decided to stay the night near the Inlet, but in order to cut off all retreat, he sent a messenger back to Fort Lauderdale, advising Wade to send troops to "Lake Tompkins".[451] The troops dispatched by Wade to Lake Tompkins left Fort Lauderdale at 3 o'clock in the morning and arrived about sunrise. Examining the eastern shore of the lake produced no evidence or recent signs, but the southern end of the lake held more promise. Led by the intrepid Lieutenant George H. Thomas [later famous to history as the "Rock of Chickamauga"], the command proceeded to follow in its canoes an old creek leading from the southern extremity. This lead was followed for three to four miles until the mangroves, which had been earlier cut by the Indians, crowded in so as to block further passage. Thomas observed no recent signs or improvements in this secluded waterway and concluded his difficult search when "the only axe we had" was lost overboard.[452] Meanwhile, Wyse waited in vain at the Inlet for the two men to return.

Throughout the month of October 1841, the troops under the command of Major Childs, now numbering eight companies of the 3rd Artillery, were on the move in the Everglades.[453] Captain Burke made one of the more memorable scouts of the southern war when he traversed the Everglades. In cooperation with Naval Lieutenant (soon to be Captain) John T. McLaughlin, Burke reached "Chikkos Island" on the 11th of October. The combined force numbered two-hundred and sixty men. This group arrived at the "Lower Landing" on the 14th, later than they had anticipated. Returning to a point between Shark River and the position supposed to be northeast of Fort Harrold, the troops paddled and slogged their way up innumerable inlets, lagoons and sloughs, one taking three quarters of the day to traverse. They did not reach the Everglades proper until the 19th of the month. On this day they first cited the enemy and gave chase. The result was the capture of only one canoe. The entire country was covered with water and trails were difficult to locate. Nine days later the entire command arrived at Punta Rassa, near the mouth of the Caloosahatchee River. On the 2nd of November, the order was given for Burke's command to return to Fort Dallas via the Caloosahatchee River, Lake Okeechobee to the Loxahatchee River and down the coast. According to John T. Sprague, this expedition caused, "much apprehension in the Big Cypress Swamp," and showed the enemy that a large force was capable of reaching anywhere in the Everglades at any time of the year. The only physical result of the expedition was the destruction of a large number of Indian huts and corn fields.[454] The reason for the cross-peninsula return, improbable as it may seem, was to possibly catch Sam Jones' group by surprise, since he had been reported in the

Loxahatchee area again. Like so many such reports of his where abouts, it proved to be false and the exhausted troops marched into Fort Jupiter nearly spent.[455]

By November, Major Childs had put into motion a large number of scouts and had brought the troops from Fort New Smyrna, under Captain Vinton, to Fort Lauderdale. The most successful of these scouts was led by Captain Richard Wade, who had left Fort Lauderdale and headed northward with three officers and sixty enlisted men in twelve canoes. In his report, Captain Wade noted, "We proceeded by the inland passage to the northward, coming out in the bay at the Hillsborough Inlet, and in such manner that our canoes were concealed from the view of an Indian, whom I there discovered fishing on the Northern point of the inlet; I made the requisite dispositions immediately to land, and succeeded in surprising him."[456] Wade, "operating on his hopes and fears," persuaded the frightened man to lead them to his encampment, which was surrounded and assaulted by the troops. The result was the capture of twenty more Indians and the killing of eight others who had attempted to escape. Following a small stream as far as possible, the command encamped. One of the prisoners, the noted guide, Chia-chee (often referred to as simply Chi), led the force to another village on the following day which resulted in the capture of an additional twenty-seven Indians and the destruction of a "large quantity of provisions." The soldiers then continued northward to Lake Worth, "where we found and destroyed a canoe, a field of pumkins, and an old hut." One additional Indian surrendered to Wade before his triumphal return to Fort Lauderdale. Upon his return, Wade allowed Chia-chee to return to the swamps and bring in a further six Indians. Wade's recapitulation showed a total of eight Indians killed, fifty-five captured and many provisions and other materials destroyed. The expedition's most important gain, however, was the acquisition of a reliable guide, who remained such throughout the remainder of the war.[457]

Major Childs was pleased with the results of Wade's actions and noted that he was assisted by Lieutenants Thomas and Ord and Assistant Surgeon Emerson.[458] Not everyone had such a glowing opinion of the operation. Captain John Rogers Vinton emphasized the role of luck and good fortune more than the abilities of those involved. "The public prints", he noted, had praised the success of Colonel Worth's entire operation and, in the usual fashion, had failed to see his faults. In this treatment, the press was repeating what it had done with every new leader who commanded in the swamps of Florida. Stating that he believed Worth a man deserving of success, for his zeal and spirit, he warned of the fates of the others before him. He concluded by declaring the war "is but a hunt after all," and that accident had as much to do with success as thorough planning and execution. Wade, he believed, had the "good fortune" to have the advice and assistance of at least twenty others. His luck was due to this outside aid more than Wade's personal attributes, zeal or military ability.[459] Vinton, it will be recalled, had been on numerous scouts without ever encountering the enemy, thus being deprived of a chance for glory or promotion.

Vinton's command had evacuated Fort New Smyrna on the 1st of November and proceeded southward, arriving at Fort Lauderdale on the November 5, 1841. By this time, Wade had already left the fort and headed northward on the scout reported above. Immediately, Vinton was advised by the Captain Cooper of the local schooner, *Francis*, that he had seen two Indians near the mouth of the Hillsborough, apparently gesturing to the schooner to come ashore. Vinton quickly dispatched Lieutenant William Harvey Churchill to the scene.[460] After marching twelve to fourteen miles to the place describe by Captain Cooper, Lieutenant Churchill found evidence of three Indians on the beach, two large and one small, possibly a child. The tracks were followed in the not so romantic moonlight until they terminated on the south shore of the Hillsborough Inlet. Having no means of crossing the inlet, and knowing that Wade's forces were in the area, the troops returned to Fort Lauderdale. There was no speculation as to the reason these Indians would expose themselves to capture on the beach this close to an active military post.[461]

While Vinton, Churchill and Wade were occupied with their endeavors, Lieutenant Francis O. Wyse was headed back to Lake Worth to destroy more of the fields on the western shore. The large number of fields, especially on the eastern margins of the lake, indicates the fertility of the area which, in later years, attracted some of the pioneers of southern Florida. It also shows the lack of accurate geographic knowledge the army actually possessed about this vicinity. Given the activities of the army during the campaigns of 1837, 1838 and 1839, this fact is surprising. Wyse's scout, operating in less of an informational vacuum, produced no prisoners or enemy casualties, only the destruction of an isolated field.[462]

Major Thomas Childs, like many of his fellow commanders, had only one real goal for his campaigns of 1841: the capture of the elusive Sam Jones and his followers. Almost every major move of the 3rd Artillery was dictated by the supposed or rumored whereabouts of this Native American master of guerrilla warfare. Abiaka's dictation of the army's movements indicates the power of the near obsession of the army with his capture or destruction. Almost every piece of correspondence from Childs denotes this. Concerning the destruction of the fields at Lake Worth: "My opinion," Childs wrote, "is that these fields belonged to Sam Jones & his party & that Indians were sent from Okeechobee to tend them."[463]    Burke's expedition into the Everglades included the capture of an Indian who, "I think will be invaluable if an expedition goes again to the Everglades for Sam Jones."[464] When Chia-chee (or "George" as the Major referred to him) was brought in, the determined Childs rewarded him with a bag containing one hundred dollars to guarantee his faithfulness to the army, even though "George", the Major reported, "cannot say where Sam [Jones] is, but some where in the Everglades."

His interviews with the others captured with Chia-chee proved equally fruitless. "Thus far," he recorded, "I have not been able to gather any information as to Sam Jones' whereabouts. They say they have not seen him for a long time." But, he continued, "I am trying to ingratiate myself into their confidence & in a few days I hope to find out how much they know. I would not advise these Indians to be removed from this so long as there is any hope of bringing in others."[465]    This tactic, like all others for gaining access to Sam Jones, ended in failure. Captain Vinton had informed Childs just two days prior to the above letter that this group of Indians had reported Sam Jones and forty-five warriors were on an island in the Everglades. However, Childs did not take heed of this and vowed, "to make a dash at Sam Jones wherever I may find him with as gallant a set of officers & soldiers as ever invaded the Everglades."

208

but Childs had one fear, that Wade's successful capture of the fifty-five would induce Sam Jones to remove further into the Everglades to another of his unknown havens.[466]

The compulsion to bring in the evasive leader and his followers gave rise to interesting and continual speculation. Whether reading the papers of Captain Vinton, the narrative of John T. Sprague or the letters of the commanders, it is hard to escape the conclusion that this wily leader had his enemies totally confused and baffled. Following reports of Jones being in the vicinity of the Loxahatchee River, troops of the 3rd Artillery were poured into the area. News that he was headed for or in the Big Cypress led Colonel Worth to order troops under Major William Belknap, Captain McLaughlin and Major Childs to converge on that region. When the expeditions under Captains Rogers and Burke had covered portions of this ground, the speculation was that Jones had fled to the prairies of the Kissimmee or southward toward Fisheating Creek. As Childs proffered again, "I think it important that troops be sent to the Kissimmee, to which place Sam Jones will probably go if routed out of the Locha-Hatchee."[467] The evasive tactics used in the midst of the uncharted wilderness of southern Florida by Jones, following the pattern set by Coacoochee, Osceola, Tiger-Tail, Alligator, King Philip, Octiarche and numerous others during this war was simply too much for those trained in set-piece military theory to handle. To their credit, the campaigns of Worth and Childs were relatively appropriate adjustments to these tactics.

An additional point does need emphasis here. The army was heavily handicapped, from an offensive orientation, by the lack of accurate geographical knowledge of South Florida. This woeful weakness of the military should not surprise us when we reflect that the best known map of the era, that of John Lee Williams (1837) does *not* show Lake Okeechobee. From what has already been written above, it will be recalled that Lake Worth was not on the charts provided to Major Childs. This virtual storehouse of agricultural supplies for the Seminoles and their allies was unrecorded on any map of the time, even though a major battle had been fought under General Thomas Jesup on the banks of the nearby Loxahatchee River. It is clear that this important area was ignored and not scouted by the army prior to the arrival of the 3rd Artillery in

1841. These examples could be multiplied in nearly every region of Florida, including the vicinity west of Tallahassee, where the last of the "renegade Creeks" under Pascoffer surrendered to Captain Ethan Allen Hitchcock in January of 1843, nearly five months after the conclusion of the war.[468] This lack of specific geographical knowledge greatly injured the army's attempts to capture and deport the agile and elusive Seminoles and their allies from the swamps of Florida.

The army was not unaware of this weakness, which greatly explains its efforts to co-opt captives at every opportunity. In the case of Chia-chee, as noted above, he was given one hundred dollars to remain loyal and lead the troops into the unknown reaches of the Everglades in the pursuit of Sam Jones. Immediately after his capture, this reliable guide led Lieutenant Wyse to the other planting grounds and villages on the western shore of Lake Worth.[469] When the Prophet was rumored to be leaving the Big Cypress for a lake guarded by mangroves near Key Biscayne, Chia-chee was officially noticed by Colonel Worth as the most reliable source to explain how to attack that position.[470] At this point in time, Chia-chee had been assigned as guide to the "Mosquito Fleet" forces under Captain John T. McLaughlin. Worth also relied upon Chia-chee's advice to inform Major Belknap of the most likely locations to find the Prophet in the Big Cypress.[471] Although this reliance upon one guide was unusual, Chia-chee had proven himself to Worth and Childs, and his knowledge and advice were eagerly sought.

Other sources of intelligence were also taken seriously and when information came that Sam Jones was definitely on the Loxahatchee, troops from Fort Lauderdale were dispatched to the vicinity. Unfavorable December weather forced a delay in the movements of the force under Captain Wade. Wade's assignment was to scour the area along the coast, past Lake Worth and toward the headwaters of the Loxahatchee River. He was then to descend the river and scout along the way to Fort Jupiter, before heading back to Fort Lauderdale. Wade's movements were to be timed to coincide with a more westerly route taken by troops under the command of Captain Vinton. Even with the aid of "two good guides" Wade could not control the weather and the two forces essentially operated independent of each other. This created a gap through which, if

210

needed, Sam Jones and his band could easily have escaped detection.[472]

John Rogers Vinton was elated to have a chance to pursue Sam Jones. Writing from Fort Lauderdale on November 29, 1841, Vinton informed his constant correspondent, his mother, of his most recent illness and incapacity, noting that it had prevented his partaking of the most recent movements by Major Childs. Yet, he was excited to be in all the "bustle & enterprise of an active campaign." His long duty at Fort New Smyrna, while not totally devoid of action, was less active than posts like Fort Lauderdale, further southward. Vinton felt that the upcoming campaign was vital for the 3rd Artillery in that unless the Indians were captured and removed, the regiment would be stuck in Florida indefinitely.[473] By the 15th of December, Vinton was writing home to inform his family that he was just leaving Fort Lauderdale and that his command numbered one hundred and twenty men in nineteen boats. The goal was the usual one, the capture of "the old fox" Sam Jones.[474] Once again, Captain Vinton was to be disappointed in the results of his efforts, noting, "it has not been my good fortune to meet & capture Sam Jones." The dejected Captain could only speculate as to his time of departure from Florida and complain about the sameness of the Florida landscape.[475] However, for John Rogers Vinton, his active campaigning in Florida was over. He soon shipped out to Georgia and points more northerly.

Vinton's route, if such it can be called, was up the western side of the waters of Lake Worth to the Loxahatchee River (where he was scheduled to meet Captain Wade) and thence westerly over the wet prairies of the "Halpatioka" swamp, west of Fort Pierce. Guided by "old Georgy" and Johnny Tigertail, with Negro John as his interpreter, Vinton was sure he would meet with success. But as the days wore on and the waters of the swamps got cooler, Vinton's forces were forced to find whatever signs they could and follow them to their conclusions. The only "capture" was the Indian known as Katsa Micco, "a wild & eccentric Character, associated with no party - though an actual relative of Sam Jones himself." West of Fort Pierce, the command did find some villages, abandoned, but still occasionally farmed. Some of the islands in this swamp contained old camp sites, with old canoes and some more or less wild crops still producing (all of which were destroyed). Vinton's last campaign in Florida was to find only old camps, worn out tools, and one semi-exiled Indian.[476] Held up by winds, rising water, numerous cypress swamps and low marsh, Captain Richard Wade fared no better.[477] The last major scouts from Fort Lauderdale had proven barren of results.

Neither Childs, Worth, Vinton, Wade or McLaughlin ever found or captured the elusive Sam Jones. As the war wound down and the eastern posts, like Fort Lauderdale, were abandoned, there was no word of his capture or whereabouts. Indian guides, upon whose advice so much depended in the absence of accurate maps, had failed to lead the army to its goal. Communication with Sam Jones was effectively precluded, as Childs informed Worth: "All the Indians refuse to go to Sam Jones they say if they know where he was they would not dare to go, as he would kill them, this in view of a bag of dollars I exhibited belonging to the Q'master."[478] No inducement could persuade the guides to take the army to Sam Jones. With poor, inaccurate maps, very reluctant guides, a Congress eager to end a political nightmare and thousands of troops broken or dead, it was time for another solution. The result was the continued freedom of a small number of Seminoles, Miccosukees, escaped African-Americans and other "remnants" left in the vastness of the uncharted lands of South Florida.

# Cantonment Morgan:
# Cedar Keys 1841-1843

Fort Armistead stood on the shores of lovely Sarasota Bay overlooking the tranquil waters of the Gulf of Mexico. It was situated high enough to catch most of the daily on-shore breezes and had a fine source of fresh water not far away. Named for the commanding general in Florida at the time, Walker K. Armistead, it had all the markings of a successful location for a permanent fortification. Occupied in early 1841 by the forces of the First U. S. Infantry, it was commanded by the capable veteran of the War of 1812, William Davenport. The commanding officer had paid his dues in the service of the country, and even though he did not attend the Military Academy at West Point he had commanded men in some of the toughest terrains. Davenport had been raised to the colonelcy in 1838. What more could be asked for from a finely situated post and a fine commanding officer?

One of the primary problems was the quality of the recruits sent to the frontier as replacements for casualties, resignations and discharges. The frequent letters from all front line commanders during these difficult years of the Second Seminole War (1835-1842) indicated that many of the recruits were not officially sworn into the service until they reached the far flung outposts of the frontier.[479] By the time they arrived they were debilitated and discouraged and often deserted at the first opportunity. Many were physically unfit for any kind of service and were rejected by the boards of administration made up of officers and physicians at the time of their arrival. A large number were recruited right off the boat from whatever their homeland was and shuffled off into the service of their new country. A great percentage of these recruits could not speak English. As Colonel Davenport acknowledged, "May of these men are Germans & Hollanders and entirely ignorant of the English language, but this objection will become less every day, & I am well aware that it is difficult to fill the ranks of the Army without receiving such men."[479]

Recruits, raw and untrained, were a difficult problem but minor compared to the problems of disease. This was a day and age when physicians worried more about "miasma" and damp, rainy weather than with the actual causes of the fevers that killed so many. Nothing was known about germs or viruses or how they were transmitted. Infection and sterilization were concepts not yet fully grasped. The only thing done to prevent the spread of disease was to move the garrison to another location and bury the dead far from the site. In mid-February 1841, Davenport was stricken by the "fever & Ague" and had not the strength to even sign his name to official reports. By the end of April of that year, Fort Armistead numbered over two hundred men on its sick list.[480] The number of healthy men able to maintain the routine of scouts and garrison duty was not sufficient to accomplish these tasks. Something had to be done if these men were to survive. The only solution offered by the medical practice of the day was to remove the garrison to a healthier place.

There was one additional problem that commanders of posts often ascribed to outsiders: alcohol. Fort Armistead could be reached by land or sea and was open to the evil influences of nearby Fort Brooke (Tampa). Nearly every commander in Florida (and everywhere else) had problems with this age-old evil. On 27 February 1841, Davenport wrote Acting Adjutant General G. Bliss that a certain Captain Babcock of the Schooner *Van Buren* was illegally delivering alcoholic beverages to the garrison. Indeed, the vessel contained only twenty-six barrels of whiskey, while both the consignment sheet and the collector of customs showed that twenty-eight barrels had entered port. One barrel was sold to the officers of the post, but the other was alleged to have been sold to either common soldiers or the Indians, both of which were prohibited from having liquor in their possession. Davenport ordered the cargo seized and held in the public stores until proper legal authorities could handle the disposition of the remaining twenty-six barrels. The irate Colonel even boldly declared that, "a large part of the Garrison at Fort Brooke being constantly kept in a state of intoxication and thus rendered perfectly incapable of any service, besides being prostrated by disease induced by this continued debauch." [481] Davenport was not going to allow such a state of affairs to continue. Thus the wily veteran had two very logical reasons for transferring the garrison to a more healthy environment.

On 5 May 1841 the garrison of Fort Armistead left the confines of Sarasota Bay and headed northward. The afternoon of the following day found them at the "Outer Key" in the Cedar Keys group. The regiment had listed with it two hundred and five sick men and the hospital equipment. The island was high and dry and appeared pure. It was hoped that this location would bring better health to the soldiers. Because they came direct from the mainland they had nothing for cover except the tents, many of which were old and dry rotted. They did find some fresh water on the island but the cautious Colonel decided to sink a well for better quality water. Colonel Davenport and his unhealthy regiment even contemplated being sent to a northern assignment to improve the well being of the troops. [482]

"The post which I am about establishing on the Island," wrote Colonel Davenport, "with the hope of restoring the Corps I have called Cantonment Morgan after our late commander."[483] The reference here is to Willoughby Morgan, Colonel of the First Infantry Regiment who passed away on 4 April 1832. Colonel Morgan was another of the War of 1812 veterans to rise in the ranks of the U. S. Army. Like Davenport and most of the leadership of the U. S. military, he had been appointed during that war and remained in the army following the inevitable retrenchment Congress demanded after each war. He was a career infantry man and was apparently well-respected by his peers.

It should be remembered that the U. S. Army was less than ten thousand men when the Second Seminole War broke out and this limited force had to cover the volatile Texas border, a line of fortifications stretching to Minnesota and all of the newly established coastal batteries. Almost every commander and all of the upper level officers received their training under fire during the War of 1812. Included in this list of outstanding military talent were Thomas Jesup, Winfield Scott, Zachary Taylor and William Jenkins Worth. The two former were to remain on the scene until the outbreak of the Civil War and all were to command the forces in Florida during the Second Seminole War.

By the end of May, Davenport was asking for a leave of absence, having served in the field continuously for over two years. Always the commander to look to the health of his troops, he requested that his leave not be granted until the quarters at Cedar Key (on Seahorse Key) were suitable and the hospital in good shape. Also in the Colonel's thinking was getting leave to visit St. Louis (Jefferson Barracks) and inquiring about making his brevet rank permanent. The idea of being out of touch with the politics of the military establishment was grating on the nerves of nearly every officer who served in Florida, and Davenport was particularly interested in maintaining his contacts. His wish was soon granted and the regiment was sent northward to Jefferson Barracks in July of 1841. [484]

Cantonment Morgan was reoccupied by Companies D and K of the Sixth Infantry in August under the command of Captain William Hoffman. The New York born Hoffman was a career military man and graduated from West Point in the class of 1829. With one short break (in 1852) Hoffman served most of his career with the Sixth Infantry until just prior to the Civil War, when he was promoted to Lieutenant Colonel with the Eighth Infantry. He was the son of Lieutenant Colonel William Hoffman who served in the War of 1812 on the Niagara frontier. Captain Hoffman's career lasted forty years and saw him serving with distinction in the Mexican War (Brevet Major for Gallant and Meritorious Service at Battles of Contreras and Churubusco and a Brevet Lieutenant Colonel for service in Molino del Rey), on the frontier during the Sioux Campaign of 1855 and in the Utah Expedition during the "Mormon War" in 1858. At the outbreak of the Civil War he was in San Antonio, Texas when General David Twiggs surrendered the forces to the Texas army. He was not exchanged until August 1862, when he was assigned to the Commissary Generalship for prisoners in the Washington area, providing food and sustenance to

216

keep them alive. He resigned from the army on May 1, 1870, having served steadily since his graduation in 1829. William Hoffman was a brave and steady commander, especially during his career in Florida where so many careers were ruined or side-tracked.[485]

The transfer of the First Infantry to St. Louis and the movement of the Sixth Infantry to Cantonment Morgan created problems of another sort. Who was to be the fort's sutler? Often lost in the annals of history is the role played by the post sutler. These intrepid entrepreneurs of the frontier provided the soldiers with goods not provided for by the army. Things like sewing needles, civilian style clothing, exotic fruits or fresh vegetables, basic furniture and treats for the children. For all of these things and more, the soldier and his family (if he brought them along) looked to the sutler for provisioning. During the Seminole Wars the army bid out these contracts to various individuals (often former army officers) and assigned them to a regiment. The problem faced by the sutler was the division of these regiments to various outposts. If only part of the regiment remained in the Territory of Florida and the other part out of the region, where did the sutler establish his store? When a unit was shipped out to another state or territory, how was the sutler to collect his bills? If two different regiments shared a facility or were at forts nearby, which sutler gets the business? With the establishment of Cantonment Morgan on Sea Horse Key and Fort Poinsett at Depot Key, which sutler was to provision these posts? These were the questions that vexed Mr. P. G. Hambaugh who had the contract for the Sixth Infantry. Mr. Hambaugh had to appeal to Secretary of War, John Bell, to get his answers. [486]

1841 is one of the more interesting years in the history of the Florida wars with the Seminoles. In July of that year, Colonel William Jenkins Worth assumed command of the forces in the Territory and immediately began pushing the troops into the field. His first goal was to remove the Indians from the "Cove of the Withlacoochee," an ancient and difficult defensive position often assaulted but never "pacified" during the first five years of the war. This involved a controversial summer time campaign into the swamps and bogs of the Withlacoochee River and Lake Tsala Apopka. Worth was undaunted by such a challenge and declared that such a campaign was actually good for the troops, who would otherwise remain at their posts and become bored, dissipated and become more prone to sickness than if they were on active campaign. From a strategic point of view, Worth reasoned that a "search and destroy" style mission would be appropriate with the overall goal of depriving the enemy of his winter crops. Find the villages, capture whomever you can, destroy all foods, planted crops, housing and animals and leave nothing upon which the enemy could rely for the next campaign season. To oversee this movement of his troops, Worth chose Cedar Key to be his base headquarters and for two months commanded the entire Florida war from this post.[487]

Prior to its leaving Florida, the First Infantry had one last campaign into the swamps to further Worth's goal of forcing the Indians from the region. From Cantonment Morgan units were sent out under the command of Captain Albert S. Miller to comb the waters of the Waccasassa River and its tributaries. Captain Joseph H. LaMotte commanded one of the forces that ascended the Waccasassa and Otter Creek. After getting lost trying to find the mouth of the river, LaMotte's command went up the river to the point of entry of Spring Creek. Lamotte took part of the command nine miles up this creek until it gave out in a cabbage swamp. He also explored the Otter Creek until it forked and then followed its branches until they were exhausted. Lieutenant Samuel E. Muse took the remainder of the command and ascended further up the Waccasassa River, which ran into snags of fallen timber, at which point he returned. Lieutenant William Prince was then assigned two boats to attempt to reach Fort Jennings on the Waccasassa River, which he reached after much labor and fatigue. It took Lieutenant Prince's command two and a half days to accomplish this difficult task. After all of this labor and exhaustion the command came back with no news of recent signs of the enemy.[488]

This exploration was preceded by a more recognized reconnaissance of the Crystal and Homosassa Rivers. Again, under the command of Captain Miller, the boats from Cantonment Morgan took their leave and headed south to the mouth of the Crystal River. Leaving the Steamer *Izard*, the command took the Mackinac boats and headed up stream. They went all the way up this famous stream about fifteen miles and met three companies of Captain Hoffman's Sixth Infantry. Scouring the shores of this river produced no recent signs of the Indians and the command headed downstream to find the mouth of the Homosassa River. While going along the inland route one of the boats was struck by lightning. This bolt from the blue killed Lieutenant Job R. H. Lancaster instantly and threw a number of the men overboard into the shallow waters. Captain Miller immediately returned to Cantonment Morgan and delivered the body of Lieutenant Lancaster and the injured men to the hospital. Upon returning to the area he was unable to find the mouth of the Homosassa River and returned with no results. [489]

Captain Hoffman, then stationed at Fort Harrison on Clearwater Harbor, was sent to the Homosassa River in early August, just prior to taking command of Cantonment Morgan. Arriving in the Homosassa River on the morning of 3 August 1841, part of Hoffman's command linked up with that under Captain Thomas J. Alexander and sailed up the river. Hearing dogs barking on the bank in front of them, the troops quietly headed toward the sound. Shots soon rang out and the guide, Colonel Sam Reid of Tallahassee, was just missed. The boats landed quickly and did not fall for the decoying tactics of the men in canoes. The troops immediately began to destroy whatever they found useful. They did not know it at the time, but they had found the main village of Tigertail, the famed Seminole leader in that section of the Territory. Tiger Tail had to watch from a nearby tree as his entire winter supplies were destroyed and trampled by the troops.

The boats descended the river after doing their duty and ran into those headed upstream under the direct command of Captain Hoffman. Hoffman persuaded Captain Alexander that he had not seen the entire river and both re-ascended it to the headwaters of both the Homosassa and Hall's Rivers. Upon returning downstream, they destroyed two smaller villages (as the whites called them) and actually finished the search and destroy mission with better results than even they knew at the time. According to the testimony found in John T. Sprague's classic, *The Origins, Progress and Conclusion of the Florida War*, this mission was the catalyst for the decision of Tigertail and his band to surrender. [490]

The men assigned to man Cantonment Morgan continued to scout along the mainland and search the hinterlands for the Seminoles and their allies. As late as October 1841, the Sixth Infantry controlled the Cantonment and the surrounding area. Fort Poinsett was placed under the control of the commanding officer at Sea Horse Key (Cantonment Morgan) sometime in the latter part of 1841 and was reduced to a storage area for the troops and nearby civilian population centered around Fort No. 4 on the mainland.

Here the number of potential settlers for the area was rapidly rising. By the end of the year, some of these intrepid men and women had moved on toward Chocochatti and Annutiliga Hammocks and along the now-cleared Crystal and Homosassa Rivers. There they soon enjoyed the patronage of Colonel Worth and were well on their way to establishing themselves as communities under the Armed Occupation Act of 1842. Worth had assisted them by providing guns, tents, seeds and other materials whenever possible, until ordered to stop by the Adjutant General's Office on orders from the president. Almost all of the early settlers of the areas named came from Fort No. 4 prior to their removing to their new homes.

Cantonment Morgan was "reoccupied" by troops from the Fourth Infantry on February 25, 1842, even though portions of four companies of the Sixth Infantry were occupying some of the quarters prior to their transshipment to Jefferson Barracks.[491] Commanding the post was Captain Robert Buchanan. According to a letter dated 25 February 1842, a Sergeant, one Corporal and fifteen men were stationed on Depot Key (at old Fort Poinsett) to guard the supplies at this post. This would indicate the falling significance of that installation just prior to the end of the war.[492] At the end of March 1842, Buchanan was ordered to leave one non-commissioned officer and ten men at both Fort No. 4 and Fort Poinsett and proceed with the remainder of his command to Fort Clinch on the Withlacoochee River. Exactly how many men remained at Cantonment Morgan is unknown, however it does not appear as if the post was abandoned. In July a general Courts Martial was held at the post in the case of Lieutenant R. F. Baker of the Seventh Infantry. Such proceedings are seldom held in inactive posts.[493] More important is the fact that this was toward the end of the war and Indians were coming in to all posts to surrender and move west. Major William M. Graham of the Fourth Infantry was in charge at the Cantonment when the question of how to guard these Indians came to the fore.

In an order issued on 11 May 1842, Major Graham was directed to not let any boat land on Sea Horse Key before reveille or after tattoo, "unless an Officer should be on board." All boats were to be under the control of the officer of the day and constantly guarded by a sentinel. Most telling about the preparations for the Indians is the following portion of the order: "He further directs that the Indian camp be kept free of intruders, and that no soldiers be permitted to visit it. Measures will be taken to verify the presence of every male Indian at stated periods, at least twice a day, say morning and evening, which may be conveniently done by the issue of a dram to each on those occasions." Graham was personally ordered to make a close examination of the island and designate a place where advanced pickets could be established so as to prevent the escape of any Indians. It was suggested that the water was shallow enough at low tide to ford over to Deadman's Key and that this might be the most appropriate place to put the picket. Finally, the guard should consist of no less than one Sergeant, one Corporal and twenty men, all chosen for their character and reliability. Such stringent orders indicate the strong desire of the military to get the Indians on to the boats and headed west with as little distraction as possible. [494]

The hospital at Cedar Keys was of importance to the well being of both Indians and soldiers. Some of the Indians became ill with the fever while detained at Sea Horse Key and were treated by the doctors on staff there. Of course, all of the soldiers taken ill or wounded in action were treated there as well. It is interesting to note that a guard was kept at the hospital and that it was supplied by the garrison on the adjacent Key. The muster rolls submitted to the commander show that those who may have belonged in the guard house were often given care at the hospital. The pay of the guards became an issue for Assistant Surgeon Wright in September of 1842. Wright noted that he had followed the practice of his predecessor in filling out the muster forms and that the pay of the guards was to be deducted from the accounts of the post on the adjacent Key, not from his meager accounts.[495]

Nothing in the service in Florida so stands out in the memories of the soldiers as the tropical storms they experienced. On October 5, 1842, a hurricane visited the Cedar Keys and caused great damage. Colonel Josiah H. Vose of the Fourth Infantry had assumed command of the Cantonment and the entire "Military District No. 9" while General Worth was in Washington. In his telling letter of 6 October 1842, Vose described the damage done by the winds, water and tides of this storm. The wind, he observed, was blowing constantly out of the southeast the entire day of 4 October and then shifted in the evening of the following day, all the while increasing in velocity. "The water rose to an unprecedented height," the Colonel declared, "and aided by the force of the wind, carried away houses, trees, boats and in fact every thing which could not be protected against their combined actions." Two steamboats and one small sloop were carried away to the neighboring Key and were smashed against its shore and totally wrecked. The entire store of public property and provisions were lost and no houses were fit to be inhabited. The blacksmith's shop and the carpenter's shop were total losses, including the tools. "Besides these," bemoaned the Colonel, "the Sutler's store and four other buildings occupied by employees of the Government were carried off and today the whole Island presents a scene of unrelieved desolation." Because of the extensive damage and the possibility of another storm doing further harm, Colonel Vose recommended that the Cedar Keys be abandoned and the entire operation moved to the mainland, possibly to Fort Stansbury, southwest of Tallahassee.[496]

Captain John B. Clark, commanding Cantonment Morgan, experienced similar effects. The wharf was totally gone from its position with hardly a mark left to verify its existence. The hospital was damaged beyond repair and was unsafe for use. All of the boats moored there were destroyed as were all of the sheds, guard house and other smaller buildings. Miraculously the Commissary's store remained uninjured. Like its neighboring Key, Sea Horse Key presented a picture of total destruction and ruin. But, as the Captain notes in his report, "Fortunately no lives were lost, and but one man seriously injured."[497]

General Worth returned to the Cedar Keys in November of 1842 to oversee the final operations of the war against the remaining "renegade Creeks". This group, led by Passoffkee, had been leading the army and the Florida volunteers on a merry chase for over six years. The constant raids on isolated settlements and approaches to Tallahassee frightened the Governor so much he felt obliged to request that troops be sent to protect the capital from destruction. It was not until the early part of 1843 that this intrepid warrior and his band of about twenty finally surrendered to Colonel Ethan Allen Hitchcock on the shores of the Ochlockonee River about twenty miles from Tallahassee. With the war over and the destruction of the facilities on Cedar Keys, there was no longer a need for troops to be stationed there. A few settlers from the Fort No. 4 area did, however, remain in the area. Judge Augustus Steele, of Tampa, put in a claim for an Armed Occupation Act permit for Cedar Key. After years of wrangling with the bureaucracy in Washington, Senator David Levy Yulee stepped in and assisted Steele in acquiring the land. The future of the Cedar Keys area was being assured and the next phase of its colorful history was about to be launched on the seas of history.

**Monument to Gen. William Worth,
New York**
*(Harper's Weekly, December 5, 1857)*

# William Jenkins Worth and The Military Colonization Of Florida

"Armed occupation, with land to the occupant, is the true way of settling and holding a conquered country. It is the way which has been followed in all ages, and in all countries, from the time that the children of Israel entered the promised land, with the implements of husbandry in one hand, and the weapons of war in the other. From that day to this, all conquered countries have been settled in that way." It was also the way of the Romans, the Celts, the Gauls, and our pilgrim fathers. So Senator Thomas Hart Benton, the man most responsible for drafting the Armed Occupation Act of 1842, declared to his colleagues in the session of 1840.[498] As the distinguished Senator noted, it had been tried and used by almost every conquering people, including Americans. What he was proposing as early as 1839, was not new and had been discussed in the highest circles of American government prior to its proposal. Many in Florida, especially Governor Richard K. Call, who was one of its original proponents,[499] were almost begging and pleading with the Administration of Martin Van Buren to get it passed.[500]

Colonel James Gadsden, who knew more about the Territory than almost anyone else, wrote in late 1839 to his old friend Major Samuel Cooper, then Assistant Adjutant General in the War Department, asking the pertinent question about the policies concerning the army and the proposed military colonization: "If population & settlement are to finish the work of Indian expulsion for us, surely it is important to preserve those that exist." He further stated that it was imperative that the Regulars and the militia quit fighting amongst themselves before anyone could be asked to risk their lives on the frontier of Florida.[501] Without some notion of security of force or numbers, the experiment, should it be carried forth, would end in miserable failure. Governor Robert Raymond Reid asked the question, "Should not the recompense to her Soldiers be greater than that usually allowed; should there not be an extra pay and bounties in Land for enlistments in the Florida Service; and do not the peculiarities of our condition require the use of blood hounds against the Savages?"[502] On March 14, 1840, Reid again wrote his friend, the Secretary of War, Joel Poinsett, noting the uniqueness of the Florida situation and questioning the sanguine results predicted for the bill:

An armed occupation may be in part, but it can not be wholly successful; ours is not the case of Pioneer driving the enemy from a frontier; from ancient habitations to other and distant homes. Had it been thus, we had so driven them long ago; but the situation in Florida is insular as respects the Indians, & they must be captured, subdued or exterminated. General T [Twiggs] I believe thinks with me, but if the whole army could be thrown into Florida, the end in view might be easily obtained; but if this cannot be done, as I presume it cannot, something practicable should be immediately resorted to, for our relief. But whatever may be the plan adopted, I need not suggest to you, that it must fail, unless carried out by efficient agents.[503]

Perhaps reflecting the majority of opinion at the end of December 1840, a desperate David Levy wrote to the Secretary, as a fellow Van Burenite, "By all means have the occupation bill passed at this session." As an almost polite afterthought, Levy added that he understood that the Secretary had been "hampered by Congress" in getting the "1600 Corps bill" passed and that this measure was popular in the Territory and with the army.[504] Indeed, all measures to increase the army or navy met with stiff opposition from Congress, especially in the House of Representatives.

226

Five years into the war and the Seminoles and their allies were still unconquered. There were the almost weekly reports of settlers "massacred" in their homes, roads near major settlements were unsafe to travel, and there was constant wrangling between the regular army and the militia. In short, what had been gained during those five difficult and bloody years? The army's top brass, Winfield Scott, Edmond P. Gaines, Thomas Jesup, Zachary Taylor and Duncan L. Clinch had utterly failed to remove the menace to the frontier. During the middle of the war, a national depression had struck and made payments to troops, sutlers and suppliers difficult, if not impossible. Brilliantly thought out military strategy of the best European type had faltered and collapsed in the face of the elusive enemy. A revolution had broken out in Texas and threatened to embroil the country in a foreign war. Frustrations were high and money short at the end of 1840 and something had to be done to reverse the trend.

The attractiveness of the Armed Occupation Bill for the United States is easy to understand in the context of the nation's economic difficulties and the military frustrations experienced in Florida. There was a definite trend towards "retrenchment", the earlier version of governmental downsizing, and the military budget had been bloated by the expenses of the Indian wars with the Creeks, Cherokee and Seminoles. The cost of land on the unsettled frontier was cheap and therefore of little financial burden to the Congress. The bill would allow people willing to brave the dangers "free land" in exchange for an inexpensive, armed force along the battlefront with the Indian enemy. Blame for Indian depredations on the settlements could be easily shifted to the new "sedentary army" and away from the Regulars. The burden of supporting the new settlements could be limited to the next crop season and the army could release troops to other frontiers or dismiss some from the service, thereby reducing costs to the military budget. Thus, there was much to encourage the Congress to pass the bill.

There were costs, however, in political terms as well as financial. The war was seen by many, especially in the North, as a "negro war" and it had been labeled such by none other than General Thomas Jesup. The expansion of slavery, should Florida be pacified and prosper and ask for admission to the Union, was greatly opposed by most Northern Congressmen and Senators, who feared the loss of power in the halls of Congress as much as the expansion of the "evil institution." The battle between the rising Whig Party and the Jacksonian Democratic Party also played heavily in the passage or blockage of the bill, just as it did in the funding the army expansion, which the Whigs opposed. The supporters of Richard K. Call even petitioned Congress seeking his reinstatement as Governor, blaming partisan politics and Call's strong support of the armed occupation of Florida for his dismissal.[505] The party lines in Florida, outlined in the Constitutional Convention of 1838-39, were even more clearly drawn by the Seminole conflict. This political division of the Territory reflected the national trend in the creation of two more distinctly defined parties, the Whigs and Democrats. The political costs of the war rose almost as fast as the death rate among the soldiers, civilians and Indians.

By mid-1840, the strain on the nation's resources and the internal conflicts between militia and regular troops was placing an increasing burden on the Florida frontier. General Zachary Taylor, no fan of militia forces, especially those of Florida, opposed the calling out of any more troops by the Governor. He wanted only regular troops or well trained forces from neighboring states to handle the defense of Florida. However, this blanket policy was not acceptable to Joel R. Poinsett, the Secretary of War. Poinsett, a political friend and ally of General Leigh Read, thought it best to restrict the Florida militia to the northern portion of the Territory, nearer to the settlements, and let the regular forces handle the main body of the Seminoles and their allies. As he noted, "No system of defense in the opinion of the department can succeed but one of incessant scout, attack and pursuit." For this, the regular forces were best equipped. However, he also proposed to Read the following option:

> Those people who have been driven from their homes are to be encouraged to return to their plantations, and to reestablish themselves within them, and every facility and protection is to be afforded them for that purpose. Every such settlement should be provided with a blockhouse to which the family may retire in case of danger, and every encouragement is to

be given to the settlers to raise supplies of provisions for themselves and for the use of the troops.[506]

What the Secretary was proposing was the limitation of militia duties and the establishment of outposts that would act as agricultural auxiliaries to the regular army in the field. Protection for these new settlements would fall on the militia and free the regular army for the duties previously outlined.

Taylor departed Florida with a distinct distaste for it, which is reflected by every one of his biographers. He was replaced by the amiable, but ineffective, Walker K. Armistead. Understanding Secretary Poinsett's frustrations with the disunity invited by these incessant quarrels, Armistead met with Governor Robert Raymond Reid and General Leigh Read to discuss a mutually satisfactory strategy.[507] On the 17th of August 1840, he reported to the Secretary of his conversation with Florida's leaders. General Armistead stated that obtaining foot soldiers in Florida was almost impossible and that three months had passed since the first call for a company of such and not one man had come forward. Horsemen were the only option for protecting the immediate settlements. It was proposed that the militia be employed near their homes, giving them soldiers' pay but no rations. This would give an immediate relief to the Federal budget and provide close protection to the settlements, freeing the mounted forces for action further from the settlements.[508] This did not meet with the Secretary's approval. Three days after Armistead wrote his suggestions, Indian Key suffered an attack which has become known as the Perrine Massacre.

Meanwhile the costs of the war continued to mount. Congress, seeking ways of retrenching, looked to the military budget for such sources. Finding that the costs for five depots in Florida had cost the nation $665,210 through 1840, the representatives searched for other areas of high expenditure.[509] They looked to the overall expenditures and found that the year 1838 had a total costs for the "prevention and suppression of Indian hostilities" of $5,275,682.88, which was an astronomical amount for a year following a sharp depression.[510] The projected costs of the next budget year's efforts through May of that year were already estimated at $3,748,600.[511] These figures staggered the imagination of most Congressmen, who pushed harder for cuts in the military budget, despite the continued bloodbath on the frontier. By 1840, the Quartermaster's Department total disbursements for the suppression of the Creeks, Cherokees and Seminoles totaled $11,574,477.23.[512] Add this total to the $3,076,024.29 for the Pay Department for the same period, ending in October of 1840, and one gets glimpse of the management tasks facing both Congress and the War Department.[513] Congress and the military had to find a way to lower the costs and yet provide the protection needed on the Florida frontier. Again, the answer offered by Benton and others was another Armed Occupation Act. Once more, it failed to meet with Congressional approval.

The military campaigning year for 1840-41 ended with the troops once more retreating into summer quarters and allowing the enemy to recapture or reoccupy much of the territory gained in the preceding year's operations. Armistead was beginning to settle down in Tampa and slowly prepare for the next campaign. But this would not come to pass. As a result of the Whig victory in the election of 1840, a shake-up was due in the army. Renewed vigor was sought in the Florida campaign but, because of the early death of President William Henry Harrison, change was slow in coming. However, the new administration was even more cost conscious than its predecessor and when it was reported that $2,525,399.29 had been paid to regular troops as of May 1841 and that citizen soldiers had received $3,461,622.15, the Whigs cried for the immediate reduction in a reliance on militia forces and civilian labor at military installlations.[514] The man to carry out their plan was Colonel William Jenkins Worth.

Worth was an energetic man eager to gain fame and glory on the frontier. A protegé of General Winfield Scott, he so admired his mentor that he named his only son after him. Professor John K. Mahon describes Worth as one of the most handsome men in the army and one of its premier horsemen. He was of medium height, slim and had "a martial bearing" with the appearance of physical strength.[515] Worth was not one to sit idle during any season and, upon assuming command in mid-1841 he ordered the troops to be prepared to march at a moment's notice. He began an immediate campaign to drive the remaining Seminoles out of the infamous Cove of the Withlacoochee with a three pronged attack on that

230

ancient bastion of Seminole defense. This campaign was conducted in the months of June and July of 1841. This was an innovation in Florida warfare and one calculated to surprise the Seminoles and their allies in the midst of tending their crops and in their hidden recesses in the swamps of the Tsala Apopka chain of lakes. It was a hot, difficult and arduous campaign that brought few tangible results, except that it convinced Worth and the new Commanding General of the army, his friend Winfield Scott, that there were few remaining enemy warriors in that vicinity.[516]  At the same time, Worth was beginning to push hard on the resettlement of Florida and the creation of military colonies along the frontier.

While he began a drastic cutback of civilian personnel at the military posts in Florida, Worth worked toward the reestablishment of plantations, the resettlement of the older towns and creation of new military colonies through recruitment.  The Colonel had a pool of settlers at hand in those formerly driven from their homesteads into the safe havens of Garry's Ferry, St. Augustine, Newnansville, Jacksonville and Alligator.  These individuals were often known to the military as the "Suffering Inhabitants," after the bill for their relief passed in early 1836.  Some of those who appeared at Jacksonville included Ephraim Tiner, Micaja Simmond, the Adam Tison family, Charles W. McMunn and Henry Sweeney, all listed as from Alachua County.  Among those gathered at Garry's Ferry were Gabriel, Emory and Granville Priest, Malachi Hagan, Sarah Faulk, James Crosbie, Mary Dike and Sarah Parsons, William Spires and Michael Savans, who listed his home as Tuscawilla Pond.[517]  It was this pool of individuals and families that were the primary targets of the resettlement program proposed by Colonel Worth.  They were, however, not the only targets for colonization.

In reporting his proposed program to the Adjutant General of the Army, Roger Jones, Worth described his expectations as follows:

I am sanguine of success in the efforts being made to induce the frontier settlers to return, and reoccupy their grounds. This measure to which much importance is attached will it is believed, be founded by authority to make new issues of provisions "to the unfortunate sufferers who are unable to provide for themselves," conditioned, in respect to such as have before been made establishments on the frontier; in their case when a reasonable assurance of security can be guaranteed, which it is thought may be done in most instances, I would also ask authority to extend the issues until the next crop season to such as will boldly come forward and make new settlements on the border. The number would not probably be great, but every little community of three or four bold hearted settlers would operate a powerful auxiliary aid in bringing this contest to a close. However beneficial the design, I hazard the opinion that the policy of the measure has been invented in the selection of objects, particularly those who with, or without sufficient cause, have abandoned their homes, & are fed by the government, while in many cases those who bravely maintained themselves have never been recipients of the public bounty. It might in addition be politic to supply the latter class with Arms, and put them under military pay, in which event I should not propose to organize them by appointment of officers ... The expense in my judgement would be insignificant in comparison with the object in view. ... Major Wilcox, an invalided officer ordered to report, will be placed in charge of this service.[518]

One of the devices which was to be relied upon by Colonel Worth was the joint resolution passed by Congress authorizing the President to issue rations to the "unfortunate sufferers" who could not provide for themselves because of Indian depredations. They were to be provided with rations until such time as they could return to their homes and be re-established in their possessions. Worth's proposal, which was accepted in part, included *new* settlers in the provision of rations. Many of these sufferers had been, as Captain A. B. Eaton noted, "subsisted from the public stores for several years."[519]

On June 24, 1841, Worth notified the consumptive Major Wilcox that he had asked permission to issue rations to those who had abandoned their homes and those who would step forward and make settlements and expected him to issue same until further notice. He also wrote that he had asked for soldier's pay for those willing to resettle or begin a new habitation, "Simply as encouragement to maintain their Homesteads." Worth finally indicated that the Major could expect the support of intelligent and respectable citizens in his efforts.[520]

On July 8th, Worth received notice from the Secretary of War that only those who had been driven from their homes by Indian depredations could receive rations until they could be re-established in their possessions. This wording, of course, could be variously interpreted, and was, by the inventive colonel. Worth was also informed that the soldier's pay inducement was not allowed.[521] Although he lost his bid to pay settlers, he did not lose the battle to provide provisions to those seeking to colonize. By the end of the month, he had the President's personal interpretation delivered to him which included the following: "The relief contemplated may properly embrace the cases of those in a necessitous condition who may penetrate for settlement, such portions of Florida as have been infested & desolated by the enemy, & thus deprived of the supplies essential for the support of settlers during the necessary preparations for raising the means of subsistence at their selected homes."[522] By mid-July of 1841, Major Wilcox had already achieved some success in recruiting re-settlers and new colonists, much to the delight of the Colonel Commanding.[523] One of those willing to begin a new settlement was Gabriel Priest, who appeared at the Major's door one July morning, notified that officer that he would make up a party to "go about seven or eight miles to the south or South East of Withlacoochee."[524]

By the end of the month, Wilcox's efforts were producing rapid results and a group of colonists were headed to Lake Monroe. Colonel Whiting was alerted to be ready to transport these settlers and their effects and also make himself available to facilitate any needs of these new Floridians.[525] To make matters easier to penetrate the interior of Florida, Worth directed that the Etoniah Scrub area be made safer for migration:

> In carrying out the plan of forming new settlements and the re-occupation of those abandoned, it is found necessary to erect a small building 15 or 20 feet square, in house form, on either side of the It-on-ni-ah Scrub, as near thereto as water may be found, where the old Picolati road passes that point to

intersect the Fort King & Black Creek road & also to re-open the road through the scrub, Major Wilcox, who is charged with this service, will also be charged with the constructions & their locations. You will be pleased therefore, when called upon by that Officer, to furnish an Officer & 20 men from Fort Russell, supplied with necessary tools, to proceed to that point and report to him for orders, for the execution of that part of the work lying South West of the Scrub. A command from Picolati will be instructed to execute the work lying North East.[526]

Wilcox also reported on the last day of July that five persons had reported to him to make a new settlement at Clay Hill, ten miles South of Fort Harlee on the Micanopy Road. The five leaders were Arnold Thigpen, Benjamin Mills, William Addams and John Wiggins, Sr. and Jr. The proposed colony would number twenty-five Whites and four Blacks, of which seven were capable of bearing arms.[527]

Not every one in the army was pleased by the duties now falling on their shoulders. Some questioned the continued need to feed the suffering inhabitants any longer, now that new settlements were opening up and many of the old plantations were being re-occupied. Even Wilcox, although with different motives, questioned the continued feeding from the public trough. On August 3rd, the Assistant Adjutant General, Major Samuel Cooper, informed Wilcox, who was looking for some pressure points to force some resettlement, that he could strike from the rolls of suffering inhabitants those he considered not entitled to such benefits. Cooper also gave Wilcox what he was looking for when he added, "however such as may proceed to form settlements whatever may be their condition" could still receive their provisions. Here was a tool to force those unwilling to undertake frontier settlement again to do so or face the threat of starvation.[528]

The general policy of the army in its colonization effort is seen clearly in Major Cooper's letter of August 19, 1841, to Captain Robert Bradley, then of Madison County. "In answer to that part of your letter which relates to the making of settlements, I am instructed to state that such as may enroll themselves for the purpose will on establishing their farms, be afforded protection from the Indians, & furnished with subsistence for themselves and families until at least the next crop season. Major Wilcox, the Officer assigned to this duty, will soon probably visit your section of the country, if he has not already done so. A letter will reach him directed to Palatka."[529] By early October of 1841, the newspapers were recording the success of this simple campaign to colonize the frontier. On the 9th of that month, the St. Augustine newspaper was reporting that William Townsend's settlement of fourteen Whites and four Blacks had begun four miles north of the Natural Bridge of the Santa Fe and John Tucker's, at the Natural Bridge, numbering forty-five Whites and four Blacks was also underway. Elisha Carter's group, at Fort White, listing twenty-nine Whites and six Blacks; John B. Stanley's colony ten miles north of Fort Fanning, of twenty-eight Whites and five Blacks; James Thomas' settlement at Fort No. 11, amounting to twenty-eight Whites and eight Blacks; Stanislaus Glanisky [Gelinsky is another spelling found] had his thirty-two Whites and one Black establish themselves sixteen miles southwest of Palatka; and the well known John Lee Williams also began a settlement opposite the ancient fortification at Picolata with eight Whites and three Black pioneers.[530] It was clear that the policy to attract colonists to the frontier was working.

Unfortunately, the health of Major Wilcox was failing rapidly and Worth was concerned for this intrepid gentleman. At the end of the year, Wilcox was asked, health permitting, to reassure the new settlers that "ample protection will be extended to them against this handful of marauders," who had just committed an atrocity at Mandarin on the St. Johns River, south of Jacksonville.[531]

Within a few days of receiving this request, Wilcox died and his assignment was given to Lieutenant Marsena R. Patrick of the 2nd U. S. Infantry Regiment. Patrick was an able man and an excellent choice to carry out the task. He immediately set about recruiting more settlers and attempting to get more of the inhabitants back on their former lands. At the beginning of February 1842 he was able to report eighteen of those at St. Augustine had returned, adding two more to the lists at the end of that month. Included on these lists were the names of Joseph S. Sanchez, Philip Weedman, Jack Forrester, Thomas Clark, Peter Segui, Robert Mickler and Andrew

Pascetti, all of whom had fled to the Ancient City at the outbreak of the war in 1836.[532]

By the middle of February 1842, the entire frontier seemed to be on the move towards the new colonies and the army was giving what assistance it could afford. The colonists headed toward the Annuteliga Hammock (in today's Hernando County) were assisted in erecting the blockhouses for their protection by the troops stationed at nearby Fort Cross.[533] Additional protection was given to the settlement at the Natural Bridge when Indians signs were sighted in the area.[534] Rations were directed to be given to returning settlers and new settlers alike, but governed in the following manner: "rations be furnished complete to whites, & to blacks such parts only as are usually issued to slaves." Worth admonished Patrick to warn settlers that the rations would only continue until the end of the current crop season.[535] Yet, even with such a limitation, the flow of immigration did not cease. By March 22, Colonel Whiting was instructed to assist Mr. Branch with transportation for settlers from Georgia coming to Florida from the Brunswick area and also from Mineral Springs. The latter group was to be furnished with wagons for the trip from Mineral Springs on the Suwannee River to Newnansville, thence to Wacahoota and finally arriving at Fort King, a total distance of approximately 112 miles.[536]

Fortifications were also offered to settlers as temporary homes for those willing to risk the frontier. The buildings at Fort Mellon, were granted to a Georgia group of settlers. Indeed, Captain E. K. Barnum was ordered to find sufficient space for only fifteen of his force (with one room for a hospital) and the rest were consigned to tents in order that a Mr. Gyer and his settlers could move into the old fort buildings and living quarters. Barnum was also notified to relate to Gyer that the wharf at that location was common property and would not be subject to private ownership.[537] Weapons were also issued to colonists, like those of Colonel Sam Reid's settlement at Manatee. Tents, too, were provided to this group of vigilant settlers at Florida's southernmost military colony.[538] Even forage was issued to some of the settlements for their draft animals and horses. Both the Stewart colony near Lake Jesup and that of Cornelius Taylor at Enterprise received such sustenance.[539] When danger did threaten the new settlements, as it did at Charley Emathla's Town, a guard

236

was often placed at the settlement itself.[540] In all of this supplying of food, forage, arms and other necessities, Lt. Patrick performed tireless duty and made the proper reports, especially on the number and condition of the arms supplied to the citizens of the various settlements.[541] The frontier was not only moving, but it was also supplied with as much assistance as Worth's forces and budget could afford.

The settlement of the frontier under Worth's direction was not a scattered or uncontrolled event. The Colonel was very aware of the precarious nature of these establishments and he would not allow a few miscreants to disrupt his fragile edifice. When two such individuals left Fort No. 4 without permission or escort, Worth ordered an immediate halt to their rations, thus exposing them to starvation and no protection.[542] Other settlers were warned not to disturb Halik's fields, near the Big Swamp settlement, for fear of causing that feared leader to return to the swamps and not migrate west.[543] When some of the settlers requested permission to raise a volunteer unit to chase the Seminoles thought to be in their area, Worth was quick to point out that the Regular Troops stationed around the Territory were adequate to handle such instances as may be caused by some of the remaining roving bands and that volunteer forces would not be tolerated, even if allowed by Territorial law.[544] Worth had requested that the battalion of 2nd Dragoons be maintained in Florida while the frontier was being settled under his "semi-military colonization" and that as soon as the settlements had been established, this force could be reduced, along with a number of teamsters, wagoners, etc. used in transporting the colonists to their new homes.[545] The settlement of Florida under the direction of William Jenkins Worth was an organized, controlled event which produced impressive results.

According to a report filed by Lt. Patrick in March of 1842, twelve settlements had been established at that time, totaling four hundred and ninety-three White settlers and one hundred and fifty-nine Blacks. The names of the leaders of these colonies are familiar to students of the Florida frontier and include Moses and John Curry, John Tucker, Cornelius Taylor, Samuel Sparkman, John Osteen and Stanislau Galinski. They stretched from the area of the Natural Bridge on the Santa Fe River to old Fort Mellon on Lake Monroe.

John Wiggins' party settled three miles off the Bellamy road, north of Micanopy, just seventeen miles in the direction of Fort Tarver. Samuel Sparkman's group took possession of the lands near the famed Ichnetucknee Springs, but moved to the intersection of the Alligator and Bellamy roads because the water was bad. The famed Chukuchatee Hammock was also settled at this time by the party headed by John Curry.[546]

Thus by the time of the passage of the Armed Occupation Act of 1842, Colonel William Jenkins Worth had already begun the settlement of the frontier in Florida. His energy, drive and ambition created a new society to begin the replacement of that destroyed by the long and tragic struggle known as the Second Seminole War. Many of the colonists recruited by Major Wilcox, Lt. Patrick and others remained in Florida and took up lands under the Armed Occupation Act. Many, including most of those in the Lake Jesup colony of Daniel Stewart, returned to Georgia or other homelands. The majority of those listed in the reports cited above are well known pioneer families of Florida who took advantage of Worth's proposition and the offer made later in the Armed Occupation Act. But it should be clear that the repopulation of the Florida frontier owes its origins to the efforts of the United States Army, under the dynamic command of William Jenkins Worth. Without his efforts, in the face of many obstacles, the growth of this frontier would have been much slower and statehood delayed.

238

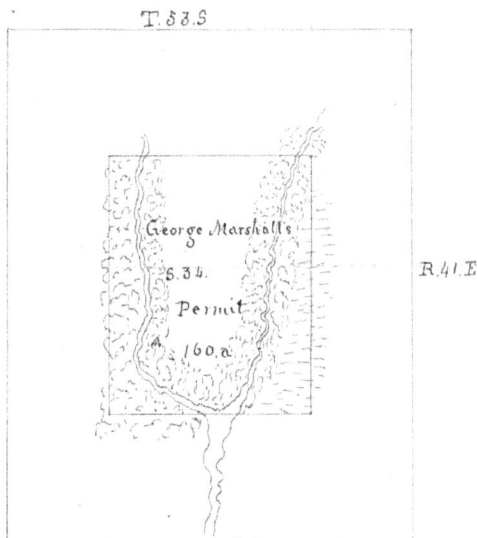

The foregoing is a survey made at my request by George Mackay Government Surveyor being land granted to me under the Armed Occupation Law of Florida in June AD 1843 by Permit in consideration of Occupation and cultivation — which survey I hereby agree to accept under said permit —

Given under my hand at Miami May 29th AD 1845

George Marshall

239

# The Impact of the Armed Occupation Act of 1842

The Armed Occupation Act of 1842 has received little attention in the history of Florida. Only James Covington and Michael Welsh have taken time to look into the language of the act and its Congressional origins. John Mahon's, *History of the Second Seminole War* draws heavily upon Covington and does not differ in interpretation. A more recent interpretation has been offered by Paul George and Joe Knetsch in their, "A Problematic Law: The Armed Occupation Act of 1842 and Its Impact on Southeast Florida." The latter's research indicates that the impact was much less, especially in Southeastern Florida, than has been previously reported. More specifically, the Knetsch-George thesis demonstrates that the lasting effect of the act in the area studied was minimal and almost nonexistent.[547] The need for a re-evaluation of the impact of the act is needed for a better understanding of the development of Florida in the mid-nineteenth century.

At the time of Dr. Covington's authoring of the first and most important article on the Armed Occupation Act, (also known at the Florida Donation Act) reliance was strongly placed upon Congressional documents, especially Senate Executive Report No. 39, 30th Congress, 1st Session, dated April 28, 1848. This document, while very important, contained a number of errors as to location of the permits. More significantly, it does not indicate all of the information contained in the permits upon which it is based. The most important omission is that of the date the permit holder entered Florida. This piece of data is tremendously important in

240

understanding the earlier interpretations. Covington, citing Commissioner of the General Land Office, Richard Young, noted the increase of Florida's population at about 6,000 souls.[548] Dr. Mahon, using Covington and other sources, and reciting the figure of 1,312 permits issued, indicated a slightly different number arrived at in the following manner: "Assuming five persons per permit, the addition to the population in those two years would have been nearly 6,500, which was more than one-tenth of the entire population."[549] Both of these figures depend upon the assumption that all of the permit holders entered Florida as a result of the passage of the Armed Occupation Act of 1842. This simply was not the case.

Although the State does not have copies of each of the over 1,300 permits, it does have over 1,100 of them. By counting each folder (arranged alphabetically at the Florida Department of Environmental Protection) and its contents, the results are quite informative. Rounded off, but without any exaggeration, the totals show that of those who received permits, one third arrived before the outset of the Second Seminole War, one third came during that conflict and the final third came after the passage of the Armed Occupation Act.[550] Thus, even by the crude method previously employed, the total number reflects only an increase of about 2,000 to 2,500. As Knetsch and George discovered in their investigation, few of those who came to the southeastern coast remained after the Indian scare of 1849. Many of those who came to the coast and up to the Indian River settlement were the more recent immigrants. Neither of these areas recovered from the 1849 scare until well into the latter half of the nineteenth century.[551]

The development of Florida was enhanced by the passage of the Armed Occupation Act of 1842, not as much by sheer numbers as by what it represented to the frontier. As many historians have noted, the act was the first act by Congress to allocate free land for settlement by meeting certain conditions. Simply put, the act required that a person be the head of a family or a single man over the age of eighteen capable of bearing arms. The residence should be one fit for man and the settler had to cultivate at least five acres of land and remain on the land for five consecutive years. Other stipulations included the proviso that a person could not cut timber on his property and sell it for profit. The only use allowed was the construction of the habitation, fences and out buildings. Women could receive a permit and have the land patented to them provided they had a son or slaves capable of bearing arms. The 160 acres given to settlers who met the above conditions were originally given in the "unsurveyed" portion of the State south of a line running roughly from Cedar Key, through Newnansville and thence south of the St. Augustine area plantations. Only 200,000 acres of public lands were allotted for the "new" inhabitants, which greatly limited the number of settlers to be attracted. Yet, the act symbolized the freedom of the frontier and represented advancement in the fight for opening up the public domain to small settlers.[552]

The act was part of a much larger movement in United States history, that of opening up of the frontier to yeomen farmers and other small landholders. It was also a part of the movement for pre-emptions, or the right to settle the land prior to government surveys and have a claim to the improvements made thereon. This struggle for right of pre-emption was one of the most dramatic in Congressional history and culminated in the "Great Pre-Emption Act of 1841." Although this act applied only to surveyed lands, it was the beginning of the opening up of the entire public domain to settlement. It marked a political passage for the country in reflecting the growth, power and influence of the frontier states against the old establishment of the Northeast and South. It is no accident that the leader of this fight in Congress was Thomas Hart Benton, the dominant Senator from Missouri. The Great Pre-Emption Act was the first formal recognition of the universality of the principle of preempting land on the frontier. There had been limited attempts and many reverses earlier, but this act finalized the principle on the American frontier.[553] The fact that the Armed Occupation Act of 1842 followed on the footsteps of this great triumph cannot be lost on even the most casual of observers.

Nationally, the Armed Occupation Act of 1842 also was the first time the government allowed a grant of free land on the frontier upon the meeting of certain settlement conditions. It was not the last. The Territory of Oregon also had problems with early settlement and, in 1843 Senator Lewis F. Linn introduced a donation act for that territory. By the time of its final passage, in September of 1850, the donation in this territory had grown to 320 acres for a single man and

640 acres for a married man. The residence on and cultivation of the land for four consecutive years was necessary to secure a patent. In 1855, this act was extended into the Washington Territory. Donation privileges were extended to the Territory of New Mexico in 1854, and had no legislated time limit. Indeed, in that territory, it lasted until 1883. But the most important act for which the Armed Occupation Act of 1842 was the model was the Homestead Act, which, significantly, reverted back to the 160 acre allotment. The long term impact of the Homestead Act upon the frontier is well documented and part of the national lore.[554] Again, the impact of the Armed Occupation Act of 1842 is much larger, even in Florida, than previously recognized.

One of the lesser known facets of this act was the role of the military in shaping the course of settlement on the Florida frontier. Early on in the conflict, Brigadier General Leigh Read strongly advocated the use of settlers, in protected communities, as a method of defense for the frontier.[555] Governors Richard Keith Call and Robert Raymond Reid both were advocates of the use of civilian forces tied to settlements as the basis for further defense against the Indians.[556] Nearly every military leader who served in Florida advocated some form of armed occupation including Zachary Taylor, Alexander Macomb, Walker Armistead, Thomas Lawson and Thomas Jesup.[557] However, it was left to William Jenkins Worth to carry out the military's ideas concerning the armed occupation of Florida.

Writing to the Adjutant General's Office in July of 1841, just two months after taking command in Florida, Worth notified General Roger Jones that Brevet Major D. Wilcox had been appointed to carry out the issuing of provisions to the "suffering inhabitants." Additionally, Worth also assigned Wilcox the task of "encouraging the reoccupancy of abandoned plantations and farms."[558] Worth desired to allow the settlers, all of whom were initially part of the suffering inhabitants, arms, ammunition, assistance with shelter and seed for the first year's crops. In late July 1841, Worth notified Lieutenant Colonel Henry Whiting of some successes accomplished by Wilcox. However, the settlers required assistance of a new kind, namely transportation to the *new* areas to be occupied. Worth wrote, "Several small companies of citizens forming under the auspices of

Major Wilcox, desiring to make settlements near Lake Monroe, on the St. Johns, will probably ask transportation for themselves and effects. Deeming the object of high public importance, it is my desire, without withdrawing the vessels from their immediate uses that you cause every facility to be afforded in the way asked."[559] On July 30, 1841, Worth gave instructions to Lieutenant Colonel B. Riley at Fort King to assist the new settlers in building homes and settlements along the old Picolata Road and other locations. Worth was quite proud of the work Major Wilcox did in getting people lined up to re-settle the frontier, either in re-occupying old plantations or in creating new ones.[560]

Wilcox did, indeed, have surprising success in recruiting occupants for the new settlements. In early August 1841, he reported to Worth that he had found fifteen settlers for the proposed occupation of Fort Mackay [Fort McCoy] on the road to Fort King. He also found occupants for the proposed positions near the natural bridge of the Santa Fe River and near "Itchetucknee" Springs.[561] Wilcox did not forget the people who sought to return to their plantations and notified Worth that Jeane Strickland and R. P. Lewis were willing to resettle their old homes by the end of August.[562] The intrepid Colonel also notified his commander that those in the neighborhood of Fort Harlee [William Addams, Arnold Thigpin, Benjamin Mills and John Wiggins, Sr. and Jr.] were also willing to reoccupy their former homes.[563] Wilcox, almost everywhere he traveled in Florida, found support for the resettlement/new settlement plans of the army. Many of the leaders of the Florida Militia were among those supporting the effort, including Gabriel Priest, William Thigpin and Captain Chamberlain. Upon receiving these reports, Worth noted, "Your reports are highly gratifying and I am greatly encouraged by the favor with which the plan is received by spirited and patriotic Citizens. Opposition was expected, yet it is gratifying to find it so limited; this only strengthens both my confidence in and resolution to carry it out."[564] Colonel Wilcox was well on the way to repopulating the frontier when word began to arrive from Washington to "retrench" and cut back on these efforts.

Worth was ambitious to get the job done and probably gave many settlers too much hope. On August 9, 1841, Worth, through his adjutant, warned Wilcox not to promise too much to the pioneers, especially the proposed offer of soldier's wages for settling on the exposed frontier. This, he noted, was dependent upon "the approbation of the Secretary of War."[565] Worth also had to dispel any notion of raising the militia to take up the tasks of the regular army. In his explanation to Captain Robert D. Bradley, then of Madison County, Worth explained the limitations:

I am instructed by the Colonel Commg. to thank you for the very patriotic offer in your letter of the 28th ult., & to inform you in reply that it is not designed to call any volunteers into the field. In answer to that part of your letter which relates to making settlements, I am instructed to state, that such as may enrol [sic] themselves for the purpose will on establishing their farms, be afforded protection from the Indians, & furnished with subsistence for themselves and families until at least the next crop season. Major Wilcox, the Officer assigned to this duty will soon probably visit your section of country, if he has not already done so.[566]

Yet, even with such casual warnings that things were about to change, Worth continued his pursuit of getting Florida settled and consistently allowed rations to be issued to these settlers under the cover of the suffering inhabitants appropriation.[567]

Worth not only provided provisions and subsistence, but he also undertook to provide arms for the new inhabitants. In September 1841, he instructed Captain J. R. J. Bradford, head of Ordinance in Florida, to provide arms for the settlers under required restrictions: "Although the description of Arms to be furnished the settlers is not designated in the enclosed Special Order No. 49, the Colonel Commanding desires you will confine the issue to second hand arms, and to such quantities of ammunition as will suffice for the defense of the settlers against Indian attack. In respect to these issues, however, he desires that the wishes of Major Wilcox may be fully complied with."[568] Wilcox did his duty well and by the end of 1841, many of the re-settlements were beginning to grow and plans were underway for new settlements, all under the protection and armed by the regular army. Unfortunately, Major Wilcox did not live to oversee the final distribution of arms, foodstuffs, tents, etc. to the new settlements. He died in early January of 1842 and his place was taken by Lieutenant Marsena R. Patrick, a New York native and graduate of West Point, Class of 1835. Patrick had served in Florida since 1837 and was familiar with many of the men who would soon lead the colonies planned by Worth and Wilcox.[569]

Lieutenant Patrick had the difficult task of helping to organize and supply the military colonies envisioned by Worth. He was given some latitude in accomplishing this goal and had permission to call out a small guard for settlements most at risk. Patrick was also encouraged to have settlers occupy and use the buildings at many of the former military posts, such as Fort King and Fort Russell.[570] The arms issued to the settlers from the military stores in Florida were, however, not turned over to the occupants on a permanent basis and each was to be accounted for and occasionally checked to maintain their preservation.[571] This fact would help to explain former Florida Governor Thomas Brown's oft quoted statement about the unarmed nature of the frontier inhabitants.[572]

By April and May of 1842, most of the "semi-military colonies" in Florida had been established. However, by this time the effects of the retrenchment minded Congress were being felt throughout the military and in the General Land Office. Cutbacks in the rations offered to new inhabitants were ordered and numerous people taken off of the roles of the suffering inhabitants for what appears to be trivial reasons [e.g. husband not living with family, etc.]. A cut off date of August 31, 1842, was established for the provision of seed crops for the next growing season.[573] The forage costs of the war, constantly mounting as the war dragged on, forced the removal of most of the Regiment of 2nd Dragoons. This unit was the one most responsible for the guarding and transportation of the colonist into the frontier areas the army wished to have settled. Worth had to write to Washington justifying the expenditures of this unit before a portion of it was allowed to remain. The number of teamsters and wagon masters were drastically cut back, as was the expenditure on building materials.[574] It was obvious that the end was near for the military colonies established by the assistance of Worth, Wilcox and Patrick.

On June 13, 1842, Colonel Worth wrote to the Adjutant General of the army informing him of the completion of the army's plan to

246

establish military colonies in Florida. More importantly, he attached a listing of the names, numbers and locations of these colonies. These lists make for very informative reading and document the success of the army's attempt to colonize and resettle Florida. In the resettlement mission, the army was able to relocate twenty families totaling ninety-three whites and sixty-six blacks. In the nineteen new settlements listed in the recapitulation, eight hundred and eighty-nine whites and two hundred and forty-six blacks became part of the new frontier colonies meant to protect the established towns and villages of the old settled areas. Two of the more notable colonies were those of Colonel Daniel M. Stewart and Colonel Sam Reid. Stewart's colony was located in the Black Hammock area on the south side of Lake Jesup (in today's Seminole County). It was described as follows:

This party dates from the 15 of April, at which time Col. Stewart landed at Fort Mellon, with the above persons. The land is of the finest quality in the Territory & the range for Cattle is unsurpassed. Already there are some hundreds of Cattle & hogs there belonging to the Settlement, & more frequently arriving. Most of the planting is in Indian Old Fields, it being too late when the party arrived to clear up new lands. A Block House has been thrown up for the protection of the Settlers, & a supply of Arms & Ammunition issued to them. Should the position prove healthy, the settlement will become one of the largest & most important in the whole Peninsula.

The colony received sixty guns [20 muskets and 40 rifled guns] as its allotment. Next to the settlement of John Curry, Daniel Stewart's military colony was the largest in Florida, numbering one hundred and forty-nine whites and thirty-nine black settlers.[575] Unfortunately, few of these colonist remained in Florida once the army's support was dropped and most returned to Georgia.

The colony of Colonel Sam Reid's was one of the more interesting and longest lasting colonies. Many of the descendants still live along the Manatee River where Reid and his group first established themselves. Reid was well known in Middle Florida and connected by marriage to the Alstons. He was a business partner with James Gamble in a dry goods store in Tallahassee and was the first purchaser of property in Port Leon. His political connections to the faction headed by Richard K. Call also found him investing in the Tallahassee to St. Marks Railroad and other internal improvement projects. Sam Reid also held the posts of collector of customs at St. Marks (and later Tampa) and U.S. Deputy Surveyor. Unlike Stewart's colony, Reid's was small, with only fifteen whites and sixteen black settlers. This colony received ten muskets, twenty flints, ten tents and seed for the coming planting season. Of the thirteen heads of families listed in the Reid colony, seven remained to receive Armed Occupation Permits (and Patents). Worth described this colony as "composed entirely of persons from Middle Florida. The lands are of Superior quality, & from the character of the gentlemen concerned, there is certainty of success." In this prediction the future hero of the Mexican War was correct.[576]

The Congress, while all of this activity was taking place on the Florida frontier, was continuing to debate the passage of the Benton sponsored Armed Occupation Act. After a close fight in the Senate, the House of Representatives, led by Speaker James K. Polk, had little trouble in passing the act. The provision about arming the new settlers was dropped as was the section dealing with free rations. The act was signed into law on August 4, 1842.[577] As noted above, the act did not have the large numbers moving into Florida as earlier reported. However, when one studies the persons taking up the permits and investigates the relationships of the settlers, it will be found that many of the permitees were directly related to their neighbors. They moved southward from homes already established in Florida to the more fertile and less exploited lands in the central portion of the peninsula. This is hardly a new story in the history of the American frontier. In many ways, Congress was simply recognizing what was already in place. As Covington noted in his ground-breaking article, those on the western and central portions of the Territory were active in the development of their portion of Florida. Yet, as Knetsch and George discovered about Southeastern Florida, the impact of the act was almost negligible. This set of uneven results needs further examination before a more complete story of the Armed Occupation Act of 1842 can be told. Too many facets of the story remain untold and unexplored for us to say we have a thorough knowledge of the impact of this act on the development of Florida. It is time that the total picture of the military colonies, Congressional intrigue, retrenchment and land development be placed in their proper contexts. There is still so much to do.

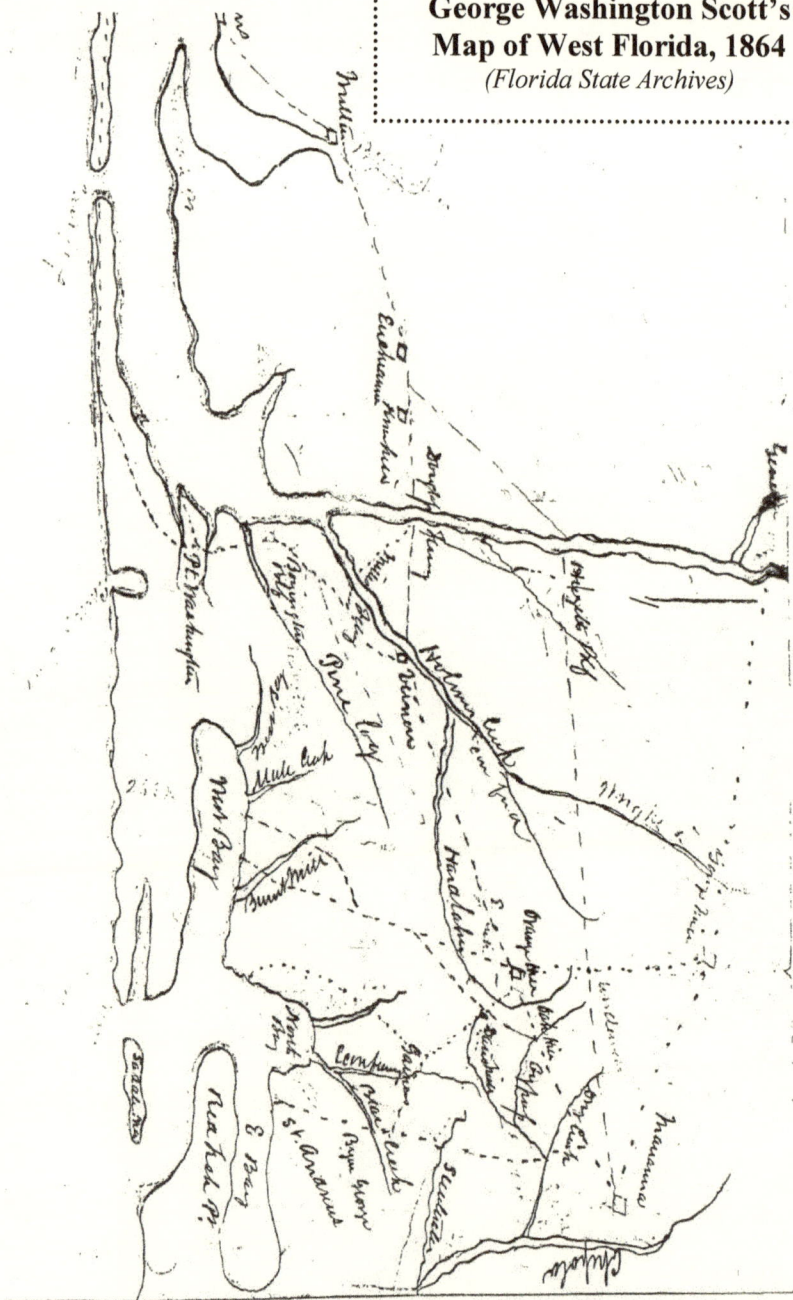

George Washington Scott's
Map of West Florida, 1864
(Florida State Archives)

# The Unknown Conflict:
# West Florida, 1835-1848

West Florida in 1835 was a vast, relatively unsettled land of pine trees, sand hills and some red clay regions near Jackson County. The Scots of the Euchee Valley had not come in great droves but settled in family orientated groups scattered far from each other. There were the fishing families along the coast from St. Andrews Bay to Santa Rosa Island who were also a distinct distance from one another. A few cotton plantations had begun along the Apalachicola and Chipola Rivers even before the Spanish had "sold" the Floridas to the United States. Marianna, Campbellton, the Holmes Valley, the lumbering hamlets along the Blackwater and lower Yellow Rivers and, of course, Pensacola were the only centers of population. At the beginning of the era under discussion, the fledgling town of St. Josephs would begin its meteoric rise and fall. There were few Native Americans around to cause much trouble and what few of them survived the diseases and intrusions of the white population were centered along the Apalachicola River and Escribano Point near Pensacola. In short, it was an area where not much trouble was anticipated between the races.

Middle Florida and East Florida were thriving areas complete with a transplanting of the southern institution of slavery. The neighboring southern states of Georgia and Alabama provided many of the immigrants to the new territory. By 1835, the pioneers from South Carolina, Virginia, Tennessee and Kentucky had also begun to migrate to Florida to take their share of the newly

251

opened and surveyed lands. With them came many of the southern attitudes toward Native Americans symbolized by the policy of Indian removal. This policy was fraught with difficulties from under-funding to incompetence to outright fraud. The Indian Bureau in Washington, for example, had only four full-time employees to oversee the immense duties of this entity. This far flung bureau had to administer to the needs of all Native Americans, their agents, the military (it was under the War Department at the time) and white politicians representing a multitude of constituencies. For those in West Florida, this meant that almost no attention would be paid to the needs of the Apalachicola bands, and the few Creeks and Choctaws who would soon be forced to leave Florida. Even less attention would be paid to the needs of whites and the few black inhabitants who would soon need military protection from those who resisted or refused emigration to the lands of the Arkansas River and beyond.[578]

While this was the situation in West Florida the neighboring states of Alabama and Georgia were experiencing the pangs of Native American emigration as a result of the 1832 Treaty of Cusseta. This treaty was designed to allow the Creeks of Alabama to receive bare title to the lands upon which they lived, and in return the Indians agreed to sell these lands under the guiding hands of the agents so as to have funds to emigrate to the new lands in the west. The details of this treaty and the role of the agents are complicated but it boiled down to the agents having the final say and many of these men were in league with land speculators, mostly out of Columbus, Georgia. When a Native American did receive money for his land he was often immediately forced to kick back some of the money to the agent or to repay imagined debts run up as a result of the land arrangement. It was a system flooded with fraud and the resentment this caused festered on this volatile frontier. The land deals clouded relationships among the various units of the Creek Confederation and bred even more distrust and hatred between the Upper and Lower Creeks. Many of the "leaders" were aligned with the speculators and some, like Paddy Carr, took full advantage of their leadership positions to enrich themselves at the expense of their kinsmen.[579]

This confusing and frustrating situation on the frontier bordering West Florida was to have dire consequences for the citizens of this region. When the Seminoles and their allies attacked Major Francis L. Dade's command near modern Bushnell, and killed Indian Agent Wiley Thompson and Lieutenant Constantine Smith near the agency at Fort King on December 28, 1835, the Second Seminole War began in earnest. The signs pointing to conflict had been clear for a number of months and both Thompson and commanding general, Duncan L. Clinch, had warned Washington about the possibilities. The Seminoles, Miccosukies and their black allies were divided on the issue and held many heated discussions about their removal.[580] The Creeks were also divided in their councils and it was the Upper Creeks who resisted the most. This was the same group that had led the opposition to Andrew Jackson's invasion of their territory in 1813-14 which led to the disastrous Battle of Horseshoe Bend and the ultimatum known as the Treaty of Fort Jackson, which gave up Creek rights to millions of acres in Alabama and southwestern Georgia. As soon as the gun barrels cooled in Florida from the first major battles, Creeks began heading south to join the Seminole resistance.[581]

The situation on the Creek frontier of Alabama deteriorated rapidly after the beginning of the Seminole War. Long pent up frustrations, frauds and hatred among the Native Americans soon led to bloodshed and murder along the entire frontier. By early May of 1836 West Floridians were panicking and demanding protection from the Creeks and whatever Seminoles would be in the vicinity. By 18 May 1836 Governor Schley of Georgia was writing the Secretary of War for assistance and noting the Creeks had begun making war on the frontier and had attacked and burnt the town of Roanoke on the Chattahoochee River.

Commodore A. J. Dallas from his ship in Havana Harbor had sent aid to the struggling remnants at Fort Brooke (Tampa) in January of 1836 and had also dispatched Lieutenant Nathan Waldron of the marines to aid that garrison.[582] Captain W. C. Bolton, commanding the Naval Station at Pensacola received requests from the citizens of Marianna for arms and ammunition for their defense to which he immediately sent an estimated one hundred and fifty guns and ammunition.[583] Governor Richard Keith Call, of Florida, also requested that Bolton send some kind of protection to the new town of St. Joseph. On 20 June 1836 Commodore Dallas informed Secretary of the Navy Mahlon Dickerson that he had that day sent the Revenue Cutter *Jefferson* to St. Joseph for the protection of that settlement.[584] The efforts of Bolton and Dallas led to the sending of the steamers *Watchman* and *Major Dade* to cruise the Chattahoochee and Apalachicola Rivers to prevent the Indians from crossing into Georgia and joining their kinsmen in Florida.[585] The steamer *American* soon joined its sister ship *Major Dade* in patrolling the Chattahoochee and Apalachicola and providing logistical help to General Thomas Jesup and Major General Winfield Scott in their campaigns in Alabama.[586] The navy was doing its part to prevent the spread of the violence.

The plan devised by Major General Winfield Scott was relatively simple and attempted to catch the Creeks in the usual vice between two forces. Although Jesup had been appointed to take the field first, he was definitely under Scott's command when the two met with Governor Schley in late May of 1836 in Augusta, Georgia. Scott had a very meticulous plan to put forth which involved Jesup taking command of the Alabama forces on the Alabama side of the Chattahoochee River while Scott waited for the regulars and Georgia volunteers to arrive in Columbus. The idea was for Jesup to hold up the Alabama advance into the Creek country from the south and wait for Scott's force to take the field. By driving the Creeks northward the plan would negate any attempt by the Creeks to flee to Florida. By stationing parts of the Georgia militia along the Georgia side of the river in fortifications strategically spaced, the hope was to prevent any crossing of the Creeks into southwestern Georgia and then onward into Florida. This was to be augmented by the navy's patrolling the river by constant moving up and down the stream between Columbus and the village of Chattahoochee in Florida. The marines were to join in the fun by attaching themselves to Scott's command and constructing Fort Henderson fifteen miles below Columbus and making constant patrols along the river to prevent crossings from the Alabama side.[587]

The federal government felt confident that Jesup and Scott could end the war quickly. Both commanders felt the same way but neither considered that a large portion of their contingents would be Georgia and Alabama militia with their own elected leaders and an agenda quite different than that of simple removal. Additionally, both militias feared that enrolling in the federal service for a certain amount of time would lead to their being sent to Florida at the quick conclusion of this conflict. No militia officer or enlisted man would tolerate service under such circumstances and made it very clear to both commanders. Scott and Jesup had to reassure these troops that none would be required to serve in Florida once the Creek problem was eliminated. Land frauds were not to be investigated at this time and the only goal, from the view of Secretary of War Lewis Cass, was to remove all Creeks from Alabama, including friendly Creeks. All of the agents were released and the operation was to be strictly military. The land speculators among the officer class in the militias thought this was good policy but the rank and file and their families were more hesitant about the removal of all Creeks, many of whom were now related by marriage or had been peaceful neighbors for many years. These conflicts within the forces opposing the Creeks made it more difficult to enforce government policy and ensure compliance among the Creeks.

The Indian leadership among the Creeks was also divided between those who saw little prospect of winning a war against the whites, those who wished to sell and resettle quickly, and those who were opposed outright. The struggle amongst the Creeks that had helped to lead to the First Creek War (1812-1814) and which divided them between Upper and Lower Creeks was once more brought to the forefront. Just at the last moment when things looked as though the Creeks might be united in opposition Opothleyahola led his bands to join the whites against the rebels in the south. Neah Micco, Neamathla and Jim Henry led the Lower Creeks against the army and the militia forces and rejected the attempts to mediate by the agents. Neamathla, who had led the fight against Gaines at Fowltown to begin the First Seminole War and resisted the attempts of Governor William Pope Duval to have him emigrate to the west in Florida, was back as the aged leader of the rebellious Creeks. Neah Micco and Jim Henry were well known leaders among the Lower Creeks and the former had been one of the dominant leaders at the Fort Mims massacre. But these were different times and the factions were more fragmented than ever. There would be no united resistance against the army, Militia and Friendly Creeks this time around. It was simply every group for themselves.[588]

Scott's plan versus this fragmented enemy should have worked to perfection. Once again, however, just like his misadventure in Florida, Scott's plan depended too much upon good supply routes, disciplined troops, near perfect timing of troop movements and everyone following through with the ideal. On the frontier this coalescing of forces and movements hardly ever happened. First, the Alabama troops under the command of Governor C. C. Clay were very anxious to move against the enemy and pushed the starting date of the whole operation up five days. Secondly, Scott's regular forces and much of the Georgia militia had not shown up at Columbus at the same time Clay and Jesup were ready to advance. Both militia groups lacked serious discipline and devoured rations faster than federal troops were allowed to consume them. Many of the Georgia militia showed up without weapons and Clay had depleted the resources of the Chattahoochee and Mt. Vernon arsenals. A wagon shortage slowed down Scott's operation and forced the general to use pack mules and horses, which consumed great quantities of forage. The impatience of the Alabama troops and the pressure from Secretary Cass on Jesup to move forward forced that general to leave his position days ahead of schedule and take a more direct course northward. Scott's set-piece, grand strategy failed again as it did in Florida for many of the same reasons. The only lesson the Major General appears to have learned from his misadventure in Florida was to not publicly criticize the militia and call the general populace cowards for running in the face of Indian depredations.[589]

Scott's biggest fears were being realized when he finally received word that Jesup had marched northward and had decided to take Neamathla's village as the main goal of his movement. Jesup did not inform his superior that his forces had already captured Neah Micco, his son and thirty-five of his people and that a few days later they had captured old Neamathla. The movement to Neamathla's village on the Hatchechubbee Creek proved to be both wise and lucky. Without their leader many of Neamathla's warriors decided it was not possible to hold their lands and they retreated into the surrounding swamps. Jesup later noted that this was very fortunate because the village was a near perfect natural fortress and would have taken many lives to gain possession of it.[590] By 12 July the *Army and Navy Chronicle* was declaring the war at an end and noting the surrender of over one thousand Creeks to Jesup and Scott's forces.[591] Two days later the same paper observed that the capture of Jim Henry and one hundred of his warriors effectively had ended the war.[592] Major General Scott was not amused or pleased by these headlines and the direct disobedience of his orders. He ordered Jesup to Fort Mitchell for a direct explanation of his actions.

General Jesup gave as his reasons for the move the shortage of rations his forces were experiencing, the impatience of the Alabama forces to get into action and the information of the Friendly Indians under Opothleyahola indicated the need for quick, determined movement. Because he was successful and the press had reported the war at an end, Scott had little choice but to accept his subordinate's explanations. For his part, the Major General decided upon a move to the south to cut off those who may have avoided the net. It was a campaign for show and accomplished little but to stir up a few isolated skirmishes for the Georgia militia and regular forces to place on their records. Jesup's success and Scott's inability to deviate from the grand plan had led to a short-lived disagreement between the two generals that would be patched up within a year. In reality, the actual glory should have gone to the Friendly Creeks as it was this group that captured two of the three major leaders of the rebellion.[593]

But was this the end to the Second Creek War or was there another phase of this conflict that filtered down into the wilds of West and Middle Florida? The reality of the "ending" of the war soon fell on the settlers and pioneers of West Florida. The denizens of the area had already begun to fear that the conflict would move south and that it was coordinated with their brethren, the Seminoles.[594] As early as 21 May 1836 the Apalachicola *Gazette* was reporting that settlers on both sides of the river were fleeing their homes. They needed to call out the militia to defend the city from suffering the same fate as Roanoke. The Charleston *Courier* for 2 July 1836 reported that the Creeks were fleeing Alabama and roaming across southern Georgia before descending into Florida to join the Seminoles. The same paper also observed in its 7 September issue that, "Hundreds, we may say, have already made their way to the Seminoles, where, prompted by the almost universal success of that nation, and in conjunction with them, they will make a bold and daring stand."[595]   Throughout the remainder of 1836, the fears of a general Indian outbreak in West Florida put a sense of urgency into the minds of everyone.

Reports from Alabama continued to flow southward to Pensacola and demonstrated that many of the Creeks allegedly defeated by Jesup and Scott had indeed escaped to the less settled areas near the Florida-Alabama line.  In February of 1836 Indian Agent Archibald Smith learned from his Alabama counterparts that a large number of Creeks had left that area and were headed toward Pensacola, specifically to visit the Escribano Indian settlement which, it was alleged, had been supplying the Creeks with arms, ammunition and foodstuffs.  On 28 February Smith heard of the murder of the Alberson family living along the Choctawhatchee River near the line between Florida and Alabama.  He was also informed that between 125 and 400 Creeks were headed down the Choctawhatchee and Yellow Rivers seeking to avoid deportation to the west.

By 9 March Colonel Jackson Morton, with Joseph Bonifay as his scout, had left Pensacola and headed up the Blackwater River to the settlement near modern Milton in search of these Indians.[596] Commodore Dallas again offered the assistance of the navy in Pensacola and sent the Revenue Cutter *Dexter* up the Blackwater River with fifty men under the command of Lieutenant Ball with orders to cooperate with Morton's mounted volunteers.[597]  Several bands of Creeks soon appeared all over West Florida and were duly reported in the press.  The Tallahassee *Floridian* for 18 March 1837 reported that the militia of Washington and Walton Counties had been mobilized and that the venerable Colonel William Wyatt had offered his services (he was also running for office that year).

An incident occurred in Lumberton (today's Milton) on 15 April that led to an attempt to detain some eight to ten Creeks.

258

This attempt led to the wounding of one warrior and the cutting of his own throat by the afflicted Indian who bade his son to follow his example. A Creek woman and a boy (probably the son of the dead man) were taken captive. Retaliation was not long in coming and on 23 April the Creeks struck at a party of seven Walton County cow hunters and killed five of the men. The other two hid in the swamps to avoid capture and torture. Captain Arch Justice led a patrol of thirty-five men after these perpetrators and found them near Shoal River. After a brief skirmish two of the Indians lay dead.[598]

By 20 May the situation in West Florida was rapidly deteriorating and the force of Creeks allegedly forced from Alabama continued to rise, threatening all of Walton County and anything in between. The Tallahassee *Floridian* for that date reported that the people of Walton had fled their plantations and that Governor Call was calling on all able bodied men to take up arms against these Native American intruders.[599] Colonel John McKinnon answered that call and raised what troops he could to meet the challenge. Colonel Morton, being incapacitated by the fever, saw his command devolve upon Colonel Levin Brown of Jackson County. Brown was a persistent man and would not give up on the trail and found his quarry near Lagrange on Choctawhatchee Bay. What happened next is still debated today. Brown reported that he had heard of McKinnon's skirmish with the Creeks near the Cow Ford on the Choctawhatchee River. About the same time he received information that a body of Creeks were near the home of J. J. Harrison on the Alaqua River. After approaching the area, Brown's force surprised one camp of the Creeks and took four men and thirteen women and children prisoners. One of the men was persuaded to take the force to another encampment of Creeks a few miles away in the swamps near the Bay. Brown informed the Indian that if he did not lead them directly to the camp he would be executed. The guide did not lead them to his fellow Creeks and he was returned to the care of Captain Daniels as a prisoner. Shortly thereafter, according to Brown's report, Daniels' men, in retaliation for the false scout, fired on and executed the man, whereupon the women and children attempted to flee. All were shot down as they tried to escape.[600] Lieutenant John G. Reynolds report of the affair differed greatly from that of Brown. He reported that the Indians were found dead within a circle of not more than fifteen feet diameter and, "that the poor devils were penned up and slaughtered like cattle."[601] The war on this frontier was no less vicious than that found in East Florida where federal troops did much of the fighting.

Numerous other skirmishes were reported throughout the remainder of 1837. By early 1838 a number of the Creeks were beginning to come in larger numbers than anticipated. Governor Call hastened to West Florida in late January and attempted to negotiate with these Native Americans.[602] Not all of the Creeks were involved in these negotiations and on 27 January 1838 the Pensacola *Gazette* reported a barge belonging to a Colonel Bright was robbed on the Choctawhatchee River for its provisions. Significantly, no one on the barge was injured or anything taken except the food. The Governor left the area in March of 1838 and reported that the area was safe and returning settlers need not fear the remaining Creeks. Indeed, many of them did surrender and emigrate west with the Apalachicola Bands in mid-1838.[603] However, the remnants of the Euchees and other Creeks did not feel that way.

Isolated incidents dot the historic landscape for the period from 1840-1842. The Pensacola *Gazette* for 19 September 1840 reported that a Mr. Jones in the Holmes Valley was away on business when a group of about twenty Indians (alleged to be Creeks) attacked his farmhouse and murdered his wife and young child. A little over a month later a report was made from Marianna where a number of "fugitive Creeks" had been committing depredations down on the Econfina River. These same Creeks were alleged to be in the vicinity of Marianna and troops had been locally raised to defend the community.[604] A 7 August 1841 report showed that not all was peaceful even at this late date. In this typical frontier report, two young daughters of Morris Simms living twelve miles south of Marianna were out in the cow pen when a group of thirty Indians (Marauding Creeks) fell upon them, shot them with spiked arrows and dashed their brains out with lightwood knots. All of this damage for a barrel of flour, a smokehouse full of bacon and other provisions.[605] Because of these isolated incidents the army

260

did establish some posts in the region at Econfina and at Fort Preston, three miles above Blountstown. These are the only federal installations found in West Florida until Pensacola was reached. In almost every instance in the history of the Creek-Seminole War in West Florida, the fighting was done by local militia or some component of the navy from Pensacola. Only after the Seminole War ended in 1842 does one find federal army troops scouting in West Florida. On 4 May 1844, for example, Lieutenant A. Montgomery of the Seventh Infantry led a scout of forty men up the Choctawhatchee River looking for some illusive Creeks.[606] The raid at St. Andrews Bay in 1847 was one of the last such incidents to be recorded in Florida, eleven years after Jesup and Scott thought they had ended the Second Creek War and five years after the proclaimed end of the Second Seminole War. Although the region of West Florida was sparsely populated and isolated from most cities, it felt the full fury of the Indian wars and survived to tell its tales. To those who survive and carry on the traditions of both Native American and white society we can say only that the full history is yet to be written from both sides.

# Hurricanes and the Conduct of War

Anyone familiar with or living near the Gulf Coast of the United States knows the impacts of hurricanes on the lives of the citizens. From the time of the sinking of the Spanish treasure fleets to the most recent calamities, the story of hurricanes on this coast has had a role in the lives of all who have called it home. Almost forgotten in all of the coverage of the recent events has been the historical role of these vast storms on the conduct of military operations in the region. This is especially true of the operations surrounding the Second Seminole War (1835-1842), America's most costly war against Native Americans in lives lost and in monetary expenditure. Operations in the swamps of Florida were bad enough without the unpredictable problems caused by these monster storms.

From the very beginning of the attempts to remove the Seminoles and Miccosukees and their allies, the Jackson administration had done little, if any, planning for the operation. There was a tacit assumption of cooperation. It appears that the simple plan was to gather all of the natives and their black allies into one or two locations, buy their cattle and horses and peaceably ship them to Indian Territory west of the Mississippi River. It was the accepted belief that the Indians would cooperate in this endeavor and some were, in fact, very willing to do so. Others, led principally by Osceola, Alligator and Coacoochee were totally opposed to this forced emigration and were willing to lead the fight against it.

In November of 1835 the entire force available to the army to protect an ever growing frontier was 7,151 men, and not all were ready for combat.[607] General Duncan L. Clinch, the commanding officer in Florida, had a force of 536 men, of whom only 26 were officers and not all of these were in Florida or fit for duty.[608] With this force Clinch was supposed to persuade or force nearly 5,000 Seminoles and Miccosukee, of whom 1,500 were classified as warriors, to emigrate west. This was an impossible task and the army would pay dearly for the assumptions of the political leaders.

In addition to the initial advantage in numbers, the Seminoles and Miccosukees and their black allies had the advantage of knowing the terrain. They were relatively familiar with the major waterways, the trails and the types of crops that could be grown and under what conditions. Like most Native American groups, they were masters of the art of guerilla warfare and how to adapt to the changing physical conditions. An additional advantage was the control of the "interior lines" of communication and defense. One of the major factors giving them a further advantage was the weather. As has been observed by military writers for centuries; "One characteristic, however, remains unchanging: in combat an environmental advantage for one side always means some degree of misfortune for the other, ..."[609] In this bloody war the advantages lay on the side of the Seminoles and their allies.

Southern Florida lies in the Inter Tropical Convergence Zone and the remainder of the peninsula is classified as semi-tropical. Its rainfall is distinctly seasonal, it is an area of high humidity year round and is frequently visited by tropical disturbances and hurricanes. It often has a surplus of moisture and has more rain than the annual evaporation potential which creates the perfect conditions for swamps, excessive humidity and poor drainage.

The heavy carpet of tropical or near tropical plant life, the large, seemingly endless swamp lands and an almost monsoonal weather pattern makes for very difficult campaigning by an invading army. Building roads in such a climate is complicated by the collection of wet alluvial soils with its mixture in the northern areas of red clay. The heat and moisture make a perfect combination for the breeding of mosquitoes and other disease-bearing insects, which bring with them typhoid, yellow, bilious fevers and malaria. The intense heat of the summer months in such climates exacerbates this situation and stresses the body to the point where its resistance to these diseases is very weak. It also brings with it a demoralizing factor of discomfort, which plays heavily upon the psychology of the average soldier and officer.[610] The Second Seminole War would lead to a large number of suicides amongst the officers and men of the army.

Military planning by the army of 1835 was not a well developed art. It was readily assumed that the regular soldier could be sent from the Falls at Niagara directly to the St. Johns River in Florida without a change of clothing, accoutrements or food. These vital resources had to be shipped to Florida on almost every occasion because the Seminoles and Miccosukees had destroyed most of the productive plantations that might have provided these items and forage for the horses, mules and oxen used to transport supplies to the interior. Since the Territory of Florida was nearly unknown to the military, sending an army into this strange world was taking a large number of risks.[611] One of the major handicaps for the Florida campaign was the lack of understanding of the scope of operation by President Andrew Jackson and his Secretary of War, Lewis Cass. Jackson's relatively successful campaign in Florida in 1817-1818 was conducted in the dry season, against a vastly outnumbered foe in an area of northern Florida unlike that where most of the campaigns of 1836-1842 were to take place. Assumptions based upon this short, politically driven campaign had little relevancy to the campaigns to be conducted further south. Jackson's 1818 campaign was comparatively self-contained and brief. This was not the case in those conducted after 1835.

Writing from Fort Drane in the northern portion of today's Marion County, Colonel James Bankhead in mid 1836 wrote, "It is painful to me to be obliged to state that the quantity of provisions here will barely suffice to sustain the troops on this frontier until the wagons can be sent & returned with further supplies; and that it would be almost impossible to afford relief to the citizens & their families at Micanopy." The Colonel then advocated the evacuation of Fort King (Ocala) and other posts that could not be readily supplied.[612] The infrastructure of Florida being almost non-existent, Bankhead's advice was typical and proper for an area devoid of

264

replenishment. All operations in Florida had to stop shortly after May when the onset of the rainy (sickly) season came over the Territory. The season coincided with the arrival of the tropical storms (hurricanes) that wrecked havoc nearly every year and made military operations and the transportation of supplies exceedingly difficult and dangerous.[613]

For most of the first year of the war, military setback after setback dogged the steps of the soldiers. The Battle of Dunlawton, where the Florida militia was forced back to St. Augustine, exposed the entire eastern coast and the plantations along the St. Johns River to Indian depredations and all were nearly destroyed in the process.[614] The near disasters along the banks of the Withlacoochee River in the first years of the war resounded throughout the Territory and to the nation's capitol. One of the few positive notes from that fateful year was the attack by troops under Major Benjamin Pierce on the force at Fort Drane led by Osceola, and that was not a complete victory in any sense. Generals Clinch, Call, Scott and Gaines had all failed to close the campaign and force the emigration so wanted by the administration. In almost every instance it must be noted that the supply of the troops, the transportation of forage and foodstuffs and the arrival of reinforcements were all delayed at some stage by the normal storms of the seasons. The terrible storms of 1837 would present even more costly delays and damage.

Of all of the military planners and generals of the army, the most qualified to take the field and command in Florida was General Thomas Jesup, the Quartermaster General of the Army. Few understood the logistical art better than this meticulous and careful man. His plan for the 1837-1838 campaign is a masterful piece of operational planning. Its major component was the encirclement of the Seminoles in the Everglades and gradually surrounding that difficult terrain and forcing them into battle or destroying them piecemeal at leisure.

The main portion of the four-pronged attack was to come down the St. Johns River and join forces with the army led by Generals Eustis and Hernandez, who were coming down between the St. Johns and the coast. Colonel Zachary Taylor was to leave Tampa, go east to the Kissimmee River and follow it to where it joined

Lake Okeechobee. A third force of Second Infantry and Louisiana Volunteers was to proceed up the Caloosahatchee River to where it emerges from Lake Okeechobee and establish a group of fortifications along the western side of the lake. The final piece was to land troops under Surgeon General Thomas Lawson at Cape Sable and from that point penetrate the Everglades and interdict the trade thought to be taking place between the Spanish fishing ranchos along the coast and the Seminoles. With the establishment of the forces along the eastern coast in a series of fortifications in conjunction with that outlined above, Jesup hoped to end the war. Constant delays in the delivery of boats, foot gear, troops and forage made what appeared on paper as a wonderful, workable plan into a logistician's nightmare. The severe storms of July to October of 1837 played a major role in these delays.[615]

The storm season began in earnest in July of 1837 even before Jesup and his men attempted their campaign. The storms of that month did not do much damage but put the military on notice that this might not be the best season to take the field. On August 12, 1837, the *Florida Herald* of St. Augustine reported, "Another Gale – On Sunday morning last we were visited with another gale, much severer than the first. The Wind commenced blowing from the N. E. and blew with violence until about 11 o'clock A.M. when it suddenly changed to the N. W." The report listed the damages done in St. Marys, Georgia where the steamboat *Florida*, a frequent carrier of goods to St. Augustine, had its side smashed in and an unnamed iron steamboat wound up in the middle of the Amelia River marsh. Another steamboat was destroyed near the town of Fernandina along with nineteen houses. Reports also reached St. Augustine that the road from Pablo to the head of North River (Tolomato River) was heavily obstructed by fallen trees.[616] The storm not only caused the immediately visible damage but it also destroyed the crops that were ripening in the fields, which deprived the soldiers and civilians of that year's produce.[617] The same storm caused the shipwreck of the Schooner *S. S. Mills* off Jekyll Island. The rough surf that accompanied the storm for a few days afterward upset a boat load of soldiers off Matanzas Inlet in which four soldiers and Colonel William S. Harney's servant drowned.[618] Writing from Savanah on September 12, 1837, Quartermaster

Thomas Hunt noted that the severe storms that were hitting the eastern coast had greatly delayed the delivery of goods to St. Augustine; goods destined for the forces then gathering for the push southward under Jesup.[619]

Writing on October 19, 1837, Surgeon Samuel Forry noted the disasters befalling the entire coast between Charleston and St. Augustine: "Disasters by sea are now every day occurrences. Half a dozen vessels are now off this coast, one of which left the mouth of the St. John's 15 days ago, bound for Charleston."[620]

The eastern coast however, was not the only scene of destruction from the storms of 1837. On August 31, 1837, the squalls picked up and the waters began to rise in the town of Apalachicola and nearby St. Joseph. Nearly every able bodied man in the town was called down to the wharves to save what they could from the oncoming storm. The tides were estimated to have risen from ten to fifteen feet in the downtown area and most of the ships tied up at the wharves found new homes, mostly inland. The scene was one of near total destruction down on Water Street. If it was made of wood it was floating in the Bay or smashed into millions of pieces. From the Promenade to above the Columbus wharves on Water Street the debris was piled at least four feet deep. Military stores and supplies along with everything else near the water were damaged beyond repair or use. The first estimates from Apalachicola put the damage at nearly $200,000. The St. Joseph *Times* reported that, "...we were visited by the severest gale felt on this coast by the earliest settlers in Florida. In fact, many of the oldest inhabitants pronounce it the most violent storm they have ever witnessed." Although most of the wooden structures in St. Joseph sustained damage, the pilings along the new wharf withstood the heavy wind and extreme tides.[621] Operations against the Creeks and Seminoles in West Florida came to a temporary halt as a result of the storms.

St. Marks, the depot for the army in northern Florida and along the coast to Cedar Key, was especially hard hit by the storms of August 7th and 31st. According to the *Floridian*, the town was totally underwater, the inhabitants fled to the old fort for protection and the light house was damaged. Eight people drowned at St. Marks and the damage to the tiny village was estimated at

$30,000.^{622}$ An account in the next issue of the newspaper noted that vast quantities of government and private stores were lost as the waves swept the town, destroying all but one wharf, damaging the light house and putting the schooner *Washington* in the marsh several hundred yards from open water. The newspaper, with the accustomed exaggeration, noted that this storm was "without its parallel in the history of the place." The body count had risen to eighteen one week later with probably many more unaccounted for at the time.[623] The loss of these supplies was a factor in delaying the start of Jesup's elaborate campaign. Even more crucial however, was the loss of needed transportation. The loss at Apalachicola of the *Henry Crowell*, *Edwin Forrest* and *Minerva*, all steamers frequently in the employ of the government along with the sloops *Plough Boy* and *Three Pollies* made moving men and materials very difficult and may have been a factor in delaying the moving of the force under General Persifor Smith to Tampa and Charlotte Harbor.[624]

The storms also dumped huge amounts of rain upon the fields of endeavor and made passage of the roadways very difficult. Dr. Jacob Rhett Motte noticed the heavy amount of timber across the path of the army as it moved southward down the southeastern coast. The water of the streams and rivers also became swollen enough to delay the army's crossing at a number of points along the route. As Motte described the scene, "… the fall of huge trees, torn up by their roots, crashing and echoing through the forests, under the influence of the powerful equinoctial storm, contributed to the dreariness and gloom of our situation."[625] Note here the physical difficulties encountered on the march plus the emphasis upon the psychological frame of mind. The low, overcast skies added greatly to the psychological depression of many soldiers during the war.

It should be remembered that the entire military effort in Florida depended chiefly upon the goods and services provided by northern cities, especially Philadelphia, New York and Washington. It was from these cities that most of the hiring arrangements were made for the transportation of the troops. Southern ports like Charleston and Savannah provided a large number of steamboats for plying the trade and carrying the troops, especially the volunteers from South Carolina and Georgia. Most of the steamboats hired or constructed in the South were designed for shallow draught, suitable for navigating Florida's coastal and inland waters. The frequent wrecking of many of these vessels contributed to the many logistical problems and storms were the common culprits. Crossing the tricky bars at the St. Johns and at St. Augustine made for numerous wrecks. This became so common that the Quartermaster's Department issued orders to its personnel to regulate their shipments to the Florida theatre and advised them to use only vessels of light draught since both of these places and at Garey's Ferry were not suitable for vessels drawing more than eight feet of water.[626] Hurricanes and other tropical storms would prove very dangerous for these shallow draught craft, but there was little that could be done to improve the situation given the technology available.

On the 19th of October, 1841, the post at Punta Rassa, at the mouth of the Caloosahatchee River, was hit by a violent storm that carried every government store, individual's belongings and every loose scrap miles inland. The entire point was swept by the waves from this tropical storm and every person of Company C, Eighth Infantry stationed there, "with difficulty escaped with their lives." The company books were later found by a detachment of sailors on a key eleven miles inland from Punta Rassa. This post was considered highly important for intercepting the suspected trade between the Seminoles and the Spanish fishermen who were thought to be supplying arms and ammunition to the Indians. This was also the departure point for patrols by the Revenue Cutters and their attached craft going southeastward down the coast to the Ten Thousand Islands and Cape Sable.[627] According to John T. Sprague, Aide to Colonel Worth, all of the tents, the hospital and store houses at Fort Dulany were destroyed and the steamer *Isis* was left high and dry in the middle of the camp. The fort was considered one of the healthiest locations on the coast and had shown no evidence of any major storm previous to this.[628] Again, operations in that quarter were greatly slowed down by the destruction of Fort Dulany and the surrender of some of the Seminoles was delayed when they took the storm as an omen not to come in at that time or place.

The omen against surrender because of a tropical storm (hurricane) was played out again in late 1842 when a hurricane hit the post at Cedar Key. For months Colonel Josiah Vose had been negotiating off and on with the local leaders of the Seminoles and their allies. By the end of September 1842 Vose's work was beginning to pay off and arrangements were made to transport these warriors and their families at Cedar Key. Sprague notes, however, "The violent gale at Cedar Key, on the 4th and 5th of October, deterred them from again visiting that post, as they superstitiously regarded it as an expression of anger by the Great Spirit, and an omen of misfortune."[629] Whether Sprague is correct or not (and his interpretation is open to speculation) the destruction at Cedar Key was great and it did hamper the removal process considerably.

As Vose described the storm, it began on the 4th of October coming in from the southeast and late in the evening shifted around and came in with even greater violence. "The water rose to an unprecedented height," the Colonel noted, "and aided by the force of the wind, carried away houses, trees, boats and in fact every thing which could not be protected against their combined actions." The entire public stores at the post were destroyed and two steamers and a government sloop were driven to the adjacent island and smashed against the shore. The tired Colonel also declared that the sutler's store and four other government buildings were all destroyed entirely and, "today the whole Island presents a scene of unrelieved desolation." Vose could do little more than recommend abandonment of the position.[630]

Commanding at the temporary post called Cantonment Morgan on Sea Horse Key, Captain John B. Clark, Sixth Infantry, observed that the wharf there had been destroyed as well as all of the small boats tied up or at anchor. All of the sheds and the guard house for the Indian prisoners were also obliterated by the storm. Miraculously, the store of the Commissary Office was nearly intact and uninjured. Clark also noted that there was no loss of life at the Cantonment.[631] The destructive storm of October 4th and 5th, 1842 at Cedar Key delayed the surrender of some of the major remaining bands of Seminoles. It also set back the settlement and development of this important Gulf port.

The impact of tropical storms and hurricanes on the conduct of the Second Seminole War was important but not necessarily vital to the over all goal of Indian removal. Planning for troop movements and resupply of the forces in the field were an iffy proposition at any time, but the storms gave this facet of logistical planning an added edge. As an integral part of the weather pattern of Florida, the hurricanes had to be taken into account. The navy had always been aware of these treacherous storms and had avoided being in the vicinity as much as possible during the known hurricane season. The army took less interest in these storms at first, but after the storms of 1837, they knew they had to be reckoned with if an operation were to take place within a given time span. The slowing of communication, the loss of needed supplies and transportation and the loss of soldiers' lives made these storms important in the conduct of the war. In the end, both the storms and a large number of Seminoles, Miccosukees and their black allies were overcome. The costs, however, were high.

# SELECTED BIBLIOGRAPHY

**Manuscript Materials:**

Letters Received by the Office of the Adjutant General (Main Series) 1822-1860. Record Group 94, National Archives and Records Service. Microcopy No. 567. This is the basic source of all the reports of actions during the Second Seminole War.

Letters Received by the Secretary of War Registered Series, 1801-1860. Record Group 108, National Archives and Records Service. Microcopy 221.

Records of the Office of the Secretary of War: Confidential and Unofficial Letters Sent, September 2, 1835-April 17, 1847. Record Group 108, National Archives and Records Service. "File Microcopies of Records in the National Archives: No. 7."

Letters Received by the Secretary of the Navy from Captains (Captain's Letters), 1805-1861 and 1866-1885. Record Group 45, National Archives and Records Service. Microcopy No. 125.

Letters Received by the Headquarters of the Army, 1827-1903. Record Group 107, National Archives and Records Service. Microcopy No. 1635.

Letters Sent by the Office of the Quartermaster General (Main Series), 1818-1870. Record Group 92, National Archives and Records Service. Microcopy No. 745.

Records of the Office of the Secretary of War Letters Sent, Indian Affairs, 1835-1842. Record Group 75, National Archives and Records Service. Microcopy No. 21.

Letters Received by the Topographical Bureau of the War Department, 1824-1865. Record Group 77, National Archives and Records Service. Microcopy No. 506.

Letters Received from Commissioned Officers Below the Rank of Commander and From Warrant Officers (Officer's Letters), 1802-1884. Record Group 45, National Archives and Records Service. Microcopy No. 148.

Office of Indian Affairs, Letters Received, Florida Superintendency, 1824-1850. Record Group 75, National Archives and Records Service. Microcopy No. 234. Rolls 286-289.

_____. Letters Received, Florida Superintendency, Emigration, 1828-1853. Microcopy No. 234. Rolls 290-291.

_____. Letters Received, Florida Superintendency, Emigration, 1827-1846. Microcopy 234. Rolls 806-807.

Letters Received by the Secretary of the Navy from Commanders, 1804-1886. Record Group No. 45, National Archives and Records Service. Microcopy No. 147.

General Land Office Records. Record Group 49. Six boxes of materials exist at the National Archives and Records Service dealing with the Armed Occupation Act of 1842. The most informative are those related to settlement under this act for both the Newnansville and St. Augustine Land Offices.

Returns from U. S. Military Posts, 1800-1916. Various Posts. Record Group 94, National Archives and Records Service. Microcopy No. 617.

United States Navy Department, "Records Relating to the Services of the Navy and Marine Corps on the Coasts of Florida, 1835-1842." Record Group No. 45. Office of Naval Records. Microfilm copy of this typescript is available at the P. K. Yonge Library of Florida History, University of Florida, Gainesville, Florida.

U. S. Revenue Cutter Log Books. Record Group 26, National Archives and Records Service. Copies of the log books for the *Dallas, Jackson* and others. Microfilm Copies of these logs are available at the P. K. Yonge Library of Florida History, University of Florida, Gainesville, Florida.

The Poinsett Papers: Papers of Joel Poinsett. Historical Society of Pennsylvania, Philadelphia, Pennsylvania.

Papers of Samuel P. Heintzelman. Manuscript Collections, Library of Congress, Washington D. C.

Papers of John Rogers Vinton. Manuscript Department, William R. Perkins Library, Duke University, Durham, North Carolina. (From Microfilm)

Lucian B. Webster Papers. St. Augustine Historical Society, St. Augustine, Florida. Copies of letters written by Webster while stationed in Florida.

J. R. Smith Diary and Reports. Microfilm copies from P. K. Yonge Library of Florida History, University of Florida, Gainesville, Florida. The diary portion runs from December of 1837 through April of 1838.

Diary of Josephus Conn Guild (1802-1883). Diary Kept During Campaign Against the Seminole Indians in Florida, September 5, 1836 – January 10, 1837. Tennessee State Archives, Manuscript Collections M74-29, Nashville, Tennessee.

Sylvester Churchill. Journal and Letter Copy Books of Sylvester Churchill, 1837-1839. Manuscript Division, Library of Congress, Washington D. C.

Hannibal Day Papers. 1839 Scout (Wacahoota to Micanopy) and Clippings from contemporary newspapers. United States Military Academy Special Collections, West Point, New York.

Records of the United States Army Continental Commands, 1821-1920: Volume I. "Report on Scouts from various officers to Colonel William Davenport, First United States Infantry,

Commanding the Right Wing of the Army of the South, West of the Suwannee, Nov. 19, 1839 to Jan. 27, 1840. Record Group 393, National Archives and Records Service, Washington D. C.

James Duncan Papers. United States Military Academy Special Collections, West Point, New York. Ms. 493 collection number. Three items in this collection deal with Dade's last battle.

Thomas Sidney Jesup Diary, 1836-1837. "Diary of Seminole Campaign October 1, 1836 to May 30, 1837." Microfilm Copy available at the State Library of Florida, Tallahassee, Florida.

John Erwin: Memoir of 1836. Tennessee State Library & Archives, Nashville, Tennessee. [THS I-E-2, Account No. 262.]

John Preston Watts Brown Papers. "Diary of J. P. W. Brown of the Independent Highlanders, August 20, 1836. Notes by the Wary of the Florida Campaign 1836." Tennessee State Library & Archives, Nashville, Tennessee.

Morris S. Miller Papers. "Three Letters, 1835-1836." United States Military Academy Special Collections, West Point, New York.

Brown Collection and Manuscripts (To Miss Ellen W. Brown from James W. Anderson). United States Military Academy Special Collections, West Point, New York.


**Published Manuscripts and Memoirs:**

*American State Papers: Military Affairs, Volumes VI and VII.* Washington: Gales & Seaton, 1861.

*American State Papers: Indian Affairs, Volumes I and II.* Washington: Gales & Seaton, 1860.

Bemrose, John. *Reminiscences of the Second Seminole War.* Edited by John K. Mahon. Gainesville: University of Florida Press, 1966.

Buchanan, Robert C. "A Journal of Lieutenant Robert C. Buchanan During the Second Seminole War." Edited by Frank F. White, Jr. *Florida Historical Quarterly*. 29(October 1950): 132-151.

_____. "A Scouting Expedition Along Lake Panasoffkee." Edited by Frank F. White, Jr. *Florida Historical Quarterly*. 31(April 1853): 282-289.

Cardwell, Guy A., Jr. "W. H. Timrod, the Charleston Volunteers and the Defense of St. Augustine." *North Carolina Historical Review*. 18(1941): 27-37.

Carter, Clarence E. (Editor). *The Territorial Papers of the United States, Volumes XXII-XVI: Florida Territory*. Washington: Government Printing Office, 1956-1962.

Cohen, Myer M. *Notices of Florida and the Campaigns*. Charleston, South Carolina, 1836. (Reprinted in the Floridiana and Reprint Series, University of Florida Press, (with introduction by O. Z. Tyler, Jr.) Gainesville, Florida, 1964.

Croffut, W. A. (Editor). *Fifty Years in Camp and Field: Diary of Major General Ethan Allen Hitchcock, U. S. A*. New York: 1909.

Forry, Samuel. "Letters of Samuel Forry, Surgeon, U. S. Army, 1837-'38." *Florida Historical Quarterly*. 6(January and April 1928): 133-148, 206-219 and 7(July 1928): 88-105.

Foster, William S. (Edited by John and Mary Lou Missall). *This Miserable Pride of a Soldier: The Letters and Journals of Col. William S. Foster in the Second Seminole War*. Tampa: Seminole Wars Historical Foundation and University of Tampa Press, 2005.

Hammond, E. Ashby (Editor). "Dr. Strobel Reports on Southeast Florida, 1836." *Tequesta*. 21(1961): 65-75.

Hollingsworth, Henry. "Tennessee Volunteers in the Seminole Campaign: The Diary of Henry Hollingsworth." Edited by Stanley F. Horn. *Tennessee Historical Quarterly*. 1(September and December 1942): 269-274, 344-366 and 2(March, June and September 1943): 61-73, 163-178, 236-256.

Hunter, Nathaniel W. "Captain Nathaniel Wyche Hunter and the Florida Indian Campaigns, 1837-1841." Edited by Reynold M. Wik. *Florida Historical Quarterly*. 39(July 1960): 62-75.

Jarvis, Nathan S. "An Army Surgeon's Notes on Frontier Service, 1833-1848." *Journal of the Military Service Institution of the United States*. (July 1906): 3-8,(September/October 1906): 275-286.

McCall, George A. *Letters from the Frontier*. Philadelphia: 1868. (Reprinted in the Bicentennial Floridiana Facsimile Series with an introduction by John K. Mahon, by University Presses of Florida Gainesville, Florida, 1974.)

Meek, A. B. "The Journal of A. B. Meek and the Second Seminole War, 1836." Edited by John K. Mahon. *Florida Historical Quarterly*. 38(April 1960): 302-318.

Mott, Jacob Rhett. *Journey Into Wilderness: An Army Surgeon's Account of Life in Camp and Field During the Creek and Seminole Wars, 1836-1838*. Edited by James F. Sunderman. Gainesville: University Press of Florida, 1953.

Phelps, John W. "Letters of Lieutenant John Phelps, U. S. A., 1837-1838." *Florida Historical Quarterly*. 6(October 1927): 67-84.

Pickell, John. "The Journals of Lieutenant John Pickell, 1836-1838." Edited by Frank F. White, Jr. *Florida Historical Quarterly* 38(October 1959): 142-171.

Potter, Woodburne. *The War in Florida, Being an Exposition of its Causes and an Accurate History of the Campaigns of Generals Clinch, Gaines, and Scott*. Baltimore: 1836.

Preble, George Henry. "A Canoe Expedition into the Everglades." *Tequesta*. 5(1945): 30-51.

Prince, Henry. *Amidst a Storm of Bullets: The Diary of Lt. Henry Prince in Florida, 1836-1842*. Edited by Frank Laumer. Tampa Seminole Wars Historical Foundation and University of Tampa Press, 1998.

Smith, Joseph R. "Letters from the Second Seminole War." Edited by John K. Mahon. *Florida Historical Quarterly*. 36(April 1958): 331-352.

Smith, W. W. *Sketch of the Seminole War and Sketches during the Campaign, by a Lieutenant of the Left Wing*. Charleston: 1836.

Sprague, John T. *Origins, Progress and Conclusion of the War in Florida*. Boston: Appleton, 1848. [This has been reprinted by the Seminole Wars Historical Foundation and the University of Tampa Press in 2000 with an introduction by John K. Mahon. It is an exact reproduction of the original with a very useful index. This is the major source of information readily available to begin any investigation of the Second Seminole War.]

*United States Congress Serial Set*. This is the index to all of the Congressional documents printed. The number well exceeds two hundred in the author's personal collection and there are more available, especially in the Committee on Claims.

Williams, John L. *The Territory of Florida*. New York: 1837. (Reprinted in the Floridiana Facsimile Reprint Series with an introduction by Herbert J. Doherty, Jr. Gainesville: University of Florida Press, 1962. William's famous map, without Lake Okee-chobee, is included in the fly-leaf.)

Woodward, A. L. "Indian Massacre in Gadsden County." *Florida Historical Quarterly.* 1(April 1908): 17-25.


## Newspapers:

*Apalachicola Gazette* (1836-1839)
*Army and Navy Chronicle*
*Charleston Currier*
*Charleston Mercury*
*The Floridian (Tallahassee)*
*The Florida Herald (St. Augustine)*
*Key West Register*
*The National Intelligencer*
*The News (Jacksonville)*
*Nile's Weekly Register*
*Pensacola Gazette*

## Secondary Sources:

Adams, George R. *Gen. William S. Harney, Prince of Dragoons.* Lincoln: University of Nebraska Press, 2001.

Amos, Alcione M. "The Life of Luis Fatio Pacheco: Last Survivor of Dade's Battle." Seminole Wars Historic Foundation, Dade City, Florida. Pamphlet Series, Volume 1, No. 1, 2006.

Bauer, K. Jack. *Zachary Taylor: Soldier, Planter, Statesman of the Old Southwest.* Baton Rouge: Louisiana State University Press, 1985.

Bernardo, C. J. and E. H. Bacon. *American Military Policy: Its Development Since 1775.* Harrisburg, PA: Stackpole Company, 1957.

Boyd, Mark F. "Asi-Yaholo, or Osceola." (Osceola Issue) *Florida Historical Quarterly.* 33( January and April 1955): 249-305.

_____. *Florida Aflame: Background and Onset of the Seminole War, 1835.* Tallahassee: 1951. Reprint from *Florida Historical Quarterly.* 30(July 1951): 1-115.

Brown, Canter Jr. *Florida's Peace River Frontier.* Orlando: University of Central Florida Press, 1991.

_____. "Persifor F. Smith, the Louisiana Volunteers, and Florida's Second Seminole War." *Louisiana History.* 34(Fall 1993): 389-410.

Buker, George E. *Swamp Sailors: Riverine Warfare in the Everglades, 1835-1842.* Gainesville: University of Florida Press, 1975.

Burbey, Louis H. *Our Worthy Commander: The Life and Times of Benjamin F. Pierce in Whose Honor Fort Pierce Was Named.* Fort Pierce, Florida: IRCC Pioneer, 1976.

Chamberlin, Donald L. *Fort Brooke: A History.* Masters of Arts, Thesis. Florida State University, Tallahassee, Florida, 1968.

Churchill, Franklin Hunter. *Sketch of the Life of Bvt. Brig. Gen. Sylvester Churchill.* New York: Willis McDonald & Co., 1888.

Coe, Charles H. *Red Patriots: The Story of the Seminoles.* Cincinnati: 1898. (Facsimile Reprint Series, Gainesville: University of Florida Press, 1974.)

Coffman: Edward M. *The Old Army: A Portrait of the American Army in Peacetime, 1784-1898.* New York: Oxford University Press, 1986.

Collins, John M. *Military Geography for Professionals and the Public.* Washington: Brassey's Edition, 1998.

Cotterill, Robert S. *The Southern Indians: The Story of the Civilized Tribes Before Removal*. Norman: University of Oklahoma Press, 1954.

Covington, James W. *The Seminoles of Florida*. Gainesville: University Press of Florida, 1993.

_____. "Cuban Bloodhounds and the Seminoles." *Florida Historical Quarterly*. 33(October 1954): 111-119.

_____. "Trade Between Southwest Florida and Cuba." *Florida Historical Quarterly*. 38(October 1959): 114-128.

_____. "The Establishment of Fort Brooke: From the Letters of Colonel George M. Brooke." *Florida Historical Quarterly*. 31(January 1953): 273-278.

Cullum, George W. *Biographical Register of the Officers and Graduates of the United States Military Academy ... 1802-1890*. (Volume 1) Boston: 1891.

Doherty, Herbert J., Jr. *Richard Keith Call: Southern Unionist*. Gainesville: University of Florida Press, 1961.

Eisenhower, John S. D. *Agent of Destiny: The Life and Times of General Winfield Scott*. New York: The Free Press, 1997.

Ellisor, John T. *The Second Creek War: The Unexplored Conflict*. Ph. D. Dissertation. University of Tennessee, Knoxville, Tennessee, 1996.

Foreman, Grant. *Indian Removal: The Emigration of the Five Civilized Tribes of Indians*. Norman: University of Oklahoma Press, 1953.

Ganoe, William A. *The History of the United States Army*. (Revised Edition) Ashton, Maryland: Eric Lundberg, 1964.

Giddings, Joshua A. *The Exiles of Florida: or the Crimes Committed by Our Government Against the Maroons, Who Fled from South Carolina and Other Slave States, Seeking Protection Under Spanish Law.* Columbus, Ohio: 1858. (Floridiana Facsimile Reprint, with introduction by Arthur W. Thompson, Gainesville, Florida, University of Florida Press, 1964.)

Groene, Bertram H. *Ante-Bellum Tallahassee* Tallahassee: The Florida Heritage Foundation, 1981.

Hamilton, Holman. *Zachary Taylor: Soldier of the Republic.* Indianapolis: Bobbs-Merrill Company, 1941.

Heidler, Jeanne T. *The Military Career of David Emanuel Twiggs.* Ph. D. Dissertation. Auburn University, Auburn, Alabama, 1988.

Heitman, Francis B. *Historical Register and Dictionary of the United States Army, 1789-1903.* Washington: Government Printing Office, 1903.

Huston, James A. *Sinews of War: Army Logistics, 1775-1953.* Washington: Office of the Chief of Military History, United States Army, 1966.

James, Marquis. *The Life of Andrew Jackson.* (Complete in One Volume) Indianapolis: Bobbs- Merrill Company, 1938.

Johnson, Timothy D. *Winfield Scott and the Quest for Military Glory.* Lawrence: University Press of Kansas, 1998.

Jumper, Betty Mae Tiger and Patsy West. *A Seminole Legend: The Life of Betty Mae Tiger Jumper.* Gainesville: University Press of Florida, 2001.

Kersey, Harry A., Jr. "The Cherokee, Creek, and Seminole Responses to Removal: A Comparison." In *Indians of the Lower South: Past and Present.* Edited by John K. Mahon. Pensacola: Gulf Coast History and Humanities Conference, 1975.

282

Kieffer, Chester L. *Maligned General: A Biography of Thomas S. Jesup.* San Rafael, California: Presidio Press, 1979

Kirk, Cooper. *William Lauderdale: General Andrew Jackson's Warrior.* Fort Lauderdale: Manatee Books, 1982.

Knetsch, Joe. *Florida's Seminole Wars: 1817-1858.* Charleston: Arcadia Books, 2003.

Laumer, Frank. *Dade's Last Command.* Gainesville: University Press of Florida, 1995.

McLaughlin, Andrew C. *Lewis Cass.* Boston: Houghton Mifflin Company, 1899.

McReynolds, Edwin C. *The Seminoles.* Norman: University of Oklahoma Press, 1957.

Mahon, John K. *History of the Second Seminole War, 1835-1842.* (Revised Edition) Gainesville: University Presses of Florida, 1985. All study of the Second Seminole War should begin with this classic study.

Martin, Sidney W. *Florida During the Territorial Days.* Athens: University of Georgia Press, 1944.

Matthews, Janet Snyder. *Edge of Wilderness: A Settlement History of Manatee River and Sarasota Bay.* Tulsa, OK: Caprine Press, 1983.

Millett, Allan R. and Peter Maslowski. *For the Common Defense: A Military History of the United States of America.* New York: The Free Press, 1984.

Missall, John and Mary Lou. *The Seminole Wars: America's Longest Indian Conflict.* Gainesville: University Press of Florida, 2004.

Patrick, Rembert W. *Aristocrat in Uniform: General Duncan L. Clinch*. Gainesville: University of Florida Press, 1963.

Peters, Virginia B. *The Florida Wars*. Hamden, CN: Archon Books, 1979.

Porter, Kenneth W. *The Black Seminoles: History of a Freedom-Seeking People*. (Revised and edited by Alcione M. Amos and Thomas P. Senter) Gainesville: University Press of Florida, 1996.

_____. "Tiger Tail." *Florida Historical Quarterly*. 24(January 1946): 216-217.

_____. "The Negro Abraham." *Florida Historical Quarterly*. 25(July 1946): 1-43.

_____. "Negroes and the Seminole War." *Journal of Southern History*. 30(1964): 427-450.

Procyk, Richard J. *Guns Across the Loxahatchee*. Cocoa, Florida: Auspices of the Florida Historical Society Press, 1999.

Prucha, Francis Paul. *The Sword of the Republic: The United States Army on the Frontier, 1783-1846*. Lincoln: University of Nebraska Press (Bison Edition), 1986.

Remini, Robert V. *Andrew Jackson: The Course of American Democracy, 1833-1845*. Baltimore: Johns Hopkins University Press, 1984.

Rippy, James Frederick. *Joel R. Poinsett: Versatile American*. Durham: Duke University Press, 1935.

Risch, Erna. *Quartermaster Support for the Army: A History of the Corps, 1775-1939*. Washington: Quartermaster Historian's Office, Office of the Quartermaster General, 1962.

Rivers, Larry E. *Slavery in Florida: Territorial Days to Emancipation.* Gainesville: University Presses of Florida, 2000.

Rogin, Michael Paul. *Fathers & Children: Andrew Jackson and the Subjugation of the American Indian.* New York: Vintage Books, 1976.

Rodenbough, Theophilus H. *From Everglades to Canyon with the Second United States Cavalry.* (Reprint) Norman: University of Oklahoma Press, 2000. (Originally published in New York in 1875.)

Satz, Ronald. *American Indian Policy in the Jacksonian Era.* Norman: University of Oklahoma Press, 2002 edition (paperback).

Schlesinger, Arthur M., Jr. *The Age of Jackson.* (Abridged by D. P. Geddes). New York: Mentor Books, 1962.

Shepard, Edward M. *Martin Van Buren.* Boston: Houghton Mifflin Company, 1899.

Silver, James W. *Edmund Pendleton Gaines: Frontier General.* Baton Rouge: Louisiana State University Press, 1949.

Sturtevant, William C. "Chakaika and the ʽSpanish Indians": Documentary Sources Compared with Seminole Tradition." *Tequesta.* 13(1953): 35-73.

Upton, Emory. *Military Policy of the United States.* Washington: Government Printing Office, 1907.

Wallace, Edward S. *General William Jenkins Worth, Monterey's Forgotten Hero.* Dallas: 1953.

Weigley, Russell F. *The American Way of War: A History of United States Military Strategy and Policy.* New York: Macmillan Publishing Company, 1973.

_____. *Toward an American Army: Military Thought from Washington to Marshall.* New York: Columbia University Press, 1962.

Weisman, Brent R. *Unconquered People: Florida's Seminole and Miccosukee Indians.* Gainesville: University Press of Florida, 1999.

Wright, J. Leitch, Jr. *Creeks and Seminoles.* Lincoln: University of Nebraska Press, 1986.

# NOTES

[1] Brent R. Weisman. Like a String of Beads: A Cultural History of the Seminole Indians in North Peninsular Florida. Tuscaloosa: University of Alabama Press, 1989. 34-35.

[2] J. Anthony Paredes and Kenneth J. Plante. "A Reexamination of Creek Indian Population Trends, 1738-1832." *American Indian Cultural and Research Journal.* 6(1983): 3-28.

[3] J. Leitch Wright, Jr. Creeks and Seminoles: The Destruction and Regeneration of the Muscogulge People. Lincoln: University of Nebraska Press, 1986. 67.

[4] William Bartram. *The Travels of William Bartram.* Salt Lake City: Peregrine Smith, Inc. 1980. 119-121.

[5] John Pope. A Tour Through the Southern and Western Territories of the United States of North America. (Facsimile Reprint) Gainesville: University Presses of Florida, 1979. 49.

[6] Benjamin W. Griffith, Jr. *McIntosh and Weatherford, Creek Indian Leaders.* Tuscaloosa: University of Alabama Press, 1988. 230.

[7] Benjamin Hawkins. *A Sketch of the Creek Country in the Years 1798 and 1799.* (Reprint of 1848 edition) New York: Kraus Reprint Company, 1971. 26, 30 and 47-48.

[8] George C. Osborn. "Relations with the Indians in West Florida." *Florida Historical Quarterly.* 13(April 1853): 244.

[9] Joel W. Martin. *Sacred Revolt: The Muskogee's Struggle for a New World.* Boston: Beacon Press, 1991. 56-57.

[10] Russell F. Weigley. *Towards an American Army: Military Thought from Washington to Marshall.* New York: Columbia University Press, 1962. 18-19.

[11] Sean Michael O'Brien. *In Bitterness and In Tears: Andrew Jackson's Destruction of the Creeks and Seminoles.* Guilford, Connecticut: The Lyons Press, 2003. 6. Also see Ulrich B. Phillips. "Georgia and States Rights." *Annual Report of the American Historical Association for the Year 1901.* Volume 1. Washington: Government Printing Office, 1902. 39-48.

[12] Jack D. L. Holmes. "The Southern Boundary Commission, the Chattahoochee River, and the Florida Seminoles in 1799." *Florida Historical Quarterly.* 44(October 1966): 312.

[13] Ibid.

[14] Rembert Patrick. Florida Fiasco: Rampant Rebels on the Georgia-Florida Border, 1810-1815. Athens: University of Georgia Press, 1954. 40-54. More recent scholarship by Dr. James G. Cusick in his The Other War of 1812: The Patriot War and the American Invasion of Spanish East Florida adds greatly to the Spanish side of this conflict and updates much of Patrick's earlier work.

[15] T. Frederick Davis. "Elotchaway, East Florida, 1814." *Florida Historical Quarterly.* 8(January 1930): 143-155.

[16] American State Papers: Foreign Affairs: Volume IV. Washington: Gales and Seaton, 1834. 550.

[17] Ibid. 844.

[18] Testimony of Horatio Dexter. Arredondo Grant File, Florida State Archives, Tallahassee, Florida.

[19] Mark F. Boyd. "Events at Prospect Bluff on the Apalachicola River: An Introduction to some Letters of Edmund Doyle, Trader." *Tallahassee Historical Society Annual, Volume III*. Tallahassee, Florida, 1937. 82-102.

[20] David and Jeanne Heidler. *Old Hickory's War: Andrew Jackson and the Quest for Empire*. Mechanicsburg, PA: Stackpole Books, 1996. The author also discusses this conflict in his *Florida's Seminole War, 1817-1858*. Charleston: Arcadia Books, 2003.

[21] John K. Mahon. "The Treaty of Moultrie Creek, 1823." *Florida Historical Quarterly*. 40(April 1962): 368-369. These pages give the basic clauses of the treaty.

[22] Letters and Reports to the Surveyor General, Volume 1: 1826-1847. 1-6. Title and Land Records Section, Division of State Lands, Florida Department of Environmental Protection, Tallahassee, Florida.

[23] House of Representatives Document No. 271. 24th Congress, 1st Session. 1836. "Seminole Hostilities."

[24] Ibid. 122-123.

[25] Edwin Carter, editor. Territorial Papers of the United States. Volume XXIII. Florida Territory. Washington. Government Printing, 1956. 847.

[26] Ibid. 329-31.

[27] Ibid. 844-45.

[28] Ibid. 856-58

[29] Ibid. 874. Gen. E. P. Gaines to Adjutant General.

[30] Ibid. 884-85.

[31] Ibid. 861-62.

[32] Ibid. 329-31.

[33.] John K. Mahon. History of the Second Seminole War, 1835-1842. (Revised edition) Gainesville: University Presses of Florida, 1985. 138.

[34.] East Florida Herald. August 8, 1826; and November 11, 1826. Both are cited in the Putnam Biographical Cards, St. Augustine Historical Society Library, St. Augustine, Florida.

[35.] East Florida Herald. April 21, 1830. Copy on file at the St. Augustine Historical Society Library, B-10 in Putnam Biographical File, St. Augustine, Florida.

[36.] St. Augustine, East Florida Herald, January 13, 1836. See Biographical file, Benjamin A. Putnam, St. Augustine Historical Society Library, St. Augustine, Florida.

[37.] Jacksonville Courier, December 10, 1835. The article announcing the commencement of the Indian War noted that Hernandez had already given the order by that date.

[38.] United States House of Representatives, Report No. 58. 28th Congress, 1st Session, January 19, 1844. "Joseph M. Hernandez." 41. Taken from the deposition of Joseph S. Sanchez.

39. Ibid. 22-23. Deposition of Benjamin A. Putnam.

40. "Letters Received by the Office of the Adjutant General (Main Series) 1822-1860. Roll No. 124. G 142-H 141, 1836." Washington: National Archives and Records Service, 1964. Microcopy No. 567. Letter of January 4, 1837, Putnam to Hernandez. Hereafter, Letters Received AGO, letter date and correspondents.

41. Michael Schene. A History of Volusia County, Florida. Ph. D. Dissertation. Florida State University, December 1976.124-25. Schene's work usefully condenses a number of reports filed in the Records of the Adjutant General's Office, Main Series, Record Group 94, National Archives. Roll 124.

42. St. Augustine. East Florida Herald. January 13, 1836. 1.

43. Ibid.

44. Ibid.

45. Charleston Courier. January 11, 1836.

46. Charleston Courier. January 12, 1836. 3.

47. Alice Strickland. The Valiant Pioneers: A History of Ormond Beach Volusia County, Florida. Miami: Center Printing Co., 1963. 26.

48. George C. Bittle. "In the Defense of Florida: The Organized Florida Militia From 1821 to 1920." Ph. D. Dissertation. Florida State University, December 1965. 10-46. Bittle's invaluable work is one of the few texts on this topic and deserves a close reading.

49. Letters Received AGO. Letter of January 7, 1836. Hernandez to Eustis.

50. Schene. 126. The actual letters are in Letters Received AGO. Letter of January 9, 1836. Putnam to Hernandez.

51. United States House of Representatives Report No. 58. 28th Congress, 1st Session. January 19, 1844. "Joseph M. Hernandez." 50. Deposition of Benjamin A. Putnam.

52. Ibid. 51. Deposition of John S. Williams.

53. United States House of Representatives Report No. 58. 28th Congress, 1st Session. January 19, 1844. 41. "Joseph M. Hernandez." Deposition of Joseph S. Sanchez. Putnam notes, on page 23, that Captains Williams and Dummett were posted at Harford Plantation, St. Joseph's was occupied by Captain Keogh's infantry company, Lieutenant Solana's mounted volunteers were stationed at Carrickfergus, while Putnam's own troops were at Bulowville. In Letters Received AGO, Letter of January 7, 1836, Putnam noted to Hernandez that he had also sent out Captain John S. Williams' command to Hartford, but had not heard from Captain Keogh. He was in an extremely isolated position and made even more vulnerable by the lack of discipline of the militia.

54. Charleston Courier. January 25, 1836. 3.

55. Charleston Courier. January 12, 1836. 3.

56. St. Augustine East Florida Herald. January 6, 1836. 1.

57. St. Augustine East Florida Herald. January 20, 1836. 2.

58. Ibid.

59. Bittle. 65; Schene. 127-28; Strickland. 26.

60. Charleston Courier. January 28, 1836. 3.

61. Letters Received AGO. Letter of January 18, 1836. Putnam to Hernandez, "PS."

62. Charleston Courier. January 27, 1836. 3.

63. United States House of Representatives Report No. 58. 28th Congress, 1st Session. January 19, 1844. 58-59. "Joseph M. Hernandez." Deposition of Benjamin A. Putnam. Also, House of Representatives Report No. 176. 27th Congress, 3d Session. February 14, 1843. 10-11. "Heirs of John J. Bulow, Jr." Deposition of Benjamin A. Putnam.

64. United States House of Representatives Report No. 104. 27th Congress, 3d Session. January 26, 1843. 20-21. "Joseph M. Hernandez."

65. Charleston Courier. February 2, 1836. 3.

66. Charleston Courier. February 12, 1836. 3.

67. Charleston Courier. February 12, 1836. 4.

68. Tallahassee Floridian. January 7, 1837. 2.

69. St. Augustine East Florida Herald. July 2, 1836. 2.

70. Benjamin A. Putnam. Letterbook & Accounts; 1836-1844. MC-16.8. Letter of July 6, 1836; and letter of July 11, 1836, to Col. John Warren and Governor Call respectively. St. Augustine Historical Society Library, St. Augustine, Florida

71. Letters Received by the Office of the Quartermaster General. Book 16, No. 23.A, 1836. Record Group 92, National Archives and Records Service. Copy from the Cooper Kirk Collection, Broward County Historical Commission, Fort Lauderdale, Florida.

72. Donald L. Chamberlin. "Fort Brooke, A History." Masters Thesis, Florida State University, Tallahassee, Florida. June 1968. 62-63.

73. National Intelligencer. January 26, 1836. 3.

74. Charleston Courier. February 16, 1836.

75. John T. Sprague. The Origins, Progress and Conclusion of the Florida War. Tampa: Seminole Wars Historic Foundation, 2000. 91. (This is a reprint of the original 1848 edition of Sprague with an excellent index and new introduction by the dean of Seminole War studies, John K. Mahon.)

76. Ronald N. Satz. American Indian Policy in the Jacksonian Era. Norman: The University of Oklahoma Press, [Red River edition], 2002. Satz's discussion is detailed and entertaining. It gives one of the finest examinations of the total policy of Indian Removal available in print.

77. Chamberlin. Fort Brooke. 7.

78. House of Representatives Document No. 74. 19th Congress, 1st Session, 1826. "Treaty with the Florida Indians." 13. This is from Gadsden's letter of June 11, 1823 to the Secretary of War.

79. Ibid. p. 49. The letter from Governor William Pope Duval to the Secretary of War dated July 29, 1824.

80. Michael A. Bellesiles. Arming America: The Origins of a National Gun Culture. New York: Alfred A. Knopf, 2002. 293-297.

81. Letters Received by the Office of the Adjutant General (Main Series), 1822-1860. Record Group 94. Roll No. 117, 1836. Washington: National Archives

and Records Service, 1964. Microcopy No. 567. Hereafter LRAG, roll number, date of letter and correspondents.

[82] LRAG. Roll No. 117. Letter of January 5, 1836. Belton to "Commander of the Naval force at Pensacola."

[83] Ibid. Second letter of January 5, 1836. Belton to Commanding Officer of the Naval force at Pensacola."

[84] LRAG. Roll No. 122. Letter of January 7, 1836. Eaton to Cass.

[85] LRAG. Roll No. 122. Letter of January 7, 1836. Call to Eaton.

[86] LRAG. Roll No. 122. Letter of January 9, 1836. Eaton to Cass.

[87] LRAG. Roll No. 117. Letter of January 14, 1836. Belton to Jones.

[88] Letters Received by the Secretary of the Navy from Captains (Captain's Letters) 1805-1861 and 1866-1885. Record Group 45. Roll No. 220, 1836. Washington: National Archives and Records Administration, 1976. Microfilm No. M125. Letter of January 15, 1836. Dallas to Secretary of the Navy Mahlon Dickerson. [Hereafter, Captains' Letters. Volume No., date of letter and correspondents.]

[89] Captains' Letters. Roll 213. Letter of January 17, 1836. Dallas to Dickerson.

[90] LRAG. Rolls 122 and 133. Letters of January 17, 1836. Eaton to Cass and Letter of January 20, 1836. White to Cass.

[91] Records Relating to the Navy and Marines in the FloridaWar, 1836-1842. Record Group 45. National Archives and Records Administration. Microcopy No. 617. Letter of January 21, 1836. Dickerson to Dallas. Copy obtained from P. K. Yonge Library of Florida History, George Smathers Libraries, University of Florida, Gainesville, Florida. The author would like to thank Dr. James Cusick for his assistance in obtaining this microfilm and that related to the Revenue Cutters.

[92] LRAG. Roll 117. Letter of January 23, 1836. Belton to Jones.

[93] LRAG. Roll 122. Letter of January 31, 1836. Eaton to Cass.

[94] Captains' Letters. Roll No. 214. Letter of February 1, 1836. Belton to Dallas.

[95] Captains' Letters. Roll No. 214. Letter of February 10, 1836. Gaines to Webb.

[96] Captains' Letters. Roll No. 214. Letter of February 13, 1836, Webb to Dallas.

[97] *National Intelligencer.* January 29, 1836. 3.

[98] John K. Mahon. *History of the Second Seminole War: 1835-1842.* Gainesville: University of Florida Press, 1985. [Revised Edition]. 153-154.

[99] Records Relating to the Navy and Marines in Florida. Letter of March 18, 1836. Powell to Webb.

[100] Records Relating to the Navy and Marines in Florida. Letter of March 28, 1836. Powell to Webb.

[101] Captains' Letters. Roll No. 216. Letter of April 1, 1836. Jones to Webb.

[102] Captains' Letters. Roll No. 216. Letter of April 12, 1836. Webb to Dallas.

[103] Records Relating to the Navy and Marines in Florida. Letter of April 27, 1836. Powell to Webb.

[104] St. Augustine *Florida Herald.* May 12, 1836. Also see Log Book of the U. S. Revenue Cutter *Dallas.* Record Group 26, "Records of the U. S. Coast

Guard." USRD *Dallas* 1836. Microfilmed for the University of Florida, P. K. Yonge Library of Florida History. Copies available at the library now housed in the Special Collections Department of the George Smathers Libraries, University of Florida, Gainesville, Florida.

[105] Charleston *Courier* April 28, 1836.

[106] John Erwin Diaries, Memoirs, etc. [Memoir, 1836) Tennessee Historical Society, State Library and Archives, Nashville, Tennessee. I-E-2. 52-53.

[107] W. F. Rowles. "Incidents and Observations in Florida in 1836." *Southron.* 1841. Galletin, Tennessee. 107. Copy obtained from the P. K. Yonge Library of Florida History, George Smathers Libraries, University of Florida, Gainesville, Florida.

[108] John K. Mahon, editor. "The Journal of A. B. Meek and the Second Seminole War, 1836." *Florida Historical Quarterly.* 38(April 1960): 307-308.

[109] House of Representatives Document No. 271. 24th Congress, 1st Session. 1836. "Seminole Hostilities". Letter of September 21, 1835. Wiley Thompson to General George Gibson. 211.

[110] Mahon. Journal of A. B. Meek. 316-317. Also see LRAG. Roll 127. Letter of May 2, 1836. Colonel William Lindsay to General Winfield Scott.

[111] LRAG. Roll 134. Letters of May 8 through 30. Mostly those between Mix and Wilson.

[112] Captains' Letters. Roll 217. Letters of May 11 and 12. E. Jones to C. Childs and Childs to Jones.

[113] LRAG. Roll 133. Letter of June 1, 1836. Wilson to Roger Jones. When Dr. Reynolds did finally receive a leave of absence, he was replaced by Dr. Lee, another assistant surgeon. See Wilson's letter of June 7, 1836 on Roll No. 134.

[114] LRAG. Roll 122. Letter of June 9, 1836. Warren to Major J. F. Heileman.

[115] LRAG. Roll 128. Letter of July 6, 1836. James Morgan to Roger Jones; and LRAG. Roll 131. Letter of June 25, 1836. William Landers to J. B. Benjamin. (The latter gives and itemized account of Captain Gardiner's debts.)

[116.] Michael G. Schene. "Indian Key." Tequesta. Historical Association of Southern Florida. 34(1976): 10-11.

[117.] Clarence E. Carter, ed. The Territorial Papers of the United States: Volume XXV, The Territory of Florida, 1834-1839. Washington: The National Archives, 1960. 169. Letter of April 24, 1835. Lt. Robert P. Smith (Acting Adjutant) to Major Francis L. Dade. [Hereafter, Territorial Papers and page number. Since this article concerns only one year in only one volume, this is deemed sufficient for proper location of the source material.]

[118.] Key West Enquirer. November 7, 1835.

[119.] Territorial Papers. 222.

[120.] Army and Navy Chronicle. February 4, 1836. 75.

[121.] Also see the accounts published in the Charleston Currier on January 23, 1836. Cooley's own account of the murders appeared in the January 27th edition.

[122.] Territorial Papers. 238-53.

[123.] Army and Navy Chronicle. February 25, 1836. 125.

[124.] United States House of Representatives. Report No. 215. 24th Congress, 2d Session. February 14, 1837. "Jacob Houseman". 1-2.

[125.] Tallahassee Floridian. April 16, 1836.

[126.] Territorial Papers. 313. Petition dated June 15, 1836. This was signed by William Marvin, W. R. Hackley, P. J. Fontane, F. A. Browne, John Dubose, James Curry, and many others.

[127.] Key West Inquirer. June 18, 1836.

[128.] Territorial Papers. 324-25. Letter of August 1, 1836.

[129.] Army and Navy Chronicle. August 4, 1836. 76.

[130.] Army and Navy Chronicle. September 29, 1836.

[131.] Charleston Courier. September 9, 1836.

[132.] Charleston Courier. October 5, 1836. Also see the same paper for October 7, 1836. The latter account noted the time the **Dexter** was alleged to have remained at Indian Key.

[133.] Charleston Courier. November 11, 1836.

[134.] Territorial Papers. 331-32. Call to Dallas, September 14, 1836.

[135.] Charleston Courier. November 12, 1836.

[136.] See Joe Knetsch. "All His Wants Must Be Provided: The Caloosahatchee Campaign of Percifer Smith, 1837-38." Sunland Tribune. Tampa Bay Historical Society, 1996; also, Joe Knetsch. "Jesup's Strategy, the Founding of Fort Lauderdale and the Role of Colonel James Bankhead." Broward Legacy. Broward County Historical Commission, Winter/Spring 1996. In both of these articles I discuss the U. S. Army's strategy for the campaign in South Florida and the foundation of many of the fortifications, including Fort Lauderdale, Fort Dallas, Fort Center, Fort Keais, Fort Poinsett, Fort Pierce, etc.

[137] National Intelligencer. December 16, 1835. 3. The Thompson warning was issued on November 30, 1835 from the Indian Agency near Fort King, today's Ocala.

[138] Clarence E. Carter, ed. The Territorial Papers of the United States, Volume XXV, The Territory of Florida: 1834-1839. Washington: The National Archives and Records Service, 1960. 189-90.

[139] National Intelligencer. December 24, 1835. 3.

[140] John K. Mahon. History of the Second Seminole War, 1835-1842 (Revised Edition) Gainesville: University of Florida Press, 1985. 102-03.

[141] Professor Mahon uses the figure of 4,000 Seminoles and 1,400 warriors and notes that President Jackson did not believe that they numbered more than 900 warriors. 5,000 is admittedly a higher estimate but one often found in contemporary sources.

[142] Army and Navy Chronicle. March 24, 1836. 181.

[143] American State Papers: Military Affairs. Volume VII. Washington: Gales & Seaton, 1861. 867.

[144] Edward M. Coffman. The Old Army: A Portrait of the American Army in Peacetime, 1784-1898. New York: Oxford University Press, 1986. 140-41.

[145] National Intelligencer. December 16, 1835. 3.

[146] Letters Received by the Office of the Adjutant General (Main Series) 1822-1860. Roll 124, G-142 – H-141. 1836. Record Group 94. National Archives and Records Service Microfilm No. 567. Washington, 1964. Letter of January 7, 1836. Hernandez to Eustis. Hereafter LRAG, Roll number and date of letter.

[147] The Diaries of Samuel P. Heintzelman. Manuscript Division of the Library of Congress. Reel No. 2. 107-111. The manuscript is misnumbered and pages 109-110 are unaccounted for but the dates are consecutive.

[148] *National Intelligencer.* January 7, 1836. 3. And, LRAG Roll 124. Letter of January 11, 1836. Hernandez to Lewis Cass.

[149] LRAG. Roll 124. Letter of January 4, 1836. Putnam to Hernandez.

[150] National Intelligencer. January 7, 1836. 3.

[151] LRAG. Roll 124. Letter of January 9, 1836. Putnam to Hernandez.

[152] LRAG. Roll 124. Letter of January 18, 1836. Putnam to Hernandez. Also see the author's "Benjamin A. Putnam: The Battle of Dunlawton." (2 parts) *Halifax Herald.* Daytona, Florida, Halifax Historical Society. Volumes 16 and 17, December 1998 – June 1999. 1-5, 1-5.

[153] Robert Hawk. *Florida's Army: Militia/State Troops/National Guard, 1565-1985.* Englewood, Florida: Pineapple Press, 1986. 65.

[154] LRAG. Roll 124. Letter of January 22, 1836. Hernandez to the officers of the 2nd Brigade, Florida Militia.

[155] Heintzelman Diaries. 115-16.

[156] The very best source for this battle is Frank Laumer's *Dade's Last Command.* Gainesville: University Press of Florida, 1995. This is an updated version of his now classic *Massacre.*

[157] Mahon. 103-04.

[158] Mahon. 108-111.

[159] Heintzelman Diaries. 118.

[160] Ibid. Reel 3. 4. The blacks were ordered to Anastasia Island for safety according to M. M. Cohen's *Notices of Florida and the Campaigns.* Gainesville: University of Florida Press, 1964 edition. (reprint). 96.

[161] Ibid. 14.

[162] *Army and Navy Chronicle.* February 25, 1836. 120.

[163] Charleston *Courier.* January 8, 1836. 3.

[164] Cohen. 110-113.

[165] Guy A. Cardwell, Jr. "William Henry Timrod, the Charleston Volunteers, and the Defense of St. Augustine." *North Carolina Historical Review.* 16(January 1941): 36-37.

[166] Cohen. 122-127.

[167] Charleston *Courier.* February 28, 1836. 4.

[168] Joe Knetsch. *Florida's Seminole Wars, 1817-1858.* 86-91. The details on the sickness in Brisbane's force see *Army and Navy Chronicle.* April 21, 1836. 253.

[169] *Army and Navy Chronicle.* August 18, 1836. 105.

[170] *Army and Navy Chronicle.* September 1, 1836. 140.

[171] George Buker. "The Americanization of St. Augustine, 1821-1865." In *The Oldest City: St. Augustine Saga of Survival*. Edited by Jean Parker Waterbury. St. Augustine: St. Augustine Historical Society, 1983. 168-170. And, Knetsch. *Florida's Seminole Wars*. 99-103.

[172] Territorial Papers of the United States:Volume XXIV, Territory of Florida, 1828-1834. Washington: National Archives, 1959. 659, 740, 788-89, 885. Also, for a description of the Caldez Island, see *Connections*, Journal of the Boca Grande Historical Society, Volume 3, No. 1, Winter 2002. 29.

[173] Maranda M. Almy. "The Cuban Fishing Ranchos of Southwest Florida: 1600s-1850s." Department of Anthropology, University of Florida, 2001. The author gratefully acknowledges the work of Ms. Almy |and having given her permission to use it in this paper. It is the best summary of the findings concerning the Ranchos yet available.

[174] Key West *Register*, July 30, 1829.

[175] Territorial Papers, Vol. XXIV. 513-14.

[176] Ibid. 659-661.

[177] Key West *Gazette*, November 2, 1831.

[178] Key West *Gazette*, March 7, 1832.

[179] Key West *Gazette*, March 21, 1832.

[180] Key West *Gazette*, April 11, 1832.

[181] Key West *Gazette*, May 30, 1832.

[182] Key West *Enquirer*, January 24, 1835.

[183] Territorial Papers of the United States; Volume XXV, Territory of Florida, 1834-1839. 168-69.

[184] Ibid. 183-84.

[185] Ibid. 190.

[186] Territorial Papers, Vol. XXIV. 134-37.

[187] Key West *Register*. December 31, 1829. Notice of Marshal's Sale.

[188] Territorial Papers. Vol. XXIV. 949.

[189] Letters Received by the Office of Indian Affairs, 1824-81. Roll No. 288, Florida Superintendency, 1824-1853: 1832-1837. Microcopy No. 234. Washington: National Archives, 1956. Letter of January 9, 1835. Bunce to Thompson.

[190] Ibid. Letter of January 10, 1835. Steele to Thompson.

[191] For the best treatment of the Dade Battle see Frank Laumer, *Dade's Last Command*. Gainesville: University Press of Florida, 1995. This an update of his classic account, *Massacre* first published in 1968.

[192] Joe Knetsch. "Benjamin A. Putnam and the Battle of Dunlawton: A Reappraisal." *Halifax Herald*, Halifax Historical Society, Daytona Beach, Florida. December 1998 and March 1999 (in two parts).

[193] Emory Upton listed the whole fighting strength of the U.S. Army at the outbreak of the Seminole War as 3,888. Upton. Senate Document No. 494. 62d Congress, 2d Session. 1912. "Military Policy of the United States." 162.

[194] Upton. 166-190.

[195] Letters Received by the Secretary of the Navy from Captains (Captain's Letters): 1805-1861 – 1866-1885, Rolls 213-215 (January to March, 1836.) Record Group 45. National Archives Microcopy No. M125. Washington, 1976. The paragraph above is a synopsis of these letters related to the west coast of Florida.

[196] Captain's Letters. Roll 216, April 1, 1836. Jones to Captain Thomas Webb.

[197] Captain's Letters. Roll 216, April 12, 1836. Captain Thomas Webb to Alexander Dallas.

[198] U. S. Navy and Marines in Florida, 1835-1842. Record Group No. 45. National Archives. Microfilm version of this collection of transcribed document is at the P. K. Yonge Library of Florida History, University of Florida, Gainesville, Florida. Letter dated April 27, 1836. Powell to Webb.

[199] U. S. Revenue Cutter Logbooks. Record Group 26, Records of the U. S. Coast Guard. Logbook of the Revenue Cutter *Dallas*, 1836. Microfilm available at the P. K. Yonge Library of Florida History, University of Florida, Gainesville, Florida.

[200] Captain's Letters. Roll 216. Letter of April 30, 1836. Mix to Dallas.

[201] Letters Received by the Office of Indian Affairs. Roll 289. Letter of April 22, 1838. Jesup to Poinsett.

[202] For one of the best discussions of the impact of climate and geography see Harold A. Winters, et. al. in *Battling the Elements: Weather and Terrain in the Conduct of War*. Baltimore: Johns Hopkins University Press, 1998. Chapters 2, 7 and 11 were most pertinent to this discussion.

[203] Clarence E. Carter. *The Territorial Papers of the United States, Volume XXV, The Territory of Florida: 1834-1839*. Washington D. C.: National Archives and Records Service, 1960. 186-87.

[204] Ibid. 192-93.

[205] Ibid. 194.

[206] Ibid. 200-01.

[207] United States Senate Document No. 152. 24th Congress, 1st Session. 1836. 2-5.

[208] John K. Mahon, editor. *Reminiscences of the Second Seminole War by John Bemrose*. Gainesville: University of Florida Press, 1966. 35-37.

[209] Morris S. Miller Papers, 1814-1870. United States Military Academy Library Special Collections, West Point, New York. Letter of 29 January 1835, Morris Miller to his brother, Rutger.

[210] Bemrose. 38,

[211] Territorial Papers XXV. 203-218.

[212] Bemrose. 39-42.

[213] Edward M. Coffman. The Old Army: A Portrait of the American Army in Peacetime, 1784-1898. New York: Oxford University Press, 1986. 141.

[214] William Barott Skelton. *The United States Army, 1821-1837: An Institutional History*. Ph. D. Dissertation, Northwestern University, Evanston, Illinois, June 1968. 327-30.

[215] Bemrose. 42.

[216] Rembert W. Patrick. *Aristocrat in Uniform: General Duncan L. Clinch.* Gainesville: University of Florida Press, 1963. 93-111. The quotation is found on page 109-110.

[217] Joe Knetsch. "Benjamin A. Putnam and the Battle of Dunlawton: A Reappraisal." *Halifax Herald.* Halifax Historical Society, Daytona Beach, Florida. Two parts, December 1998 and March 1999.

[218] John T. Sprague. *The Origins, Progress and Conclusion of the Florida War.* Tampa: University of Tampa Press and Seminole Wars Historic Foundation, 2000. (Reprint of 1848 edition). 93.

[219] Bemrose. 47-53.

[220] Letters Received by the Office of the Adjutant General (Main Series) 1822-1860, Roll 119, C 1-278, 1836. Record Group 94, National Archives and Records Service, Washington: 1964. Microcopy No. 567. Hereafter LRAG, roll number and letter date and correspondents. Letter of January 4, 1836, Clinch to Jones.

[221] LRAG. Roll 119. Letter of 11 January 1836, Clinch to Jones.

[222] Frank Laumer, editor. *Amidst a Storm of Bullets: The Diary of Lt. Henry Prince in Florida, 1836-1842.* Tampa: University of Tampa Press with the Seminole Wars Historic Foundation, 1998. 5.

[223] LRAG. Roll 119. Letter of 13 January 1836, Parish to Call.

[224] Prince Diary. 6-7.

[225] Bertram H. Groene. *Ante-Bellum Tallahassee* Tallahassee: Florida Heritage Foundation, 1971. (Second printing 1981.) 107-08.

[226] LRAG. Roll 119. Letter of 30 January 1836, Clinch to Cass.

[227] John K. Mahon. *History of the Second Seminole War, 1835-1842* (Revised edition). Gainesville: University of Florida Press, 1985. 158-59.

[228] Ibid. 140-44.

[229] Pamela N. Gibson and Joe Knetsch. "…being continually in apprehension of an attack from the Indians …':Tampa Bay in Early 1836." *Sunland Tribune.* Tampa Historical Society, Tampa, Florida. Volume XXIX, 2003. 115-128.

[230] Mahon. Second Seminole War. 146-47.

[231] Prince Diary. 8.

[232] Sprague. Florida War. 109-113.

[233] Mahon. Second Seminole War. 150.

[234] Bemrose. 79.

[235] Bemrose. 80.

[236] Mahon. Second Seminole War. 151-58.

[237] LRAG. Roll 122. Letter of 12 March 1836. Eustis to Jones.

[238] Prince Diary. 32.

[239] LRAG. Roll 122. Letter of 17 May 1836. Bankhead to Scott.

[240] Bemrose. 86.

[241] Mahon. Second Seminole War. 159.

[242] John Buchanan. Jackson's Way: Andrew Jackson and the People of the Western Waters. Hoboken: John Wiley & Sons, 2001.

[243] LRAG. Roll 122. Letter of 17 May 1836. Lieutenant A. A. Humphreys to Scott. And report of 30 June 1836. J. H. Prentiss to Jones.
[244] LRAG. Roll 122. Letter of 26 May 1836. Bankhead to R. B. Lee.
[245] LRAG. Roll 125. Letter of 9 June 1836. Heilman to Scott.
[246] LRAG. Roll 120. Letter of 3 July 1836. Call to Cass.
[247] LRAG. Roll 120. Letter of 23 July 1836. Call to Jones.
[248] Mahon. Second Seminole War. 175.
[249] Ibid. 177-78.
[250] John Erwin Papers. Manuscript. Tennessee State Library & Archives, Nashville, Tennessee. 17 and 28.
[251] Stanley Horn, editor. "Tennessee Volunteers in the Seminole Campaign of 1836: The Diary of Henry Hollingsworth." *Tennessee Historical Quarterly.* Volume 1, No. 4. December 1942. 355-57.
[252] LRAG. Roll 121. Letter of 22 October 1836. Call to Jones.
[253] W.P. Rowles. "Incidents and Observations in Florida in 1836." *The Southron.* Galletin, Tennessee. 1841. 159.
[254] Theodore F. Rodenbough. *From Everglades to Canon with the Second Dragoons.* New York: D. Van Nostrand, 1875. 23.
[255] LRAG. Roll 134. Letter of 30 November 1836. Winder to Lt. W. C. Del Hart.
[256.] Clarence E. Carter, ed. Territorial Papers of the United States: Territory of Florida. Volume XXIV. Washington: Government Printing Office, 1959. 282-87.
[257.] Joe Knetsch. "Range War in the East: Conflict over Cattle and Land on the Georgia-Florida Borderlands." Proceedings of the 90th Annual Meeting of the Florida Historical Society, May 1992. Tampa: Florida Historical Society, 1993. 108-20.
[258.] Army and Navy Chronicle. August 31, 1837. 137.
[259.] Ibid. 137.
[260.] The Courier. (Jacksonville) January 7, 1836. Letter of W. Wyatt. Wyatt describes in detail the movement of the volunteers to Hogan's house and the short battle which erupted near there.
[261.] House of Representatives Report No. 236. 25th Congress, 3d Session. 1839; and Senate Report No. 195. 25th Congress, 3d Session. 1839.
[262.] Senate Report No. 162. 24th Congress, 2d Session. 1837.
[263.] See House of Representatives Report No. 96. 33d Congress, 2d Session. 1855.
[264.] Senate Report No. 195. 25th Congress, 3d Session. 1839.
[265.] The Courier (Jacksonville). December 17, 1835. 2. "Indian Hostilities".
[266.] The Courier. (Jacksonville) December 24, 1835. 2.
[267.] Army and Navy Chronicle. January 14, 1836. 24.
[268.] Army and Navy Chronicle. April 21, 1836. 253.
[269.] Records of the Quartermaster Generals Office, Letters Sent: 1835-1842. Record Group 92. National Archives Mircofilm. Roll 1 NNO-737. 456-60.

Letter to Captain Samual Shannon, dated January 19, 1836, gives the clearest exposition of this process.

[270.] Ibid. 461-62.

[271.] Ibid. 465.

[272.] Ibid. 132, Part 2.

[273.] John Bemrose. Reminiscences of the Second Seminole War. Ed. by John K. Mahon. Gainesville: University of Florida Press, 1966. 103.

[274.] Ibid. 104-05.

[275.] Returns from U. S. Military Posts, 1800-1916. National Archives Microcopy No. 817. Roll 775. Fort Micanopy, Fla. June 1836-January 1843. Returns for June and July 1836.

[276.] Army and Navy Chronicle. June 30, 1836. 410-11.

[277.] Army and Navy Chronicle. July 21, 1836. 41.

[278.] John Preston Watts Brown Papers. State Library and Archives, Nashville, Tennessee. "Diary of J.P.W. Brown of the Independent Highlands, August 20, 1836. Notes by the Way of the Florida Campaign 1836." Transcribed version, page 11.

[279.] Army and Navy Chronicle. August 4, 1836. 76.

[280.] Army and Navy Chronicle. August 18, 1836. 105-06.

[281.] Army and Navy Chronicle. September 15, 1836. 172. This account gives an abbreviated version of Pierce's letter and an account by one George Nauman. I have mingled both in this brief recounting.

[282.] Returns from U.S. Military Posts 1800-1916. National Archives Microcopy No. 817. Roll 775. Fort Micanopy, Florida. June 1836-January 1843. Returns for April 1837.

[283.] Letters Received by the Office of the Adjutant General (Main Series) 1822-1860. National Archives Microcopy No. 567, Record Group 94. Roll 241, W 46-286, 1841. W-275.

[284.] Ibid.

[285.] Ibid.

[286.] Letters Received by the Office of the Adjutant General (Main Series) 1822-1860. Roll 223. 1841.

[287.] Letters Received by the Office of the Adjutant General (Main Series) 1822-1860. Roll 196.

[288.] Felix P. McGaughy, Jr. ed. "The Squaw Kissing War: Bartholomew M. Lynch's Journal of the Second Seminole War, 1836-1839." Unpublished M. A. thesis, Florida State University, 1965. 123-127, 179.

[289.] Letters Received by the Office of the Adjutant General (Main Series) 1822-1860. Roll 260.

[290.] For a good discussion of this fortification, see Arthur E. Francke, Jr.'s, Fort Mellon, 1837-42:A Microcosm of the Second Seminole War. Miami: Banyon Books, Inc., 1977. Two sketches of the fort appear on page 11 of the text. Note the number of "out" buildings present on the site and the cupola on the main building.

[291.] Letters Received by the Office of the Adjutant General (Main Series) 1822-1860. Record Group No. 94. Roll 198. T 235 - V 63. 1839. National Archives Microcopy No. 567. Letter of August 26, 1839. Major Thomas Childs to General Zachary Taylor. [Hereafter Letters Received Office of Adj. Gen., roll number and date of letter.]

[292.] For a general discussion of Fort Drane, see Joe Knetsch, "Marion County's Other Fort." Marion County Historical Society, Ocala, Florida, May 16, 1987; John Bemrose, Reminiscences of the Second Seminole War. ed. John Mahan. Gainesville: University of Florida Press, 1966; and Henry Prince, "Prince Diary." Typescript by Frank Laumer at P.K. Yonge Library of Florida History, University of Florida.

[293.] Albert C. Manucy. "Some Military Affairs in Territorial Florida." Florida Historical Quarterly. 25(October 1946): 205-06.

[294.] Michael G. Schene. "Fort Foster: A Second Seminole War Fort." Florida Historical Quarterly. 54(January 1976): 322-23.

[295.] Letters Received Adj. Gen. Office. 218. Letter of February 1840. (no specific date found with this letter)

[296.] Records of the Quartermaster General's Office: Letters Sent, 1835-1842. Record Group No. 92. National Archives Microfilm. Three Rolls, Roll No. 3. Letter of April 12, 1841. 382-83.

[297.] Records of the Quartermaster General's Office: Letters Sent 1835-42. Record Group No. 92. Roll No. 1, June 22, 1835 - October 4, 1838. NNO - 737. Letter of January 26, 1836. 477.

[298.] Ibid. Part 2, 132.

[299.] Ibid. Part 2, 216.

[300.] Records of the Quartermaster General's Office: Letters Sent 1835-1842. Roll 3. Letter of December 10, 1841. 376.

[301.] Ibid. no visible page number. Letter of September 28, 1841.

[302.] Ibid. 125.

[303.] Ibid. 151.

[304.] Records of the Quartermaster General's Office: Letters Sent, 1835-1842. Roll 3. Letter of May 25, 1841. 467.

[305.] Ibid. 261.

[306.] Ibid. no page number readable.

[307.] Ibid. Letter of March 25, 1841. 333-34.

[308.] Samuel Forrey. "Letters of Samuel Forrey, Surgeon, U. S. Army, 1837-1838." Florida Historical Quarterly. 6 & 7(1927-28): 138-39. Letter of Forrey to Phelps dated August 1, 1837.

[309.] John Bemrose. Reminiscences of the Second Seminole War. ed. John Mahon. Gaineville: University of Florida Press, 1966. 98-99.

[310.] Records of the Quartermaster General's Office: Letters Sent, 1835-1842. Roll 3. Letter of March 6, 1841. 276.

[311.] Bartholomew M. Lynch. "The Squaw Kissing War: Bartholomew M. Lynch's Journal of the Second Seminole War, 1836-1839." ed. Felix P.

McGaughy, Jr. Unpublished Masters Thesis, Florida State University, 1965. 179.

[312] Letters Received Office of Adj. Gen. 217. Letter of December 11, 1839.

[313] Letters Received Office of Adj. Gen. 202. Letter of October 2, 1840.

[314] Letters Received Office of Adj. Gen. 218. Document dated April 28, 1840. Signed by Colonel David Twiggs.

[315] Letters Received Office of Adj. Gen. 202. Most of the correspondence in this series is dated November 9 and 18, 1840.

[316] Letters Received Office of Adj. Gen. 241. Letter of January 20, 1841.

[317] Letters Received Office of Adj. Gen. 201. Letter of May 28, 1840.

[318] Ibid. Letter of June 22, 1840.

[319] Letters Received Office of Adj. Gen. 202. Letter of November 10, 1840.

[320] Letters Received Office of Adj. Gen. 217. Letter of January 11, 1841.

[321] One of the best discussions of the impact of climate and terrain upon military operations is found in Harold A. Winters, et. al. *Battling the Elements: Weather and Terrain in the Conduct of War*. Baltimore: Johns Hopkins University Press, 1998. I have relied upon Chapters 2, 5, 7 and 11 in this discussion.

[322] Allan R. Millett and Peter Maslowski. *For the Common Defense: A Military History of the United States of America*. New York: The Free Press, 1984. 136.

[323] Clarence E. Carter ed. *The Territorial Papers of the United States, Volume XXV, The Territory of Florida: 1834-1839*. Washington: The National Archives and Records Service, 1960. 189-90.

[324] The Jacksonville *Courier*. December 10, 1835. 2.

[325] Letters Received by the Office of the Adjutant General (Main Series) 1822-1860. Roll 124, Record Group 94, G 142 – H 141, 1836. Letter of 7 January 1836. Hernandez to Abraham Eustis. Hereafter LRAG, date of letter and correspondents.

[326] Jacksonville *Courier*. 24 December 1835.

[327] T. Frederick Davis. *History of Jacksonville, Florida and Vicinity: 1513-1924*. St. Augustine: The Florida Historical Society, 1925. 77.

[328] Joe Knetsch. "Benjamin A. Putnam and the Battle of Dunlawton: A Reappraisal." *Halifax Herald*. Halifax Historical Society, Daytona Beach, Florida. December 1998 and March 1999 issues.

[329] Joe Knetsch and Pamela N. Gibson. "being continually in apprehension of an attack from the Indians: Tampa Bay in Early 1836." *Sunland Tribune*. Volume 29. Tampa Historical Society, Tampa, Florida, 2003.

[330] LRAG. Roll 124. Letter of 19 January 1836. Warren to Hernandez.

[331] LRAG. Roll 124. Letter of 20 January 1836. Warren to Hernandez.

[332] Territorial Papers, Volume XXV. 257-58.

[333] Territorial Papers, Volume XXV. 411-12.

[334] See Returns from U. S. Military Posts, 1800-1916. Roll 437, Fort Heilman, Fla. May 1836-May 1841. National Archives Microcopy No. 617. The Historical Information Relating to Military Posts and other Installations ca. 1700-1900, Roll No. 4, Volumes I-L, National Archives Microcopy No. 661. list the date 8 August 1837 as the founding date for the federal installation in

Jacksonville. Some of the officers listed as serving at Jacksonville during 1837 include George Forsyth, John H. Winder and J. A. E'Lagnel.
[335] LRAG. Roll 120. Letter of 8 July 1836. Moses Curry to Thomas Hunt.
[336] LRAG. Roll 120. Letter of 18 September 1836. John Warren to R. K. Call.
[337] Territorial Papers. Volume XXVI. 38 and 64.
[338] Mary A. Graff. *Mandarin on the St. Johns*. Gainesville: University of Florida Press, 1953. 21.
[339] Ibid. 24. Ms. Graff's account closely matches the facts reported in John T. Sprague's *The Origins, Progress, and Conclusion of the Florida War*, originally published by Appleton's in Boston in 1848 and recently reprinted by the Seminole Wars Historic Foundation. 400.
[340] Ibid. Graff 26 and Sprague 401.
[341] House of Representatives Report No. 903. 27th Congress, 2d Session. July 6, 1842. "Cost of Depots in Florida." 2.
[342] Ibid. 5-6.
[343] John Bemrose. *Reminiscences of the Second Seminole War*. Ed. By John K. Mahon. Gainesville: University of Florida Press, 1966.
[344] Henry Prince. *Amidst a Storm of Bullets: The Diary of Lt. Henry Prince in Florida, 1836-1842*. Ed. By Frank Laumer. Tampa: University of Tampa Press and the Seminole Wars Historic Foundation, 1998. 121.
[345] Jacob Rhett Mott. Journey Into Wilderness: An Army Surgeon's Account of Life in Camp and Field during the Creek and Seminole Wars, 1836-1838. Ed. By James F. Sunderman. Gainesville: University of Florida Press, 1963. 105.
[346.] Francis B. Heitman. Historical Register and Dictionary of the United States Army, Volume 1. Washington: Government Printing Office, 1903. 344. The writer would like to than Ms. Leslie Lawhon and Mr. Wilburn Bell for their assistance in the preparation of this piece.
[347.] Canter Brown, Jr. Florida's Peace River Frontier. Orlando: University of Central Florida Press, 1991. 53-54.
[348.] Letters Received by the Office of the Adjutant General (Main Series), Record Group 94, Roll 167, I-J, 1-90, 1838. National Archives Microcopy No. 567. Washington D. C.: National Archives, 1964. Letter of December 28, 1837. Jesup to Brant. Hereafter LRAG, date of letter and correspondents. The author would like to thank Mr. Rodney Dillon and the Broward County Historical Commission for their assistance in the research for this piece.
[349.] Robert McHenry, editor. Webster's American Military Biographies. Springfield, Massachusetts: G. & C. Merriam Company, 1978. 400.
[350.] Canter Brown, Jr. "Persifor F. Smith, the Louisiana Volunteers, and Florida's Second Seminole War." Louisiana History 34(Fall 1993): 391-93. The author would like to thank Dr. Brown for a copy of his article and for his informal discussions of Smith's role in Louisiana and Florida.
[351.] Ibid. 393-99.
[352.] Ibid. 407-10. Also see Brown's Florida's Peace River Frontier. Orlando: University of Central Florida Press, 1991. 44-45.

302

353. House of Representatives Document No. 760, 25th Congress, 2d Session, 1838. In American State Papers Volume VII: Military Affairs. Washington: Gales & Seaton, 1861. 880. Hereafter, ASP, date of letter, correspondents and page number.

354. Ibid. 880-81.

355. ASP. Letter of September 2, 1837. 848. Poinsett to Jesup.

356. ASP. Letter of July 25, 1837. Poinsett to Jesup. 811. While not specifically naming Persifor Smith in the letter, Poinsett discussed the nature and pitfalls of using volunteer forces.

357. ASP. Letter of July 30, 1837. Smith to Jesup. 881.

358. Army and Navy Chronicle. Volume V. November 16, 1837. 315.

359. ASP. Letter of October 7, 1837. Poinsett to Jesup. 852. This letter specifically notes that five hundred men were to be raised in Philadelphia and meet Smith in Tampa. The Secretary also noted here that as other units were formed, he would forward them to Tampa, clearly making this the central point for all forces headed into the interior of Florida from the west coast.

360. There is a difference between two of the leading experts on this point. John Mahon, in his history of the war [History of the Second Seminole War 1835-1842. (Revised Edition) Gainesville: University Presses of Florida, 1985. 219-220.] notes seven columns, while Jesup's biographer, Chester L. Kieffer, clearly states that there were nine columns in motion.[Kieffer. Maligned General: The Biography of Thomas Sidney Jesup. San Rafael, California: Presidio Press, 1979. 191.] My reading of Jesup's report, [found in Senate Executive Document No. 263. 25th Congress, 2d Session, July 7, 1838. 253-54.] indicates that there were at least nine columns. These were led by Smith, Zachary Taylor, Brigadier General Nelson (with his Georgia volunteers), Colonel Snodgrass (with his Alabama volunteers), Lieutenant Colonel Coffee's Alabama volunteers, General Joseph Hernandez and his Florida militia units, Major William Lauderdale with his unit of Tennessee volunteers (Spies), General Abraham Eustis and Lieutenant L. Powell's naval contingent. If one were to include in the total operation, the "scouring actions" of Colonel David Twiggs and Colonel Mills prior to uniting with Eustis and Jesup at Volusia, the number is even higher. The main thrust, however one views the actions, was carried out by four major columns.

361. Senate Executive Document No. 263. 25th Congress, 2d Session, July 7, 1838. 253. It will be noted by the reader that Smith's force arrived in Tampa about or on November 6, 1837. His force of nearly eight hundred men, which is mentioned in the opening paragraph, is noted in a letter dated December 28, 1837. This would indicate that Smith's column had not reached the main area of his operation at the time of Taylor's battle with Sam Jones, Alligator and others at Okeechobee on Christmas Day of that year. Adding to Jesup's frustration with this campaign is the fact that Colonel Thomas Lawson's unit of Pennsylvania volunteers, destined for assignment under Smith, only reached Florida on the same day, December 25, 1837.

362. Ibid. 254. Fort Dallas, which became the site for the present-day city of Miami, was founded after the fort on Key Biscayne.

363. Ibid. 253.

364. Ibid. 253. The loss to the enemy, in men killed or wounded is unknown. The Seminoles and their allies, if time and the action permitted, removed their dead from the field and secreted them from enemy view. Therefore, as in certain modern wars, the exact number of enemy killed is uncertain.

365. Mahon. 219-40; Kieffer. 190-212. Also see, Kenneth J. Hughes, "Warriors from the Sea, the Second Seminole War Navy and Their Exploits in Southeast Florida," Parts I and II, Broward Legacy, Volume 11, Nos. 3 & 4 (Summer/Fall 1988) and Volume 12, Nos. 1 & 2, (Winter/Spring 1989). This two-part article gives a fine overview of the entire campaign, with an emphasis on southeastern Florida. Hughes also does yeoman's work in explaining the strategy of Jesup in readable terms.

366. Army and Navy Chronicle. January 11, 1838. 30.

367. LRAG. Letter of January 2, 1838. Jesup to Major Collins.

368. LRAG. Letter of December 22, 1837. Jesup to Major Henry Whiting.

369. LRAG. Letter of January 28, 1838. Jesup to Lieutenant L. Powell.

370. LRAG. Letter of December 29, 1837. Jesup to Lieutenant George Watson.

371. LRAG. Letter of December 30, 1837. Jesup to Taylor.

372. For an excellent discussion of his early career, see Keiffer's Maligned General, 1-66.

373. LRAG. Letter of January 18, 1838. Jesup to Taylor.

374. LRAG. Letter of January 18, 1838. Jesup to Major I. B. Brant.

375. Army and Navy Chronicle. February 8, 1838. 94.

376. LRAG. Letter of January 15, 1838. Jesup to General Walker K. Armistead, who was technically in command of forces south of the Withlacoochee River, headquartered at Tampa Bay. See also LRAG, letter of January 18, 1838. Jesup to Smith. This letter gave Smith the power to establish Fort Poinsett, "so soon as you can spare the force." Lawson arrived in Tampa on December 23, 1837, at the head of a force of 270 Pennsylvania volunteers and left to join Smith on December 27, 1837. See House of Representatives Document No. 78. 25th Congress, 2d Session, January 8, 1838. Letter of December 25, 1837. General W. K. Armistead to Jesup. 205-06.

377. U. S. Congress, House of Representatives Document No. 78. 25th Congress, 2d Session. January 8, 1838. Letter of December 6, 1837. Jesup to Poinsett. 197-98.

378. Ibid. Letter of November 29, 1837. Jesup to Poinsett. 197.

379. LRAG. Letter of February 3, 1838. Jesup to Taylor.

380. LRAG. Letter of February 2, 1838. Jesup to Taylor. The Army and Navy Chronicle for March 8, 1838 (159), reported that Taylor had taken about six hundred head of cattle immediately after the Battle of Lake Okeechobee. This would indicate a substantial supply of fresh beef available to the Indians at this period, even though it was reported that this capture had nearly "exhausted" the Indian's overall supply.

304

381. LRAG. Letter of March 6, 1838. Jesup to Smith.

382. LRAG. Letter of February 14, 1838. Jesup to Taylor.

383. LRAG. Letter of March 25, 1838. Jesup to Colonel James Bankhead, then commanding officer at Fort Lauderdale.

384. John T. Sprague. Origins, Progress and Conclusion of the Florida War. New York: Appleton & Co., 1848. 199-200. Sprague quoted Jesup's letter to Joel Poinsett, dated February 11, 1838.

385. Army and Navy Chronicle. March 1, 1838. 136.

386. LRAG. Letter of March 8, 1838. J. A. Chambers to Smith.

387. LRAG. Letter of March 14, 1838. J. A. Chambers to Smith. Also, Letter of March 14, 1838. Chambers to Taylor.

388. LARG. Letter of March 17, 1838. Smith to Chambers.

389. LRAG. Letter of April 7, 1838. Jesup to Armistead.

390. LRAG. Letter of April 16, 1838. Smith to Chambers. This letter was sent from Fort Keais.

391. Army and Navy Chronicle. May 17, 1838. 315.

392. LRAG. Letter of March 22, 1838. Chambers to Smith. Also, see letter of April 20, 1838. Taylor to Jesup.

393. LRAG. Letter of March 30, 1838. Jesup to Colonel W. I. Mills, Florida Militia, then in Washington D.C. Jesup urged Mills to see his Delegate about the matter.

394. Army and Navy Chronicle. May 24, 1838. 334.

395. Sprague. 189.

396. Brown. "Persifor F. Smith ..." 410.

397. Kenneth J. Hughes. "Warriors from the Sea, the Second Seminole War Navy and Their Exploits in Southeast Florida Parts I and II." Broward Legacy. Volumes 11 and 12, Summer/Fall 1988 and Winter/Spring 1989. These two articles give and excellent overview of the operations of the Army and Navy in Southeast Florida and well explain Jesup's campaign of 1837-38.

398. Ibid. See Part 1, page 39 for Hughes' discussion of this specific campaign.

399. The majority of the correspondence regarding this campaign is found in "Letters Received by the Office of the Adjutant General (Main Series) 1822-1860. Record Group 94, Roll 167. I-J, 1-90. National Archives Microcopy 567. Washington D. C.: 1964. The most telling letter concerning the supply of shoes to the troops, sent by General Jesup to Lt. Powell on January 28, 1838, states: "In consequence of more than four hundred of the foot troops being without shoes, and General Eustis having expressed the opinion that the greater part of them would be entirely disabled by the Saw Palmetto, in forty-eight hours, I have been compelled to postpone my movement south until a supply of shoes be obtained, or until the first regiment return, when all the men who have shoes will be put in march." From here on out, this correspondence will be referred to as LRAG, roll number and date of letter with the names of the correspondents.

400. LRAG, Roll 167. Letter of December 28, 1837. Jesup to Major Henry Whiting.

401. LRAG. Roll 167. Letter of January 2, 1838. Jesup to Collins.

[402.] Senate Executive Document No. 1. 25th Congress, 2d Session. 1838. Reprinted in the New American State Papers: Military Affairs, Volume 9; Combat Operations. Wilmington, Delaware: Scholarly Resources Inc., 1979. 257.

[403.] LRAG. Letter of February 3, 1838. J. A. Chambers to Brig. General A. Eustis.

[404.] Francis B. Heitman. Historical Register and Dictionary of the United States Army, Volume 1. Washington: Government Printing Office, 1903. 189.

[405.] Tommy Richard Young II. "The United States Army in the South, Volume 1." Dissertation, Louisiana State University, August 1973. 265-283.

[406.] Heitman. 189.

[407.] Robert Anderson. "Robert Anderson Fights Indians in South Florida." Broward Legacy. Summer/Fall, 1986. 12-14.

[408.] Kenneth J. Hughes. "Warriors from the Sea ..." Part 1. 42.

[409.] LRAG. Roll 167. Letter of March 3, 1838. Jesup to Lauderdale.

[410.] LRAG. Roll 167. Letter of March 28, 1838. J. A. Chambers to Bankhead.

[411.] Robert Anderson Diary. 13-14.

[412.] LRAG. Roll 167. Letter of March 31, 1838. Jesup to Harney.

[413.] Robert Anderson Diary. 13-15; and LRAG. Roll 167. A thorough search of this correspondence found no further reference to a move of the fort site.

[414.] LRAG. Roll 167. Letter of March 29, 1838. Bankhead to Jesup.

[415.] LRAG. Roll 167. Letter of March 30, 1838. Jesup to Mills.

[416.] David A. Clary and J. W. A. Whitehorne. The Inspectors General of the United States Army, 1777-1903. Washington: Center of Military History, United States Army, 1987. 120.

[417.] Heitman. 189.

[418.] Justin H. Smith. The War With Mexico, Volume II. Glouster, Mass.: Peter Smith, 1963. 184, 222, 335 and 432.

[419.] Heitman. 189.

[420.] Letters Received by the Office of the Adjutant General (Main Series) 1822-1860. Record Group 94. Roll 242, W 287-396, 1841. Washington: National Archives Microcopy 567, 1964. Letter of July 24, 1841. Worth to Adjutant General. [No. 30] Hereafter, LRAG, roll number, date and correspondents.

[421.] LRAG. Roll 241. Letter of May 31, 1841. Worth to Adjutant General R. Jones. This was the date upon which Worth officially took command of the troops in Florida.

[422.] LRAG. Roll 241. Letter of June 1, 1841. Worth to Loomis.

[423.] LRAG. Roll 241. Letter of June 16, 1841. Worth to Lt. Cols. Clarke, Riley and Loomis. (W-230)

[424.] LRAG. Roll 241. Letter of June 28, 1841. Worth to Riley.

[425.] LRAG. Roll 241. Letter of July 1, 1841. Worth to Clarke.

[426.] LRAG. Roll 241. Letter of July 3, 1841. Worth to Sibley.

[427.] LRAG. Roll 241. Letter of July 3, 1841. S. J. Johnson to Lt. Col. N. S. Clarke.

428. LRAG. Roll 241. Letter of July 5, 1841. Worth to Brigadier General R. Jones, Adjutant General of the Army.

429. LRAG. Roll 241. Letter of July 23, 1841. Worth to Major Samuel Cooper.

430. George W. Cullum. Biographical Register of the Officers and Graduates of the U. S. Military Academy at West Point, New York. Boston: Houghton, Mifflin and Company, 1891. 657.

431. For an account of the life of Rear Admiral John Rodgers, see, Robert Erwin Johnson. Rear Admiral John Rodgers, 1812-1882. Annapolis: United States Naval Institute, 1967. Interestingly, Johnson makes no mention of this expedition, assuming, instead, that he immediately went south to join in the campaigns around Lake Okeechobee, were Rodgers served later in 1841-42, under John T. McLaughlin, commander of the "Mosquito Fleet". Sprague's life is covered in Cullum and in the introduction to his work, by the noted historian of the Second Seminole War, Dr. John Mahon, republished by the University Press of Florida, in 1964.

432. Record Group 94, "Letters Received by the Office of the Adjutant General (Main Series) 1822-1860. Roll No. 241, W 46-286, 1841." Washington: National Archives Microcopy 567, 1964.

433. Captain Lloyd J. Beall, according to Cullum, was a graduate of West Point in the class of 1830, having been appointed as a cadet from Maryland in 1826. He saw extensive duty on the frontier including the Black Hawk war in 1832. He was promoted to 1st Lieutenant of the 2D Dragoons on June 11, 1836. Beall served on the Regimental Staff in 1836-37 and was promoted to Captain. He was sent to France to study dragoon tactics, returning to teach same at the Carlisle Military Barracks. After a short sojourn in Washington D. C., he was on the Board of Visitors to the Military Academy at West Point. In 1844, he promoted to Major with the Paymaster's Office. He served in the Mexican War but saw no battle action as a member of the Paymaster's Corps. Major Beall then served in numerous posts prior to his resignation to participate in the Civil War on the side of the South. Again, his services were mostly administrative as the South had many capable fighting leaders, but few of the bureaucratic type necessary to make the army function. After the War, Beall remained in Richmond as a prominent merchant and served as an Alderman. Upon his retirement from business, he was the Superintendent of the Westmoreland Club and remained in that position until his death on November 10, 1887. [Cullum. 459-60]

434. Cullum notes that Franklin D. Callender was born in appointed to West Point from New York. He graduated eighth in his class (1839) and was immediately appointed to the Ordinance Service, in which he served for almost his entire long and meritorious service. Like many who survived the Seminole War, he served in the War with Mexico, where he saw action in the Battles of Contreras and Churubusco, being severly wounded twice in the latter. Callender rose to Captain in 1853, and after many years service, remained in the Army during the War of the Rebellion, serving in the Ordinance Department and commanding same in Missouri. His service also included parts in the campaigns in Tennessee

and Mississippi, especially during the siege of Corinth, Mississippi. Callender was rewarded with the Brevet Brigadier Generalship at the War's end. He continued in the Regular Army until his retirement in 1879. Franklin Callender died on December 13, 1882, in Daysville, Illinois at the age of sixty-six. [Cullum 743-44.]

435. Letters Received by the Office of the Adjutant General (Main Series) 1822-1860. Record Group 94, Roll 244, W 434-Z, 1841. Washington: National Archives and Records Service, 1964. Microcopy No. 567. Letter of July 24, 1841. Worth to Jones. Hereafter, LRAG, date of letter and correspondents. All letters quoted from this source are from Roll Number 244.

436. Vinton Papers. Manuscript Department, William R. Perkins Library, Duke University, Durham, North Carolina. Letter of October 31, 1841. Vinton to "Friend". A microfilm copy of these papers related to his Florida service is available at the Broward County Historical Commission, which the author wishes to thank for making them accessible for this article.

Vinton was a graduate of the Military Academy, at West Point New York, Class of 1817. Appointed from Rhode Island, he was assigned as "Third Lieutenant" in the Corps of Artillery. Rising to Second Lieutenant in late 1817, he spent many of his early years on garrison duty in the South, particularly Charleston, South Carolina. He transferred to the Third Artillery in late 1821 and remained with this unit until his death, at the seige of Vera Cruz, March 22, 1847. Although he had served as Aide-de-Camp to Major General Brown, his fortunes did not rise until he was made Captain in December of 1835. Transferred with his regiment to Florida, he served here throughout the entire war, much of the time as commander at Fort New Smyrna. His service during the Mexican War, prior to his death, was rewarded with the rank of Brevet Major for his gallant conduct during the Battle of Monterey, in September of 1846. [See. George W. Cullum. *Biographical Register of the Officers and Graduates of the U. S. Military Academy at West Point, N. Y.*. Volume 1. Boston: Houghton, Mifflin and Company, 1891. 159-60.

437. Ibid. [Vinton Papers]

438. Cullum. 115-116. Cullum also includes a short biographical sketch of this remarkable man. After leaving Florida in 1842, he served at a number of posts on garrison duty, before being transferred to the Texas frontier. During the Mexican War, Childs saw extended action in the Battles of Reseca-de-la-Palma, Monterey, Vera Cruz, Cerro Gordo and in the defense of Puebla. For his services in Mexico he was promoted to Brevet Colonel, Major (full service rank) and Brevet Brigadier General for his "gallant and meritorious service in the defense of Puebla". After this war, he continued to command in various capacities, including the garrison at Fort McHenry, Maryland. Transferred to Florida in early 1852, he was charged with the command of all of East Florida. However, while at Fort Brooke (Tampa), he contracted the dreaded Yellow Fever and died there on October 8, 1853.

439. John T. Sprague. The Origins, Progress, and Conclusion of the Florida War. New York: D. Appleton & Company, 1848. 277-78.

440. Sprague. 280. Cullum reports that the New York born Burke was a graduate of the Academy in the Class of 1836. Upon graduation he was immediately sent to Florida as a Brevet Second Lieutenant in the 1st Artillery. During his service in Florida, he saw action in the Battle of the Wahoo Swamp and other skirmishes. When he transferred to the 3rd Artillery is uncertain as Cullum, uncharacteristically, has him terminating his Florida service in 1836-37, with no return. This is in error, as Burke's numerous signatures appear on much of the correspondence of this 1841 campaign out of Fort Dallas (Miami). He did serve in the Mexican War and received a promotion to Captain in March of 1847. Unfortunately, he was killed in action during the Battle of Churabusco, on August 20, 1847. [Cullum. 649.]

441. Sprague. 298. Also see, Kenneth J. Hughes. "Warriors from the Sea, the Second Seminole War Navy and Their Exploits in Southeast Florida, Part II." Broward Legacy. 12(Winter/Spring 1989.): 32-33.

442. Sprague. 273.

443. Edward J. Steptoe was a member of the Class of 1837. Like many others of his class, he was immediately sent to Florida upon graduation. In recognition of his service, he was promoted to First Lieutenant on July 9, 1838. After the war, he served as an instructor of infantry tactics at the Academy and additional garrison duty. His service in the Mexican War included the Battles of Vera Cruz, Cerro Gordo (receiving a Brevet Major's rank for gallantry) and the seige and capture of Mexico City. He returned to Florida during the Indian Scare of 1849-50. After duties in the East, he was transferred to the Washington Territory (after refusing a governorship of the Utah Territory). Steptoe saw extensive action against the Indians of this territory. For his service in the Northwest, he was promoted to Lieutenant Colonel in 1863. Because of ill health, he was forced to resign his position in November of 1861 and he died at his home near Lynchburg, Virginia, on April 1, 1865. [Cullum. 689.]

444. Richard Dean Arden Wade was appointed to the Corps of Artillery on October 27, 1820. The New York born Lieutenant transferred to the 3rd Artillery in 1822 and received his promotion to First Lieutenant in 1828. Wade was promoted to Captain on December 26, 1840, and was awarded a promotion to Brevet Major for his gallant services during the war against the Florida Indians. During the Mexican War, he received a promotion to Lieutenant Colonel for his gallant and meritorious service at the Battle of Molino del Rey, in 1847. He did not live long after his promotion, passing away on February 13, 1850. [Francis B. Heitman. Historical Register and Dictionary of the United States Army. Volume 1. Washington: Government Printing Office, 1903. 991.]

445. Edward Otho Cresap Ord of Maryland, graduated from the Academy in the Class of 1835 and was promoted to First Lieutenant in July of 1841. He received his promotion to Captain in 1850. Ord's career in the service found him extensively involved in the War Between the States, being mustered out of volunteer service with the rank of Major General. He received much recognition for his gallantry and leadership during that bitter conflict. Returning to the service after the war, he was promoted to Brigadier General in 1866 and

retired from active service at the rank of Major General of the United States Army in January 1881. He died two years later on July 22, 1883. [Heitman. 759.]

Thomas W. Sherman graduated from the Academy in 1836, having been appointed from his native Rhode Island in 1832. Like many of his class, he spent much of the time from graduation until the end of the Seminole War in active service in Florida. During 1838, he received his promotion to First Lieutenant. At the beginning of the Mexican War, in 1846, he was promoted to Captain of the 3rd Artillery. He served with distinction and commanded a battery during the Battle of Buena Vista, for which he received a Brevet Major promotion. After this war, he was assigned to the western frontier, especially in Kansas, where he played a role in quelling some of the outbursts in that area prior to the Civil War. During the War Between the States, Sherman served in the Maryland and Capitol areas helping to shore up Washington's defenses and keeping open the lines of communication. He organized part of the expedition which siezed Fernandina, Florida, and commanded a division in the siege of Port Royal. Transferred to the Army of the Tennessee, he saw almost continuous action on that front until sent to the Department of the Gulf, in late 1862. In May of 1863, he led a division in the expedition to Port Hudson, Louisiana, where, on May 27th, he lost his right leg leading an assault on the town. For his services during the war, he received a Brevet Major Generalship. Returning to active service after the war, he saw little but garrison duty, ending his last assignment, Key West, Florida, in 1870. He retired from active service on December 31, 1870, and died nine years later at New Port, Rhode Island. [Cullum. 642-43.]

Georgia born George Taylor was a member of the Academy Class of 1837. He was promoted to First Lieutenant on July 7, 1838, in recognition of his service in Florida. Further service, like that detailed in this article, earned him a promotion to Brevet Captain in 1842. After a stint as Assistant Professor of Mathematics at the Academy, he saw extensive service in the Mexican War. Taylor was involved in the Battles of Resaca-de-la-Palma, Monterey, Palo Alto, Cerro Gordo, Huamantla and Atlixo. For his bravery and meritorious conduct he was promoted to Brevet Major. George Taylor, along with 180 others and his wife, met a tragic end, all drowning off the Capes of the Delaware when a violent storm raked the steamer *San Francisco* on December 24, 1853. He was age 37 at the time of his death. [Cullum. 679-80.]

[446.] LRAG. Letter of September 18, 1841. Childs to Samuel Cooper. Cooper was the Acting Adjutant to Colonel Worth.

[447.] Ibid.

[448.] LRAG. Letter of September 19, 1841. Burke to Ord.

[449.] Ibid.

[450.] Maryland born Francis O. Wyse was another member of the Class of 1837 who was sent, almost upon graduation, into the heat and discomfort of Florida. Like others, he rose in the ranks to First Lieutenant, on July 31, 1838. After his Florida service, he spent much time in garrison duty until the outbreak of the

310

Mexican War.  After a promotion to Captain of the 3rd Artillery in March of 1847, Wyse saw action in the affair at Calabaza River, for which he received a Brevet Major rank.  He spent much of the time between this war and the War Between the States in garrison duty along the Northwest coast and participated in the Spokane expedition of 1858.  On the eve of the Civil War, he was promoted to Major, 4th Artillery.  By the end of the year, he had been further promoted to the rank of Lieutenant Colonel.  During the first two years of the war, he was on recruiting duty and was the disbursing officer in Baltimore.  He resigned his commission on July 25, 1863.  Wyse was later reinstated as an additional Lieutenant Colonel, 4th Artillery, on February 19, 1879 and officially retired by an act of Congress on February 28, 1879. [Government reduction in the Army and clearing of the rolls.]  He spent the remainder of his life on his farm near Pikesville, Maryland. [Cullum. 693-94.]  For Wade's report of the dispatch of Wyse's command, see LRAG. Letter of September 27, 1841. Wade to Childs.

451. LRAG. Letter of September 19, 1841. Wyse to Wade.

452. LRAG. Letter of September 19, 1841. Thomas to Wade.

453. LRAG. Letter of October 9, 1841. Worth to Jones.

454. Sprague. 333-35.

455. LRAG. Letter of October 30, 1841. Cooper to Childs.  This letter was the order given for the return trip.

456. LRAG. Letter of November 13, 1841. Wade to Childs.  Also see Sprague, 392-93.

457. Ibid.

458. LRAG. Letter of November 15, 1841. Childs to Cooper.

459. Vinton Papers. Letter of January 27, 1842. Vinton to his mother.

460. William Hunter Churchill, a native of New York, was a member of the Military Academy Class of 1840 and earned the rank of Second Lieutenant of the 3rd Artillery on July 1, 1840.  After his service in Florida, he remained with the regiment and rose to First Lieutenant in 1843.  He saw a quantity of action during the Mexican War and was breveted Captain in 1846 for his actions during the battles of Palo Alto and Resaca-de-la-Palma.  He died while on service in Mexico, on October 10, 1847. [Heightman. 301.]

461. Vinton Papers. Letter of November 6, 1841. Vinton to Childs.

462. LRAG. Letter of November 15, 1841. Childs to Cooper.

463. LRAG. Letter of September 18, 1841. Childs to Cooper.

464. LRAG. Letter of September 29, 1841. Childs to Cooper.

465. LRAG. Letter of November 15, 1841. Childs to Cooper.

466. LRAG. Letter of November 13, 1841. Childs to Cooper.

467. LRAG. Letter of December 4, 1841. Childs to Worth.

468. Sprague. 501.

469. Vinton Papers. Letter of November 14, 1841. Vinton to Childs.

470. LRAG. Letter of December 8, 1841. Worth to J. T. McLaughlin.

471. LRAG. Letter of December 9, 1841. Worth to Belknap.

472. LRAG. Letter of December 19, 1841. Childs to Cooper.

[473.] Vinton Papers. Letter of November 29, 1841. Vinton to Mother.

[474.] Vinton Papers. Letter of December 15, 1841. Vinton to Mother.

[475.] Vinton Papers. Letter of January 27, 1842. Vinton to Mother.

[476.] LRAG. Roll 260. Letter of January 2, 1842. Vinton to Childs.

[477.] LRAG. Roll 260. Letter of January 7, 1842. Wade to Childs.

[478.] LRAG. Letter of December 19, 1841. Childs to Worth.

[479] Letters Received by the Office of the Adjutant General (Main Series) 1822-1860, Roll No. 227, "D", 1841. Record Group 94, National Archives and Records Administration, Microcopy No. 567. Washington: D. C., 1964. Letters of January 29, 1841 and February 20, 1841. Davenport to Adjutant General Roger Jones.

[480] LRAG. Roll No. 227, Letter of May 8, 1841. Davenport to Jones.

[481] LRAG. Roll No. 227, Letter of February 27, 1841. Davenport to Bliss.

[482] LRAG. Roll No. 227, Letter of May 8, 1841. Davenport to Jones.

[483] LRAG. Roll No. 227, Letter of May 11, 1841. Davenport to Jones.

[484] LRAG. Roll No. 227. Letters of May 17 and July 5, 1841. Davenport to Jones.

[485] Culllum, George W. *Biographical Register of the Officers and Graduates of the U.S. Military Academy, Volume 1*. Boston: Houghton, Mifflin and Company, 1891, Third Edition. 433-434.

[486] LRAG. Roll No. 231. Letter of August 5, 1841. Hambaugh to Bell.

[487] LRAG. Roll 242. See Worth letters for the months of July and August 1841.

[488] LRAG. Roll 242. Letters of July 28 and July 30, 1841. LaMotte to Miller and Prince to Jones.

[489] LRAG. Roll 241. Letter of July 18 (?), 1841. Miller to Davenport.

[490] Joe Knetsch. "Worth's Southern Prong and the Exploration of the Homosassa River." *At Home*, Citrus County Historical Society, Inverness, Florida, Volume 17, No. 3, May/June 2000. I have also covered part of this story in "The Second Seminole War and the Founding of Fort Harrison." *Punta Pinal*, Pinellas County Historical Society, Seminole, Florida, Volume 27, No. 4, Winter 2002.

[491] Returns from Military Posts, 1800-1916. Cantonment Morgan, Florida. National Archives and Records Service, Microcopy No. 617. 1965.

[492] LRAG. Roll No. 245. Letter of February 25, 1842. Buchanan to Jones.

[493] LRAG. Roll No. 246. Letter of July 17, 1842. M. Barbour to Jones.

[494] LRAG. Roll No. 262. Letter of May 11, 1842. Samuel Cooper to Major Graham.

[495] LRAG. Roll No. 263. Letter of September 30, 1842. Wright to Capt. J. M. Hill.

[496] LRAG Roll No. 260. Letter of October 6, 1842. Vose to Jones.

[497] LRAG. Roll 260. Letter of October 6, 1842. Clark to Lieutenant Barbour.

[498.] Thomas Hart Benton. <u>Thirty Years View</u>. Volume II. New York: D. Appleton and Company, 1856. 167-68.

[499.] United States Senate Document No. 139. 25th Congress, 3d Session. 1839. "Extracts from the Message of Governor Call." 4.

[500.] The best article on the passage of the act is Michael E. Welsh. "Legislating a Homestead Bill: Thomas Hart Benton and the Second Seminole War." Florida Historical Quarterly. 57(October 1978): 157-72.

[501.] Joel R. Poinsett Papers. Historical Society of Pennsylvania, Philadelphia, Pennsylvania. Letter of November 29, 1839. James Gadsden to Samuel Cooper. 13-151. Hereafter, simply Poinsett Papers, correspondents, date of letter and index number.

[502.] Poinsett Papers: Letter of November 25th, 1839. Reid to Poinsett. 13-147.

[503.] Poinsett Papers: Letter of March 14, 1840. Reid to Poinsett. 14-74.

[504.] Poinsett Papers: Letter of December 14, 1840. Levy to Poinsett. 15-172.

[505.] Clarence E. Carter. Ed. The Territorial Papers of the United States, Volume XXVI: The Territory of Florida, 1839-1845. Washington D. C.: Government Printing Office, 1962. 81-88.

[506.] Territorial Papers. 169.

[507.] Poinsett's biographer, Fred Rippy notes specifically that these constant bickerings and contests divided the various factions and "made a unified and efficient policy impossible." J. Fred Rippy. Joel R. Poinsett, Versatile American. New York: Greenwood Press, 1968. 189.

[508.] Territorial Papers. 197.

[509.] United States House of Representatives Report No. 903. 27th Congress, 2d Session. July 6, 1842. "Costs of Depots in Florida." 2.

[510.] Benjamin F. Cooling, Ed. The New American State Papers: Military Affairs, Volume 9, Combat Operations. Wilmington, Delaware: Scholarly Resources Inc., 1979. 215. [House of Representatives Report No. 253. 25th Congress, 2d Session. March 21, 1838.]

[511.] New American State Papers. 244. [House of Representatives Report No. 259. 25th Congress, 2d Session.]

[512.] New American State Papers. 329. [House of Representatives Report No. 296. 26th Congress, 2d Session.]

[513.] Ibid. 330.

[514.] John K. Mahon. History of the Second Seminole War, 1835-1842 (Revised Edition). Gainesville: University of Florida Press, 1985. 293. Dr. Mahon cites a letter of the Paymaster General to the Secretary of War, May 20, 1841, Paymaster General's Digest, page 395, as the source for these figures.

[515.] Mahon. 295.

[516.] Joe Knetsch. "Into the Cove Again: Worth's 1841 Campaign." At Home. Citrus County Historical Society, Inverness, Florida. Volume 16(November-December 1999):1, 10-11. Also, see Mahon. 300-01.

[517.] Letters Received by the Office of the Adjutant General (Main Series) 1822-1860. W 46-286, 1841. Record Group 94, Roll 241. Washington: National Archives Micro Copy 567, 1964. Hereafter, LRAG, roll number, date of letter and correspondents. The rolls containing the names cited in this text are oversized prints.

[518.] LRAG. Roll No. 241. Letter of June 24, 1841. Worth to Jones.

[519.] LRAG. Roll 241. Letter of June 16, 1841. Eaton to Captain G. Wright.

[520.] LRAG. Roll 241. Letter of June 24, 1841. Worth to Wilcox.

[521.] LRAG. Roll 241. Letter of July 8, 1841. Jones to Worth.

[522.] LRAG. Roll 241. Letter of July 31, 1841. E. Schriver, Acting Adjutant General to Worth.

[523.] LRAG. Roll 241. Letter of July 17, 1841. Worth to Wilcox.

[524.] LRAG. Roll 242. Letter of July 22, 1841. Wilcox to S. Cooper.

[525.] LRAG. Roll 242. Letters of July 29, 1841. Worth to Whiting and Worth to Wilcox.

[526.] LRAG. Roll 242. Letter of July 30, 1841. Worth to Col. B. Riley.

[527.] LRAG. Roll 242. Letter of July 30, 1841. Wilcox to Cooper.

[528.] LRAG. Roll 242. Letter of August 3, 1841. Cooper to Wilcox.

[529.] LRAG. Roll 244. Letter of August 19, 1841. Cooper to Bradley.

[530.] Florida Herald & Southern Democrat [St. Augustine] October 8, 1841. 3.

[531.] LRAG. Roll 260. Letter of December 30, 1841. Cooper to Wilcox.

[532.] United States Military History Institute, Carlisle Barracks, Pennsylvania. Archives. Ralph G. Newman Collection. The author would like to thank Dr. Richard Sommers and his staff for their assistance in locating this source.

[533.] LRAG. Roll 261. Letter of February 19, 1842. John T. Sprague to "Commanding Officer at Fort Cross".

[534.] LRAG. Roll 261. Letter of March 21, 1842. Worth to Judge J. H. Bronson.

[535.] LRAG. Roll 261. Letter of March 21, 1842. Cooper to Patrick.

[536.] LRAG. Roll 261. Letter of March 22, 1842. J. T. Sprague to Whiting.

[537.] LRAG. Roll 261. Letter of April 22, 1842. Cooper to Barnum.

[538.] Joe Knetsch. "Colonel Sam Reid: The Founding of the Manatee Colony and Surveying the Manatee Country, 1841-1847." Sunland Tribune. Tampa Historical Society. 21(November 1995): 29-34.

[539.] LRAG. Roll 261. Letter of April 22, 1842. Cooper to Whiting.

[540.] LRAG. Roll 261. Letter of April 23, 1842. Cooper to Lt. Col. Whistler.

[541.] LRAG. Roll 262. Letter of April 27, 1842. Cooper to Patrick.

[542.] LRAG. Roll 262. Letter of May 21, 1842. Cooper to Whistler.

[543.] LRAG. Roll 261. Letter of April 22, 1842. Cooper to Lt. J. McKinstry.

[544.] LRAG. Roll 262. Letter of June 8, 1842. Cooper to Cornelius Taylor.

[545.] United States House of Representatives Document No. 262. 27th Congress, 2d Session. July 7, 1842. 39.

[546.] LRAG. Roll 261. "Consolidated Report" of March 26, 1842. Worth to the Secretary of War.

[547.] Joe Knetsch and Paul George. "A Problematic Law: The Armed Occupation Act of 1842 and Its Impact on Southeast Florida." Tequesta. LIII(1993): 63-80.

[548.] James W. Covington. "The Armed Occupation Act of 1842." Florida Historical Quarterly. 40(July 1961): 51.

[549.] John K. Mahon. History of the Second Seminole War 1835-1842 (Revised Edition). Gainseville: University Presses of Florida, 1985. 314.

[550.] The count was done by the author, twice, in the summer of 1991. I have copies of almost all of the permits granted in Florida which are on file in the

314

Deparment of Environmental Protection, Division of State Lands, Land Records and Title Section, Tallahassee, Florida.
[551.] See Knetsch and George. Also, Joseph D. Cushman, Jr. "The Indian River Settlement: 1842-1849." Florida Historical Quarterly. 43(July 1964): 34-35.
[552.] See Covington. Also see, Roy M. Robbins. Our Landed Heritage: The Public Domain 1776-1936. Lincoln: University of Nebraska Press, 1962. 153; and Paul W. Gates. History of Public Land Law Development. Washington: Public Land Law Review Commission, 1968. 388.
[553.] Paul Wallace Gates. History of Public Land Law Development. 219-48. Gates' discussion of this issue is one of the landmark writings on the opening of the frontier.
[554.] See discussion in Roy M. Robbins. Our Landed Heritage. 153-55.
[555.] Letters from Commissioner, Volume 3: 1840-43. 161-66, 225 and 265. Land Records and Title Section, Division of State Lands, Florida Department of Environmental Protection, Tallahassee, Florida.
[556.] Letters Received by the Office of the Adjutant General (Main Series) 1822-1860. Rolls 184 and 194. Record Group 94. 1839. Washington: National Archives, 1964. Call's letters are dated August 29, 1839 and October 4, 1839. Reid wrote to Secretary of War Joel Poinsett on August 15, 1839. Professor Mahon has gone so far as crediting Call with the initiation of the concept in Florida as early as 1838. See Mahon. 313.
[557.] See Mahon. 313-14. Professor Mahon notes that this worked against the passing of the bill in Congress when the opposition cited the facts that none of these gentlemen had been able to finish the war. Also see, Letters Received by the Office of the Adjutant General (Main Series) 1822-1860. Rolls 196 [Taylor], 240 [Armistead] and 191 [Macomb]. Record Group 94. Washington: National Archives, 1964. [Hereafter LRAG, date and correspondents.]
[558.] LRAG. Roll 242. "Order No. 27", July 20, 1841. Worth to Jones.
[559.] LRAG. Roll 242. July 29, 1841. Worth to Whiting.
[560.] LRAG. Roll 242. Letter of August 11, 1841. Worth to Jones.
[561.] LRAG. Roll 242. Letter of August 4, 1841. Wilcox to Worth.
[562.] LRAG. Roll 242. Letter of July 30, 1841. Wilcox to Worth.
[563.] Ibid.
[564.] LRAG. Roll 242. Letters of July 22, 1841. Wilcox to Worth: and July 17, 1841. Worth to Wilcox.
[565.] LRAG. Roll 242. Letter of August 9, 1841. S. Cooper to Wilcox.
[566.] LRAG. Roll 242. Letter of August 19, 1841. Cooper to Bradley.
[567.] LRAG. Roll 244. Letter of October 2, 1841. Cooper to Captain L. N. Morris.
[568.] LRAG. Roll 243. Letter of September 17, 1841. Cooper to Bradford.
[569.] LRAG. Roll 260. Letter of January 6, 1842. Cooper to Patrick. Biographical information on Patrick can be found in George W. Cullum. Biographical Register of the Officers and Graduates of the U. S. Military Academy. Volume I. Boston: Houghton, Mifflin and Company, 1891. 622-23.
[570.] Ibid.

[571.] LRAG. Roll 260. Letter of September 14, 1842. Lt. P. N. Barbour to Capt. William Seawell. Also see LRAG. Roll 262. Letter of April 27, 1842. Cooper to Patrick. This letter specifically assigned Patrick to maintain these second hand weapons and make a full report on their condition.

[572.] See Covington. 51.

[573.] LRAG. Roll 262. Letter of June 8, 1842. Cooper to Major R. B. Lee. Other letters in this roll also refer to this cut off date.

[574.] LRAG. Roll 262. See letters of May 11, 18, and 21, 1842.

[575.] LRAG. Roll 262. Attachment to Letter of June 13, 1842. Worth to "The Adj. Genl U.S. Army" (R. Jones)

[576.] Joe Knetsch. "Colonel Sam Reid: The Founding of the Manatee Colony and Surveying the Manatee Country, 1841-1847." Sunland Tribune. Tampa Bay Historical Society. 21(November 1995):29-34.

[577.] See Covington. Also see Michael E. Welsh. "Legislating a Homestead Bill: Thomas Hart Benton and the Second Seminole War." Florida Historical Quarterly. 57(October 1978): 157-72.

[578] Ronald N. Satz's American Indian Policy in the Jacksonian Era [Norman: University of Oklahoma Press, 1975.] gives one of the best discussions of the confusion and maladministration of the removal policy.

[579] See John T. Ellisor. "The Second Creek War: The Unexplored Conflict." Ph. D. dissertation from University of Tennessee, 1996. Ellisor's discussions of these frauds is concise and clear.

[580] United States Senate Executive Document No. 152, 24th Congress, 1st Session, 1836. 8-9

[581] Ibid. 14-15.

[582] Edwin N. McClellan. Typescript for a chapter on the History of the United States Marine Corps to be published as Chapter VI of Volume 2, dated January 5, 1932. 7. Typescript in the Florida Historical Society Collections, Alma Clyde Field Library of Florida History, Cocoa, Florida.

[583] Letters Received by the Secretary of the Navy from Captains (Captain's Letters) 1805-1861 and 1866-1885. Roll 218, June 1-30, 1836. National Archives and Records Service Microcopy M125, Record Group 45. Washington: National Archives and Records Service, 1976. Letter of 12 June 1836, Bolton to Richard K. Call, Governor of Florida. [Hereafter Captain's Letters, date and correspondents.]

[584] Captain's Letters. Roll 218. Letter of 20 June 1836. Dallas to Dickerson.

[585] Captain's Letters. Roll 218. Letters of 16 and 30 June 1836. Bolton and Dallas to Dickerson.

[586] Captain's Letters. Roll 219. Letter of 10 July 1836. Lieutenant S. Johnston to Dallas.

[587] Ellisor. 152-164: McClellan. 9: and Kenneth L. Valliere. "The Creek War of 1836: A Military History." The Chronicles of Okalahoma. 57(Winter, 1979080): 474-481.

[588] Ellisor. 163-180.

[589] Valliere. 474-477: and Ellisor. 171-195.

316

[590] Valliere. 477-479.

[591] Army and Navy Chronicle. 12 July 1836. 13.

[592] Army and Navy Chronicle. 14 July 1836. 25.

[593] Ellisor. 184-195.

[594] Pensacola *Gazette*. 28 May 1836. 1.

[595] Charleston *Courier*. 7 September 1836. 3.

[596] Brian Rucker. "West Florida's Creek Indian Crisis of 1837." *Florida Historical Quarterly*. 69(January 1991): 321-323.

[597] Records Relating to the Navy and Marines in the Florida War. National Archives Microcopy M617, Record Group 45. Washington: National Archives and Records Service. 86. Letter of 9 March 1837. Dallas to Mahlon Dickerson.

[598] Rucker 324-325.

[599] Tallahassee *Floridian*. 20 May 1837. 3.

[600] Brown's Report was published in the Tallahassee *Floridian*. 1 July 1837. 3.

[601] Quoted by Rucker. 329.

[602] Pensacola *Gazette*. 20 January 1838. 3.

[603] Pensacola *Gazette*. 31 March 1838. 2. and Tallahassee *Floridian* 28 April 1838.

[604] Pensacola *Gazette*. 24 October 1840. 2.

[605] Pensacola *Gazette*. 7 August 1841. 3.

[606] Niles National Register. 4 May 1841. 160.

[607] United States House of Representatives Executive Document No. 23. 45th Congress, 3d Session. 1879. "Strength of the Army." 5.

[608] John K. Mahon. *History of the Second Seminole War, 1835-1842.* Gainesville: University Press of Florida (Revised Edition), 1986. 102.

[609] Harold A. Winters and Gerald E. Galloway, Jr., et. al. *Battling the Elements: Weather and Terrain in the Conduct of War.* Baltimore: Johns Hopkins University Press, 1998. 1.

[610] Ibid. 233-235.

[611] John M. Collins. *Military Geography for Professionals and the Public.* Washington: Brassey's Edition, 1998. 79.

[612] Letters Received by the Office of the Adjutant General (Main Series) 1822-1860. Record Group 94. Microfilm Roll No. 122. D-E, 1836. Washington: National Archives and Records Service, 1964. Microcopy No. 567. Letter of May 26, 1836. Bankhead to Captain R. B. Lee. [Hereafter Adjutant General's Records, roll number and date and correspondents.]

[613] Ibid. Letters of January 26, 1836, Governor John Eaton to Lewis Cass and January 23, 2836, General Abraham Eustis to Lewis Cass. Eaton and Eustis both advised the Secretary of War about the onset of the sickly season and the stormy weather which often accompanied it.

[614] Joe Knetsch. "Benjamin A. Putnam and the Battle of Dunlawton: A Reppraisal." *Halifax Herald.* Halifax Historical Society, Daytona Beach, Florida. December 1998 and March 1999. The author herein discusses the battle and its impact upon the inhabitants of East Florida.

[615] The author has discussed Jesup's plan in two articles: "Jesup's Strategy, the Founding of Fort Lauderdale and the Role of Colonel James Bankhead." *Broward Legacy.* Broward County Historical Commission, Fort Lauderdale, Florida. Winter/Spring 1996: and in "All His Wants Must Be Provided: The Caloosahatchee Campaign of Persifor Smith, 1837-38." *Sunland Tribune.* Tampa Historical Society, Tampa, Florida. 1996.

[616] *The Florida Herald and Southern Democrat.* St. Augustine Florida. August 12, 1837.

[617] *The Florida Herald and Southern Democrat.* St. Augustine, Florida. August 29, 1837.

[618] Ibid.

[619] Adjutant General's Letters Received. Roll 143. 1837. Letter of September 12, 1837, Thomas Hunt to Adjutant General Roger Jones.

[620] "Letters of Samuel Forry, Surgeon U. S. Army, 1837-1838." (Part III) *Florida Historical Quarterly.* 7(July 1928): 90.

[621] *The Floridian.* Tallahassee, Florida. September 9, 1837.

[622] *The Floridian.* Tallahassee, Florida. September 2, 1837.

[623] *The Floridian.* Tallahassee, Florida. September 9, 1837.

[624] Ibid. Also see the author's article, "All His Wants Must Be Supplied..."

[625] James Sunderman, editor. Journey into Wilderness: An Army Surgeon's Account of Life in Camp and Field during the Creek and Seminole Wars 1836-1838. By Jacob Rhett Mott. Gainesville: University Press of Florida, 1963. 133.

[626] Erna Risch. *Quartermaster Support of the Army: A History of the Corps, 1775-1939.* Quartermaster Historian's Office, Office of the Quartermaster General. Washington D. C., 1962. 231-232.

[627] Adjutant General's Letters Received. Roll 233. 1841. Letters of October 21st and November 6th 1841. Lieutenant George Lincoln to General Roger Jones.

[628] John T. Sprague. *Origins, Progress and Conclusion of the Florida War.* Boston: Appleton Press, 1848. (Reprint edition by the Seminole Wars Historical Foundation with introduction by John K. Mahon, University of Tampa Press, 2000.) 332.

[629] Ibid. 496-497.

[630] Adjutant General's Letters Received. Roll 260. Letter of October 6, 1842. Vose to Jones.

[631] Ibid. Clark to Lieutenant Barbour.

# INDEX

## A

Abiaka, 76, 180, 208
Adams, John Quincy, 8
*Ajax*, 48
Alligator, 34, 76, 92, 147, 209, 231, 238, 262
Alvord, Benjamin, 32, 80, 99
American Revolution, 3, 4
Anclote River, 41
Andrew Jackson, 93
Armistead, Walker, 47, 138, 140, 152, 187, 201, 243
Arredondo Grant, 7

## B

Bartram, William, 2
Battle of Dunlawton, 16, 23, 26, 29, 63, 79, 91, 120, 146, 265
Battle of the Withlacoochee, 64, 79, 91, 120, 121, 145, 146, 149
Battle of Thonotosassa, 44
Bell, John, 8
Belton, Francis S., 32
Benton, Thomas Hart, 225
Black Dirt, 46
Blunt, Reading, 9
Boca Grande, 73
Bowlegs, 7
Browne, J. B., 50
Bulowville, 22, 23, 24, 27, 289
Bunce's Rancho, 45
Butler, Robert, 8

## C

Caldes Rancho, 45
Call, Richard K., 30, 36, 64, 100, 121, 150, 191, 225, 253
Camp King, 13
Cantonment King, 14

## C (continued)

Cape Florida, 37, 48, 49, 50, 52, 53, 55, 80
Cape Sable, 50, 52
Cass, Lewis, 144
Ceasar, John, 19
Cedar Key, 270
Charlotte Harbor, 38, 41, 48, 71, 72, 73, 74, 75, 77, 79, 80, 81, 82, 83, 151, 163, 164, 268
Chattachoochee River, 6
Cherokees, *1*, 5, 193, 230
Chester, Peter, 3
Childs, Charles P., 45
Chisolm, William, 44
Chocachatti, 40
Choctaws, *1*, 4, 252
Clinch, Duncan L., 14, 33, 58, 64, 77, 86, 88, 105, 142, 263
Coacoochee, 69, 76, 201, 209, 262
Colonel John Warren, 89
Constellation, 37, 38, 80
Cooley Massacre, 50
Cooley, William, 17, 49, 80, 183
*Courier*, 20, 23, 26, 48, 50, 54, 63, 67, 143, 144, 145, 148, 258
Cowford, 7, 147
Creek War, *2*, 255, 257, 261
Creeks, *1, 2*, 3, 4, 5, 6, 7, 43, 72, 102, 142, 210, 223, 227, 230, 252, 253, 254, 255, 257, 258, 259, 260, 267
Cross, Thomas, 13
Cruger, Henry, 19

## D

Dade Massacre, 14, 16, 105
Dade, Francis L., 16, 48, 63, 77, 78, 87, 119, 137, 146, 253
*Dallas*, 38, 39, 43, 49, 50, 52, 55, 77, 82, 167, 184, 201, 203, 204, 205, 254, 258
Dallas, A. J., 37, 41, 92, 253
Dancy, Francis L., 64, 108, 121
de Fongueres, Marquis, 18

Timrod, William Henry, 66
Treaty of Fort Gibson, 9
Treaty of New York, 5
Treaty of Payne's Landing, 9, 143

# U

U. S. S. *Concord*, 41

# V

*Vandalia*, 38, 39, 41, 43, 55, 80-82

# W

Waldron, N. S., 38
Walton, George, 13

War of 1812, 6, 40, 109, 150, 155, 181,
    200, 213, 215, 216
Warren, John, 46, 61, 63, 144
Wayne, Anthony, 5
Whiting, Henry, 243
William & Frederic, 73
William Bartram, 2
William Stewart, 73
Williams, William H., 26
Wilson, Henry, 45
Winfield Scott, 67
Withlacoochee River, 33, 64, 79, 88,
    90, 96, 99, 157, 188, 192, 217, 220,
    265
Worth, William Jenkins, 46, 47, 140,
    152, 187, 192, 199, 216, 217, 230,
    237, 243, 269
Wy-ho-kee, 41, 81

www.ingramcontent.com/pod-product-compliance
Lightning Source LLC
Chambersburg PA
CBHW031233090426
42742CB00007B/184

* 9 7 8 0 9 8 2 1 1 0 5 4 6 *